Just when you thought the *Connecting Core Competencies Series* couldn't get any better... it did.

Each book has been enhanced with these features:

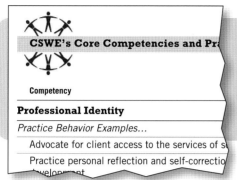

- A grid indicates where **competencies** and **practice behaviors** are highlighted in the text

- Highlighted **core competencies,** throughout the text, with:
  - a **practice behavior** example for that competency
  - a **critical thinking question** to help students apply the competency through a critical thinking lens

- **Practice Test** questions build on each other with three types of questions. Students go from —
  1. assessing basic knowledge, to
  2. understanding larger themes and concepts, to
  3. applying the concepts and themes with mini-case study questions.

MySearchLab®

- **MySearchLab Connections** indicate correlated chapter-specific online videos, cases, assessment, and more.

  Learn more about MySearchLab on the next page...

MySearchLab

MySearchLab provides engaging experiences that personalize, stimulate, and measure student learning.

Features in MySearchLab include:

- **A complete eText—** Just like the printed text, you can highlight and add notes to the eText online or download it to your iPad.

- **Assessment—**chapter quizzes, topic-specific assessment and flashcards offer immediate feedback and report directly to your grade book.

- **Chapter-specific learning applications—**ranging from **videos** to **case studies,** and more.

- **Writing and Research Assistance—** A wide range of writing, grammar and research tools and access to a variety of academic journals, census data, Associated Press newsfeeds, and discipline-specific readings help you hone your writing and research skills.

Students: if your text did not come with bundled with MySearchLab, you can purchase access at: www.mysearchlab.com

Instructors: Your students will get access to MySearchLab at no extra cost only when you use the bundle ISBN. See back cover for ISBN to give to your bookstore.

www.mysearchlab.com

CSWE's Core Competencies and Practice Behavior Examples in this Text

Competency	Chapter
Professional Identity	
Practice Behavior Examples	
Serve as representatives of the profession, its mission, and its core values	1, 3, 11, 13
Know the profession's history	2, 11
Commit themselves to the profession's enhancement and to their own professional conduct and growth	9
Advocate for client access to the services of social work	
Practice personal reflection and self-correction to assure continual professional development	13
Attend to professional roles and boundaries	
Demonstrate professional demeanor in behavior, appearance, and communication	
Engage in career-long learning	
Use supervision and consultation	
Ethical Practice	
Practice Behavior Example	
Obligation to conduct themselves ethically and engage in ethical decision making	11
Know about the value base of the profession, its ethical standards, and relevant law	1
Recognize and manage personal values in a way that allows professional values to guide practice	3, 10
Make ethical decisions by applying standards of the National Association of Social Workers *Code of Ethics* and, as applicable, of the International Federation of Social Workers/International Association of Schools of Social Work Ethics in Social Work, Statement of Principles	
Tolerate ambiguity in resolving ethical conflicts	
Apply strategies of ethical reasoning to arrive at principled decisions	
Critical Thinking	
Practice Behavior Examples	
Know about the principles of logic, scientific inquiry, and reasoned discernment	2
Use critical thinking augmented by creativity and curiosity	2, 5, 13
Requires the synthesis and communication of relevant information	6, 10
Distinguish, appraise, and integrate multiple sources of knowledge, including research-based knowledge and practice wisdom	3
Analyze models of assessment, prevention, intervention, and evaluation	
Demonstrate effective oral and written communication in working with individuals, families, groups, organizations, communities, and colleagues	6, 7, 12

Adapted with the permission of Council on Social Work Education

CSWE's Core Competencies and Practice Behavior Examples in this Text

Competency	Chapter
Diversity in Practice	
Practice Behavior Examples	
Understand how diversity characterizes and shapes the human experience and is critical to the formation of identity	
Understand the dimensions of diversity as the intersectionality of multiple factors including age, class, color, culture, disability, ethnicity, gender, gender identity and expression, immigration status, political ideology, race, religion, sex, and sexual orientation	3
Appreciate that, as a consequence of difference, a person's life experiences may include oppression, poverty, marginalization, and alienation as well as privilege, power, and acclaim	4, 7
Recognize the extent to which a culture's structures and values may oppress, marginalize, alienate, create, or enhance privilege and power	12
Gain sufficient self-awareness to eliminate the influence of personal biases and values in working with diverse groups	8
Recognize and communicate their understanding of the importance of difference in shaping life experiences	
View themselves as learners and engage those with whom they work as informants	
Human Rights & Justice	
Practice Behavior Examples	
Understand that each person, regardless of his or her position in society, has basic human rights, such as freedom, safety, privacy, an adequate standard of living, health care, and education	2, 8, 9
Recognize the global interconnections of oppression and are knowledgeable about theories of justice and strategies to promote human and civil rights	9
Incorporates social justice practices in organizations, institutions, and society to ensure that these basic human rights are distributed equitably and without prejudice	
Understand the forms and mechanisms of oppression and discrimination	6
Advocate for human rights and social and economic justice	1, 12
Engage in practices that advance social and economic justice	5, 11, 12
Research-Based Practice	
Practice Behavior Examples	
Use practice experience to inform research, employ evidence-based interventions, evaluate their own practice, and use research findings to improve practice, policy, and social service delivery	
Comprehend quantitative and qualitative research and understand scientific and ethical approaches to building knowledge	5
Use practice experience to inform scientific inquiry	
Use research evidence to inform practice	4

Competency	Chapter
Human Behavior	
Practice Behavior Examples	
Know about human behavior across the life course; the range of social systems in which people live; and the ways social systems promote or deter people in maintaining or achieving health and well-being	
Apply theories and knowledge from the liberal arts to understand biological, social, cultural, psychological, and spiritual development	
Utilize conceptual frameworks to guide the processes of assessment, intervention, and evaluation	
Critique and apply knowledge to understand person and environment	
Policy Practice	
Practice Behavior Examples	
Understand that policy affects service delivery and they actively engage in policy practice	
Know the history and current structures of social policies and services; the role of policy in service delivery; and the role of practice in policy development	7
Analyze, formulate, and advocate for policies that advance social well-being	1, 5, 8, 10, 13
Collaborate with colleagues and clients for effective policy action	4, 6, 7, 8, 9, 10
Practice Contexts	
Practice Behavior Examples	
Keep informed, resourceful, and proactive in responding to evolving organizational, community, and societal contexts at all levels of practice	
Recognize that the context of practice is dynamic, and use knowledge and skill to respond proactively	4
Continuously discover, appraise, and attend to changing locales, populations, scientific and technological developments, and emerging societal trends to provide relevant services	
Provide leadership in promoting sustainable changes in service delivery and practice to improve the quality of social services	

Competency	Chapter
Engage, Assess, Intervene, Evaluate	
Practice Behavior Examples	
Identify, analyze, and implement evidence-based interventions designed to achieve client goals	
Use research and technological advances	
Evaluate program outcomes and practice effectiveness	
Develop, analyze, advocate, and provide leadership for policies and services	
Promote social and economic justice	
A) ENGAGEMENT	
Substantively and effectively prepare for action with individuals, families, groups, organizations, and communities	
Use empathy and other interpersonal skills	
Develop a mutually agreed- n focus of work and desired outcomes	
B) ASSESSMENT	
Collect, organize, and interpret client data	
Assess client strengths and limitations	
Develop mutually agreed-on intervention goals and objectives	
Select appropriate intervention strategies	
C) INTERVENTION	
Initiate actions to achieve organizational goals	
Implement prevention interventions that enhance client capacities	
Help clients resolve problems	
Negotiate, mediate, and advocate for clients	
Facilitate transitions and endings	
D) EVALUATION	
Critically analyze, monitor, and evaluate interventions	

MySearchLab Connections in this Text

In addition to the outstanding research and writing tools and a complete eText in **MySearchLab**, this site contains a wealth of resources for social work students.

Following is a listing of the videos and readings found in **MySearchLab**, keyed to each chapter in this text.

In addition, a wealth of assessment questions (including those based on CSWE's core competencies) and useful online resources can be found under the appropriate chapters in **MySearchLab**.

VIDEOS

* Advocating for Human Rights and Social and Economic Justice (1)
  Ellis Island Immigrants, 1903 (2)
  Responding to the Great Depression: Whose New Deal? (2)
  Historical Significance of the 2008 Presidential Election, The (2)
  Tea Party Victories Concern for GOP (2008) (3)
  Battle Between Faith and Science (3)
  Abortion Wars (3)
* Participating in Policy Changes (4)
* Collaborate With Colleagues and Clients for Effective Policy Action in Community Organization (5)
  The 2010 Health Care Legislation (2010) (6)
  Vaccines: Mandatory Protection (2007) (6)
  Hidden Addictions (Nightline, 8-14-09) (7)
* Social and Economic Justice: Understanding Forms of Oppression and Discrimination (8)
  Photographing the Civil Rights Movement (8)
  The Real ID (2008) (8)
  Rev. Martin Luther King, Jr.'s Speech (8)
  Grandmothers Raising Grandchildren (9)
* Recognizing Personal Values (10)
* Managing Personal Values: The Code of Ethics (10)
  America's Aging Population (10)
  Court Rules on Hazelton's Immigration Laws (2010) (11)
  Funeral Protesters Push the Limit of Free Speech (2007) (11)
  Proposition 8 (11)
  Supreme Court: No Race-Based Admissions (2007) (11)
  Working Poor (12)
  Republicans and Democrats Divide on Tax Cut (2008) (12)
  Raising the Minimum Wage (12)
  The Bailout Hearings (12)
  Military Families (13)
  Gay Marriage (13)
  Who Is The Middle Class? (2008) (13)

---

* = **CSWE Core Competency Asset**
Δ = **Case Study**

MySearchLab Connections in this Text

READINGS

* Policy Practice (1)
  Jane Addams, The Subjective Necessity of Social Settlements (1892) (2)
  Meridel Le Sueur, Women on the Breadlines (1932) (2)
  Frances Perkins and the Social Security Act (1935, 1960) (2)
  Lyndon B. Johnson, The War on Poverty (1964) (2)
  Franklin Roosevelt's Radio Address Unveiling the Second Half of the New Deal (1936) (2)
  Herbert Croly, From Progressive Democracy (1914) (3)
  Social Workers Involved in Political Action (4)
Δ Community to Community (5)
Δ What's Medically Wrong With This? (6)
Δ A Community Coalition (6)
Δ Mental Health Services Consumers (7)
Δ The Chronically Mentally Ill Young Adult (7)
  Cesar Chavez, From "He Showed Us the Way" (1978) (8)
  The Gay Liberation Front, Come Out (1970) (8)
Δ Undocumented Mexicans (8)
  John Lewis, Address at the March on Washington (1963) (8)
  Fannie Lou Hammer, Voting Rights in Mississippi (1962–64) (8)
Δ The Impact of Childhood Trauma on Development (9)
Δ Crisis and Kinship in Foster Care (9)
  Keating-Owen Child Labor Act of 1916 (9)
  United Nations, Universal Declaration of Human Rights (1948) (9)
Δ Elderly People (10)
Δ Residents' Rights to Intimacy in an Assisted Living Residence (10)
Δ End-of-Life Decisions in an Intensive Care Unit (10)
  Brown v. Board of Education of Topeka, Kansas (1954) (11)
  Plessy v. Ferguson (1896) (11)
  Roe v. Wade (1973) (11)
Δ Andrew Carnegie, "Wealth," North American Review (1889) (12)
  Bob Stinson, Flint Sit-Down Strike (1936) (12)
  Caroline Manning, The Immigrant Woman and Her Job (1930) (12)
  Huey Long, "Share Our Wealth" (1935) (12)
* Human Rights and Justice (13)

---

* = CSWE Core Competency Asset
Δ = Case Study

Social Work Policy Practice

Changing Our Community, Nation, and the World

Jessica A. Ritter, Ph.D., MSSW, BSW
Pacific University Oregon

PEARSON

Boston Columbus Indianapolis New York San Francisco Upper Saddle River
Amsterdam Cape Town Dubai London Madrid Milan Munich Paris Montréal Toronto
Delhi Mexico City São Paulo Sydney Hong Kong Seoul Singapore Taipei Tokyo

Editorial Director: Craig Campanella
Editor in Chief: Ashley Dodge
Editorial Project Manager: Carly Czech
Editorial Assistant: Nicole Suddeth
Vice President/Director of Marketing:
  Brandy Dawson
Executive Marketing Manager:
  Wendy Albert
Marketing Assistant: Frank Alarcon
Digital Media Editor: Paul DeLuca
Production Project Manager: Liz
  Napolitano

Manager, Central Design: Jayne Conte
Cover Designer: Karen Noferi
Cover Image: ©Turkishblue/Shutterstock
Interior Design: Joyce Weston Design
**Full-Service Editorial Production
  Service:** Shree Mohanambal
  Inbakumar/PreMediaGlobal
Cover Printer: Lehigh-Phoenix Color/
  Hagerstown
Printer/Binder: Edwards Brothers
Text Font: Melior 10/12

Credits appear on page 265, which constitutes an extension of the copyright page.

Library of Congress Cataloging-in-Publication Data

Ritter, Jessica A.
  Social work policy practice : changing our community, nation, and the world / Jessica A. Ritter.
      p. cm.
  Includes bibliographical references and index.
  ISBN-13: 978-0-205-82851-7
  ISBN-10: 0-205-82851-5
  1. Social service—Political aspects—United States.   2. Social service—United States.   3. United States—Social policy.   4. Social justice—United States.   I. Title.
  HV91.R58 2013
  361.6'10973—dc23   2012027629

10 9 8 7 6 5 4 3 2 1

Student Edition
ISBN-10: 0-205-82851-5
ISBN-13: 978-0-205-82851-7
Instructor's Review Copy
ISBN-10: 0-205-18292-5
ISBN-13: 978-0-205-18292-3
à la Carte Edition
ISBN-10: 0-205-03279-6
ISBN-13: 978-0-205-03279-2

Contents

PART II

4. Social Workers in Action: The Six Stages of the Policy Change Process   53

5. When Wearing Buttons Isn't Enough   77

PART III

PART IV

Preface

Some social work majors are not exactly overjoyed when they learn that they will be required to take one, or sometimes two, courses focused on social welfare policy. They find this perplexing because they want to work with individuals, families, and communities. If they wanted to understand the political process and how laws are enacted, they would have majored in political science after all! The purpose of this book is to demystify the world of policy-making and demonstrate why this is an exciting and critical dimension of social work practice. After all, social work's mission of social justice and person-in-environment perspective sets it apart from almost all other helping professions in the United States.

Part I includes three chapters that provide an introduction to social work policy practice in the United States. Chapter 1 sets the stage by exploring the social work profession's mission of social justice and how policy practice helps fulfill that mission. It highlights the tensions that exist within the profession, which have led some social work scholars to argue that social work has largely neglected the macro realm. Finally, it defines policy practice and social welfare policy. Chapter 2 provides a brief history of social welfare legislation in the United States and the role of social workers in the development of policies that have advanced human rights and the well-being of vulnerable, underserved populations. Finally, Chapter 3 explores the role of values that are inherent in political debate surrounding social welfare policy.

Part II of this book includes Chapters 4 and 5. The purpose of these two chapters is to provide concrete information about how policies get enacted into law and *how* to engage in policy practice.

Part III has six chapters that include compelling stories of advocates, activists, and organizations in their efforts to make changes in the political and/or legal arenas on behalf of vulnerable populations in the United States. The topical areas covered include child welfare, children's rights, end-of-life decisions, rights for the disabled, health care, mental health, discrimination, gay rights, immigrant rights, and the social work profession itself. By critically evaluating these stories, we can learn from the tactics and strategies used by these advocates, activists, and change agents. Chapter 11 focuses on the use of lawsuits to effect social change.

Part IV includes the two final chapters of the book. Chapter 12 focuses on the economics that surrounds the policy change process, and Chapter 13 takes a look toward the future.

Get Connected With MySearchLab With eText

Provided with this text, MySearchLab with eText provides engaging experiences that personalize, stimulate, and measure student learning. Pearson's MySearchLab Connections deliver proven results from a trusted partner in helping students succeed. Features available with this text include:

- A **complete eText**—Just like the printed text, you can highlight and add notes to the eText online or download it to your iPad.

- **Assessment**—Chapter quizzes, topic-specific assessment, and flashcards offer and report directly to your grade book.
- Chapter-specific **learning applications**—Ranging from videos to case studies and more.
- **Writing and Research Assistance**—A wide range of writing, grammar and research tools and access to a variety of academic journals, census data, Associated Press newsfeeds, and discipline-specific readings help you hone your writing and research skills.

MySearchLab with eText can be packaged with this text at no additional cost—just order the ISBN on the back cover. Instructors can also request access to preview MySearchLab by contacting your local Pearson sales representative or visiting www.mysearchlab.com.

To my family, my everything. Mom, Dad, Alissa, thank you for continually supporting my dreams and passions in life.

And to all the social justice activists and advocates who work tirelessly to change the world, every day, one small step at a time.

1

Policy Practice: The Hidden Side of Social Work

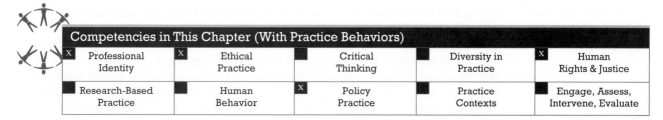

Competencies in This Chapter (With Practice Behaviors)				
x Professional Identity	x Ethical Practice	Critical Thinking	Diversity in Practice	x Human Rights & Justice
Research-Based Practice	Human Behavior	x Policy Practice	Practice Contexts	Engage, Assess, Intervene, Evaluate

> Action indeed is the sole medium of expression for ethics.

Jane Addams (1860–1935),
early social worker,
founder of Hull House, Chicago

Most people have no idea that there is a political dimension to social work practice in the United States and around the world. When people think about social workers, the most common image that comes to mind is that of a professional who is trained to assist individuals and families experiencing a range of problems such as poverty, child abuse, family violence, substance abuse, illness, and other problems of daily living. They envision trained professionals who work in a range of settings such as government agencies, hospitals, domestic violence programs, homeless shelters, schools, residential settings for older adults, and various nonprofit and community organizations. Even college students, who enter social work programs in universities across the country, are often surprised (and later delighted) to learn that social work includes macro practice and that one of the core values of the social work profession is **social justice**. In fact, a workforce study conducted by the National Association of Social Workers in 2007 found that 14% of NASW members are engaged in macro-level social work because their interventions are aimed at social change or policy/planning/administration (Whitaker & Arrington, 2008).

SOCIAL WORK'S COMMITMENT TO SOCIAL JUSTICE

A basic tenet of social work is that when helping individuals, sometimes the appropriate target of intervention is the individual, whereas at other times it is necessary to target various social conditions and injustices within the individual's environment.

Social justice has been written about and defined by countless scholars. From a social work perspective, social justice is the view that all members of society deserve equal economic, political, and social rights and opportunities. The social work profession has long recognized that to help people, change efforts must be directed both at the **micro level**, that is, the individual, and at the **macro level**, which can include the neighborhood, community, or broader society where one resides. Thus, one of the defining features of the profession is a dual focus on individuals and their respective environments. A basic tenet of social work is that when helping individuals, sometimes the appropriate target of intervention is the individual (e.g., when individuals need assistance with various problems of daily living), whereas at other times it is necessary to target various social conditions and injustices (e.g., discrimination, violence, poverty, income inequality) within the individual's environment, which may cause or exacerbate an individual's problems. This dual commitment to individuals and their social environment is clearly articulated in the preamble of the *Code of Ethics* of the National Association of Social Workers (NASW) (2008).

Most are aware of social workers' activities at the individual level, but do not realize that social workers have a rich history of working in a political context on behalf of various social causes and client populations. Since the profession's beginning, social workers have engaged in political advocacy in efforts to achieve social justice for the poor and disenfranchised in society. Some of the most politically active social workers were the **settlement house workers** during the late 1800s and early 1900s. In their efforts to improve living conditions for immigrants and the poor, they influenced state and federal legislation on issues such as child labor, women's suffrage, occupational safety, and immigrant rights. During the Great Depression, social workers were involved in the development of humane policies for the millions thrown into poverty, and during the 1960s many social workers engaged in **community organizing** and worked to support the developing fight for welfare rights and civil rights (see Chapter 2 for a more detailed history). Today, you can find social workers working in a vast array of settings (e.g., advocacy organizations, legislators' offices) that are focused on legislative advocacy and policy change efforts.

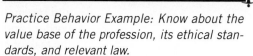

Ethical Practice

Practice Behavior Example: Know about the value base of the profession, its ethical standards, and relevant law.

Critical Thinking Question: Visit the NASW website and read section 6.04, which speaks to social workers' ethical obligation to engage in social and political action. What does this mean to you? If you are working in direct services, how will you meet this ethical obligation?

Evidence of the social work profession's commitment to social change and political action on behalf of the poor and disenfranchised can be seen in various sections of the National Association of Social Workers' (2008) *Code of Ethics*, particularly in section 6, which outlines social workers' ethical obligation to engage in social and political action in order to advocate for policies and legislation that promote social justice and improve individuals' capacity to develop and meet their basic human needs. Additionally, the Council on Social Work Education's (2008) "Educational Policy and Accreditation Standards"* require accredited social work programs to prepare students for policy practice and to help them understand the impact of policies and legislation on service delivery in the United States.

The Debate Between the "Micro Changers" and the "Macro Changers"

However, despite social work's history of political advocacy and the language that is included in a few of the most important documents of the social work profession, some have argued that this commitment to social justice and political action is not carried out in practice (Byers & Stone, 1999; Figueira-McDonough, 1993; Harding, 2004; Haynes & Mickelson, 2009; Ritter, 2007, 2008; Shamai & Boehm, 2001; Specht & Courtney, 1994). The social work profession has historically had a love–hate relationship with politics, and depending on the decade, has alternated between being very active in advocacy and legislative efforts and being relatively absent from the political arena. Figueira-McDonough (1993) and Harding (2004) discuss the consequences of social workers' absence from the legislative process at home and abroad:

> Most often, the decision makers who define the contexts within which social workers practice their profession tend to have backgrounds in economics, law, management, and politics. This fact raises two problems. First, it subordinates the exercise of the social work profession to purposes and regulations that are not informed by and often not consistent with the goals and values of social work. Second, decisions that are likely to have enormous impact on the lives of the recipients are made by people who have little or no direct knowledge of that constituency or contact with their circumstances. Policy decisions are predominantly made from the top down without input from the ground up. In sum, the absence of social workers from social policy practice is damaging to the identity of the profession and to the clients whose interest they should represent and defend (Figueira-McDonough, 1993, p. 180).**

*Adapted with the permission of the Council on Social Work Education.
**Figueira-McDonough, J. (1993). Policy practice: The neglected side of social work intervention. Social Work, 38(2), 179–188.

Silence on global problems, especially those dealing with overtly political issues, reinforces the false notion that politics—especially on the international stage—has little bearing on the social work profession, education,
and research. Given the numerous social problems that transcend national
borders and impact human well being, and in the wake of September 11,
the task of engagement with such issues is vital to creating policies world-
wide that reflect the values of the profession (Harding, 2004, pp. 180–181).*

So, whereas some social workers are uncomfortable with the profession taking political stands and would prefer to operate above the political fray, others
argue that social work is intrinsically political because of its quest for social
change and social justice. Others assert that social workers must often advocate for individuals, such as children, who cannot advocate for themselves in
the political or legislative arena (Andrews, 1998).

Has Social Work Abandoned Its Mission of Social Justice?

Since the beginning, the profession has grappled with tensions between social
workers who prefer radical political approaches versus moderates who believe
in the adaptability of the American political system and are uneasy with radical
thoughts and behaviors. In recent years, the social work profession has been accused of neglecting its commitment to social problems such as racism, sexism,
poverty, and access to health care and of being more committed to private practice and efforts to enhance the status of the profession. Epstein (1992) argued
that social work disengaged from the economically disadvantaged as a result of
being tempted into a "Faustian bargain"—professional gain at the expense of its
obligation to marginal populations (p. 154). Specht and Courtney's (1994) controversial book *Unfaithful Angels* claimed that social work has abandoned its
historic mission to the poor in favor of popular psychotherapies with the middle
class. The authors argued that social work is at risk of being undifferentiated
from other mental health or counseling professions. Social work has been criticized by those outside of the profession as well. In 1945, the famous community
organizer Saul Alinsky made his views about social workers abundantly clear:

> They come to the people of the slums not to help them rebel and fight
> their way out of the muck.... Most social work does not even reach the
> submerged masses. Social work is largely a middle class activity and
> guided by a middle class psychology. In the rare instances where it
> reaches the slum dwellers it seeks to get them adjusted to their environ-
> ment so they will live in hell and like it. A higher form of treason would
> be difficult to conceive (Meyer, 1945).**

Thus, a fundamental criticism that the social work profession has long grappled
with concerns whether it has been more committed to improving people's lives
via individual interventions at the expense of working to create needed social
and political change at the local, national, and international levels. It appears
that the "**person-in-environment**" perspective that defines the social work profession, and sets it apart from other helping professions, has also created tension
between social workers with a clinical orientation and those with a social policy
focus. Some have characterized this conflict as a profession "at war with itself"

*Harding, S. (2004). The sound of silence: Social work, the academy, and Iraq. Journal of
Sociology & Social Welfare, 31, 179–197.
**Meyer, Agnes Elizabeth Ernst. Out of These Roots. 1980. New Hampshire: Ayer Publishing.

(Thompson, 1994, p. 457), whereas others have described it as a healthy debate between the "micro changers" and the "macro changers," which, however, becomes destructive only when one approach declares itself to be "the profession" (Abramovitz & Bardill, 1993, p. 14).

This debate has been argued on a number of levels: What is the appropriate role of a profession in political activity and social change? Should social work have a political ideology, or does it require professional impartiality? Because most social workers come from the middle class or majority culture, do the values of the social work profession lean toward preservation of the status quo rather than social change? Is social work a dissenting profession or an acquiescing profession? Is the mission primarily to serve those who are poor and disenfranchised, or should the profession be open to assisting all members of society regardless of their social or economic status? In short, how political should the social work profession be?

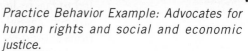
Human Rights and Justice

Practice Behavior Example: Advocates for human rights and social and economic justice.

Critical Thinking Question: There are many critics who allege that the social work profession has neglected its social justice mission in recent years. Do you agree with these criticisms? Why or why not? How can the profession improve in this regard?

Are Social Workers Adequately Prepared for Policy Work?

It has been suggested that social workers do not receive sufficient preparation for work in the political arena. In other words, they must acquire the knowledge and skills necessary so they feel competent performing this role. One recent national study that surveyed licensed social workers from 11 states found that roughly half of social workers (47%) do not feel that they were adequately prepared by their social work program for work in the legislative arena (Ritter, 2007). Additional research should be conducted to examine this topic in more depth.

IS ALL SOCIAL WORK POLITICAL?

Some social work scholars, such as Haynes and Mickelson (2009), have argued that "all social work is political" and that political advocacy is central to the mission of the profession. However, social services are provided through a political process over which social workers seem to have little influence. As Epstein (1992) observed, "Physicians are in charge of medical care; lawyers of legal practice; but social workers are not in charge of social service agencies" (p. 160). Ortiz, Wirz, Semion, and Rodriguez (2004) further argue, "As a profession wholly dependent on social policy for practice, the profession needs to continue to find ways to increase its presence in the policy arena" (p. 67).

Despite the many criticisms that have been leveled at the social work profession, there is evidence of the profession's dedication to political action. All social work programs accredited by the Council on Social Work Education are required to prepare students to engage in policy practice, and there are a small number of social work programs in the United States that offer concentrations in macro-level social work, which includes policy change. In 1997, Influencing State Policy was formed by 30 social work practitioners and educators. The mission of this organization is to assist faculty and students in learning how to effectively influence the formation, implementation, and evaluation of state-level policy and legislation. It accomplishes this by holding policy conferences, by sending information to its member database via email, and by giving monetary awards to recognize the political action activities undertaken by social work students and faculty.

The Social Welfare Action Alliance (SWAA) is a "national organization of progressive workers in social welfare" that works primarily on issues of peace and social justice. Furthermore, a significant number of social workers feel committed to macro-level change efforts. A 2007 study found that 83% of social workers strongly agreed or agreed with the statement, "Actions for improving social conditions should be a primary responsibility for all social workers" (Dickinson, 2007).

Indeed, the NASW has embraced the view that the profession should be involved in both the legislative and the electoral process. NASW, and many of its state chapters, employs professional lobbyists who work on legislation that impacts professional practice and various social welfare policy initiatives. In 1976, NASW established a political action committee called PACE, Political Action for Candidate Election, which endorses and financially contributes to candidates from any party that supports NASW's legislative agenda. Many state chapters also have formally organized PACs (political action committees), which is the legal designation for groups that want to be involved in candidate electioneering activities. States require formation of these entities for the purposes of reporting contributions and expenditures to campaigns. NASW publishes a book titled *Social Work Speaks* every 3 years, which includes its policy positions on various political issues such as capital punishment, end-of-life care, health care, immigration, human trafficking, environmental policy, economic justice, and family planning and reproductive choice, just to name a few. And a significant portion of the NASW website is dedicated to advocacy and includes information on current legislation, tips on communicating with elected officials, and enables members to sign up for legislative action alerts.

What Exactly Is "Policy Practice"?

Some social work scholars argue that policy practice is as integral to the social work profession as is the study of human behavior.

Some social work scholars argue that policy practice is as integral to the social work profession as is the study of human behavior. Social workers recognize that most social problems require interventions at both the micro level and macro level, and sometimes they demand a policy solution. For example, many social workers work with parents to help them address problems that are occurring within their family, such as substance abuse or harmful discipline practices that are placing their children at risk of child abuse and/or neglect. These adults may receive a range of services such as individual counseling, parenting classes, and substance abuse treatment. However, there are times when child welfare workers must enter the legislative arena to propose legislation, or advocate for legislation, that addresses the social problem of child abuse and neglect at the community, state, or federal level. Examples of legislation might include requesting increased funding for parent education, substance abuse programs, or other prevention programs; improved training and support for child welfare workers; harsher penalties for those who harm children; incentives for people who foster or adopt children in the foster care system; or assistance to foster youth who age out of the foster care system after graduating from high school.

For social workers, "**policy practice**" means being able to analyze, formulate, and advocate for policies that affect social well being (Council on Social Work Education, 2008). There are many levels of policy change that social workers may try to impact, such as laws and policies at the local, state, and federal level; laws within the domain of the judicial system (see Chapter 11); and even agency or administrative policies (see Figure 1.1). Policy practice may also include working to elect legislators with similar values, concerns, and priorities who are likely to support legislative efforts benefitting the

---

Macro level
(broad laws and policies from state and federal level)

Mezzo level
(administrative policy within organizations)

Micro level
(what happens when social workers translate macro- and mezzo-level policy into actual services for clients)

Figure 1.1
Three Levels of Social Welfare Policy.

various vulnerable populations that social workers represent. Finally, it should be noted that in order to be a successful change agent in this area of social work practice, many skills are necessary, such as organizing people, using the media, building a compelling argument, skillfully framing an issue, building coalitions, conducting research, and producing written communication and/or campaign tools (see Chapters 4 and 5 for more on this).

Social work students often wonder why they have to learn about politics in their social policy courses. Is it not enough to learn about the American system of government, how laws are enacted, and how to logically navigate through that process? **Politics** at its most basic definition is the process by which groups make decisions (see http://en.wikipedia.org/wiki/Politics_disambiguation). Politics can be found in all kinds of groups, organizations, and institutions— even in families! We often see politics playing out in the workplace or any environment where there are power dynamics at play. People who are good at politics are skilled at using their power to get what they want. Merriam-Webster online defines *politics* as "the art or science concerned with guiding or influencing governmental policy" and "... winning and holding control over a government" (see http://www.merriam-webster.com/dictionary/politics).

Some may like the idea of legislators using some sort of objective or rational problem-solving model when they are making policy decisions. Legislators would learn about the problem, discuss various alternatives that could be used to address the problem, and choose the best option based on the available research and evidence. However, the legislative process is embedded in a larger political process that involves personal values, political ideology, political parties vying for power, compromise, and powerful special interest groups that have a great deal of influence with legislators.

It is understandable that many Americans are turned off by politics because the American political system often does not operate the way many Americans wish it did. It is an imperfect system that is sometimes corrupt and often operates in the interests of special interests rather than the interests of ordinary people. The unfortunate outcome is that large numbers of citizens feel alienated from the political process and do not participate in the civic and political affairs of their community or government. Although social workers often find politics to be corrupt and distasteful, and the legislative process to be intimidating, it is important that they share their expertise with elected officials in order to help shape crucial policies that benefit the individuals and families whom they serve. To be effective change agents in the legislative arena, social workers must understand the policy process and develop the advocacy skills that are needed to be effective in this exciting, yet challenging, environment.

To be effective change agents in the legislative arena, social workers must understand the policy process and develop the advocacy skills that are needed to be effective in this exciting, yet challenging, environment.

You are a social worker working in a community counseling center that serves individuals from the surrounding community, most of whom are Hispanic. You work with them on a range of issues including depression and other mental disorders, family problems, and other challenges of daily living. You see your role as working directly with individuals and families in a micro context because this is where you feel most skilled and passionate.

However, a new law is being proposed in your border state to address some of the public's concerns about illegal immigration. This issue has been heating up in the last couple of years and has divided people living in various communities across the state. Racial tensions are at an all-time high. The new law proposed by the state legislature would do the following: Address the perceived problem of "anchor babies" (i.e., children who were born in the United States but whose parents are not legal citizens) by denying these children social services from many state programs.

Questions

1. Think about your own values and the values of the social work profession. How does this proposed law fit within those values? *Personally*, do you agree or disagree with this law? *Professionally*, do you agree or disagree with this law?

2. Google the term "anchor babies" to see what this phrase refers to and the various opinions out there regarding this loaded terminology.

3. According to the NASW's *Code of Ethics*, what is your responsibility if you believe that this new law would be harmful to the clients you serve?

4. If you believe this new law would cause harm, what actions would you take, if any? Brainstorm some possibilities.

5. How do you feel about taking on this challenge? Does it seem scary or intimidating? Or, does this kind of work feel thrilling and energizing?

6. Should this be part of your job even though your work is primarily clinical? Why or why not?

Social Welfare Policy

There are many different types or categories of legislation: tax policy, transportation policy, environmental policy, education policy, energy policy, agriculture policy, labor policy, and foreign policy, just to name a few. However, this text will focus primarily on *social welfare* policy. The **social welfare system** in the United States refers to the nation's complex set of programs and services that address the health, social, economic, and educational needs of its citizens. There are a vast array of social welfare programs in this country that are offered at the local, state, and federal level, such as Social Security, Head Start, SNAP (formerly known as the food stamps program), unemployment compensation, Medicare, Medicaid, public education, college financial aid, TANF, public housing, the U.S. Department of Veterans Affairs, and many more. Although there are many government-funded social welfare programs, there are also many private organizations that assist people with these needs (e.g., faith-based organizations; nonprofit organizations; and for-profit organizations).

Thus, **social welfare policy** specifically refers to legislation, laws, rules, and regulations that govern the social welfare system in the United States (Figure 1.2). Scholar Diana DiNitto (2011) defines social welfare policy as "anything a government chooses to do, or not to do, which affects the quality of life of its people" (p. 2). This is an interesting definition because it points out that there are some programs and services that government may choose not to offer to its citizens. One of the biggest political debates in the United States concerns what the role of government should be in regard to providing for the general welfare of its citizens. Social welfare policy includes many topics that are of interest to social workers, such as health, mental health, poverty and homelessness, criminal justice, family violence, education, civil rights, child welfare, and issues that

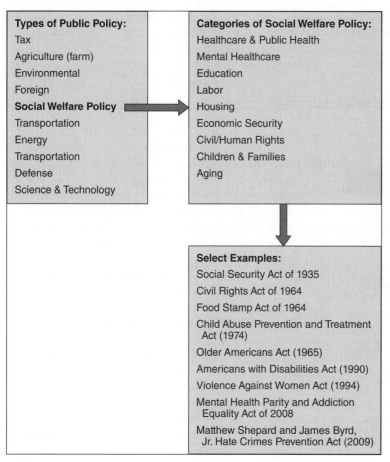

Types of Public Policy:
Tax
Agriculture (farm)
Environmental
Foreign
Social Welfare Policy
Transportation
Energy
Transportation
Defense
Science & Technology

Categories of Social Welfare Policy:
Healthcare & Public Health
Mental Healthcare
Education
Labor
Housing
Economic Security
Civil/Human Rights
Children & Families
Aging

Select Examples:
Social Security Act of 1935
Civil Rights Act of 1964
Food Stamp Act of 1964
Child Abuse Prevention and Treatment Act (1974)
Older Americans Act (1965)
Americans with Disabilities Act (1990)
Violence Against Women Act (1994)
Mental Health Parity and Addiction Equality Act of 2008
Matthew Shepard and James Byrd, Jr. Hate Crimes Prevention Act (2009)

Figure 1.2
Social Welfare Policy Flow Chart.

affect women, older adults, sexual minorities, and people with disabilities. When social workers are not involved with political advocacy, they are neglecting to use an important tool in their toolbox. Policies are powerful for the following reasons:

- Legislation can **create new social programs** or improve existing ones.
- Policies **determine funding levels** for many social welfare programs; many legislative efforts by social workers involve asking the government to preserve funding or appropriate additional resources for various programs and/or initiatives.
- Policies often **determine the goals** of social welfare programs, how they operate, and who is eligible to receive services.
- Legislation can be designed to **provide protections to vulnerable populations** and advance human rights.
- Policies can **cause harm**.

Although policies have the capacity to improve people's lives for the better, it is important for us to keep in mind that throughout U.S. history there are many examples of policies that have been harmful to groups of people, such as laws that legalized slavery; President Franklin Delano Roosevelt's Executive Order that forced thousands of Japanese Americans into internment camps during World War II; laws that forced Native Americans to give up their land and resettle (e.g., Indian Removal Act); Jim Crow laws that restricted the civil rights of African Americans and legally mandated racial segregation; laws that barred women from voting and made birth control illegal; and the don't ask don't tell policy used in the military as well as laws that bar same sex couples from getting married or adopting children.

Are Social Workers Active Enough Politically?

A common critique from prominent academics in the field has been that there are low levels of political participation by practicing professionals. However, this critique should be put into context because Americans in general are criticized for their lack of civic and political engagement. Though many social work academics have written about the importance of social workers' engagement in the political process, surprisingly few empirical studies have examined this topic. The social work literature is full of studies and evaluations of clinical interventions, but strikingly few have assessed how well social workers are faring in the policy arena. This has been examined in only a handful of studies (see Figure 1.3).

The studies listed in Figure 1.3 show that social workers are more politically active than the general public, though there are a number of political activities where their participation is quite low (e.g., volunteering for a political campaign, contributing money to a campaign, testifying before a legislative committee). The most recent analysis of social workers' political participation was a national study that surveyed licensed social workers from 11 states. This study found that approximately 46% of survey respondents can be characterized as "active" or "very active," whereas 54% can be considered "inactive" or "somewhat active" (Ritter, 2007).

This study also found that social workers are twice as active than the public when it comes to advertising for a party or candidate during an election year, three times as active in contributing financially to a candidate or party,

Policy Practice

Practice Behavior Example: Analyze, formulate, and advocate for policies that advance social well-being.

Critical Thinking Question: Do you agree with the statement that "all social work is political" and the argument that the profession should take political stands and be involved in policy change efforts? Or, do you believe that the profession should be neutral politically?

- Social workers are more politically active than the general population and as active as other professional groups (Andrews, 1998; Ezell, 1993; Hamilton & Fauri, 2001; Parker and Sherraden, 1992; Ritter, 2007, 2008; Wolk, 1981).
- Most common political activities are voting; communicating directly with legislators; belonging to an organization that takes public stands; and attending political meetings or rallies (Andrews, 1998; Ezell, 1993; Hamilton & Fauri, 2001; Ritter, 2007, 2008; Wolk, 1981).
- Least common political activities are volunteering for a political campaign, contributing financially to a campaign, and testifying before a legislative committee (Wolk, 1981; Ezell, 1993; Andrews, 1998; Ritter, 2007; Ritter, 2008).
- The most active social workers tend to be macro practitioners; be older and more experienced; be African American; belong to NASW or other professional associations; have a high degree of political interest and efficacy; and have higher incomes and educational levels (Andrews, 1998; Ezell, 1993; Hamilton & Fauri, 2001; Parker and Sherraden, 1992; Ritter, 2007, 2008; Wolk, 1981).

Figure 1.3
Findings From Studies of Social Workers' Political Participation.

Practice Activity 1.2   Assess Your Own Level of Political Participation by Completing the Following Survey

1. Did you happen to vote in the last presidential election?
   ☐ Yes   ☐ No

2. During the 2012 campaign, did you volunteer to work for **any** candidate who was running for political office, or for a political party (local, state, or national)?
   ☐ Yes   ☐ No

3. During the 2012 campaign, did you talk to any people and try to persuade them why they should vote for or against one of the parties or candidates running for political office (local, state, or national)?
   ☐ Yes   ☐ No

4. During the 2012 campaign, did you wear a campaign button or T-shirt, put a campaign sticker on your car, or place a sign in your window or in front of your residence?
   ☐ Yes   ☐ No

5. During the 2012 campaign, did you attend any political meetings, rallies, speeches, dinners, or similar events in support of a particular candidate who was running?
   ☐ Yes   ☐ No

6. During the 2012 campaign, did you make a financial contribution to a candidate, a political party, or any organization that was supporting candidates?
   ☐ Yes   ☐ No

7. Are you currently a member of a political party or an organization that takes public stands on public issues (e.g., NASW)?
   ☐ Yes   ☐ No

8. In the last year, did you contact any local or federal officials about an issue you were concerned about—in person, by phone, via letter, or via email?
   ☐ Yes   ☐ No

9. In the past 2 years, have you taken part in a protest, consumer boycott, march, or demonstration on some national or local issue?
   ☐ Yes   ☐ No

10. In the past year, have you gotten together informally with others in your community or neighborhood to try to deal with some issue or problem in the community?
    ☐ Yes   ☐ No

11. In the last 2 years, did you take part in forming a new group or a new organization to try to solve some problem in the community?
    ☐ Yes   ☐ No

12. In the past year did you lobby legislators or work to get legislation passed *as part of your job*?
    ☐ Yes   ☐ No

Now count the number of yeses that you marked
My score: _____

0–4	Not Very Active
5–8	Active
9–12	Very Active

and four times as active when it comes to attending political meetings or rallies and volunteering for political campaigns.

BEING THE VOICE OF THE VOICELESS

This book will demonstrate how social workers can impact the lives of many vulnerable populations by being advocates and working for policy change. Perhaps the biggest strength of the social work profession is the opportunity to effect change with individuals, families, groups, organizations, communities—and even at the national and international levels. There is no doubt that many social workers are motivated by the idea that you can change the world by changing the lives of individuals and families at the micro level. However, other social workers are motivated by the idea of changing the world by using the legislative or judicial system for large-scale social and/or political change. Most social workers will end up doing both micro- and macro-level work over the course of their careers because the two are so intertwined.

Many social workers who want to work in direct services or clinical practice often wonder why they need to learn about the legislative process because their main desire is to help people one on one. This is a good question with multiple answers. First, all social workers are ethically bound to engage in social and political action as indicated in the NASW *Code of Ethics.* Furthermore, policies and laws impact the programs where social workers are employed and the clients they serve. For example, in recent years, federal legislators made significant changes to the U.S. welfare system and the child welfare system. The **Personal Responsibility and Work Opportunity Act of 1996** created a new 5-year time limit for families receiving welfare, whereas the **Adoption and Safe Families Act of 1997** required states to follow a much shorter time line when filing for the termination of parental rights. These were huge changes that dramatically changed the work of social workers in child protection services agencies as well as the lives of many vulnerable children and families. However, we should ask: How many social workers were at the table, sharing their expertise with lawmakers, when these policies were being debated and considered?

Because social workers have firsthand experience working with individuals, families, and communities, they should weigh in on whether proposed policies are sound: Will the policy be effective in solving the identified problem? Is the policy supported by research and people with expertise? Does the policy operate in the best interests of the individuals whom we serve? How will the policy impact populations at risk? Does the policy support social justice, or does it seek to oppress?

Perhaps the most powerful reason to be engaged in political action is that it is an opportunity for social workers to be advocates—to be the voice of the voiceless. Legislation can be extremely powerful and can create dramatic changes in our society. There are numerous examples of this: the **Social Security Act of 1935**, which created the social security program in the United States, lifting millions of older adults out of poverty; the **Civil Rights Act of 1964**, which outlawed racial segregation; legislation in the 1960s that created the **Medicare** and **Medicaid** programs; the **Americans with Disabilities Act**, which outlawed discrimination against people with disabilities; **the 2008 Mental Health Parity and Addiction Equality Act**, which requires that insurers provide coverage for mental illness and chemical addiction treatment that is comparable to

> **All social workers are ethically bound to engage in social and political action as indicated in the NASW *Code of Ethics.***

Young woman providing testimony.

that which they provide for physical illnesses; and in 2009 President Obama signed a bill into law (the **Matthew Shepard and James Byrd, Jr. Hate Crimes Prevention Act**) that expanded federal hate crimes laws to include cases where a perpetrator targets a victim on the basis of his or her perceived gender, sexual orientation, gender identity, or disability (named after Matthew Shepard and James Byrd, Jr., who were both killed in a violent hate crime incident).

Can All Problems Be Solved With Legislation?

This chapter has provided numerous examples where policies have been instrumental in improving conditions for various groups of people. However, it is important to keep in mind that not all problems can be legislated or solved through the legal system. Social work programs prepare students to be **generalist social work practitioners**, which means that they are prepared to effect change with individuals, families, groups, organizations, and communities using a **planned change process** whereby the most appropriate intervention method(s) is determined. Sometimes policies that have little chance of success are proposed to solve the problem at hand. A skilled social worker has the knowledge and experience to understand when a problem requires a policy solution and when there is a more appropriate alternative.

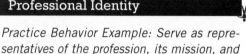

Professional Identity

Practice Behavior Example: Serve as representatives of the profession, its mission, and its core values.

Critical Thinking Question: There are a number of descriptors that could be used to describe social workers, such as caseworker, therapist, activist, researcher, and counselor. Which ones do you think most people would ascribe to social workers? Which ones are not commonly cited? Is this problematic?

For example, in recent years a number of cities and states have proposed legislation to ban smoking in cars when children are present, and it is believed that Bangor, Maine, was the first state to outlaw this practice, in 2007 (see Belluck, 2007). Parents who are caught are typically fined. Now, some people think this is an example of a brilliant piece of legislation that has the power to protect children from harmful secondhand smoke. Others disagree and believe there are better alternatives to punishing parents for this type of behavior. Some may argue that it would be more effective for cities or states to create an effective public education campaign to raise awareness about this issue (similar to campaigns that aimed to educate parents about shaken baby syndrome or the dangers of leaving children in a hot car). Perhaps there are other options. What ideas can you come up with as a way to address this problem? There are no easy answers, but social workers are trained to weigh the alternatives and to select the method with the best possible outcome.

Work Settings for Social Workers Engaged in Policy Practice

Social workers engaged in policy practice are interested in creating social change and political change. Social and political action often go hand in hand, and both are critical to advancing the health and welfare of oppressed groups. **Social action** involves promoting social change by advocating for the rights of marginalized or oppressed groups. A strong component of this work involves educating the public, raising awareness about important social problems, and helping to change societal attitudes. **Political action** typically involves a range of activities that are designed to (a) pass legislation on behalf of a particular group and (b) elect legislators who support your organization's mission and political agenda. One question that may arise is,

"Which one comes first—social change or political change?" Is it necessary to change attitudes before making progress politically on a particular issue, or will political change lead to social change? There is no easy answer to this question, and there are many examples throughout history to support both of these scenarios. Social workers who wish to engage in policy practice will most likely find employment working in an advocacy organization at the local, state, or national level. Examples of prominent advocacy organizations include the following:

- The American Civil Liberties Union (ACLU)
- Amnesty International
- Campaign to End the Death Penalty
- Child Welfare League of America
- Children's Rights
- Coalition on Human Needs
- Children's Defense Fund
- Death with Dignity National Center
- Disability Rights Advocates
- Dream Activist
- Every Child Matters
- Gray Panthers
- Human Rights Campaign (HRC)
- Human Rights Watch
- The Innocence Project
- Mothers Against Drunk Driving
- The National Alliance on Mental Illness (NAMI)
- National Association for the Advancement of Colored People (NAACP)
- National Association of Social Workers
- National Center for Victims of Crime
- National Coalition Against Domestic Violence
- National Coalition for the Homeless
- National Council of La Raza
- National Network for Immigrant and Refugee Rights
- National Organization for Women (NOW)
- National Urban League
- Physicians for a National Health Program
- Planned Parenthood
- Save the Children
- Service Employees International Union
- Stand for Children
- The Transgender Law Center
- United Farm Workers

Every day, social workers and advocates in the United States, and around the world, fight for laws and policies that advance social and economic justice for many vulnerable groups such as children, older adults, women, ethnic and sexual minorities, the disabled, and the poor. In this book, a number of their stories will be told. However, first it is important to revisit three critical periods in recent U.S. history, when significant efforts were made to radically improve the social welfare of its citizens.

CHAPTER 1 PRACTICE TEST

The following questions will test your knowledge of the content found within this chapter. For additional assessment, including licensing-exam-type questions on applying chapter content to practice behaviors, visit **MySearchLab**.

1. Which of the following was mentioned as a historical period when social workers were very politically active in the United States?
   a. World War I
   b. The Clinton presidency
   c. The Reagan presidency
   d. The Settlement House movement in the United States

2. The definition of "policy practice" for social workers would include which of the following?
   a. Referring clients to the local community mental health center
   b. Using the judicial system to effect social change
   c. Facilitating group therapy for women who have experienced domestic violence
   d. Casework practice

3. According to one national study measuring licensed social workers' levels of political participation, _____% were considered "active" or "very active."
   a. 15
   b. 36
   c. 46
   d. 52

4. You are working with foster youth and learn that many of them are upset with the Department of Human Services for not doing enough to help prepare them for adulthood after they are emancipated from the state's care and custody. You decide to advocate for a change in agency policy that would place more emphasis on "preparation for adult living" services for these youth. What level of social welfare policy would this fall under?
   a. micro level
   b. mezzo level
   c. macro level
   d. community level

5. According to the NASW *Code of Ethics*, the following types of social workers are obligated to engage in social and political action:
   a. Clinical social workers
   b. Community organizers
   c. Those who work in direct practice
   d. All social workers have this ethical obligation

6. According to this chapter, which of the following statements is false:
   a. Policies do not have the capacity to cause harm.
   b. Policies greatly impact the settings where social workers work.
   c. Policies determine funding levels for many social welfare programs.
   d. Policies can be used to advance social justice and human rights.

7. At any given time, there are social workers who are elected to public office at the local, state, and national level. If you were ever to run for public office, what issues would you prioritize? How would your values as a social worker inform your work as a public official?

Reinforce what you learned in this chapter by studying videos, cases, documents, and more available at **www.MySearchLab.com**.

Watch and Review

Watch these Videos

* Advocating for Human Rights and Social and Economic Justice

Read and Review

Read these Cases/Documents

* Policy Practice

Explore and Assess

Explore these Assets

* Interactive Case Study: What Are American Civic Values?

Research these Topics

Social Work's Commitment to Social Justice

What Exactly Is Policy Practice?

Is All Social Work Political?

Assess Your Knowledge

Go to **MySearchLab** to test your knowledge of key topics in this chapter with topic-specific quizzes. Conclude your assessment by completing the chapter exam.

---

* = CSWE Core Competency Asset   Δ = Case Study

2

Social Workers and Political Action: Three Relevant Historical Periods

CHAPTER OUTLINE

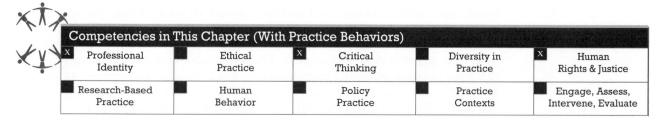

Competencies in This Chapter (With Practice Behaviors)				
x Professional Identity	Ethical Practice	x Critical Thinking	Diversity in Practice	x Human Rights & Justice
Research-Based Practice	Human Behavior	Policy Practice	Practice Contexts	Engage, Assess, Intervene, Evaluate

In these days of difficulty, we Americans everywhere must and
shall choose the path of social justice, the path of faith,
the path of hope and the path of love toward our fellow men.

—President Franklin Delano Roosevelt,
Campaign Address, Detroit,
Michigan, October 2, 1932.

Countries around the world have been faced with the dilemma of how to best assist citizens in need or in times of crisis. Some countries, such as many in Western Europe and Scandinavia, are known for having very generous social welfare systems, whereas others, such as many developing countries, cannot afford the luxury of having a social safety net for their citizens. The United States has been called "the reluctant welfare state" by one scholar (Jansson, 2008) because the government and the American public have been quite ambivalent when it comes to answering the question, "Is it the role of the government to help provide for the general welfare of its citizens, and if so, to what extent?" In fact, the United States did not have large-scale, federal social welfare programs until the presidency of Franklin Delano Roosevelt (FDR), when his administration was faced with a country reeling from the devastation caused by the Great Depression. Entire books have been written on the history of social welfare policies in the United States; this chapter provides an overview and highlights three very significant time periods in recent U.S. history when major advancements were made regarding how the U.S. government responded to the needs of vulnerable and struggling people by enacting historic, landmark social welfare legislation. These time periods are also noteworthy because they mark a time when social workers were highly politically active and made efforts to push policymakers toward needed social change. Figure 2.1 provides a list of important social welfare policies and court decisions that social workers should be familiar with.

For most of the country's early history, the U.S. federal government did not play a significant role in assisting Americans in need. Help was provided by one's relatives. If this was not an option, it was the role of the community to step in, and churches or private philanthropic organizations helped those deemed "worthy" of assistance. The able-bodied poor who needed relief were often punished and treated as criminals and were considered to be going against God's law (Day, 2008). Common approaches to dealing with the poor included the practice of indentured servitude, being forced to leave town, being auctioned off, flogging, branding, and jailing (Day, 2008). Children were often apprenticed out and were forced to labor.

When cities began to be overwhelmed with those in need, the United States saw the rise of institutions such as asylums, orphanages, correctional facilities, and **workhouses/poorhouses/almshouses**, where the poor and destitute were warehoused. When a poor person was required to enter an institution such as a poorhouse, he or she was provided with **indoor relief**. The conditions of poorhouses were wretched and included people of all ages with all kinds of problems who were often mistreated by staff. Residents were poorly clothed and fed, had no privacy, and were not afforded proper medical care; many died from malnutrition and neglect. The almshouse was a popular option at this time because residents were forced to work; thus, it was seen as an economical option that would promote better morals among the poor. However, **outdoor relief** (providing alms to people in their own homes) was also used in many cities. The first time in U.S. history when federal funds were used to

1930s–1950s: FDR's New Deal and Beyond
Social Security Act of 1935 (created public assistance; unemployment compensation; social security; aid to the blind and disabled)
Fair Labor Standards Act (1938)
GI Bill of Rights (1944)
UN Declaration of Human Rights (1948)
Brown v. Board of Education (1954)

1960s: LBJ's Great Society
Equal Pay Act of 1963
Civil Rights Act of 1964
Economic Opportunity Act of 1964
Food Stamp Act of 1964
Voting Rights Act of 1965
Elementary and Secondary Education Act of 1965
Higher Education Act of 1965
Older Americans Act (1965)
Creation of Medicare and Medicaid programs (1965)
Age Discrimination in Employment Act of 1967

1970s: Policies Affecting Women and Children
Roe v. Wade (1973)
Child Abuse Prevention and Treatment Act (1974)
Individuals With Disabilities Education Act (1975)
UN Convention on the Elimination of All Forms of Discrimination Against Women (1979)

1990s: A Mix of Progressive and Conservative Policies Passed Into Law
UN Convention on the Rights of the Child (1990)
Americans With Disabilities Act (1990)
Ryan White Care Act (1990)
Family and Medical Leave Act (1993)
Violence Against Women Act (1994)
Defense of Marriage Act (1996)
The Personal Responsibility and Work Opportunity Reconciliation Act of 1996
Adoption and Safe Families Act (1997)
State Children's Health Insurance Program (1997)
Oregon's Death With Dignity Act (1997)

Notable Policies and Court Decisions in the New Millennium
No Child Left Behind (2001)
Atkins v. Virginia (2002) Supreme Court ruling that it is unconstitutional to execute those with mental retardation
Medicare Prescription Drug Modernization Act (2003)
Same sex marriage licenses (2004) issued in Massachusetts (the first U.S. state to do so)
Roper v. Simmons (2005) Supreme Court ruling that the death penalty for those who committed crimes as juveniles is cruel and unusual punishment and a violation of the Constitution
The Paul Wellstone and Pete Domenici Mental Health Parity and Addiction Equality Act of 2008
Lilly Ledbetter Fair Pay Act (2009)
Matthew Shepard and James Byrd, Jr. Hate Crimes Prevention Act (2009)
Repeal of "don't ask, don't tell" (2010)
Patient Protection and Affordable Care Act (2010) (health care reform law)
Supreme Court's controversial Citizens United (2010) ruling that the government may not ban political spending by corporations in candidate elections, arguing that this would violate the First Amendment's free speech principle

Figure 2.1
Important Social Welfare Legislation and Court Decisions.

Activist Spotlight: Dorothea Dix*

In the 1840s, Dorothea Dix began her life's work, advocating on behalf of the mentally ill in the Unites States. She traveled all across the United States (more than 60,000 miles) documenting the deplorable condition of the mentally ill who were housed in prisons, poorhouses, and other types of institutions. In her appeal to the U.S. Congress, where she suggested federal aid to the states so that they could provide humane treatment to the mentally ill, she stated,

> I myself have seen more than nine thousand idiots, epileptics, and insane, in the United States, destitute of appropriate care and protection; and of this vast and most miserable company, sought out in jails, in poorhouses, and in private dwellings, there have been hundreds, nay, rather thousands, bound with galling chains, bowed beneath fetters and heavy iron balls, attached to drag-chains, lacerated with ropes, scourged with rods, and terrified beneath storms of profane execrations and cruel blows; now subject to jibes and scorn, and torturing kicks—now abandoned to the most loathsome necessities, or subject to the vilest and most outrageous violations. These are strong terms, but language fails to convey the astounding truths (Dorothea L. Dix and Federal Aid, 1927, p. 120).

Her measure passed both houses of Congress but was vetoed by President Franklin Pierce. Her first success came in 1843 when she presented the state of Massachusetts with her findings and the state legislature agreed to fund a state hospital in Worchester. Other states were soon to follow.

Illustration 2.1

help people in need occurred in 1865 when the Freedman's Bureau was established to help free slaves make the transition from slavery to freedom. Social reformers, like Dorothea Dix, helped to persuade the government to do more for vulnerable people who needed better care and protection, such as those suffering from mental illness (see Illustration 2.1).

THE SETTLEMENT HOUSE MOVEMENT (LATE 1800s)

The **Progressive Era** in the United States (1890–1920) is known for rapid economic growth due to the move from an agrarian economy to one increasingly reliant on machine-based manufacturing. During this period, millions of people moved to large urban cities in the north to take jobs in factories where goods were manufactured. Cities such as Boston, Chicago, and New York were suddenly overwhelmed with these new inhabitants from eastern and western Europe and rural areas of the U.S. south who were looking for work and opportunity. It is called the Progressive Era because of the work of progressive social reformers who rejected the idea of **social Darwinism** and instead worked toward resolving the social and economic problems of the day that were brought on by corporate greed, government corruption, rapid industrialization, and social inequality. **Social Darwinism** was an idea that was popular during this time and was espoused by some prominent thinkers of the day who took Darwin's ideas of natural selection and applied them to sociology in efforts to develop a theory of social evolution. The basic idea was that life is a struggle and only the fittest or strongest people will survive. Social Darwinism provided

*Editors, Social Service Review. "Dorothea L. Dix and Federal Aid" 1:1 (1927), pp. 117–137.

a moral justification for vast inequalities between rich and poor and was used as an argument for not providing people with public assistance because it would lead to dependency and interfere with the notion of "survival of the fittest." During this same time, a whole host of new social problems emerged:

- Housing structures called **tenement buildings** that were unsafe, unsanitary, and overcrowded
- The development of **sweatshops** (characterized by low wages, long hours, and exploitation) where people labored under poor and often dangerous working conditions
- **Child labor**; many young children and adolescents worked in factories instead of going to school
- An abundance of orphaned, abandoned, and homeless children on the streets (This prompted the founding of the **Orphan Trains** by Charles Loring Brace of the Children's Aid Society, by which thousands of children from New York City were transported to other states to live with rural Christian families.) (See Illustration 9.1 in Chapter 9)
- Millions of immigrants moving to large cities in the United States, unfamiliar with local customs, who experienced serious hardships and discrimination
- Congested **city slums** that were riddled with garbage, crime, violence, and prostitution
- Illness, death, and disease caused by poor sanitation, inferior hospitals, and factories (e.g., lead poisoning)
- A range of problems affecting working women (lack of day care; job discrimination; little information about birth control; their being legally barred from voting or joining trade unions)

The work of these progressives of the day included the pioneering work of the settlement house workers. The **U.S. settlement houses** were patterned after Toynbee Hall, a settlement house in London. The purpose of settlement houses was to provide a less patronizing form of charity whereby middle to upper class volunteers would live alongside poor immigrants as equal participants as they delivered a range of recreation, education, and health programs to its inhabitants.

The Settlement House movement differed in practice and philosophy from the **Charity Organization Societies (COS)** movement, which was also very prominent during this time period. The COS model was also borrowed from England and embraced the common ideas and values of the time, including social Darwinism, Christian charity, worries that relief promotes dependency, and the belief that poverty was due to a moral flaw in the individual. It was an individual approach to helping. First, an investigation was made by a paid worker to determine whether the individual was "worthy" of being provided services. The COS was against providing direct relief (money). Instead, it believed that individuals could be cured by being in contact with middle and upper class "friendly visitors" who could uplift the poor by teaching values of hard work and thrift. Although it is easy to be critical of these early social workers, it is important to note that the views of COS leaders did evolve over time as they came to have a more sophisticated understanding of the causes of poverty. COS workers, such as **Mary Richmond**, helped to further professionalize social work in the United States by calling on schools to train professional social workers. Richmond's *Social Diagnosis* laid the groundwork for casework in social work practice.

Instead of trying to change individuals, the settlement house workers wanted to change neighborhoods and expand opportunities for people. The women who founded the settlement houses in the United States were from privileged

The purpose of settlement houses was to provide a less patronizing form of charity whereby middle to upper class volunteers would live alongside poor immigrants as equal participants as they delivered a range of recreation, education, and health programs to its inhabitants.

backgrounds and were among the first women in the United States to attend college. Many earned advanced degrees in academic fields, such as medicine, sociology, and economics. They were attracted to live and work in settlement homes in order to participate in social reform, seek solutions to the social problems of the day, and escape the rigid gender roles that were common during this time. The most famous settlement house in the United States is Chicago's Hull House, founded by **Jane Addams** and her friend **Ellen Gates Starr** in 1889.

Jane Addams relied on several principles that guided the work of Hull House: (a) It was important to live in the community alongside the people the settlement house workers were assisting; (b) individuals should be treated with dignity and respect, and their culture and customs should be honored; (c) the goal would be to help people to help themselves; and finally, (d) there was a strong belief that poverty, lack of opportunity, and economic desperation were the cause of people's problems, not some moral flaw in their character. Hull House was decorated in Victorian style, and art from the European masters was displayed. It greatly expanded over the years due to financial contributions from wealthy women, and eventually the Hull House compound covered an entire city block.

Hull House offered an impressive array of programs and services to the people of the surrounding neighborhood, including art classes; day nurseries, day care, kindergarten, and social clubs; cooking, sewing, and housekeeping classes; citizenship and literacy classes; lending libraries and reading rooms; theater and dance programs; political discussion groups; health clinics; and a visiting nurse program. One criticism of the settlement house workers, however, was their sole focus on serving immigrants, thereby ignoring the plight of urban African Americans.

The hallmark of the Settlement House movement was the recognition that macro-level change efforts were needed to improve conditions for women, children, and the newly arriving immigrants. A large part of the Hull House volunteers' work involved conducting investigations (i.e., survey research) of various social problems and then working to change laws that would improve life for many in the urban slums. The settlement house workers lobbied on behalf of legislation that today is taken for granted, such as the 8-hour work day, the minimum wage, worker's compensation, old age pensions, health insurance, outlawing child labor and sweatshops, safe housing, and laws protecting the public's health from industrial hazards such as lead poisoning. They established the world's first juvenile court and improved neighborhood conditions by adding public baths, gyms, and playgrounds and improving sanitation and garbage removal. Their work led to the establishment of clinics to diagnose and treat venereal disease and efforts to provide birth control information to women.

Many of the settlement house workers picketed in various labor strikes and marched for women's suffrage and peace. Some were offered important positions in government. The governor of Illinois appointed **Florence Kelley** as Chicago's first chief factory inspector with a staff of 12. Kelley also served as head of the National Consumers League. Jane Addams served as a

Jane Addams

garbage inspector, one of the only salaried positions she held. **Julia Lathrop** was the first person to head the U.S. Children's Bureau, and she was later succeeded by **Grace Abbott**. Ms. Abbott had an important role in ensuring that children's services were included in the social security program and in helping to get the Social Security Act through Congress in 1935. **Dr. Alice Hamilton** worked for the U.S. Bureau of Labor studying industrial diseases and was a pioneer in the field of toxicology and industrial poisons.

Jane Addams became a well-known peace activist and traveled the world espousing pacifist ideals. In 1919, she helped found the Women's International League for Peace and Freedom. In 1931, Jane Addams became the first U.S. woman to be awarded the Nobel Peace Prize. In 2010, *Time* magazine included Jane Addams on its list of the "25 Most Powerful Women of the Past Century." Many social workers today cite the settlement house period as the birth of policy practice and community practice in social work, although some critics believe that social work's commitment to these areas of practice has waned in recent years (Specht & Courtney, 1994).

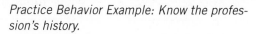

Professional Identity

Practice Behavior Example: Know the profession's history.

Critical Thinking Question: After reading about the early settlement house workers, what do you see as their contribution and legacy to social work practice in the United States? How has social work practice changed since then?

FRANKLIN DELANO ROOSEVELT'S NEW DEAL

Prior to 1935, the U.S. federal government played a very limited role in protecting its most vulnerable citizens from poverty and fluctuations in the economy. This was left largely to local communities and the states. The strong value of individualism in the United States goes back to the country's founding, and citizens who were poor or struggling were often blamed for their circumstances and personal failings. This stood in contrast to European countries, which had some form of social insurance by the 1900s. However, this all changed with the Stock Market Crash of 1929 and the ensuing **Great Depression**. The Great Depression left millions of Americans destitute and disillusioned; at its height, one in four American workers were unemployed. When the American economy collapsed, there was a new focus on the structural causes of poverty, and the idea took root that sometimes bad things happen to people that are beyond their control. Social workers saw firsthand the desperation and hardship caused when millions of Americans were thrown into poverty. They began lobbying the government for reform and action, including an unemployment program. They also gathered data on the effects of the Great Depression on communities.

FDR was a member of the Democratic Party and took office in 1933 at a time when Americans were desperate for help from their government. Roosevelt's optimism, charisma, and ability to take action stood in stark contrast to the disposition of his predecessor Hebert Hoover, who believed that government aid to the people went against the principle of self-sufficiency. FDR was known for his skill in communicating with the American public through his speeches and radio fireside chats. Americans elected FDR president four times, clear evidence of his popularity and the public's confidence in his leadership during this turbulent time.

The theme of Roosevelt's administration was **The New Deal**, and the focus would be on providing immediate relief to the suffering, reforming the financial system to prevent future economic catastrophes, and passing legislation

> **I see one-third of a nation ill-housed, ill-clad, and ill-nourished. The test of our progress is not whether we add more to the abundance of those who have much; it is whether we provide enough for those who have too little.**
>
> *—President Franklin Delano Roosevelt, Second Inaugural Address, Washington, DC, January 20, 1937.*

that would create a safety net for the needy. Work relief programs, such as the **Works Progress Administration (WPA)** and the **Civilian Conservation Corps (CCC)**, were created to give the unemployed a job until the economy recovered. Workers were paid by the government to work on a variety of public works projects, such as the construction of roads, schools, hospitals, libraries, bridges, state parks, public buildings, and public utilities. These New Deal jobs programs also included cultural projects for unemployed artists, sewing projects for women, as well as jobs for teachers, doctors, and nurses. WPA wages were higher than poor relief, and by 1936, the WPA employed one third of all unemployed Americans (Day, 2008). In its 8 years of operation, the WPA spent almost $11 billion employing eight-and-a-half million jobless Americans. One unfortunate aspect of these work programs was the discrimination faced by women and ethnic minorities who sought equal participation.

In response to the suffering and economic hardships being experienced by millions of Americans, FDR worked with the Congress to pass the **Social Security Act of 1935**, a landmark social welfare policy. At the signing of the Social Security Act, on August 14, 1935, FDR stated, "We can never insure one hundred percent of the population against one hundred percent of the hazards and vicissitudes of life, but we have tried to frame a law which will give some measure of protection to the average citizen and to his family against the loss of a job and against poverty-ridden old age" (see http://docs.fdrlibrary.marist.edu/odssast.html). The Social Security Act of 1935 attempted to protect those most vulnerable in society, including older adults, the unemployed, the poor, the disabled, widows, and children. The Act would create a combination of social insurance (for those participating in the workforce) and public assistance programs (for nonworking and dependent individuals). The key program would be social security, a program that would insure people against poverty in old age. The Social Security Act included the following:

- Grants to states for old age assistance (Title I)
- Federal old age benefits (Title II)
- Unemployment compensation (Title III)
- Aid to dependent children (Title IV)
- Maternal and child welfare (Title V)
- Public health work (Title VI)
- Aid to the blind (Title X)

The Social Security Act of 1935 attempted to protect those most vulnerable in society, including older adults, the unemployed, the poor, the disabled, widows, and children.

Two key figures in FDR's administration were **Frances Perkins** and **Harry Hopkins**, both of whom were social workers in their early careers. Hopkins was one of FDR's closest advisors and was hired to oversee the Federal Emergency Relief Administration (FERA), the Civil Works Administration (CWA), and the WPA, all of which were focused on creating work relief programs for the unemployed. Perkins was a remarkable woman. Early in her career, she volunteered her time in the Settlement House movement and soon became a passionate advocate for the rights of laborers. An event that had great impact on her was watching 146 people (mostly young women) jump to their death in the Triangle Shirtwaist fire of 1911. Before working for President Roosevelt, she had a distinguished career in social work that focused on forced prostitution; child labor; creating health clinics to decrease the number of poor women and babies who were dying in child birth; and holding various positions where she advocated for worker's rights and workplace protections. She was able to get many pieces of legislation passed into law in New York State that improved working conditions for factory workers of the day (e.g., limiting the number of hours women and children could work per week; requiring sprinklers and fire escapes).

Frances Perkins served as the secretary of labor under FDR, the first woman to hold a U.S. cabinet post. FDR appointed her chairman of the Committee on Economic Security, which was tasked with conducting an investigation of social insurance. Ms. Perkins was one of the chief architects of the Social Security Act and championed this legislation until its passage in 1935. After the passage of the Social Security Act, she spoke about the capacity of this policy to provide economic security for not only the individual but also the nation because it is better for the economy when lower income people have purchasing power. In addition to her work on the Social Security Act, she is known for working on behalf of other important New Deal reform legislations such as the abolition of child labor, the minimum wage, and a maximum workweek.

The passage of the Social Security Act of 1935 is considered the **birth of the welfare state** in the United States. FDR was opposed by some conservatives of the day who viewed it as government intervention that was overly intrusive; it was their hope that the programs created by this Act would end once the economy recovered. Throughout U.S. history, many have agreed with the philosophy that "the dole" would lead to idleness and dependency and reduce people's incentive to work. However, to the delight of those on the Left, almost all of the federal social welfare programs created by the Social Security Act were expanded over time and are still in existence today.

The Social Security Act, however, was not a perfect piece of legislation. The benefits to the poor were very low and did not include health insurance (due to heavy resistance from the AMA) or disability coverage. Some were excluded from coverage, such as farm workers, domestic workers, and many people of color, who were discriminated against. Finally, the Act continued the notions of worthy and unworthy poor because the public assistance programs created by the Act mandated means testing and gave welfare staff much discretion in deciding who would be given aid. However, many of these problems were addressed in subsequent years through the policy-making process.

Whether the United States would have passed a Social Security Act without a Great Depression is an interesting question. Frances Perkins did not believe so as she explained in a speech to the Social Security Administration, titled "The Roots of Social Security," when she was 80 years old. In her view, although many brilliant thinkers had studied and written about the need for such a policy, only something as terrifying as the Great Depression could have led the United States to pass the Social Security Act (Perkins, 1962).

The philosophical differences between liberals and conservatives over what role, if any, the government should play in protecting the general welfare of its people are still with us today. In 1944, President Roosevelt laid out an **Economic Bill of Rights** in his State of the Union speech (Roosevelt, 1944), in which he stated that people cannot be free without economic security. Among the rights he felt should be included in this second Bill of Rights were the right to a job, an adequate salary, a good education, adequate medical care, and a good home. See Figure 2.2 for an excerpt of this speech.

> **The passage of the Social Security Act of 1935 is considered the birth of the welfare state in the United States.**

Critical Thinking

Practice Behavior Example: Use critical thinking augmented by creativity and curiosity.

Critical Thinking Question: The United States has been called a "reluctant welfare state." Do you agree with social worker Frances Perkins that the United States would not have been able to pass the Social Security Act without a cataclysmic event such as the Great Depression? Why or why not?

"It is our duty now to begin to lay the plans and determine the strategy for the winning of a lasting peace and the establishment of an American standard of living higher than ever before known. We cannot be content, no matter how high that general standard of living may be, if some fraction of our people—whether it be one-third or one-fifth or one-tenth—is ill-fed, ill-clothed, ill housed, and insecure.

This Republic had its beginning, and grew to its present strength, under the protection of certain inalienable political rights—among them the right of free speech, free press, free worship, trial by jury, freedom from unreasonable searches and seizures. They were our rights to life and liberty.

As our Nation has grown in size and stature, however—as our industrial economy expanded—these political rights proved inadequate to assure us equality in the pursuit of happiness.

We have come to a clear realization of the fact that true individual freedom cannot exist without economic security and independence. Necessitous men are not free men. People who are hungry and out of a job are the stuff of which dictatorships are made.

In our day these economic truths have become accepted as self-evident. We have accepted, so to speak, a second Bill of Rights under which a new basis of security and prosperity can be established for all regardless of station, race, or creed.

Among these are:

The right to a useful and remunerative job in the industries or shops or farms or mines of the Nation;

The right to earn enough to provide adequate food and clothing and recreation;

The right of every farmer to raise and sell his products at a return which will give him and his family a decent living;

The right of every businessman, large and small, to trade in an atmosphere of freedom from unfair competition and domination by monopolies at home or abroad;

The right of every family to a decent home;

The right to adequate medical care and the opportunity to achieve and enjoy good health;

The right to adequate protection from the economic fears of old age, sickness, accident, and unemployment;

The right to a good education.

All of these rights spell security. And after this war is won we must be prepared to move forward, in the implementation of these rights, to new goals of human happiness and well-being.

America's own rightful place in the world depends in large part upon how fully these and similar rights have been carried into practice for our citizens. For unless there is security here at home there cannot be lasting peace in the world.

One of the great American industrialists of our day—a man who has rendered yeoman service to his country in this crisis-recently emphasized the grave dangers of "rightist reaction" in this Nation. All clear-thinking businessmen share his concern. Indeed, if such reaction should develop—if history were to repeat itself and we were to return to the so-called "normalcy" of the 1920's—then it is certain that even though we shall have conquered our enemies on the battlefields abroad, we shall have yielded to the spirit of Fascism here at home.

I ask the Congress to explore the means for implementing this economic bill of rights—for it is definitely the responsibility of the Congress so to do. Many of these problems are already before committees of the Congress in the form of proposed legislation. I shall from time to time communicate with the Congress with respect to these and further proposals. In the event that no adequate program of progress is evolved, I am certain that the Nation will be conscious of the fact.

Our fighting men abroad—and their families at home—expect such a program and have the right to insist upon it. It is to their demands that this Government should pay heed rather than to the whining demands of selfish pressure groups who seek to feather their nests while young Americans are dying."

Figure 2.2

FDR's Bill of Economic Rights, From 1944 State of the Union.

Source: http://www.presidency.ucsb.edu/ws/index.php?pid =16518

LYNDON B. JOHNSON'S GREAT SOCIETY AND WAR ON POVERTY

Another very significant time period when the country moved forward in the way it responded to the needs of those on the margins of society was the 1960s, under the leadership of Democratic **President Lyndon B. Johnson** (LBJ). All of the social upheavals of the 1960s led to many social workers' involvement in social movements along with a renewed commitment to the need for social change in order to achieve social and economic justice. This was an interesting time for social workers because the Great Society programs created by the LBJ administration created thousands of new community-based programs across the country that sought to create a more just society for those who have been left out. Many social workers began to view the community as their client. Social work programs also responded to the changing landscape by offering more courses and concentrations in community practice and community organizing.

Lyndon Johnson was John. F. Kennedy's vice president and was sworn in as president after Kennedy's assassination. Johnson hailed from Texas and often felt out of place among the Kennedys, who were educated at Ivy League universities and had grown up among great wealth and privilege. President Johnson served in office during extremely turbulent times in the United States that were marked by race riots; the Civil Rights Movement; the Women's Movement; the Gay Liberation Movement; the Vietnam War and the resulting antiwar movement; the publication of Michael Harrington's book *The Other America* (which exposed high rates of poverty in the United States); and the assassinations of President Kennedy, his brother Bobby, and Dr. Martin Luther King, Jr.

LBJ lived and breathed politics and is one of only a few U.S. presidents who held office as a congressman, senator, vice president, and president. Some point to his over 20 years of experience in the U.S. Congress as critical to his success in getting a voluminous amount of legislation passed as president. Johnson was a skilled politician and was not above using intimidation or shaming others to vote his way. FDR was his political hero, but unlike Roosevelt, LBJ was not privileged. He grew up in rural Texas in a family that experienced economic hardship and saw poverty around him. He also taught public school in an elementary school in Cotulla, Texas, where he taught Mexican American children, most of whom were from poor families.

I shall never forget the faces of the boys and the girls in that little Welhausen Mexican School, and I remember even yet the pain of realizing and knowing then that college was closed to practically every one of those children because they were too poor. And I think it was then that I made up my mind that this Nation could never rest while the door to knowledge remained closed to any American. So here, today, back on the campus of my youth, that door is swinging open far wider than it ever did before.

—President Johnson's remarks at Southwest Texas State College upon signing the Higher Education Act of 1965, November 8, 1965 (see http://www.lbjlib.utexas. edu/johnson/lbjforkids/edu_whca370-text.shtm)

This experience seemed to make a large impression on him and how he viewed the importance of education in order to rise above poverty.

The theme of LBJ's administration would be **The Great Society**, and the focus would be tackling the social problems of poverty and racial injustice. Johnson would declare a **War on Poverty** with the lofty goal of eliminating poverty in the United States. In terms of passing progressive social welfare legislation, few U.S. presidents have surpassed Johnson; the number of bills passed by the Johnson administration is truly astounding by any measure. The focus of the Great Society was to remove barriers for the disadvantaged and to create a plethora of social programs that would provide them with the opportunity to rise out of poverty.

Johnson supported and signed two of the most famous pieces of civil rights legislation in the United States: the Civil Rights Act of 1964 and the Voting Rights Act of 1965. The **Civil Rights Act of 1964** made discrimination based on race, color, religion, sex, or national origin illegal and included the following:

The focus of the Great Society was to remove barriers for the disadvantaged and to create a plethora of social programs that would provide them with the opportunity to rise out of poverty.

- Voting rights (Title I)
- Made segregation and discrimination in places of public accommodation illegal (e.g., hotels, restaurants, theaters) (Title II)
- The attorney general was empowered to undertake civil action on behalf of anyone being denied equal protection of the laws (Title III)
- Called for the desegregation of public schools (Title IV)
- Expanded the powers and rules of the Commission on Civil Rights (Title V)
- Nondiscrimination in federally assisted programs (Title VI)
- Equal Employment Opportunity (discrimination in employment was prohibited) (Title VII).

The **Voting Rights Act of 1965** outlawed discriminatory voting practices used in many states to prevent African Americans from voting, such as poll taxes, literacy tests, harassment, intimidation, and violence, and empowered the federal government to oversee voter registration and elections. This law had an immediate impact as hundreds of thousands of African Americans were registered to vote over the next couple of years following passage.

Johnson relished using the power of the federal government to create programs that would help people in need. His administration focused on the structural causes of poverty and the idea that people needed access to resources and opportunity in order to be successful. The legislation that he signed into law focused on health care, job training programs, education, food programs, and housing. Perhaps his greatest legacy is creating social programs for the poor, the vulnerable, and the disadvantaged, many of which are still in existence today, such as Medicare, Medicaid, VISTA, federal aid to public schools to equalize funding to less affluent schools, federal money given to universities to provide financial assistance to students, and Head Start (for a full list see Figure 2.3).

This was an extremely interesting time for the social work profession in the United States because many of these new and expanded social welfare programs needed the expertise from social workers. Prominent social workers during this time included **Whitney Young** and **Dorothy Height**. Whitney Young was the executive director of the National Urban League, president of NASW, and was awarded the Medal of Freedom by President Lyndon Johnson for his civil rights accomplishments. (Please see opening chapter photo of Mr. Young with President Johnson and Dr. Martin Luther King, Jr.). Dorothy Height was a civil rights leader, a champion of women's rights, and served as president of the National Council of Negro Women. She passed away in April 2010, and President Obama delivered a eulogy at her funeral service.

The **Economic Opportunity Act of 1964** was one of the cornerstones of LBJ's War on Poverty. It established the Office of Economic Opportunity (OEO), which was charged with directing and coordinating antipoverty programs that were focused on education, job training, and employment for the poor and people of color. The Act had many components and included the following:

- Training people for better jobs (e.g., **Job Corps** training centers).
- Adult education.
- Providing incentives to encourage industries to move to depressed areas with high unemployment.
- **Work study programs** to enable young people to go to college.
- Providing small business loans to African American entrepreneurs to increase African American–owned businesses.
- Providing incentives to employers to hire low income and minority individuals, including those on welfare.
- The **VISTA program**, which is a domestic version of the Peace Corps (VISTA volunteers were assigned to work in community programs designed to assist communities in need).
- The creation of thousands of **Community Action Agencies** across the country; these were grassroots public or nonprofit community organizations that offered an array of programs that were designed to address the causes of poverty, such as job training and employment services, **Head Start**, **Upward Bound**, preparing young people for college, day care centers for working parents,

> Freedom is the right to share, share fully and equally, in American society: to vote, to hold a job, to enter a public place, to go to school. It is the right to be treated in every part of our national life as a person equal in dignity and promise to all others.
>
> But freedom is not enough. You do not wipe away the scars of centuries by saying, "Now you are free to go where you want, and do as you desire, and choose the leaders you please.
>
> You do not take a person who, for years, has been hobbled by chains and liberate him, bring him up to the starting line of a race and then say, "You are free to compete with all the others," and still justly believe that you have been completely fair.
>
> Thus it is not enough just to open the gates of opportunity. All our citizens must have the ability to walk through those gates.
>
> *—President Johnson delivering the commencement address at Howard University on June 4, 1965*

> I want to be the president who educated young children to the wonders of their world. I want to be the president who helped to feed the hungry and to prepare them to be taxpayers instead of tax eaters. I want to be the president who helped the poor to find their own way and who protected the right of every citizen to vote in every election.
>
> *—President Johnson's voting rights address to Congress, March 15, 1965.*

(Aimed at the elimination of poverty and racial injustice)
Civil Rights Act of 1964
Voting Rights Act of 1965
Law banning housing discrimination (fair housing)
Established the Department of Housing and Urban Development
Economic Opportunity Act of 1964
Medicare
Medicaid
VISTA Program (domestic version of the Peace Corps)
Vocational and job training programs (e.g., Job Corps)
Community Action Programs
Economic Opportunity Act of 1964
Food Stamp Act of 1964
Minimum wage increase
Age Discrimination in Employment Act of 1967
Older Americans Act
Public Broadcasting Act of 1967 (allowed creation of PBS and NPR)
School breakfast program
National Endowment for the Arts
National Product Safety Commission
Air Quality Act
Wilderness Act
Land and Water Conservation Fund Act
Wild and Scenic Rivers Act
National Trails Systems Act
Immigration and Nationality Services Act of 1965 (abolished strict immigration quotas)
Education (60 bills to improve schools and access to education):

   Head Start
   Upward Bound program (helps low income high school students go to college)
   Elementary and Secondary Education Act of 1965
   Higher Education Act of 1965
   College Work Study Program
   Bilingual Education Act of 1968

Figure 2.3
Great Society Legislation/Programs During the LBJ Administration.

recreation centers for children, and health and family planning centers. An important principle of community action agencies was termed **maximum feasible participation**, meaning that programs were developed, conducted, and administered by the actual residents of the areas served.

The creation of the **Medicare** and **Medicaid** programs during this time was a major achievement in health care. The Medicare program would be a social insurance program and would provide health care coverage for those over 65 and people with disabilities on Social Security. In contrast, the Medicaid program would be a means-tested, public assistance health care program for the poor. This was a significant achievement as previous U.S. presidents, most notably Franklin Roosevelt and Harry Truman, had been unsuccessful in their efforts to expand health care coverage to the poor and aged. LBJ signed Medicare into law at the Truman Library on July 30, 1965, with Truman and his wife in attendance. President Johnson enrolled Truman as the first Medicare beneficiary and issued him the first Medicare card.

On March 31, 1968, LBJ announced to the nation that he would not be running for reelection. His presidency and beloved Great Society were done in by the war in Vietnam. Many scholars have debated whether Johnson's War on Poverty was a success or a failure, and the data are somewhat mixed. Of course, his policies were not successful in eradicating poverty in America, but the poverty rate was greatly decreased. According to Census data, the overall poverty rate was almost cut in half from 1959 (before the War on Poverty) to 1970 (from 22% to 12%). And the poverty rate for African Americans and older adults also decreased significantly during this time period (from 55% to 33% for Blacks; from 35% to 25% for those over 65). This decrease has been attributed to the combination of rapid economic growth and concerted government efforts to invest in the human capital of its citizens. The downside was that although living standards for the poor were greatly improved, some now found themselves on the welfare rolls. This was not LBJ's vision; he wanted to see people rising out of poverty and earning a decent salary as a result of new skills and education provided by Great Society programs. Unfortunately, LBJ's beloved War on Poverty suffered as more federal dollars were being committed to fight another war—in Vietnam.

LBJ's Great Society slowly became overshadowed by the war in Vietnam. It seems that the War on Poverty could not compete with the attention, time, and resources that were devoted to this war. However, many of the programs that his administration created are still with us today (e.g., Head Start, Medicaid, Medicare, the food stamp program, federal funding for public and higher education, AmeriCorps VISTA program). It is unfortunate that Johnson's commitment to ending poverty and historic achievement of shepherding through an impressive array of domestic social welfare legislation is often overshadowed by his failure in Vietnam.

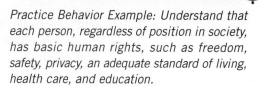

Human Rights & Justice

Practice Behavior Example: Understand that each person, regardless of position in society, has basic human rights, such as freedom, safety, privacy, an adequate standard of living, health care, and education.

Critical Thinking Question: What do you think about the legislative priorities and accomplishments of President Lyndon Johnson? Can you imagine another U.S. president declaring a War on Poverty? How was he able to successfully pass all of the Great Society legislation, which was focused primarily on the disadvantaged?

THE RISE OF CONSERVATISM AND THE DECLINE OF SOCIAL RESPONSIBILITY

In many respects, the heyday of progressive social welfare legislation ended with the LBJ administration. The rise of conservatism in the 1980s through the present day in the United States has coincided with decreasing levels of social and political action by the country's social workers. Despite a number of issues and social problems that are of concern to the social work profession, such as rising income inequality and poverty rates, the wars in Iraq and Afghanistan, health care reform, and efforts to dismantle the social safety net, social workers largely retreated to their micro roles.

By today's standards, Presidents Nixon (R), Ford (R), and Carter (D) were political moderates. A conservative backlash in the United States began with the presidential election of **Ronald Reagan**, as Republican lawmakers began arguing that large-scale, federal social welfare programs were incapable of solving the problems of the poor. President Reagan championed low taxes, government deregulation, and small government. His opinion of government's ability to operate effectively and efficiently was clear when he famously stated that "government is not the solution to our problems, it is the problem." He also advocated **supply side** or **trickle-down economics**, which is the idea that giving tax cuts and other benefits to the wealthy is good for the middle class and the poor because it leads to job creation, lower prices, and other societal benefits. He angered liberals by making significant cuts to government spending in the area of social welfare, and during his administration, the federal government began devolving responsibility for social welfare to the states and the private sector. During the 1980s and 1990s, Americans saw the rise of the **Christian Right** and their increasing influence in the Republican Party. Leaders and organizations in this movement emerged, such as Focus on the Family and the Moral Majority, and gained increasing prominence as they contributed to the national discourse on issues such as prayer in the schools, abstinence-only sex education, abortion, and same-sex marriage.

During this same time, the Democratic Party was also moving to the Right, as evidenced by the founding of the **Democratic Leadership Council (DLC)** in 1985 and increasing numbers of Democrats who began embracing an ideology of **neoliberalism** (see Chapter 3 for more on this). These new, more centrist Democrats, such as Bill Clinton, were embracing a more conservative view of economics, and they began aligning themselves with U.S. corporate interests. Some were glad to see the Democratic Party moving away from their "bleeding heart," leftist policies of the past, whereas others referred to them as "corporatist Democrats" who were now indistinguishable from their Republican colleagues on the Hill. Many on the Left were dismayed to see **Bill Clinton**, a Democratic president, sign policies into law that had been passionately promoted by conservatives, such as the **Defense of Marriage Act (DOMA)**, the **1996 welfare reform law**, government deregulation of private industry, and the **North American Free Trade Agreement (NAFTA)**. When Clinton made good on his promise to "end welfare as we knew it" by signing the 1996 welfare reform into law, three high ranking officials at the Department of Health and Human Services resigned in protest. The middle class flourished under Clinton, but many liberals were disappointed that the plight of the poor was not a major policy focus of his administration.

Progressives were further dismayed to witness the election of **George W. Bush**, an unabashed conservative who espoused government funding of faith-based social services and led the country to war against Iraq and Afghanistan in the aftermath of the September 11 attacks. President George W. Bush shared the same philosophy as his father, George Bush Sr., and President Reagan—that government should have a limited role in ensuring the social welfare of its citizens. Notable policies under President George W. Bush were **No Child Left Behind** and the largest expansion of Medicare since the program was created, the **Medicare Prescription Drug Modernization Act**, a bill focused on making prescription drugs more affordable for seniors. Both of these bills were controversial.

However, despite this conservative era of U.S. politics, there have been some notable progressive social policies passed into law, such as the Americans with Disabilities Act, the Violence Against Women Act, the creation of the State Children's Health Insurance Program (S-CHIP), the Mental Health Parity Act of 2008, and the Matthew Shepard and James Byrd, Jr. Hate Crimes Prevention Act of 2009. The 2008 presidential election was historic as Americans witnessed the election of the first African American president, in **Barack Obama**.

The theme of Senator Obama's campaign was *change*, the importance of bipartisanship in order to solve the country's most pressing problems, and putting the United States on a very different path from the previous 8 years under George W. Bush. Obama made a lot of campaign promises, including passing health care reform, ending the don't ask don't tell policy in the military, getting U.S. troops out of Iraq, repairing America's tarnished reputation in the international community, getting an immigration bill passed, and closing down Guantanamo Bay. Many social workers were hopeful that this would be a new era in U.S. politics that would tackle issues of social justice and economic inequality.

The 2008 presidential election between Senators Barack Obama and John McCain was the most expensive campaign in history, and voter turnout was high as record numbers of young people and Independents turned out. However, President Obama came into office facing immense challenges, including the biggest economic recession since the Great Depression and the continuing wars in Iraq and Afghanistan. Progressives have been split when it comes to grading the new president. Some point to his many legislative achievements, such as appointing two women to the Supreme Court; withdrawing troops from Iraq; and signing a number of bills into law that cover topics ranging from economic stimulus, health care reform, hate crimes, financial reform, and gender pay discrimination. Others have been disappointed that the dramatic change that Obama promised has not materialized and that much of the legislation passed has been too compromised and incremental to do much good (see Chapter 6 for an overview of the health care bill that Obama signed into law). During Obama's first 4 years in office, Americans witnessed the birth of two new and wildly opposing social movements, the **Tea Party movement** and the **Occupy Wall Street movement**. The country seems as polarized as ever as those on opposite sides of the political spectrum continue to disagree about the best way to move the country forward and address the country's most pressing social and economic problems. Meanwhile, there are various views regarding what kind of Democratic president Obama has been. Perhaps only history will be able to judge whether he was a president who championed progressive social welfare legislation in the mold of FDR or LBJ, whether he was a centrist and pragmatist like President Bill Clinton, or whether he blazed his own path.

Critical Thinking

Practice Behavior Example: Requires the synthesis and communication of relevant information.

Critical Thinking Question: As soon as President Obama came into office, he had to respond to a severe economic recession. In your opinion, how do his legislative goals and strategies compare with those of FDR, who was faced with the Great Depression? Compare and contrast the approaches used by these two presidents.

The following questions will test your knowledge of the content found within this chapter. For additional assessment, including licensing-exam-type questions on applying chapter content to practice behaviors, visit **MySearchLab**.

1. The first time in U.S. history when the federal government provided funds to assist people in need was
   a. the establishment of the Freedman's Bureau after the abolition of slavery.
   b. during the Great Depression.
   c. during the Settlement House movement.
   d. during World War I.

2. This chapter highlighted three time periods that are very relevant for social work practice due to progressive approaches used to help those who were poor and/or marginalized in the United States. A commonality among the settlement house workers, President Roosevelt, and President Johnson was
   a. direct experience living in poverty.
   b. a strong focus on criminalization as a cure for social ills.
   c. the belief that the best way to help those living in poverty is to provide therapy.
   d. the belief that government has a responsibility to help provide for the social welfare and protection of its citizens.

3. What defining historical event led to the United States becoming a welfare state?
   a. The American Revolution
   b. World War I
   c. The Great Depression
   d. World War II

4. Who was the first American woman to be awarded the Nobel Peace Prize?
   a. Jane Addams
   b. Florence Kelley
   c. Eleanor Roosevelt
   d. Frances Perkins

5. Which of the following was left out of the Social Security Act of 1935 passed by the FDR administration?
   a. Social security for the aged
   b. Health insurance
   c. Public assistance for low income families with children
   d. Unemployment compensation

6. According to this chapter, which of the following statements is false regarding the beliefs of the settlement house workers?
   a. The culture and customs of immigrants should be honored.
   b. It is important for people helping the poor to live in the same community with those they are assisting.
   c. Poverty is sometimes due to a flaw in one's moral character.
   d. Macro-level change efforts are needed to improve the lives of those living in poverty.

7. Why do you think most Americans do not know about the important accomplishments and social reforms of social workers over the course of U.S. history such as Jane Addams, Harry Hopkins, Frances Perkins, and Whitney Young? What can the social work profession do better to educate the public about the profession's contributions to society?

Reinforce what you learned in this chapter by studying videos, cases, documents, and more available at **www.MySearchLab.com**.

Watch and Review

Watch these Videos

* Ellis Island Immigrants, 1903
* Responding to the Great Depression: Whose New Deal?
* The Historical Significance of the 2008 Presidential Election

Read and Review

Read these Cases/Documents

* Jane Addams, The Subjective Necessity of Social Settlements (1892)
* Meridel Le Sueur, Women on the Breadlines (1932)
* Frances Perkins and the Social Security Act (1935, 1960)
* Lyndon B. Johnson, The War on Poverty (1964)
* Franklin Roosevelt's Radio Address Unveiling the Second Half of the New Deal (1936)

Explore and Assess

Explore these Assets

* Timelines: The Evolution of Social Welfare Policy

Research these Topics

Know the profession's history

Understand that each person, regardless of position in society, has basic human rights, such as freedom, safety, privacy, an adequate standard of living, health care, and education.

Understand the development of social welfare policies in the United States.

Assess Your Knowledge

Go to **MySearchLab** to test your knowledge of key topics in this chapter with topic-specific quizzes. Conclude your assessment by completing the chapter exam.

---

* = CSWE Core Competency Asset   Δ = Case Study

3

The Role of Values in the Political Arena

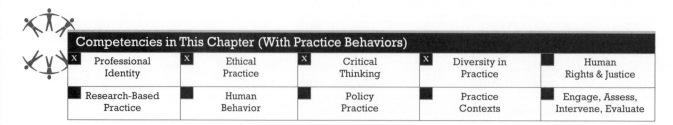

Competencies in This Chapter (With Practice Behaviors)				
[x] Professional Identity	[x] Ethical Practice	[x] Critical Thinking	[x] Diversity in Practice	Human Rights & Justice
Research-Based Practice	Human Behavior	Policy Practice	Practice Contexts	Engage, Assess, Intervene, Evaluate

> If you're not a liberal at 20 you have no heart,
> if you're not a conservative at 40 you have no brain.
>
> —*Winston Churchill*

Today, U.S. politics seems more divisive than ever. During the 8 years of the George W. Bush presidency, progressives were disillusioned and believed the country was on the wrong track as they witnessed U.S. troops being sent to Iraq and Afghanistan in the aftermath of 9/11, the approval of the use of torture termed *enhanced interrogation techniques*, the erosion of civil liberties after the passage of the USA Patriot Act, further deregulation of the private sector, and the diminished reputation of the United States on the world stage.

In 2008, Barack Obama became the 44th president of the United States after a record number of Americans went to the polls, and conservatives were inconsolable. Soon after the new president and his administration went into action to deal with the biggest economic recession since the Great Depression, the country witnessed the emergence of the Tea Party movement. Tea Party activists overwhelmed town hall meetings around the country and took to the streets to express their outrage at "out-of-control" government spending and the ballooning deficit due to the passage of the stimulus package, the bailout of the U.S. financial system, and President Obama's plans to reform the health care system. A few years later, another protest movement emerged called Occupy Wall Street with the rallying call, "We are the 99 percent!" On the 24-hour cable news cycle, political pundits often reduce Americans to either red state, salt-of-the-earth Americans who tune into Fox News to watch Glenn Beck call President Obama a socialist, or blue state, latte-drinking intellectuals whose favorite pastime is watching Jon Stewart chiding conservatives on his "fake" news show, *The Daily Show*.

IT'S ALL ABOUT VALUES

In social work education, **values** are discussed quite frequently. Students learn about important social work values such as service, social justice, the dignity and worth of individuals, and self-determination, and are encouraged to explore their own personal values. There are times when personal values and professional values conflict, and social workers must find a way to sort this out. "The personal is political" is a famous saying that came out of the women's movement in the 1960s, though this is true for many people. The idea behind this phrase is that people tend to be politically active about issues that affect their lives directly (e.g., discrimination, gun ownership, sexual violence, lack of health insurance, funding for public education). Our personal values are influenced by family members, the community where we were raised, people we admire, such as teachers and mentors, dominant societal values, and our spiritual or religious beliefs.

It should not be a surprise then that our personal value system affects our political beliefs. For example, our personal values shape our thinking about how

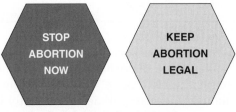

Stop Abortion Now, Keep Abortion Legal

Politics is personal, and many political issues have to do with values that we hold very dear.

our country should help people, especially the more vulnerable members of our society, what kinds of problems we should be addressing in our country, and where the government should intervene and when it should stay out of our lives. They also affect our opinions on hot-button issues such as abortion rights, the death penalty, and same sex marriage. Many of us can recall occasions in our life where we got into heated political arguments with others. Why is this? Politics is personal, and many political issues have to do with values that we hold very dear.

Many astute observers of the political process will tell you that social policies are based primarily on values, and that the development of these policies is often not a rational process based on evidence or the careful consideration of alternative policies. Many Americans may prefer that their legislators use a logical problem-solving model when making policy. It would look something like the following: (a) examine the problem; (b) identify various courses of action to solve the problem; (c) consult experts and available research on the topic; (d) select the best option based on available information; and (e) evaluate the outcome and revise as needed. Sometimes policies are made in this manner. However, much of the time, legislators make decisions based on their values and what is moral or right, in their view. For example, based on their religious convictions, some conservative lawmakers advocate the use of abstinence-based sex education in public schools. Many of these lawmakers would not be persuaded by research showing that comprehensive sex education is more effective in preventing teen pregnancy. On the other side, some liberals would hesitate to support capital punishment even if they were presented with evidence that it was an effective deterrent. Time and again, values and ideology trump rationality when it comes to making public policy.

AMERICAN VALUES

Some have argued that values constitute the most important dimension for understanding social welfare policy. According to Prigmore and Atherton (1986), the following 15 American values influence their social policies:

- Achievement and success
- Activity and work
- Public morality
- Humanitarian concerns
- Efficiency and practicality
- Progress
- Material comfort
- Marketplace capitalism
- Equality
- Freedom
- Conformity versus individualism
- Science and rationality
- Nationalism and patriotism
- Democracy
- Racism and group superiority

When a particular policy embraces some of the above values, it is more likely to pass. Policies that violate these cherished values will face strong opposition. Some are surprised to see the last "value" on the list; however, Prigmore and Atherton argue that many American policies historically have been based on the belief that some groups are superior to other groups.

> **Capital.** The stock of capacity to do something.
> **Human Capital.** Skills and talents that increase one's value in the marketplace; investments in human capital can include education, job training, and experience.
> **Social Capital.** The concept of social capital is applied to communities; communities with a substantial stock of social capital are healthy communities; you will see established social networks, social connectedness, high levels of civic engagement, collaboration, reciprocity, social trust, a value of less *I* and more *We*. Robert Putnam is one of the gurus of social capital and has written best-selling books on the topic, including *Bowling Alone: The Collapse and Revival of the American Community* (2001) and *Better Together: Restoring the American Community* (2004).

Figure 3.1
Defining Terms

Sometimes American values and social work values are at odds with each other, which can be challenging when social workers are trying to get certain types of legislation passed. For example, legislation to expand funding for social programs that serve those living in poverty, such as early childhood education programs, Medicaid, housing programs, or food stamps, are often not popular with the public because they are perceived as going against American values of individualism, hard work, and success. Policy work from a social work perspective often involves asking the public to be willing to support public policies and social programs (via taxation) that are investments in human and social capital (see Figure 3.1 for definitions).

Ethical Practice

Practice Behavior Example: Recognize and manage personal values in a way that allows professional values to guide practice.

Critical Thinking Question: What has influenced your value system? What political issues are you passionate about? How are your political beliefs informed by your personal values?

POLITICAL IDEOLOGY

In the political arena, people often refer to "ideology." **Ideology**, in a general sense, means a way of looking at things, or one's world view. It may include beliefs through which we view the world, how the world works, what has value, what is worth living and dying for, what is good and true, and what is right. **Political ideology** largely concerns itself with how society should work and the best way to achieve this ideal arrangement. Political ideology includes ideas on what is considered to be the best form of government, the best economic system, and often identifies where someone falls on the political spectrum (e.g., Left, Center, or Right). Even though there are a number of political ideologies, the two dominant ideologies in the United States are **liberalism** and **conservatism**. In recent years, fewer people identify as belonging to a particular political party and are more likely to use one of the following terms to describe themselves politically: *conservative*, *liberal*, *progressive*, or *moderate*. As Self-reflection Exercise 3.1 indicates, political ideology can be conceptualized as a continuum from extremely liberal to extremely conservative.

WHY CAN'T LIBERALS AND CONSERVATIVES GET ALONG?

Americans frequently state their desire for their legislators to work together on various issues and to find areas of compromise. Often, the desire for more **"bipartisanship"** is voiced. However, this is a fairly stiff challenge to overcome

Perhaps the biggest difference between conservatives and liberals concerns what the role of government should be and where Americans should spend federal resources.

in light of the fact that conservatives and liberals have starkly different world-views or ideologies. Perhaps the biggest difference between **conservatives** and **liberals** concerns what the role of government should be and where Americans should spend federal resources (see Table 3.1). Conservatives value tradition, individual responsibility, minimal government intervention into the lives of individuals and corporations, privatization, competition, and low taxes. President Ronald Reagan, a conservative icon in the Republican Party, is a good example of espousing conservative ideology because he championed supply side economics and small government.

Liberals, on the other hand, value social change, social justice, progress, social responsibility, and strong government intervention via taxation, regulation, and government programs to address social and economic inequality and to bring about a more level playing field. President Franklin Delano Roosevelt is a hero to many liberals because he was responsible for the creation of large-scale social programs such as Social Security, worker's compensation, unemployment compensation, and public assistance in the aftermath of the Great Depression. Some on the Left prefer to describe themselves as "progressives" because the term *liberal* has been tainted by conservatives (e.g., "tax and spend liberal," "bleeding heart liberal," the "liberal elite").

Radicalism is another political ideology that sometimes gets confused with liberalism; however, there are important philosophical differences between the two. Liberals strive to improve society by changing the social order, but they strive to make the system more fair, not change the system altogether. In other words, liberals want to bring people into the system who have traditionally been left out. Radicals, on the other hand, believe that the system itself is flawed and thus seek more fundamental changes in society. Radicals are critical of free market economies and believe they result in the exploitation of labor and the poor. Often socialist economic systems are advocated by people with a radical worldview. There are a couple of interesting points of discussion concerning the last two rows of Table 3.1. During the last 20 to 30 years, the United States has witnessed the growth and development of new factions within both conservative and liberal

Table 3.1   Political Ideology

	Conservatism	Liberalism
Change	Change is generally not desirable; it is better to keep things as they are.	Change is generally good; it brings progress.
	Preserving the status quo is more important than social change.	Supports social change and institutional reform (but not structural change, as in radicalism)
View of Society	Society is inherently fair and functions well on its own.	Society needs regulation to ensure fair competition between various interests.
Responsibility	*Individual responsibility*: Individuals have free will and are responsible for their own lives and problems. They have the right and responsibility to pursue their own self-interest and to receive a fair share of societal resources based on merit and hard work.	*Social responsibility*: Individuals are not entirely autonomous because the environment plays a part in problems people face. Collective responsibility for ensuring the social welfare of its citizens; individuals need to be afforded a fair chance to secure societal resources.
Role of Government	Freedom means freedom from government coercion; government should not interfere with the free play of economic and political forces; strong focus on states' rights	Government is needed to bring about a more level playing field and to compensate for the market's inability to meet basic needs; strong federal government.

Table 3.1   (*continued*)

	Conservatism	Liberalism
	• Government should have a minimal role in ensuring the social welfare of its citizens. • "Government is not the solution to our problems, it is the problem." (Ronald Reagan) • Prefer private sector approaches over government welfare.	• Government programs needed to ensure a minimum standard of living below which no one should fall. • The state protects people from the following risks: loss of income due to illness, old age, death, disability, economic downturns, and globalization. • Social welfare expenditures are investments in human capital that increase the nation's wealth.
Size of Government	*Small government*: • Reduce the size and power of government programs. • Focus on privatization of social services. • "Starve the beast" through high deficits.	*Large, active government*: *Expanded government programs such as:* • Social Security • Medicare • Medicaid • Public assistance • Health care
View of the Free Market	Free market economy is the best mechanism for distributing a fair share of societal resources; strongly values competition. Opposed to the rights of unions to bargain collectively and government regulation of corporations and industries.	Market is not equipped to meet basic needs of citizens; produces an unequal distribution of income, resources, and life chances; and fails to account for discriminatory barriers that stand in people's way. Government regulation and unions are needed to protect workers and average citizens (e.g., FDA, consumer protections).
Taxes	Lower taxes for corporations and the rich; Reagan's notion of "trickle-down economics."	Tax the wealthy and corporations to fund programs for the middle class and the poor; redistribution of wealth.
View of Inequality	Historically, has been opposed to extending civil rights legislation (e.g., women; non-Whites; gays and lesbians) and supporting workers' right to unionize. Inequality is inevitable and necessary. Equality, or leveling the playing field, rewards a lack of initiative, reduces work effort, and leads to economic stagnation.	Strong focus on social/economic justice and equality, or leveling the playing field. Too much inequality is problematic. Large gap between haves and have-nots creates tensions that undermines individual life changes, economic productivity, and social harmony.
Church	Separation of church and state.	Separation of church and state.
New Factions	Cultural conservatives.	Neoliberals.

camps. Today, cultural conservatives differ from traditional conservatives with regard to the separation of church and state.

RELIGION AND POLITICS

Historically, conservatives have strongly valued the separation of church and state because this supports the idea of limited government intrusion in the lives of individuals. However, the 1980s saw the birth of the Christian Right movement in the United States and a new kind of conservative—the **cultural conservative**. The religious Right movement was a grassroots movement that included groups such as Jerry Falwell's Moral Majority, Pat Robertson's Christian Coalition, Phyllis Schlafly's Eagle Forum, and James Dobson's Focus on the Family, which embrace traditional conservatives' laissez-faire approach to economics, yet argue for government intervention into citizens' private lives when it comes to issues such as same sex marriage, abortion, prayer in the schools, and end-of-life decisions.

The Christian Coalition is a political organization that seeks to mobilize pro-family Christians for political action. The mission of Focus on the Family is to spread the gospel of Jesus Christ. The organization is based around

Stop Abortion Sign

the following six pillars: the preeminence of evangelism; the permanence of marriage; the value of children; the sanctity of human life; the importance of social responsibility; and the value of male and female (see http://www .focusonthefamily.com/about_us/guiding-principles.aspx). Cultural conservatives are a very powerful force within the Republican Party and today outnumber traditional or classic conservatives.

A good example to illustrate the difference between traditional conservatives and cultural conservatives is the famous case of Terri Schiavo. In 1990, Ms. Schiavo suffered from severe brain damage after collapsing in her home and experiencing respiratory and cardiac arrest. She lived in a persistent vegetative state and required institutionalized care for 15 years until her feeding tube was removed at the request of her husband Michael Schiavo, her legal guardian. But this was only after a lengthy legal battle between Michael and Terri's parents, Robert and Mary Schindler, who fought against the removal of the feeding tube. The nation soon became spectators to one of the most fascinating, yet heartwrenching, right-to-die battles in recent U.S. history that included vigorous protests by various right-to-life groups and the involvement of the Florida state legislature; the U.S. Congress; Florida governor Jeb Bush; the President of the United States, George W. Bush; and the U.S. Supreme Court. See Illustration 3.1 for a time line of the events that unfolded in this case.

American public opinion on the Terri Schiavo case varied widely. Some, because of their religious beliefs, which include a right-to-life philosophy,

---

Time Line of the Terri Schiavo Case

- February 11, 2000: Circuit Judge George W. Greer approves Michael Schiavo's request to have Terri's feeding tube removed, agreeing that she had told her husband that she would not want to be kept alive artificially.
- April 2001: Terri's feeding tube is removed but another judge orders it reinserted 2 days later.
- November 2002: Judge Greer finds no evidence that Terri has any hope of recovery and again orders tube removed.
- October 15, 2003: Feeding tube removed for second time.
- October 21, 2003: Republican Governor Jeb Bush signs a bill called *Terri's Law*, allowing him to intervene, and then orders that the tube be reinserted.
- September 23, 2004: Florida Supreme Court rules that *Terri's Law* is unconstitutional.
- February 25, 2005: Judge Greer gives permission for tube removal at 1 p.m.
- March 18, 2005: Feeding tube removed. Judge Greer rules against congressional Republicans who had tried to put off tube removal by seeking Terri's appearance at hearings.
- March 20–21, 2005: U.S. Congress passes bill that would allow a federal court to review the case. President Bush signs the bill. Terri's parents file an emergency request with a federal judge to have the tube reconnected.
- March 22, 2005: U.S. District Judge James Whittemore refuses to order the reinsertion of the tube. Terri's parents appeal to the 11th U.S. Circuit Court of Appeals.
- March 23, 2005: The 11th Circuit declines to order the reinsertion of the tube. Terri's parents then appeal to the U.S. Supreme Court.
- March 24, 2005: U.S. Supreme Court denies the appeal.
- March 31, 2005: Terri Schiavo dies, at age 41.

Illustration 3.1

Diversity in Practice

Practice Behavior Example: Understand the dimensions of diversity as the intersectionality of multiple factors including age, class, color, culture, disability, ethnicity, gender, gender identity and expression, immigration status, political ideology, race, religion, sex, and sexual orientation.

Critical Thinking Question: Because the political process is often a fight over values, do you think it is possible to divorce political views from religious and/or spiritual beliefs? Or, is it acceptable to allow one's spiritual/religious beliefs to inform his or her political views? Why or why not?

sided with Terri's parents. Others believed that Terri had no quality of life and that Terri's husband was upholding her wishes and right to die. Many liberals and traditional conservatives were horrified as they watched lawmakers at the state and federal level intervene in a family's private life, which in their view, should have been left to the family to battle it out in court.

Secularism is freedom from government imposition of religion on its citizens. Many Americans are uncomfortable with the idea of religion and politics mixing, especially when it is perceived as a particular religion pushing its beliefs onto others and codifying these beliefs into law. On the other hand, it is hard to imagine not relying on one's spiritual or religious convictions when entering the political arena when so many of our stances on political issues are informed by our personal value systems. For some of us, the way we want the world to be stems from beliefs that are secular in nature, whereas for others, they are strongly rooted in spiritual or religious beliefs. It is not unusual for churches in the United States to enter the political fray. For example, the Catholic church takes political stands on issues such as abortion, the death penalty, and how governments should do more to take care of the poor. And the Civil Rights movement in the United States was led by the Reverend Dr. Martin Luther King, Jr. and other church leaders in the South.

Even though conservative religious groups tend to get a lot of attention in this country, there are also liberal religious organizations, such as The Red Letter Christians and the Interfaith Alliance, which advocate addressing poverty, caring for the environment, and advancing peace and religious freedom. Finally, there are several prominent secular organizations such as the American Civil Liberties Union (ACLU) and the Texas Freedom Network that fight against religious extremism and promote the separation of church and state. The mission of the Texas Freedom Network is to defeat initiatives backed by the religious Right, such as textbook censorship, abstinence-only sex education, defining marriage as between a man and a woman, and using tax dollars to fund religious schools and faith-based organizations.

Practice Exercise 3.1   Religion and Politics

Look at the websites for the following groups and organizations to learn more about these organizations, their mission statement, and their message:

Christian Coalition:	http://www.cc.org
Eagle Forum:	http://www.eagleforum.org
Focus on the Family:	http://www.focusonthefamily.com
Red Letter Christians:	http://www.redletterchristians.org
Interfaith Alliance:	http://www.interfaithalliance.org
Texas Freedom Network:	http://www.tfn.org
ACLU:	http://www.aclu.org

NEOLIBERALS

Neoliberal refers to a "new" type of liberal. After the defeat of President Jimmy Carter in 1980, liberal Democrats began a process of reevaluating their party's traditional stances, particularly in relation to domestic policy. This was the beginning of the party's "move to the middle" and a new philosophy that was more cautious of large-scale federal government programs for the poor and vulnerable and more embracing of big business, including less government regulation. In 1985, the **Democratic Leadership Council (DLC)** was founded by these new centrist Democrats who were focused on issues such as welfare reform, fiscal responsibility, expanding trade, and catering to the middle class. They called themselves "New Democrats." The DLC espouses the idea that economic growth generated in the private sector is the prerequisite for opportunity, and that government's role is to promote growth and to equip Americans with the tools they need to prosper in the New Economy. It also argues that government programs should be grounded in the values most Americans share: work, family, personal responsibility, individual liberty, faith, tolerance, and inclusion. Some Democrats embraced this new strategy, whereas others derided this new group of "corporate" Democrats for abandoning some of the core values of the Democratic Party.

Bill Clinton is a good example of a politician who embraced the goals and philosophy of **neoliberalism**. Although conservatives branded Clinton a liberal, many progressives were greatly disillusioned by many policy decisions of the Clinton administration, including its support for the North American Free Trade Agreement (NAFTA), deregulation of the private sector, the don't ask don't tell policy in the military, and the Defense of Marriage Act (DOMA), which defined marriage as a union between a man and a woman. But perhaps the decision that was most upsetting to some liberals was Clinton's support for welfare reform and his goal to "end welfare as we know it." The **Personal Responsibility and Work Opportunity Reconciliation Act of 1996** ended the 60-year-old federal entitlement to welfare in the United States and was an effort by conservatives to reduce dependence on government assistance. The new law replaced the **Aid to Families with Dependent Children (AFDC)** program with the **Temporary Assistance for Needy Families (TANF)** program and included the following features:

- States would now receive federal block grants and would have much more discretion in designing and operating their welfare and work programs;
- Instituted a 5-year lifetime limit on cash assistance, though states can set shorter time limits;
- Included new work requirements for parents receiving cash benefits. Adults are required to participate in work activities 2 years after they start receiving assistance;
- Permitted states to impose a family cap, to deny cash benefits to children born into families already receiving assistance;
- Required unmarried parents under age 18 to live with an adult and stay in school in order to receive benefits;
- Prohibited parents who have been convicted of felony drug offenses from receiving benefits for life under TANF or the Food Stamp Program;
- Denied benefits to most legal immigrants entering the country for 5 years, or until they attain citizenship, with states having the option of extending the ban for a longer time period.

THINK TANKS

Think tanks, or policy institutes, are extremely influential when it comes to shaping social policy in the United States. **Think tanks** are policy-oriented research organizations that engage in advocacy and provide expertise to politicians, including U.S. presidents. They employ experts and researchers who write policy briefs on a range of social issues and provide advice and ideas about how to solve social, political, or economic problems. Think tanks in the United States are privately funded, and they are often criticized for being biased because a number of them are aligned with a particular political party or ideology. It is fairly common for legislators to cite a report from one of these think tanks when they are working toward the passage or defeat of a particular piece of legislation.

Examples of prominent Right-of-Center think tanks are the American Enterprise Institute, The Heritage Foundation, the Hoover Institution, The National Policy Institute, and The Cato Institute. The mission of The Heritage Foundation is to promote conservative public policies based on the following principles: free enterprise, limited government, individual freedom, traditional American values, and a strong national defense. Examples of prominent Left-leaning think tanks are the Center on Budget and Policy Priorities, the Center for American Progress, the Progressive Policy Institute, Brookings Institution, Urban Institute, Institute for Policy Studies, and the Economic Policy Institute. The mission of the Center on Budget and Policy Priorities is to develop policy options to alleviate poverty and to focus lawmakers' attention on the needs of low income individuals and families.

POLITICAL PARTIES IN THE UNITED STATES

Partisanship, or identifying as a member of a particular political party, has waned significantly in recent years as more and more people identify themselves as an **Independent**. The United States is dominated by two political parties, the Democratic and Republican parties. In recent times, the **Democratic Party** has been the home of liberal or progressive politics, whereas the **Republican Party** is the home base of conservatives. Some see differences between these two political parties, whereas others feel that there are fewer differences in recent years because they both get accused of catering primarily to corporate interests. With the increase of cultural conservatives in the Republican Party and neoliberals in the Democratic Party, it can be argued that both political parties have moved to the Right in the last 20 to 30 years.

Social workers who are involved in policy change efforts must understand the two dominant political parties, what they stand for, and how they differ. One way to do this is to examine each party's political platform, a lengthy document that lays out each party's priorities and concerns. It is important to note not only what is emphasized but also what is not emphasized in these party platforms. These party platforms change over time and are not static.

Many would like to see the development of third parties as a way to challenge the two-party system in the United States. The only two political parties that have gained some traction in recent years are the **Green Party** on the Left and the **Libertarian Party** on the Right. Libertarians believe in extremely limited government intervention in all areas of human and social life. According to the Libertarian Party's website, "Libertarians believe the answer to America's political problems is the same commitment to freedom that earned America its greatness: a free-market economy and the abundance and prosperity it brings; a dedication to civil liberties and personal freedom that marks this country above all others; and a foreign policy of non-intervention, peace, and free trade as prescribed by America's founders" (http://www.lp.org/issues). Because Libertarians emphasize individual freedom and personal responsibility, they advocate for minimal taxation (only for police and military defense), the legalization of drugs, and do not oppose same sex marriage because they believe the government should not interfere with the personal affairs of Americans as long as they are not harming others.

The **Green Party** includes many Americans who are disillusioned with the Democratic Party, which they believe has abandoned its commitment to poor and working families. Famous activist and consumer advocate Ralph Nader ran for president as a Green Party candidate in 1996 and 2000. The Green Party's website lists the following 10 core values (www.gp.org): grassroots democracy; social justice and equal opportunity; ecological wisdom; nonviolence; decentralization [of wealth and power]; community-based economics and economic justice; feminism and gender equity; respect for diversity; personal and global responsibility; and future focus and sustainability.

Critical Thinking

Practice Behavior Example: Distinguish, appraise, and integrate multiple sources of knowledge, including research-based knowledge, and practice wisdom.

Critical Thinking Question: Visit the websites of the Democratic Party (www.democrats.org), the Republican Party (www.gop.com), and the Green Party (www.gp.org). What is emphasized and not emphasized by each party? Which party is most naturally aligned with the values of the social work profession?

THE TEA PARTY MOVEMENT

A very recent development in U.S. politics is the birth of the **Tea Party**, an ultraconservative movement that developed as a reaction to the presidency of Barack Obama and his administration's policies, in particular legislation that allocated a huge amount of federal dollars to bail out the financial system and stimulate the economy, as well as health care reform. The party's name is a reference to the Boston Tea Party of 1773, a protest of the ruling British government by disenfranchised American colonists. The Tea Party is a decentralized movement, though it is supported by wealthy donors, a number of prominent individuals inside the Republican Party, such as former speaker of the House Newt Gingrich, and conservative organizations such as FreedomWorks and Americans for Prosperity.

The Tea Party Patriots call themselves the official home of the Tea Party movement, and their mission statement is to fight against excessive government spending and taxation, which is in line with their three core values of fiscal responsibility, constitutionally limited government, and free markets. Leaders within this movement have developed a Contract From America, which includes 10 agenda items that they are asking candidates to sign (see http://www.contractfromamerica.com). There has been a lot of activity across the country at the local and national levels, including local protests, a national Tea Party convention hosted by Tea Party Nation where Sarah Palin was the keynote speaker, and a Taxpayer March on Washington in September 2009. In the 2010 midterm elections, a number of Tea Party candidates were elected to political office at the state and national levels.

A very recent development in U.S. politics is the birth of the Tea Party, an ultraconservative movement that developed as a reaction to the presidency of Barack Obama and his administration's policies.

OCCUPY WALL STREET

The Tea Party movement was not the only new movement to emerge during the Obama administration. In September 2011, the United States witnessed the emergence of the Occupy Wall Street movement on the Left. The first protest was in Manhattan's financial district, but protests soon spread to other major cities in the United States and around the globe. Many media pundits have criticized this movement for not having a clear agenda with a list of specific goals or demands. But the protesters thus far have resisted doing this. Instead, they are communicating a broad message of fighting against the immense power amassed by banks, the financial industry, and multinational corporations, which has distorted the democratic process in the United States and led to rising levels of economic inequality and injustice. According to the Occupy Wall Street website, the movement was inspired by the popular uprisings in Egypt and Tunisia.

The slogan the protestors have embraced is "We are the 99%" to make the point that it is the 1% of the richest Americans who have enjoyed most of the financial gains in recent years at the expense of average working Americans as well as those at the bottom of the economic ladder. This movement is in large part a reaction to the 2008 financial collapse of Wall Street and the resulting economic recession that threw millions of Americans out of work and out of their homes. Many Americans were further outraged when the government decided that the banks would be bailed out by the American taxpayer. Soon it appeared that the financial industry was back to business as usual with no serious reforms of the system to prevent something like 2008 from happening again. Feelings of helplessness and anger have helped to fuel this movement for those who feel that the rich and powerful collude with politicians to bend the rules in their favor with no one looking out for the interests of average Americans.

The Occupy Wall Street movement is using nonviolent civil disobedience tactics, such as peaceful assembly, and tent cities can be seen in many major cities where protesters have organized and are carrying out their work. The decision-making process used by Occupy Wall Street is called a People's Assembly, a nonhierarchical, consensus-building model that encourages dialogue and where all opinions are heard.

Even though the protests have been nonviolent, there have been a number of incidents of police brutality where protesters have been pepper-sprayed and beaten and arrested by police as mayors have grown impatient. The protests have even spread to some U.S. college campuses, and one incident made

Self-reflection Exercise 3.2

Where would you place yourself on the following scale?

- [ ] Strong Democrat
- [ ] Weak Democrat
- [ ] Independent Leaning to the Democrats
- [ ] Pure Independent
- [ ] Independent Leaning to the Republicans
- [ ] Weak Republican
- [ ] Strong Republican
- [ ] Other Political Party (e.g., Green Party; Libertarian Party)

Why do you think people are less partisan today—that is, they are less likely to identify with any particular political party—than in previous decades?

national news when police in riot gear pepper-sprayed students at the University of California Davis. Other clashes with police have occurred in cities such as Oakland and Manhattan when the authorities have attempted to forcibly remove protesters by using tear gas, forcibly tearing down the camp sites, and arresting those who refuse to leave.

It is too soon to assess the success of the Occupy Wall Street movement and how it may change the political landscape and impact the next elections. But the movement has been successful in gaining extensive media coverage.

ARE ALL SOCIAL WORKERS LIBERAL?

In 2007, conservative journalist George Will published a scathing indictment of the social work profession in *The Washington Post* and referred to social work programs as schools of indoctrination with a sign on the door proclaiming "conservatives need not apply." He cited the social work profession's mission of social and economic justice and many of the constructs that are commonly examined in social work courses such as diversity, classism, White privilege, inclusion, and racism as evidence of the profession's liberal bias and opposition to conservative thought.

NASW Executive Director Elizabeth J. Clark responded in her piece to *The Washington Post*, "Social work students learn to use advocacy for the benefit of individuals, families, and populations that are most vulnerable to the unresolved problems of the day." She went on to say:

> Members of NASW hold a diverse array of opinions on many social issues, including abortion and homosexuality as mentioned in Will's column. However, professional social workers are united in their commitment to respecting the rights of clients to access services and expand options available to them. Social workers do not apologize for caring about people who are marginalized by society, nor do we apologize for holding members of our profession to high standards (Clark, 2007).*

The social work profession certainly has a reputation for being associated with liberal causes and for embracing a progressive political ideology. Many social work scholars argue that social work's mission of working for social and economic justice makes it impossible to be neutral politically. A 2007 national study that surveyed 396 licensed social workers from 11 states found that almost 50% of respondents affiliate themselves with the Democratic Party, 22% describe themselves as "Independents leaning to the Democratic Party," a little over 6% identify as Independents, almost 6% describe themselves as "Independents leaning to the Republican Party," and 13% affiliate themselves with the Republican Party (Ritter, 2007). According to this study's findings, when compared to the general public, social workers identify more with the Democratic Party and less with the Republican Party.

Respondents were also asked to place themselves on a scale from extremely liberal to extremely conservative. The majority of respondents (60%) described themselves as liberal, 16% as moderate, and roughly 20% as conservative

Many social work scholars argue that social work's mission of working for social and economic justice makes it impossible to be neutral politically.

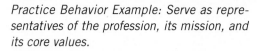

Professional Identity

Practice Behavior Example: Serve as representatives of the profession, its mission, and its core values.

Critical Thinking Question: What do you think about the criticisms of liberal bias leveled against social work education by columnist George Will? Do you agree or disagree with his assessment? Why or why not?

*Courtesy of Elizabeth J. Clark, National Association of Social Workers, Washington, D.C.

(Ritter, 2007). When compared to the general public at that time, more social workers rated themselves as liberal (60% versus 23%) (National Election
Studies, 2004). A study of 294 licensed social workers in Maryland found
that 55% ranked their political ideology from liberal to radical Left, 34% as
moderate, and 10% as Right of Center (Rosenwald, 2006).

As described in Chapter 1, the social work profession has a long history of
being active in progressive political causes and embraces the idea of advocacy
on behalf of marginalized populations as documented in the NASW *Code of
Ethics*. NASW also takes political stands on a number of political issues and
includes these in its book, *Social Work Speaks* (National Association of Social
Workers, 2012), published by the NASW Press. *Social Work Speaks* describes
the association's position on a wide range of public policy issues such as reproductive choice, health care, the death penalty, human trafficking, affirmative action, immigration, and lesbian, gay, and bisexual issues, to name a few.
However, as the above research shows, there is a significant minority of social
workers who identify as being politically conservative, including social work
professor Bruce Thyer, who argues that "conservative political ideology is both
largely ignored and demonized by mainstream social work" and that "conservative principles are completely congruent with the value of social justice"
(Thyer, 2010, p. 272). This creates some interesting tensions within the profession, but also creates an opportunity for debate, reflection, tolerance, and critical thinking.

The following questions will test your knowledge of the content found within this chapter. For additional assessment, including licensing-exam-type questions on applying chapter content to practice behaviors, visit **MySearchLab**.

1. According to this chapter, some argue that _____ is the most important factor in the development of social welfare policies.
   a. research
   b. rational decision making
   c. personal values
   d. public opinion

2. One's beliefs about how the world works, what has value, and what is right and true is
   a. ideology.
   b. partisanship.
   c. neoliberalism.
   d. secularism.

3. Which of the following political ideologies advocates personal responsibility, small government, and low taxes?
   a. Liberalism
   b. Radicalism
   c. Conservatism
   d. Secularism

4. This chapter discussed trends in the Democratic and Republican parties in recent years. What assessment can be made from these observations?

   a. Neoliberals and neoconservatives have very similar belief systems.
   b. Both the Democratic Party and the Republican Party have grown more conservative in recent years.
   c. They have both supported the development of third parties in the United States.
   d. They have both been increasingly responsive to the needs of lower income Americans.

5. Which of the following statements about think tanks in the United States is false?
   a. Most are politically neutral.
   b. They shape social policy in the United States.
   c. They employ experts and researchers.
   d. They issue policy briefs and research reports covering a range of important social issues.

6. A 2007 study of licensed social workers found that _____% describe themselves as conservative.
   a. 5
   b. 10
   c. 16
   d. 20

7. This chapter talks about the importance of values in the political arena. If you were advocating for a new policy in your state that would mandate that new mothers are entitled to 6 months of paid parental leave after the birth of a child (at 80% of normal salary), what cherished American values could you emphasize to sway people to your side of the issue? What American values might the opposition emphasize in order to defeat this policy change effort?

Reinforce what you learned in this chapter by studying videos, cases, documents, and more available at **www.MySearchLab.com**.

Watch and Review

Watch these Videos

* Tea Party Victories Concern for GOP (2008)
* Battle Between Faith and Science
* Abortion Wars

Read and Review

Read these Cases/Documents

* Herbert Croly, from Progressive Democracy (1914)

Explore and Assess

Explore these Assets

* Interactive Case Study: Comparing Political Parties
* Interactive Case Study: Presidential Leadership: Which Hat Do You Wear?
* Timelines: The Evolution of Political Parties in the United States
* Timelines: Third Parties in American History
* Interactive Case Study: Who Are Liberals and Conservatives?

Research these Topics

Exploring the role of values in political debate involving social welfare policy

Understanding political ideology and political parties

Exploring the intersection of religion and politics

Assess Your Knowledge

Go to **MySearchLab** to test your knowledge of key topics in this chapter with topic-specific quizzes. Conclude your assessment by completing the chapter exam.

* = CSWE Core Competency Asset   Δ = Case Study

4

Social Workers in Action: The Six Stages of the Policy Change Process

with Maura Roche and Lisa Horowitz

CHAPTER OUTLINE

Competencies in This Chapter (With Practice Behaviors)				
☐ Professional Identity	☐ Ethical Practice	☒ Critical Thinking	☒ Diversity in Practice	☐ Human Rights & Justice
☒ Research-Based Practice	☐ Human Behavior	☒ Policy Practice	☒ Practice Contexts	☐ Engage, Assess, Intervene, Evaluate

> About one-third of the American population can be characterized
> as politically apathetic or passive; in most cases they are unaware
> literally of the political part of the world around them. Another
> 60 percent play largely spectator roles in the political process;
> they watch, they cheer, they vote, but they do not battle. In
> the purest sense of the world, probably 1 or 2 percent of the
> American population could be called gladiators.
>
> —*Political scientist Lester Milbrath, 1965*[*]

Social workers are in a unique position to play an important role in policy change efforts because they often work closely with populations who find it challenging to advocate for themselves before Congress, state legislatures, or in other policy-making settings. Social workers can either act as a second-hand validator to a problem or concern or organize marginalized individuals or groups and assist them in speaking for themselves, or work in some combination of both. Many social workers initially find the legislative arena intimidating, but once they learn how the process works they realize it is not as daunting as originally perceived.

WHO MAKES POLICY IN THE UNITED STATES?

Take a minute to think about the above question. What comes to mind for you? Unfortunately, most Americans picture political elites, and the average citizen does not easily come to mind when we think about who makes public policy in the United States. However, in order for a democracy to thrive, it is crucial to have high levels of civic and political participation among citizens from all walks of life, including social workers and the clients that they serve. You may be surprised to learn that average citizens do affect the political process every day, though we often do not hear these stories. After her son Matthew was murdered in a hate crime incident, Judy Shepard (see Illustration 8.1) worked tirelessly to get the Matthew Shepard and James Byrd, Jr. Hate Crimes Prevention Act passed into law. However, depending on whom you ask, you will get various perspectives regarding who actually makes policy in the United States.

There are a variety of political science theoretical perspectives or approaches to explain who makes policy. According to the Pluralism approach, numerous interest groups compete for influence in making policy but all voices are heard equally and power is widely diffused. Other approaches are more cynical. For example, Public Choice theorists argue that all actors in the political arena are rational actors who pursue their own private self-interests (e.g., voters vote based on what is best for them personally and politicians support policies that will get them the most votes in order to get reelected and to expand their base of power). Finally, the Elitism approach posits that policies are made primarily by political elites that include the wealthy, corporations, military institutions, and well-financed interest groups. Policies flow from elites to the masses. Each of these perspectives probably has some truth to it. There are a number of important actors in the policy-making arena, which we discuss next.

---

*Milbrath, L. W. (1965). *Political participation: How and why do people get involved in politics.* Chicago: Rand McNally.

Legislators and Their Staffers

It is imperative for social workers to build good relationships with elected officials and the staff who work in their offices. Legislators are very busy, so, much of the time you will be meeting with a member of their staff who has public policy expertise in a variety of subject areas. These staffers (also called legislative aides) are very influential and can convince their boss to support you if you present a convincing policy proposal. Legislative staffers come from a variety of educational backgrounds, including social work.

Advocacy Groups

There are thousands of advocacy groups across the country whose mission is to advocate for a specific cause or population. Most of these are nonprofit organizations, and their focus in social work ranges from gay rights, the poor, children, older adults, and those with mental illness. They are also sometimes referred to as interest groups or special interests (see list of U.S. advocacy organizations in Chapter 1).

Political Action Committees

Political action committees are commonly referred to as PACs, and their sole purpose is to work to get people elected to public office who support their mission and goals. They do this by endorsing candidates, providing message or campaign training, engaging in grassroots activities (making calls or knocking on doors), and providing financial contributions. PACs in and of themselves do not directly influence policy. Structurally, a PAC is a controlled entity of an advocacy group, professional association, labor union, or industry. Many states have strict laws (or legislative rules) prohibiting or discouraging overt connections between policy making and PAC contributions—such as prohibiting campaign contributions while the legislature is in session. Generally what PACs "buy" is access, an open door, or clout that comes from the gratitude of an elected official for the efforts put forward during the election by an interest group. The NASW has a federal PAC called PACE (Political Action for Candidate Election), and every election cycle it makes endorsements and donates money to candidates running for political office. State chapters of NASW have state PACs and are able to donate funds to political candidates running for office at the state level.

Lobbyists

Some people get confused about the difference between a PAC and a lobbyist, although each tries to influence different parts of the policy-making process. PACs try to affect who gets elected, whereas lobbyists try to influence actual legislation. Every day, lobbyists representing various interests (from corporations to grassroots organizations) can be found at the state Capitol and the nation's capital trying to convince legislators to support their policy initiatives and legislative agenda. Social workers can become registered lobbyists. Most NASW state chapters employ registered lobbyists, some of whom have a degree in social work and some of whom do not (see Figure 4.1).

As a lobbyist for a statewide group of social work professionals, I have experienced real challenges in getting social workers to narrow their policy focus enough to accomplish concrete changes at the state legislative level. Often when asked for policy priorities, what emerge are goals that are overly broad: improve the child welfare system or health care access for all. Of course, these are desirable to achieve, but not quite the right fit for a professional association of social workers to accomplish as the lead. Instead, it would be more productive to choose a smaller, more achievable goal such as increasing access to health care for low-income children with a concrete policy step of simplifying the state enrollment process for the State Children's Health Insurance Program or trying to secure a small amount of funding for better outreach so that more families who would qualify actually know about the program. Who better than a social worker to identify that the eligibility determination process has some resolvable glitches or to recognize that far too many families don't know they are eligible for the service at all?

—*Maura C. Roche, registered lobbyist, Oregon Chapter, National Association of Social Workers*

Figure 4.1
Lobbyist Spotlight: Maura Roche, Contract Lobbyist, NASW Oregon.
Source: Courtesy of the National Association of Social Workers.

Policy Institutes or Think Tanks

Think tanks have grown increasingly influential over the years in their efforts to shape public policy, both foreign and domestic. They are staffed by scholars and researchers who have developed an expertise on a range of important social or economic issues. Although some policy institutes claim to be impartial, many of these policy institutes lean left or right and operate from a distinct ideological framework—and are financially backed by individuals or organizations with a political agenda. Lawmakers, particularly at the federal level, have come to rely on the position papers and policy briefs produced by these policy institutes when deliberating on important public policy issues.

POLICY-MAKING SETTINGS IN THE UNITED STATES

When working toward a particular change, it is critical to identify how the issue fits into the American system of government. If policy change is the right course to address the issue that has been identified, the branch of government where the change should occur must be determined. Are you seeking a change in federal law or regulation, state law or regulation, local law or regulation, or is there a way to change a policy or procedure without having to change the law directly? Could litigation cause the law or policy to be changed (i.e., using the judicial branch)? Or, could the often broad authority of an Executive Order issued by a governor or the president bring about the change you are seeking? And sometimes state or federal agencies have the authority by law to modify rules or regulations without requiring a change in the law at all.

Determining where the change should occur is one of the early pieces of research that will have to be done. Often, a policy change can be made at more than one level of government or by more than one route. Figuring this out is often part of the challenge. A couple of important factors to consider would be (a) where you can garner the most support for the change, and (b) where the change can be achieved most quickly. Or in the case of litigation, how will it be paid for?

CIVICS 101: LEVELS AND BRANCHES OF GOVERNMENT

Although you received this content in government or social studies class, it is always helpful to review the topic, particularly in light of the fact that these days we receive little education on civics skills or what it means to be an active and engaged citizen. There are three branches of government at the federal, state, and local levels: executive, legislative, and judicial. Having these separate branches ensures a separation of powers and provides for checks and balances in the system. The elected/appointed officials serve terms ranging from 2 years (U.S. House, state house, local elected officials), 4 years (presidents, mayors), 6 years (U.S. Senate, some state judges), to life (federal judges). Please see Chapter 11 for an overview of the U.S. judicial system.

The Federal Government

The federal government can be the toughest to impact as an advocate, in part because of its size and distance from many local communities and the sheer volume of constituents the branches have to respond to, and because it has the most expensive and complex rules of engagement. Although change at this level can be slower than at other levels, on the upside, it tends to trump state and local laws or regulation, so changes in federal law can be the most profound and far reaching.

Executive Branch: The President of the United States, Cabinet, and Federal Agencies

The U.S. president is elected every 4 years through a nationwide election and is limited to two terms of service for a total of 8 years. The election is conducted through the Electoral College instead of by popular vote (simple majority of 50% plus 1), which is a system based on each state providing a number of votes determined by its representation in Congress. The president chooses his or her running mate, who will be second in command as vice president. The president appoints the head of each of the federal agencies and positions, such as the U.S. Surgeon General.

The President's Cabinet

The president's cabinet includes the vice president and the heads of 15 executive departments: the secretaries of Agriculture, Commerce, Defense, Education, Energy, Health and Human Services, Homeland Security, Housing and Urban Development, Interior, Labor, State, Transportation, Treasury, and Veterans Affairs, as well as the Attorney General. The president also has the power to reorganize federal agencies and their duties or create new ones. The most recent example of a newly created federal agency would be the Office of Homeland Security. The agency directors then have broad authority in hiring staff and

President Barack Obama and Vice President Joe Biden pose with the full Cabinet for an official group photo in the East Room of the White House, Sept. 10, 2009.

> **Social workers should be familiar with the U.S. Department of Health and Human Services because this agency has a lot of impact on social service delivery in the United States.**

setting policy within their agency's authority. This has a profound effect on how federal programs operate. Social workers should be familiar with the U.S. Department of Health and Human Services because this agency has a lot of impact on social service delivery in the United States. The secretary under President Obama is Kathleen Sebelius. To learn more about her, visit www.hhs.gov/secretary/index.html.

Legislative Branch: The United States Congress

The U.S. House of Representatives and the U.S. Senate are the two legislative chambers at the federal level and are referred to as the U.S. Congress. There are no term limits for members of Congress.

- **U.S. Senate:** Each state elects two members to the U.S. Senate (regardless of the state's population) every 6 years for a total of 100 members—also known as "The Club of 100."
- **U.S. House of Representatives:** Each state elects members to the U.S. House of Representatives every 2 years; the number of members representing a state is based on population and recalculated with the national census every decade. Each state gets one member per roughly 600,000 people in population, and each state is accorded at least one representative even if the state's population is less. There are 435 members of the U.S. House.

The structure and size of each chamber affects how it operates, and in a sense the chambers have different personalities. The U.S. Senate is considered the upper body. It is smaller than the U.S. House of Representatives, and therefore more power is concentrated in each member. It sits for reelection less often, and it is the body that is considered more deliberative and less reactive. The members tend to be more politically experienced because many of them have served in the U.S. House or other high office in their home state. The U.S. House can be much more raucous, and it can be difficult for a member (or his or her policy issues) to stand out or make his or her way into leadership due simply to the sheer number of members. The two bodies each have 20 committees with four joint committees, so obviously a higher percentage of Senate members are chairing committees than House members, and House committees have more members than Senate committees.

Partisanship and seniority matter in Congress and it shows, right down to the placement of the furniture. The party holding the most seats in each chamber occupies all of the presiding officer roles, such as Speaker of the House or President of the Senate. The presiding officers decide who will chair each committee, make all committee assignments for every member, and assign a majority of each committee's membership to the majority party. In fact, the desks on the floor of each chamber are arranged by party membership with the center aisle moving left or right depending on the makeup of the chamber and perhaps the mood of the country.

Generally, to change or make policy via federal law, a legislative concept must be introduced in both chambers and pass with a simple majority of 50% plus 1. If the language that passes each chamber is not exactly the same, then the bills must go through a process to iron out the differences in language, and this is usually done through a conference committee.

Before each body can vote on a bill, the legislation will be assigned to a committee to be "worked." During this time, the committee will take testimony on the bill and entertain amendments. However, this is not the last opportunity for changes to the bill because amendments can be offered in either chamber at the time the bill is up for debate and final passage before the entire body. In fact, the rules pertaining to "germanity" are incredibly loose at the federal level and that can lead to attaching amendments to bills on topics that are seemingly unrelated.

Examples of committees that are most relevant to social workers can be seen in Table 4.1. Some of these committees also have a number of smaller subcommittees attached to them. For example, the House Committee on Ways and Means has a subcommittee called the Subcommittee on Income Security and Family Support, and the Senate Committee on Finance has a subcommittee called the Subcommittee on Health Care.

Table 4.1   U.S. House and Senate Committees Most Relevant to Social Workers

U.S. House Committees	U.S. Senate Committees
Appropriations	Appropriations
Budget	Budget
Education and Labor	Health, Education, Labor, and Pensions
Judiciary	Judiciary
Veterans' Affairs	Veterans' Affairs
Ways and Means	Agriculture, Nutrition and Forestry
Financial Services	Finance
	Banking, Housing, and Urban Affairs
	Indian Affairs
	Aging (Special)

State Government

State government is often much more accessible to citizen advocates as compared to the federal process, so this can be a good place for beginning social workers to get experience. Advocates can have a great deal of influence at this level because policy changes at the state level impact the entire state. Similar to the federal government, state government has an executive branch overseen by the governor, a judicial branch with a state supreme court and state court of appeals as well as state trial courts. Each state also has a state legislative body.

Executive Branch: Governors and State Agencies

The governor is the top elected official in a state's executive branch of government. In some states, the second-ranking state official (typically the lieutenant governor) runs on the same ticket as the governor, whereas in other states the lieutenant governor is elected separately so that the two top-ranking officials could be from different political parties. Six states do not have a lieutenant governor (Arizona, Maine, New Hampshire, Oregon, West Virginia, and Wyoming); thus the next person in line to succeed the governor is the secretary of state, the president of the Senate, or the speaker of the House. Governors appoint most state "agency heads" (though a few states have some positions that are elected) who oversee state programs, and the people appointed to run those programs have a profound effect on the philosophy and policies that are put in place in the state.

Legislative Branch: State Legislatures

State legislatures vary widely from state to state in size, structure, and rules of procedure. Some are structured similarly to Congress, and some operate very differently. All but one state in the United States are bicameral institutions, meaning that they have a Senate and a House of Representatives or Assembly. Nebraska is the only U.S. state with a unicameral system (only one legislative body).

How state legislatures structure representation of their populace can vary widely as well. It is fairly common to have representation based on population, which is reconfigured every decade with the U.S. Census. Most states have a roughly 2:1 or 3:1 House-to-Senate ratio with numbers such as 98 House to 49 Senate as in Washington State, or 110 House to 38 Senate as in Michigan. Some are structured very differently, such as Vermont, which has a House of Representatives with 150 members (a representative for every 4,100 people) and a Senate with only 30 members.

Many aspects with regard to partisan issues and majority rule are similar between the state and federal level process. The majority party usually elects the presiding officers, such as the speaker of the House or Assembly, the president of the Senate, and the whips and assistant leaders. Generally, the majority party gets to chair all of the committees and have numerical majorities on every committee. However, some states, such as Vermont, assign some committee chairmanships to minority party members (usually based on seniority) for a few committees as a way to create a more cohesive and less rancorous relationship between the majority and the minority parties.

The rules of procedure vary a great deal as well. Some common differences between state and federal rules of procedure have to do with the roles of committees, amendment procedures, and transparency of process. Many states do not allow amendments to be made on the floor while the entire body is deliberating on the bill. In those states, the committees are more powerful and there is

---

Practice Activity 4.1

Take a few minutes to find out who represents you in the U.S. Congress and who represents you in your state legislature. In most cases, this will be a total of five people. Two websites that may be helpful are Project Vote Smart (www.votesmart.org) and Congress.org (www.congress.org). Next, do some research on your City Council. How many members are there, and who is the mayor?

---

a need to cultivate a champion for your issue on the "committee of jurisdiction." In states that allow amendments on the floor, committee structure is usually less powerful and a legislator who is passionate about an issue but does not sit on the committee of those bills can still play a very powerful role on the issue.

Local Government: Councils, Commissions, Mayors, and Chairs

This is the level of government that is the closest and most personal to us. It tends to have a more limited scope of issues it addresses, with a fairly strong focus on law enforcement, transportation, land use and development, public works, and infrastructure (sewer and water). However, some state programs are administered through local government. For example, advocates working on mental health issues often need to interact with local government because some of these programs may be administered at the local level. Additionally, as states face tough budget times and cut state programs serving the mentally ill, these clients may come into greater contact with local law enforcement who are often ill-equipped to address their needs.

Local governments have policy-making functions similar to state or federal government, but most of these bodies are much smaller and do not share the bicameral structure. They often range from 3 to 15 elected officials in size and have both legislative and administrative functions (legislative and executive rolled into one); however, there are often county level trial courts creating some separation of powers.

The size and scope of local government varies widely from state to state. Louisiana has 302 municipal governments and Alaska has 145. Wyoming has 23 counties and 98 municipalities. Local governments have counties (in Louisiana they are called parishes and are headed by a parish president), which may be governed by boards of aldermen or county commissions. Cities may have districts, wards, or boroughs. These may be governed by city councils and usually have a presiding officer, a mayor. School boards are also a local government function and are a good way for those interested in education policy to have some decision-making power regarding how local schools operate.

SIX STAGES OF THE POLICY CHANGE PROCESS

In most social work courses, the planned change process is emphasized, and students learn that this process is used at the micro, mezzo, and macro levels; thus, the planned change process is the same whether the target of intervention is an individual, family, group, organization, community, or society at large. The six stages of the planned change process typically are engagement,

1. **Problem Definition:** Identify the problem and possible solutions
2. **Agenda Setting:** Getting your issue on the political agenda
3. **Policy Formulation:** Translating the solution into proposed policy
4. **Adoption/Passage of Proposed Policy:** How a bill becomes a law
5. **Policy Implementation:** How the new law is implemented
6. **Evaluating the Policy Change:** What was the outcome?

Figure 4.2
Stages of the Policy Change Process.

assessment, planning, implementation, evaluation, and termination. The **policy change process** also has six stages and is similar in some ways to the planned change process used by social workers, though the terminology is somewhat different (see Figure 4.2).

When most people think about policy change, they usually focus primarily on stage 4, which is the "how a bill becomes a law" stage. However, it is important to know that there are five other important stages to creating change in the legislative arena. Similar to the planned change process used in social work, the policy change process outlined below is not always successfully achieved. This process involves a series of stages or steps, and it is possible to get derailed at each step along the way. It is not an easy, simple process and can be achieved only with concerted effort, persistence, and a little bit of luck. Like any job, doing policy practice requires gaining the requisite knowledge and skills, and you will need to receive training from someone with experience in this field (e.g., internship; field practicum; on-the-job training). Finding a good mentor can be extremely valuable. Chapters 6–10 contain real-life stories that bring these policy stages to life.

I. Problem Definition Stage

A proposed policy change always begins with the identification of a problem or need.

A proposed policy change always begins with the identification of a problem or need. Polices are proposed in order to address an **actual** or **perceived problem** that is affecting a significant number of people. This is a critically important stage of the process because before a policy can be formulated, the cause(s) of the problem must be very clearly understood. Oftentimes, people will agree that there is a problem, but disagree about the causes of the problem, and therefore have very different ideas regarding how that problem should be solved. This may be due to differences in political ideology. For example, liberals and conservatives may agree that the health care system needs to be reformed, the immigration system is broken, or that poverty is a significant social problem in the United States, but they would propose very different approaches to solving these problems based on their values, philosophical orientation, and perception regarding the nature of these problems.

It is often easier to identify a problem than to come up with a solution. Some policy change efforts are aimed at improving large systems so that they work better for people, such as the child welfare system or the mental health system. However, because the causes of some problems are multifaceted and very complex, it is harder than one would think to identify the best fix for the problem. One major decision that must be made during this stage is whether a large-scale, sweeping change will be sought or whether it makes more sense to use an incremental approach. Even though social workers often prefer the idea of making significant changes, it may be more politically feasible to identify a series of small, meaningful steps that build to significant change over time because this will result in less opposition from political opponents.

For example, in your state, social work leaders may identify the problem that social work salaries are too low and that social workers are burdened by high levels of student loan debt. At first glance, the state chapter of NASW may want to pursue student loan forgiveness legislation. However, if the state is currently experiencing a budget crisis, it is very unlikely that this legislation will pass because it is not revenue neutral. Instead, as a first step, legislation could be proposed that would create a task force to examine workforce needs in the state as relates to the social work profession and come up with recommendations to improve the social work workforce in the coming years. One of these recommendations would likely include student loan forgiveness for social workers.

How Do We Know That Something is a Problem?

Experts and researchers often feel frustrated when policy makers fail to consult the latest research when designing a proposed policy change. As discussed earlier in the book, sometimes legislation gets proposed based on one's values or even one's "hunch" about what may solve a particular problem. Ideally, a policy would not be proposed until sufficient time has been devoted to studying the problem and the causes of the problem; however, the policy-making process is not a perfect process and this is often not the case. However, because social workers are required to complete coursework on research methods, they understand how important it is that interventions are based on evidence and solid research whenever possible. Thus, proposed policy solutions that are backed up by a **needs assessment**, a **program evaluation**, or a **scientific research** study will have a better chance of successfully addressing the problem that has been identified. Social workers can help educate policy makers on this important point. These methods can be strengthened or enhanced with the addition of a social worker's **practice experience** and **anecdotal evidence**. Having clients tell their stories to legislators can be very impactful.

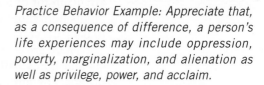

Diversity in Practice

Practice Behavior Example: Appreciate that, as a consequence of difference, a person's life experiences may include oppression, poverty, marginalization, and alienation as well as privilege, power, and acclaim.

Critical Thinking Question: When people are working in the political arena, "problems" are often the focus. How can this process be more strengths-based and rooted in principles of empowerment because we often advocate on behalf of groups who are oppressed and marginalized?

Policy Analysis

For social workers, and others working in the policy arena, an important skill to have is the ability to conduct policy analysis. This work requires strong research, writing, and analytic skills. In its strictest definition, **policy analysis** means studying a proposed policy solution (or a set or policy solutions) to a social problem. For example, every day we hear lawmakers and other stakeholders advocate certain policies in order to address a problem, such as single-payer health care, funding for home visiting programs to prevent child abuse, or comprehensive immigration reform. But often, these are complicated issues with many nuances that are not easy to understand at first glance.

For example, let's say that a legislator at the federal level proposes a piece of legislation that would make it illegal for any community-based social service program in the United States to operate needle exchange programs because of the belief that this perpetuates drug abuse and increases criminal activity.

Public opinion polls find that Americans are divided over this issue. Staff at the National Institute on Drug Abuse (NIDA) may then decide to conduct a policy analysis in order to study the issue in a comprehensive and systematic way. Policy analysts at NIDA will start researching and reading as much as they can about needle exchange programs in the United States and around the world. They will want to read every research study that has been conducted on needle exchange and harm reduction programs, consult experts in the field, and discuss the problem of drug abuse in the United States more generally, including other strategies that have been used to combat the problem.

Policy analysis is an important service to provide because it helps stakeholders and interested individuals understand the complexities surrounding a proposed piece of legislation. The analyst will evaluate whether the proposed policy is a sound response to the problem, whether the benefit derived from the policy outweighs the cost of the policy (i.e., cost benefit analysis), and whether there are better alternatives out there to address the problem. Those who perform policy analysis often work for legislators, policy think tanks, or advocacy organizations. Legislative staff conduct policy analysis to inform the policy makers they serve. It is also commonly performed by advocacy organizations and think tanks in order to inform those who have a strong interest in the issue at hand. It may also be performed by staff working in various federal, state, or local government agencies as they seek to better understand the complexities of a policy issue and to provide some input. The results of the analysis can be used as an advocacy tool by some organizations that wish to advocate for or against various strategies that are being proposed. Your arguments hold more sway when you can show that you did the research necessary to back up your claims.

There are numerous ways to organize your work when doing policy analysis and many different frameworks exist, some that are more extensive than others. The culmination of this type of analysis is often the production of a **policy analysis brief**. The framework used to organize the information in your brief can vary based on the type of public policy (e.g., social welfare policy, environmental policy, foreign policy, transportation policy) and also the audience. For example, if your readers are policy wonks, the policy analysis brief can be more sophisticated than if the audience consists of members of the general public. Entire courses and books have been developed that focus on how to conduct policy analysis. A policy analysis framework from a social work perspective (see Figure 4.3) would typically include the following pieces:

- **Description of the Legislation:** Detailing the ins and outs of the proposed policy that would eliminate needle exchange programs in the United States, including the cost of the policy. Explains to the reader what the bill would do exactly and fleshes out the goals of the proposed policy. It includes some concrete information such as the bill's sponsor and the current status of the legislation.
- **Description of the Problem That Necessitated the Introduction of the Legislation:** This is where the analyst examines the social problem of drug abuse and interventions more broadly. How widespread is the problem, and how many people are affected by drug abuse? What are the causes of drug abuse? It is important to cite the latest research and experts in the field. What do studies evaluating needle exchange programs tell us about their effectiveness?
- **Historical Background of This Legislation:** Here, it is important to examine the policy in an historical context by examining previous

I. Description of the Legislation

- Who is the sponsor(s) of the legislation, and what political party is he or she from?
- What is the current status of this bill?
- What does the policy do exactly? Is this a controversial piece of legislation?
- What are the short-term and long-term goals of the policy?
- What evidence are the advocates of this policy using in their claims that it will solve this problem?
- Is it based on research findings?
- Does this bill have a funding or appropriations request attached to it?
- Who will be charged with implementing and/or evaluating the policy?

II. Description of the Problem That Necessitated the Introduction of the Legislation

- What is the social problem being addressed by this legislation, according to the sponsors of this legislation?
- Who is the target population?
- Who is affected by this problem, and how? How many people are affected by it? Provide data and statistics.
- Is this a new social problem, or has this been a problem for some time?
- How does this problem affect vulnerable populations?
- What are the causes of the problem? Include diverse perspectives.
- What does the research say about the causes of this social problem? Make sure to cite experts and research studies.

III. Historical Background of This Legislation

Analyze this piece of legislation in a historical context:

- Describe the policies and programs that were previously developed to address this social problem and how effective or ineffective these initiatives were.
- What have policy makers, and others, tried in the past in terms of legislation and programs?
- Is there precedence for this type of policy? When did the United States first attempt to address this problem through policy and programs?
- What other important legislation has attempted to address this problem previously?
- Are there any demographic changes relevant to this policy topic? Can you identify any major shifts in public attitudes over the past 20 to 50 years?
- Does this current policy take into account previous efforts to solve the problem?
- How have our efforts to address this problem changed over time?
- How does the United States compare with other countries on this policy issue? Have they approached this issue in a different way?

IV. Social and Political Context of This Legislation

Examine the social and political environment surrounding this policy:

- Describe which political forces (legislators, prominent individuals, groups, organizations) support and oppose the policy, and what their positions are.
- Which party or ideology is informing this policy? Or, is this a bipartisan piece of legislation?
- What American social values have influenced the development of this policy?
- Describe arguments on both sides of this issue. Is there a "values debate"?
- Describe the resources possessed by the different groups involved in this policy debate in terms of money they are able to spend on lobbying and campaign contributions.

(*continued*)

- How successful have the sponsors of the policy been in getting attention on this policy out to the public and covered by the media? In which media outlets has this issue gotten coverage?
- What strategies are they using to try to get this policy passed?
- What strategies is the opposition using to try to defeat passage of this bill?
- What is public opinion on this issue?

V. Policy Analysis and Recommendations

- Based on your analysis, what conclusions have you reached about the (proposed) policy?
- Are the goals feasible?
- Do the goals contribute to social justice and greater social equality?
- Can you identify any unintended consequences?
- Do the goals contribute to a better quality of life for the target population, or do they adversely affect the quality of life for these individuals?
- Are the goals of this policy consistent with the values and ethics of the social work profession?
- Is the policy important enough to justify spending scarce funding on this policy? Would the cost outweigh the benefit?
- Do you recommend this policy as currently stated or would you suggest modifications to improve it? Or is this bad public policy, in your opinion?
- Are there alternative policies that might better achieve the goals?

Figure 4.3
Policy Analysis Framework.

policies and programs that were developed to address this problem. Does this policy represent a new strategy in dealing with the problem of drug abuse, or is it reinventing the wheel? How have efforts to address and/or treat this problem changed over time due to new knowledge?

- **Social and Political Context of This Legislation:** This is an interesting part of the analysis that brings us back to the present day. This is where the analyst has the opportunity to objectively examine who supports the policy, who opposes it, and what arguments are used on each side of the debate. If this is a controversial issue, it is important to include all relevant groups so that you can represent divergent views and opinions. It can be helpful to use quotes from prominent groups, organizations, experts, and other individuals. What ideology and values are informing this policy? Finally, who are the major actors involved, and what strategies are they using to defeat the policy or to win passage?

- **Policy Analysis and Recommendations:** Finally, this is where the analyst has the opportunity to take everything learned in order to come to some conclusion about the merits of the proposed policy. From a social work perspective, it is important to discuss whether the legislation is aligned with the values of the social work profession and whether it contributes to greater social and/or economic justice. This is also where you can do a cost-benefit analysis to assess whether this issue warrants spending scarce public resources. Finally, are there other policies that could better address this social problem?

Seeking Input From Political Allies and Opponents

During the problem definition stage, it is wise to seek input from allied individuals, groups, or organizations. Reaching out to allies is an important step and can help avoid problems later and hopefully identify unanticipated issues both with the politics of the issue and even with the technical aspects of what might be proposed. You may find a supportive legislator to forward your idea, but if the state's leading advocacy group shows up at the legislature to lobby or testify against your bill or point out a myriad of problems and unintended consequences, that is often the end of the road. Sometimes even if the differences are resolvable, it cannot be done within the time line of that legislative session, and you will be delayed a year or more before you can come back with a modified proposal.

Plan to begin identifying allies and meeting with them anywhere from 6 months to a year in advance of when the legislation would be introduced to start working to build support (or achieve neutrality, if that is the best that can be hoped for) and identify challenges with an eye toward resolving them in advance of getting into the more public arena of the legislative or rule-making process. In the process of identifying and reaching out to allies, it is important to anticipate which organizations or individuals (including policy makers) might lead the charge in opposition to what you are trying to accomplish. It is best to anticipate all the challenges and objections to your proposal so they might be resolved, or if irresolvable, so you can be better prepared to defend your proposal.

Often when seeking change in the social services world, money is the enemy rather than any real opposition to the concept. Frequently, an issue you are working on is in need of greater financial resources to improve outcomes. When state budgets are tight, this can prove to be the greatest challenge of all. Anticipating this in advance is critical. Most legislative processes have a method for calculating and attaching a "fiscal" estimate to all bills, and sometimes you can obtain these estimates informally in advance of legislation being introduced.

Finally, at this stage, it is important to ask a very critical question: Can this problem be resolved through the legislative process? There is a saying that when you have a hammer, every problem looks like a nail. However, not all problems can be solved via legislation. For example, a child advocacy organization may believe that it is harmful to spank children and may wish to follow the lead of other countries that have made it illegal for caregivers to hit or spank a child. However, a bill making spanking illegal is unlikely to pass in the United States, and some would argue that it is bad public policy to criminalize parents for this type of behavior. Perhaps a better approach might include seeking societal or attitudinal changes by applying for grant money to run a creative anti-spanking public education campaign.

The successful outcome of this stage depends on the ability of the participants to come to an adequate understanding of the problem, to consider various solutions to the problem, and to come up with a policy change proposal that has a reasonable success of passage. However, this is only the first step. The next step involves getting others to care about your issue.

II. Agenda Setting

This stage of the policy change process is often described as the "deciding what is to be decided" stage (DiNitto, 2011, p. 14). This is where you need to convince lawmakers that of all of the pressing issues facing our community or state or country, they should care about this one. Those seeking policy change must think carefully about how to propel their issue onto the political agenda because the number of bills that can be considered in any given legislative session is not infinite. Agenda setting may be the most important stage of the process because some issues get onto the "political agenda," and many issues do not make it there. Social workers often feel that many issues that affect poor and vulnerable people have a difficult time getting on the agenda. There are numerous historical examples of issues that took a long time to get seriously considered by state and federal lawmakers, such as civil rights for women, people of color, gays and lesbians, and people with disabilities.

Agenda setting may be the most important stage of the process because some issues get onto the "political agenda," and many issues do not make it there. Social workers often feel that many issues that affect poor and vulnerable people have a difficult time getting on the agenda.

One strategy to getting your issue onto the political agenda is to get a strong, savvy statewide organization with professional lobby support to adopt the issue you are trying to forward as one of their legislative priorities. This is the best and easiest way to get the technical support in the legislative process for your policy concept. However, do your homework, because if your concept gets picked up by a group that is not well regarded in the legislative process it can be very damaging. **Coalition building** is another strategy that can be useful during this stage because it can indicate to legislators that there are a number of prominent or influential allied individuals, groups, and organizations that are supportive of your legislative proposal (see Chapter 5 for more on coalition building).

Another strategy is to **use the power of the mass media** to help propel your issue onto the agenda and to create the pressure needed to get state and/or federal lawmakers to pay attention. Sometimes an issue can suddenly be viewed as a "crisis" as a result of a sensational news story. For example, child welfare advocates may be able to get a piece of legislation to be taken more seriously after a serious case of child abuse is in the news. Gay rights advocates may have an easier time introducing a piece of legislation focused on bullying after a series of news stories covering stories of adolescents who have committed suicide after being bullied by classmates. Unfortunately, it sometimes takes a tragic circumstance to create an opportunity to modify public policy, and occasionally circumstances align to help move an important social issue forward.

Policy Practice

Practice Behavior Example: Collaborate with colleagues and clients for effective policy action.

Critical Thinking Question: Agenda setting is a critical phase in the policy-making process. If you wanted to get a bill passed to improve services for those with severe mental illness in your state, what strategies might you use to propel this issue onto the political agenda?

Finding a Champion

During the agenda-setting stage, it is critical to find a legislator who will champion your policy proposal. In most states, thousands of bills are introduced each session, and legislators have to vote on hundreds of them. Legislators are like the rest of us in that they gravitate toward working on things that they care about the most. When trying to find a champion, a good starting place is to utilize legislative guides (often published by the state legislature itself and available for free or a nominal fee) or legislative websites to scan legislators' educational backgrounds, occupations or work histories, and personal biographies. It would be important to know whether there are any legislators in your state with a degree in social work because they will be your natural allies. Their biographies may reveal important details, such as experience being a foster parent, having a child with special needs, or a background as a mental health professional.

It is also important to get to know which legislators are assigned to committees or subcommittees with titles including "health care," "human services," "children," and "judiciary" (frequently addresses child welfare issues) because they are made up of people with an interest or expertise in those issues. Most state websites list the committees and legislators who serve on each committee. One advantage to working with professional lobbyists and advocacy organizations is that you can learn from those with more experience which legislators are known to be an advocate on a particular issue. Finally, once you get more experience doing policy work in your community and/or state, you will slowly build relationships with legislators and the staff who work in their offices. When you are able to build a solid relationship based on mutual respect, a legislator will be more willing to spend her or his political capital on your issue.

Once you have a list of possibilities, start with the most obvious legislator (e.g., known to care about or work on the issue, sits on or chairs committee that deals with the issue), present your concept, and see if he or she would be willing to lead the charge. If this legislator is unwilling, go to the next person on your list. It is ideal to have at least one champion in each chamber—House and Senate. Obviously it is easier to find legislative champions than to build them, but usually some combination is necessary in order to achieve the legislative support needed to pass a bill into law. Every now and then, an individual with an incredibly compelling personal story gets matched up with a legislator who is tenacious about resolving the issue. And sometimes we see the convergence of a high profile media story, a compelling constituent, and a persistent legislator—the perfect storm.

> **Sometimes we see the convergence of a high profile media story, a compelling constituent, and a persistent legislator—the perfect storm.**

III. Policy Formulation

In the previous two stages, the problem was studied, a solution to the problem was identified, relevant stakeholders were consulted, and a legislative champion(s) was secured. The third stage of the process involves getting the policy proposal drafted into an actual bill with the appropriate format and language. In some cases, the actual bill drafting will be done by paid staff (legislative counsel), whose job it is to take a legislative concept and turn it into a bill or resolution. In other cases, the bill will be drafted by the very advocates who are proposing the legislation. In either case, it is important to be involved in this part of the process to check the language for accuracy because sometimes mistakes get made or things get lost in translation when the legislative concept gets drafted into bill form. Sometimes despite everyone's best intentions, a bill can have grave, unintended consequences when it is not written correctly, as seen in Figure 4.4.

In 2008, a safe haven law was passed in Nebraska. Safe haven laws have been passed in every state and provide a safe process for parents to surrender their newborn infants to the proper authorities without facing prosecution. Most of the laws are written to apply to children less than 1 year of age, but the Nebraska law failed to include an age limit. As a result, Nebraska saw a rash of cases where parents used the new law to abandon their children (ages 0–18) to the state. It was not long before the news media began reporting these stories, including the case of a father who dropped his nine children off (ranging in age from 20 months to 17 years) at the hospital after his wife died. The Nebraska state legislature later passed a fix to this law by stipulating that it applies only to children 30 days of age or younger.

Figure 4.4
Nebraska's Safe Haven Law.

There are a number of ways that bills can be structured, and different terms are used for those structures. These structures and terms also vary by level of government (federal, state, and local). However, at the federal level, there are four types of legislative measures: **bills**, **joint resolutions**, **concurrent resolutions**, and **simple resolutions**. The key distinction among them is that two make law (bills and joint resolutions) and two do not (concurrent and simple resolutions). There is little practical difference between a bill and a joint resolution, though bills are the most common. A bill originating in the House of Representatives is designated by the letters "H.R.," followed by a bill number, whereas a bill originating in the U.S. Senate is designated by "S" followed by a bill number. Concurrent and simple resolutions normally are not legislative in character because they are not presented to the president for approval. They are often viewed as symbolic because they are used merely for expressing facts, principles, and opinions (e.g., proclaiming April as "National Child Abuse Prevention Month").

IV. Passage of the Policy

This is the part of the policy change process that gets the most attention because this is when (potentially) a bill becomes a law. You may recall the song, *I'm Just a Bill*, made famous on a Schoolhouse Rock video, which shows the steps involved in this long, rather circuitous process at the federal level. During this stage, a proposed policy gets further refined and shaped through an ongoing process of compromise and negotiation. It is often said that politics is the art of compromise, so it is not unusual for a bill to change form as it makes its way through the process. It is remarkable that of the tens of thousands of bills that are presented in the U.S. Congress each session, only about 5% become law. Some find this statistic depressing because it is clear that it is not easy to successfully usher a piece of legislation through the legislative process; however, others point out that it should not be too easy to pass legislation because then we might see a lot of bad ideas passed into law (though this still happens sometimes, unfortunately).

An overview of the process follows (see also Figure 4.5). Note, however, that this process may vary slightly from state to state.

- Bill is introduced in at least one chamber of the legislature (House or Senate).
- It is then assigned to the committee that oversees the issue addressed by the bill.
- Sometimes a committee may refer a bill to a subcommittee for deeper consideration.
- Public hearings may be held.
- The committee decides whether to approve, amend, defeat, or table a bill (many bills die in committee).
- If the bill goes forward in either its original or amended form, the full chamber considers it—which means the entire body votes on the bill (additional amendments may be offered at that time).
- The bill is introduced in the other chamber and goes through this same process.
- If both chambers approve the bill, it goes to a conference committee that works out any differences between the two bills.
- If both chambers approve the final bill, it goes to the executive (governor or president) for signature or veto.

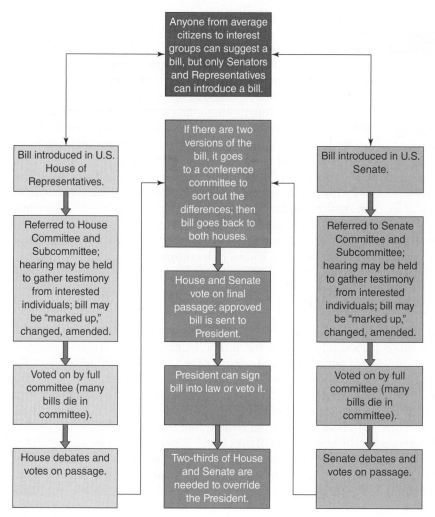

Figure 4.5
How a Bill Becomes a Law.

- If the executive signs it, it becomes law.
- If the executive vetoes the bill, legislators may then attempt to override the veto; in the U.S. Congress, it must be passed by a two-thirds vote in both chambers.
- The third branch of government, the judiciary, can legally challenge existing legislation if it is deemed to violate the federal constitution and is presented to it in the form of a law suit.

Legislative bodies also have different rules about bill passage. Some, such as the U.S. Congress, typically have a bill introduced in both chambers, and then the bill goes through each chamber and may accumulate any number of amendments. Thus, two different versions of the bill emerge. The two versions then must be reconciled via a conference committee. **Conference committees** are generally made up of members of the House and Senate committees who worked on the bill earlier in the process and are charged with ironing out the differences between the two bills. However, this may work differently in many state legislatures where bills start

in one chamber, pass through the originating chamber, and then cross over to the other chamber where the bill may be amended further. Then there is usually a concurrence process (a simple vote whereby the original chamber agrees to the changes made by the second chamber). Many, if not most, bills die in committee.

During this fourth stage, advocates of the policy work diligently to move their bill through the process. They lobby legislators, mobilize others to contact legislators to urge passage of the bill, try to get media coverage of their bill, and testify in public committee hearings. It can be very helpful to work with a professional lobbyist because he or she has the expertise needed to move the bill forward and to help it get unstuck at various points along the way. Social workers involved in policy change efforts become skilled in the art of persuasion and learn how to frame issues in a compelling way so that legislators are convinced to vote "yes."

V. Policy Implementation

This fifth stage is about what happens after a bill is passed into law. Many assume that once a bill is passed into law it is the end of the process, but this is a common misconception. Many complications may arise after a bill is passed into law, making implementation of the law problematic. In some cases, the language of the law was confusing or vague and those charged with implementing the law are not sure how to proceed, or they end up implementing the law incorrectly. For example, in the child welfare field, policies are often written that instruct child welfare professionals to operate "in the best interest of the child." What does that mean exactly? Is it possible that people would have different ideas about what is in the best interest of a child? Sometimes conflict continues when opponents decide to fight the new law by challenging it in court e.g., President Obama's Affordable Care Act being challenged by opponents, as covered in Chapter 6). A series of endless court battles may ensue, which delays the implementation of the new law (see Chapter 11 for more on this). Many times, the financial resources that are allocated to implement the law are inadequate. Finally, this is when the rule-making process occurs.

The Rule-Making Process

Most social workers have never heard of **rule making**, yet it is a part of the process in which important decisions get made, and sometimes competing interests come to the table to try to influence the new rules. Legislatures are charged with passing legislation, but then state and federal agencies have the power and the responsibility of creating more detailed **rules** or **regulations** in order to implement the new law (see Figure 4.6). Often advocates or lawmakers do not want statutes to be highly specific in terms of implementation because it can mean having to amend the law repeatedly to keep it updated and current; laws should be crafted in a way to make them as timeless as possible. For example, many states have passed laws that require social workers to get licensed by the state, but the rule-making process is where many of the details get worked out (e.g., how much the fees will be; how often social workers have to renew their license; whether there will be an exam; how many CEUs will be required each year). State and federal agencies usually have fairly transparent and rigid rules of procedure for rule making—though this process is more obscure and might be harder to find out about than legislation, which is more public.

In 2007, Oregon passed a bill prohibiting discrimination based on sexual orientation and gender identity and a bill establishing Oregon Registered Domestic Partnerships for same-sex couples. Afterward, about a dozen state agencies had to promulgate rules in order to implement these new laws. For example, Oregon's Department of Human Services, Vital Records Office (the agency charged with recording births and deaths), had to change the form and procedure for collecting parents' names at the hospital after a birth for the purpose of birth certificates. The forms needed to say "birth parent" and "other parent" instead of "Mother's Name" and "Father's Name." This is a clear example of an implementation detail that would be inappropriate to write into law, but needed to be addressed in rule. This example may sound somewhat minor, but there were a number of glitches in the process that resulted in lesbian partners of birth mothers being told by hospital staff that they could not be listed as a parent on the paperwork for their child's birth certificate. Because these couples had anticipated being listed, they had not arranged for second-parent adoption in advance of the birth. Not being listed was painful and made partners feel legally vulnerable.

Figure 4.6
Rule-Making Example at the State Level.

The rule-making process usually entails the writing of draft rules, the publication of the draft rules, a written comment period (typically 30, 60, or 90 days), and sometimes rule-making hearings. Some states have rule advisory groups made up of stakeholders convened by the agency charged with implementing the rule. Advocates can try to get a seat at that table or at least observe the meetings. In most cases, advocates will need to contact the state or federal agency charged with rule making to find out what the process is and how they can be notified about participating. Rule making is not always the sexiest part of the policy-making process, but it is an area where advocates can exert much influence in fleshing out critical details of a piece of legislation that has been passed into law.

VI. Evaluating the Policy Change

This final phase of the policy change process is often overlooked, but it is crucial to conduct formal evaluations of social policies in order to determine the impact of new laws. In other words, did the new policy achieve what the sponsors hoped it would achieve, and was it ultimately successful? For example, in recent years, federal lawmakers passed legislation that limits the amount of time that parents can receive welfare benefits as well as legislation that shortens the time frame for the filing of termination of parental rights for those whose children have been removed from the home by child protection authorities. Afterward, it would be important to find out how these new laws affected these vulnerable or at-risk populations. Did a law that sought to get tough on people on welfare result in better or worse outcomes for these children and families? Did a law that sought to free children in the custody of the state sooner result in better or worse outcomes for these children?

In social work, we focus heavily on the need to evaluate our practice interventions and this should be no different when it comes to evaluating the impact of social policies on the vulnerable individuals, families, and communities that

Research-Based Practice

Practice Behavior Example: Use research evidence to inform practice.

Critical Thinking Question: Suppose that a bill was passed that sought to decrease unnecessary barriers for those who wish to adopt children from the foster care system. How would you evaluate the outcome of this policy? How and where would you gather your data and evidence?

we serve. This type of research is commonly conducted in universities, government agencies, and policy institutes or think tanks. Important questions for those who conduct this type of evaluation research from a social work perspective should include the following: "How did the new law impact vulnerable populations?" "Did the legislation result in any harmful, unintended consequences?" "Did the new law operate from a strengths perspective?" "Was the new law successful in achieving the specified goals?"

FINAL THOUGHTS

It may seem overwhelming to read about the various levels of policy-making settings and the stages of the policy change process, but do not be daunted. Like anything else, it just takes some firsthand experience in these environments to learn how it works. Many advocates begin by working at the local or state level because these levels of government tend to be more open and accessible. As a social worker seeking to engage in policy practice, it is important to have a working knowledge of the systems of government and the procedures for getting a policy passed into law. Because there is an ethical obligation for social workers to engage in political advocacy, every social worker needs to decide at what level he or she will engage. Some will certainly choose to be more active, and some "political junkies" will make a career out of this field of social work practice. Being successful in this environment requires strong skills in communication, consensus building, and cultivating relationships—and these are certainly strengths for social workers.

The following questions will test your knowledge of the content found within this chapter. For additional assessment, including licensing-exam type questions on applying chapter content to practice behaviors, visit **MySearchLab**.

1. During which stage of the policy change process does rule making occur?
   a. Policy formulation
   b. Passage of the policy
   c. Policy implementation
   d. Evaluating the policy change

2. Sometimes those engaged in policy practice end up advocating for a flawed policy solution because they miss important steps along the way. If you were wanting to develop a policy to deal with the increasing rates of students who are dropping out of high school in your city, what is the best place to begin?
   a. Identifying potential opponents
   b. Identifying allies so that you can begin building a strong coalition
   c. Finding a legislative champion
   d. Coming up with a plan in order to learn about the causes of the dropout rate

3. During which stage of the policy change process should you seek input from political allies and opponents?
   a. Problem definition
   b. Agenda setting
   c. Policy formulation
   d. Passage of the policy

4. What is the major difference between a lobbyist and a PAC?
   a. A lobbyist is much more influential than a PAC.
   b. PACs are much more interested in influencing specific legislation.
   c. The difference lies in the part of the political process each is trying to influence.
   d. There is no difference between lobbyists and PACs.

5. During which stage of the policy change process should you engage in coalition building and find a legislative champion?
   a. Agenda setting
   b. Passage of the policy
   c. Policy implementation
   d. Evaluating the policy change

6. Which of the following statements about rule making is false?
   a. This is where important details of a policy are fleshed out.
   b. It is not a crucial part of the policy change process.
   c. It can be more challenging to find out how to participate in rule-making compared to the regular legislative process.
   d. Competing interests can come in and influence the intent of the policy that was passed during rule making.

7. You are a social worker in the field of gerontology and have a strong passion for decreasing elder abuse in the United States because this is a problem that is somewhat neglected by policy makers and the general public. Before working with others to develop a strong piece of legislation to address this problem, you first need to understand the underlying causes of this social problem. How would you begin? What kinds of information and resources would be most helpful in terms of making sure that you develop a policy that adequately addresses the root causes of this problem?

Reinforce what you learned in this chapter by studying videos, cases, documents, and more available at **www.MySearchLab.com**.

Watch and Review

Watch these Videos

* Participating in Policy Changes

Read and Review

Read these Cases/Documents

* Social Workers Involved in Political Action

Explore and Assess

Explore these Assets

* American System of Checks and Balances (interactive case study)
* Interactive Case Study: Interest Groups and Campaign Finance
* Interactive Case Study: Executive Order over Time, The
* Interactive Case Study: History of Constitutional Amendments
* Interactive Case Study: How a Bill Becomes a Law

Research These Topics

Who Makes Policy in the United States?

Knowing the Range of Policy-Making Settings in the United States.

Understanding How Policies Get Passed Into Law

Assess Your Knowledge

Go to **MySearchLab** to test your knowledge of key topics in this chapter with topic-specific quizzes. Conclude your assessment by completing the chapter exam.

---

* = CSWE Core Competency Asset   Δ = Case Study

5

When Wearing Buttons Isn't Enough

with Lisa Horowitz and Maura Roche

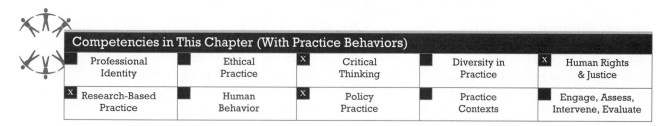

Competencies in This Chapter (With Practice Behaviors)				
☐ Professional Identity	☐ Ethical Practice	☒ Critical Thinking	☐ Diversity in Practice	☒ Human Rights & Justice
☒ Research-Based Practice	☐ Human Behavior	☒ Policy Practice	☐ Practice Contexts	☐ Engage, Assess, Intervene, Evaluate

> Never doubt that a small group of thoughtful people can change
> the world. Indeed it's the only thing that ever has.
>
> —*Margaret Mead*

Most Americans would agree that high levels of "civic engagement" (being an active participant in identifying and addressing issues of public concern) lead to stronger communities and societies. However, the news from researchers studying civic engagement in the United States has not been positive in recent years. Since the 1950s, voter turnout for presidential elections has ranged between 50% and 65%, which is much lower than in many other Western nations. Harvard University Professor Robert Putnam published the widely read book *Bowling Alone* in 2001, which documented declining levels of civic engagement in the United States over the previous three decades. In the book, he cites data showing substantial decreases in voting and other forms of political participation, and declining membership in all kinds of clubs and organizations such as the Parent Teacher Association, religions organizations, labor unions, civic organizations, and even recreational clubs such as bowling leagues. Putnam describes communities with decreasing levels of trust, cohesion, connectiveness, and reciprocity, which is often referred to as **social capital**. And the latest data from American National Election Studies (ANES) show that in 2008:

- Sixty-nine percent of Americans felt the government is run by a few big interests looking out for themselves, whereas only 29% felt it is run for the benefit of all people.
- Forty-nine percent agreed with the statement: "People like me don't have any say about what the government does." In 1960, only 27% agreed with this statement.
- Sixty percent of Americans agreed with the statement: "I don't think public officials care much what people like me think." In 1960, only 25% agreed with this statement.
- Only 25% of Americans felt that they can trust the federal government to do what is right *most of the time.* In 1964, 62% of Americans felt this way.

Additionally, according to the Center for Information and Research on Civic Learning and Engagement (CIRCLE) at Tufts University (Lopez, Levine, Both, Kiesa, Kirby, & Marcelo, 2006):

- Only 39% of youth say that changing society is a responsibility, whereas 57% say that it is a choice;
- Nearly two-thirds of young people aged 15–25 are civically and politically disengaged;
- Twenty-seven percent of Americans define citizenship in terms of being born or naturalized in the United States, whereas only 6% define citizenship in terms of local engagement or helping others.

Human Rights & Justice

Practice Behavior Example: Engage in practices that advance social and economic justice.

Critical Thinking Question: In the United States, people often talk about what rights people should have, but in your opinion, what are the responsibilities of being a citizen? Should there be an expectation when it comes to civic engagement and contributing to American communities and/or the country?

It is understandable that many Americans feel frustrated and alienated from the political process and believe that the political system in the United States is broken and needs to be reformed. However, social workers cannot get off the hook that easily. Chapter 1 of this book details social work's special dedication to social and political change. Social work is the only profession in the United States that has a **mission of social justice**. The person-in-environment perspective

1. I don't have enough time.
2. It won't make a difference since I am not rich or powerful.
3. I don't have the confidence or the skills to do this work.
4. I don't know where to start.
5. I want to help people directly; I don't see myself as an activist or expert.

Figure 5.1

Obstacles to Being Engaged Politically.

embraced by social workers means that social workers assist individuals so that individuals can function better within their environment, but they also work on changing the environment so that it works better for many vulnerable populations—and changing the larger social environment often involves social and political action by committed social workers and others who are actively engaged in policy change efforts.

However, social workers may feel ambivalent about being involved with politics and legislation for a number of reasons (see Figure 5.1). In the early 1990s, social work professor Mark Ezell (1993) observed that social workers avoid politics because: (a) politics has to do with the pursuit and use of power, whereas social workers value equality; and (b) social workers believe politics is a dirty business and they want nothing to do with the process, or the people involved in it. Social work training, which stresses a cooperative, strengths-based approach, may be viewed by some as incompatible with politics, an often adversarial process that involves skills in assertiveness and oral persuasion.

Social workers may also be reluctant due to fears of breaking legal codes that restrict the political activities of social workers in certain government and nonprofit settings and concerns that political activity will compromise their professional values or standing within the community or one's place of employment. A recent article in *Social Work* by Rocha, Poe, and Thomas (2010) concluded that social workers employed in government and nonprofit organizations can be much more politically active than they realize. Their article explains in detail lobbying activities permitted by the Internal Revenue Service (IRS) for those working in nonprofits as well as political activities permitted by the **Hatch Act** for those working for the government. According to the authors:

> Even after social workers feel competent to perform policy-related activities, it is important for them to know the laws regarding lobbying for nonprofit organizations, understand permitted and prohibited activities as state or federal employees, and not be afraid to participate in political advocacy. . . . Educating legislative bodies on issues important to clients and working with the executive branch agencies to implement regulations of laws are both important activities on which there are no restrictions whatsoever for either nonprofit organizations or public and private employees. Lobbying can be done legally by any employee and by nonprofits, as long as they watch how much they spend on these activities. The only real restriction that applies to public employees and some nonprofit employees is working in partisan political campaigns, and even these restrictions have been liberalized since 1993. The bottom line is

Social work is the only profession in the United States that has a mission of social justice.

that social workers, in organizations and individually, can advocate politically much more than they realize.*

Many social workers who lead busy lives find it challenging to find the time needed to devote to political activity. Others wonder whether their efforts can really make a difference. And then there are social workers who feel that political change takes too long, and they are not patient enough to fight for an issue or a cause for years on end. They forget that helping individuals change can be equally daunting and difficult. Finally, some social workers find the political arena intimidating and do not have confidence in their skills and abilities when it comes to doing this kind of advocacy work, referred to as **political efficacy**. According to DiNitto (2011), "It is not enough for human service professionals to know the needs of people and to want to pass policies and provide services to help them. Policy advocates for the disenfranchised must both understand the political process and be adept at working within it if they are to have a voice in shaping social policy" (p. 32). Wolk and colleagues (1996) state that, "Like any social work endeavor, political activity requires commitment, expertise, and training to be successful" (p. 91). Social work programs have an important role to play in order to ensure that students leave social work programs with the skills and knowledge needed to do work in the legislative arena (Ritter, 2007, 2008).

Most policy junkies will advise you to find an issue that you are passionate about and then figure out how you can best contribute to that cause. This chapter will provide a range of ideas and suggestions regarding how social workers can get involved in policy change efforts on issues of interest (see Figure 5.2 for 10 reasons why social workers should be politically engaged). The three broad categories include the following: (a) Opportunities for social work students; (b) Volunteering your time; and (c) Career options in the political arena.

Research-Based Practice

Practice Behavior Example: Comprehend quantitative and qualitative research and understand scientific and ethical approaches to building knowledge.

Critical Thinking Question: Research shows very clearly that U.S. citizens' confidence and trust in their government and in government officials has decreased significantly over the past 30–40 years. This creates many challenges for those working for social change. Why do you think this is the case, and how might this be overcome?

---

1. Activism can be fun!
2. There is an issue that you are passionate about.
3. Someone you care about is affected by this issue.
4. You have the expertise to contribute to this cause.
5. It is an opportunity to gain new skills.
6. Policy change can result in change for a large number of vulnerable people.
7. Social workers have an ethical duty to do so.
8. It is a great way to develop relationships with others who are also passionate about your cause.
9. Policies can dramatically improve the lives of people we serve.
10. Some policies can be harmful to those we serve and should be changed.

Figure 5.2

Top 10 Reasons for Social Workers to Be Engaged Politically.

*Rocha, C., Poe, B., & Thomas, V. (2010). Political activities of social workers: Addressing perceived barriers to political participation. Social Work, 55(4), 317–325.

I. OPPORTUNITIES FOR SOCIAL WORK STUDENTS

The first step while a student is to choose a social issue that you are truly passionate about. There are a number of ways to get informed on a range of social problems and the politics surrounding these issues:

- Tune in to news/political programming on television (e.g., ABC's *This Week*, NBC's *Meet the Press*, Comedy Central's *The Daily Show*, or a local public affairs program in your area);
- Read the political section of reputable newspapers (e.g., *New York Times*, *Washington Post*) and the local public affairs section of your local newspaper;
- Regularly read articles/blogs on reputable political websites (e.g., Politico, RealClearPolitics, Huffington Post; local blogs in your state);
- Get a copy of *Social Work Speaks* published by the National Association of Social Workers (NASW) to find out where NASW stands on a number of political issues;
- Attend "Lobby Day" if it is offered by your social work program;
- Become a member of NASW while a student when it is most affordable and then inquire about how to join your state chapter's legislative committee or political action committee (PAC);
- Listen to National Public Radio (NPR) and alternative media such as *Democracy Now*;
- Join, or start, a student group on campus that focuses on advocating for a vulnerable population (some social work programs have a student organization called the Social Welfare Action Alliance);
- Sign up for legislative alerts from local and national advocacy organizations that you care about; this is a great way to get informed about legislative issues;
- Visit the "Advocacy" section of NASW's website to learn more about legislative issues of interest to the social work profession;
- Attend community forums, town hall meetings, and other meetings in your community where important local issues are being discussed. (Tip: Go to your state legislature's website and use the "find your legislator" tab to find out who your state representatives are. Then get on the e-list for your local representatives, and they will send you invites for town hall meetings in your area.)

However, perhaps the most effective way to gain knowledge and skills in political advocacy is to choose a policy-focused practicum for the field education component of your social work education. Most social work programs have placement options for students interested in policy change efforts that may include legislator's offices and a range of diverse advocacy organizations at the local, state, national, and even international level (see list of advocacy organizations in Chapter 1). Additionally, there are a number of master of social work (MSW) programs that specialize in preparing students for social work in the political arena.

If you are interested in getting into the political arena as a career, completing a policy-focused internship or practicum will make you much more competitive on the job market because you will be able to demonstrate that you have acquired a beginning level of knowledge and skills in advocacy or legislative work. It is also a great opportunity to network and meet some of the key people who do this work in your city or state. Practicum experiences are invaluable because they give you the opportunity to discover whether you are well suited for this type of work. Additionally, you begin to learn the lingo and culture of this environment. Your practicum may provide you with the opportunity to learn how to lobby legislators, develop media and public education materials, recruit and organize volunteers, provide written and oral testimony, work on a campaign (issue or candidate), and bring groups of people together to work on an issue of concern.

II. VOLUNTEERING YOUR TIME

Join an Organization

While you are a social work student, and once you become a practicing social worker, there are a number of ways to volunteer your time in order to meet the ethical duty of engaging in social and political action. The best piece of advice is to join an organization so that you are not doing this work alone.

While you are a social work student, and once you become a practicing social worker, there are a number of ways to volunteer your time in order to meet the ethical duty of engaging in social and political action. The best piece of advice is to join an organization so that you are not doing this work alone. Although people often hear stories of remarkable individuals who made a huge impact when it comes to social and political change (e.g., Gandhi; Margaret Sanger; Rosa Parks; Cesar Chavez; Dr. Martin Luther King, Jr.; and Dorothea Dix), the reality is that most people who engage in social change efforts do not work in isolation.

Many choose to volunteer their time and expertise for an advocacy organization in their field of interest. Social workers who work in mental health, for example, may want to donate some of their time to the National Alliance on Mental Illness, whereas social workers who work with low-income children or children in foster care may want to join forces with a local advocacy organization that is working on behalf of children (e.g., Children First for Oregon; Court Appointed Special Advocates, or CASA). Once you find an organization that you believe in and want to support with your time and energy, it is a good idea to sign up to receive legislative action alerts via email so that you stay up-to-date on the legislative "hot topics" in your chosen field.

Elections

Another important way to effect change is to volunteer to work on a political campaign. There are two types of political campaigns: "people" campaigns (aka "candidate" campaigns) and "issue" campaigns. An important component of political work is electing people who share your commitment to various issues and concerns in society. Social workers typically want to elect candidates who care about the needs of vulnerable people in society and are willing to dedicate financial resources to support social service programs that serve these populations. Social workers may also work on an issue campaign in their state when there is a ballot measure that is being considered by voters. Voters may be voting on whether to allow same-sex couples to marry or enter into civil unions or whether to raise certain types of taxes in order to pay for vital state social services.

There are three main phases to election work: **voter identification** (learning where individual voters stand), **voter persuasion** (moving people from undecided to your side), and **getting out the vote**, or GOTV (turning out your base on election day). Social workers interested in this type of political work are typically engaged in the following activities: phone banking, creating and distributing campaign materials, canvassing neighborhoods and persuading voters to support an issue or candidate, organizing events that bring people together to educate them about an issue or candidate, using social media, and engaging in fund-raising activities such as hosting a house party or "dialing for dollars."

Fund-Raising

Organizations cannot survive or be effective without resources, thus grassroots fund-raising can be incredibly effective. The cornerstone of **grassroots fund-raising** is individual people asking people they know to make a contribution to a cause, campaign, or organization. A lot of people find it uncomfortable to ask friends to give money, and this is understandable. However, many organizations provide the training that is needed to give participants the confidence they need to be effective. There's a basic principle in grassroots fund-raising referred to as the ABCs:

- A: asking people who have the *a*bility to give.
- B: asking people who have a *b*elief in the issue or cause to give.
- C: asking people who have a *c*onnection to the person asking or the organization itself to give.

Influencing Legislation

Once candidates have been elected and government is in session, the focus shifts to participating in various activities in order to influence legislation. Sometimes, social workers are in the position of trying to get legislation passed into law, and other times, they are trying to defeat legislation that has been deemed harmful to a particular group or population. Social workers are often in the position of being the voice of others who are not able to advocate for themselves; however, it is very important to support clients in speaking for themselves whenever possible (see Chapter 8 on the DREAM Act activists). When clients are able to speak directly to legislators about their struggles, it can be an empowering experience for them. It can also be very effective because legislators are often moved when they hear a personal story. When social workers think about influencing legislation at the federal level, this seems very intimidating, not to mention that many citizens live far away from Washington, DC. However, social workers are often surprised to learn how easy it is to impact legislation locally (e.g., school board, city council, state legislature) because local and state lawmakers are often more responsive and accessible. There are a number of ways to influence legislation that is being considered, and some activities are more time consuming than others.

Policy Practice

Practice Behavior Example: Analyze, formulate, and advocate for policies that advance social well-being.

Critical Thinking Question: Some have debated whether social work programs prepare students adequately for work in the political arena. However, there are social workers across the country who hold public office. What social work skills lend themselves well for doing this kind of work?

Lobbying

There are basically two types of lobbying—**direct lobbying** and **grassroots lobbying**. Direct lobbying occurs when a paid professional lobbies on behalf of a cause or issue or when individuals lobby decision makers personally. Grassroots lobbying is when an organization or campaign calls upon its members to lobby decision makers through email alerts, letter writing campaigns, and other means. Social workers can be involved in both direct and grassroots lobbying.

Generally, lobbying involves contacting or meeting with an elected official and asking him or her to support or oppose

1. Be on time and organized. If you are going as a group, meet 15 minutes early near your appointment and get organized. Who is going to say what? Do a practice run-through.
2. Be informed. Go to the meeting having done preliminary research on where the decision maker stands on your issue. If that is not possible to figure out, know what committees the member sits on.
3. Be prepared. Know what you are going to say in advance and stick to those points.
4. Be brief. Most office visits with a member are 15–20 minutes. If you meet with staff, you might get 30 minutes.
5. Start a visit with a round of introductions; clearly state the bill number and brief description and the position you hold. "Hi, my name is Sally Johnson. I am with Child Advocates Utah, and we are here today to talk about SB 201, the Children's Health Bill, and to ask for your support." Then use a personal story. The more personal the better, but not too personal. If you are unsure, try to get feedback from someone with more experience.
6. Do not be afraid to say you do not know. If you don't know the answer to one of their questions, tell them you will get back to them. Then be sure you do it!
7. Leave them with a one-page fact sheet restating your main points that includes the bill number and your position on the legislation.
8. Never threaten members with backing an opponent or launching a campaign against them if they say they are voting in opposition to your position.
9. Close your meeting by trying to get the member to actually say how he or she will vote. Elected officials are pretty good at not answering questions. You might say, "Representative So & So, can we count on you to vote in favor of SB 201?" Or if the member is noncommittal, ask what other information he or she might need to move to a yes/no position on the bill.
10. Thank them at the end of the meeting, and then send a personal thank-you note afterward.

Figure 5.3

How to Make an Effective Lobby Visit.

a piece of legislation. A personal visit to a legislator or elected official has the most influence. The degree of influence tends to correspond to the amount of effort a constituent puts into the lobbying effort. For example, a personal phone call into an office has more influence than a letter. A personal letter has more influence than a form letter or email.

Many citizens are intimated by the idea of "lobbying" an elected official; however, the reality is that there is nothing to fear (see Figure 5.3). The staff members who work in legislative offices are paid to listen to their constituents and to be polite and considerate. The very essence of living in a democracy means that citizens have the right (some would say the obligation) to voice their concerns and opinions to those who were elected to represent them.

Paid Media and Earned Media

Advocates involved in policy change efforts understand the importance of getting media coverage. Many organizations and campaigns have professional or paid staff who are in charge of their messaging and media program. Maintaining "message discipline" can be critical to winning a victory. Political campaigns tend to be more effective when they are able to pay for television and radio ads (i.e., **paid media**), particularly when the opposition is using this as a strategy;

1. Keep the focus on one single issue.
2. Write it clearly, and use language the general public will understand (avoid professional jargon).
3. Know your word limit and other submission rules (usually posted on the publication's website). You must be able to write succinctly.
4. Be very timely if you are responding to a recent story in the paper because you will only get published if the editor views your piece as "newsworthy."
5. The most compelling letters and op-eds are personal.
6. Include your contact information so the paper can contact you about publishing your piece.
7. Be professional. Extreme, outrageous views are not likely to be published.

Figure 5.4

Tips for Writing an Effective Letter to the Editor or Op-Ed.

however, paid media are very expensive. Grassroots organizations do not often have the resources necessary to buy ads and will often need to engage in various fund-raising activities in order to finance this political strategy.

However, effective campaigns and organizations also understand and value the role that volunteers play in generating **earned media**. This includes writing letters to the editor, submitting opinion editorials (op-eds), using social media effectively (e.g., Facebook, posting comments on blogs), and participating in actions with the goal of "getting" media attention such as rallies, marches, or civil disobedience. Publishing a letter to the editor or op-ed in a newspaper can be an extremely effective way to get attention focused on an issue because they are widely read by the public (see Figure 5.4). Letters to the editor are very brief (a couple of paragraphs) and are written in response to a previously published article. Op-eds are longer, comment on a current issue, and do not have to be in response to a previously published article in the newspaper. However, op-eds are more difficult to get published because you need to be viewed as someone with expertise on the topic.

Coalition Building

Bringing together groups of people can be an effective tactic when trying to influence legislation. It is often said that there is power in numbers. When facing an opponent who is much better financed, often the only way to overcome this is through "power in numbers." For example, when an organization is lobbying on behalf of a particular piece of legislation, it speaks loudly when it is able to say that there are 200 organizations that have signed on in support of the bill. There are advantages and disadvantages when working in coalition.

The main advantages of coalitions is that they can increase the critical mass and visibility of an issue or campaign, help build relationships among member groups, help save resources, and duties are delegated across the participants. The potential downside of coalitions is that they take time to form and maintain, groups differ in resources and may not be able to contribute equally, and compromises may have to be reached. Prior to joining a coalition, an organization may want to consider the following: Will it gain positive visibility from participating in the coalition? Will its membership increase because of the coalition? Will relationships be strengthened with other partners? Does it have the necessary resources to commit to the coalition? Will it have decision-making power as part of this coalition?

One of the most powerful ways that social workers can influence legislation is by sharing their experience and expertise with legislators on a particular issue.

Providing Testimony

One of the most powerful ways that social workers can influence legislation is by sharing their experience and expertise with legislators on a particular issue. A very powerful action is to provide written and oral testimony on a bill when it has reached the stage of having a public hearing before a legislative committee (see Figure 5.5). Often, legislators do not have direct experience with the kinds of social problems that social workers are exposed to everyday, so it is extremely helpful to them to hear directly from social workers. When this does not happen, legislators are forced to make important decisions without the luxury of having all of the relevant facts and information. It is important to keep in mind that legislators vote on thousands of bills covering hundreds of issues; thus, they are "kindergarten experts" on a wide range of issues, but only true experts on a few. Therefore, a social worker is likely to be more of an expert than a legislator on any given issue.

1. Prepare your written testimony in advance, and bring the correct number of copies with you the day of the hearing.
2. Check your state's legislative website, because there may be tips for testifying or video examples of effective testimony. There may be audio/visual streaming of testimony in active committees or archived. Take a few moments to watch these so that you know the correct salutation/introduction to your testimony. "Chair Smith, members of the committee, my name is Jane Doe. I am here today on behalf of Child Advocates Montana to testify in favor of House Bill 2482."
3. It is best to prepare written testimony that is not too lengthy; in most cases, 1–2 pages should be sufficient.
4. You can use notes, but do not read your testimony word for word. If possible, you should paraphrase what you have written so that it sounds as conversational as possible.
5. Good eye contact is essential! You need to connect with the committee members.
6. Use the sandwich approach: Clearly state your position right away; find creative ways to argue your position; then end by stating your position once again.
7. Do not be negative. Optimism always plays better. Do not talk down to the committee.
8. Back up your argument with empirical data whenever possible, however, do not overwhelm people with stats. Using a few key pieces of data can be very powerful.
9. Know the other side of the argument very well. One technique that can be effective is to preemptively respond to your opponent's argument. "The other side will tell you, . . . however, this flies in the face of all recent available research on this topic."
10. Use creative or strong language to frame the debate or to create a narrative. Stories resonate with people. When possible, use catchy phrases, colorful metaphors, or analogies.
11. Pull at people's heart strings: A human interest angle can be effective, but choose carefully. Legislators respond better to an inspirational story rather than a "doom and gloom" story.
12. If a committee member asks you a question that you don't know the answer to, be honest, say you don't know but that you will find out and get back to him or her. Then make sure you follow up.
13. Make sure to thank the members of the committee for the opportunity to testify.

Figure 5.5

Tips for Providing Effective Testimony in a Legislative Committee Hearing.

Providing testimony is an important activity, yet very few social workers perform this critical role when their city council or state legislature is in session. The most likely reason is that it is perceived as an intimidating task to speak before a committee of legislators. For most people, this can be somewhat nerve-wracking, but with experience, many social workers actually come to enjoy it.

Social Worker Spotlight: Elaine Charpentier Philippi, BSW
Testifying Before the State Legislature

As a BSW student, I believed that Policy would be among my least favorite classes. I prematurely associated it with other required undergraduate credits like my early nemesis—Algebra. Knowing this you can imagine my surprise when I sat through my first Policy lecture where my professor shared with us her goal—to turn us all into policy geeks by the end of the semester. What I came to rapidly understand in those early weeks of policy class was that my distaste for social policy could be more accurately translated as a misunderstanding of it.

Our class project was a great vehicle for converting me to a "policy geek." Our local NASW chapter was drafting a joint memorial bill that would be introduced in that year's legislative session asking our local congressional leaders to urge the White House to convene a White House Conference on Children and Youth—something that had not been done in more than four decades.

Our assignment was to create a fact sheet for the joint memorial and then to meet with representatives in our districts to ask for their support of it. We ended the semester with a mock committee hearing in class where we were given the opportunity to sit before a "pretend" panel of legislators and offer testimony for the memorial. I was initially pretty intimidated by this assignment, but as I spent time researching child welfare issues for my testimony I became deeply passionate about the need for the convening of a White House Conference on Children. I would soon discover that when you are passionate about an issue, and can translate that passion into an effective and eloquent piece of testimony, others will listen. An advocate was born.

Then a unique opportunity was presented to me at the end of the semester when I was asked by the NASW state chapter to read the testimony I had written for class before the House Committee on Human Services in my state. I was initially really excited about being part of a team of social workers who were petitioning our state legislators to give overdue attention to children affected by the child welfare system. Yet, at the same time, I was pretty sure that I would come off to the Committee as nervous, stammering, and inexperienced. I decided to drag my family along—partially for moral support and also because it was a great opportunity to demonstrate to my children the power of being an active constituent and advocate. The experience was nothing short of fabulous! A committee co-chair spoke directly to my children after I finished testifying, thanking them for being there and telling them that they should be very proud of their mom. The experience eliminated my fear of the unknown and gave life to one of our profession's ethical standards—social and political action.

The more that I understand social policy and the diverse ways that social workers can engage in social and political action, the less afraid and more passionate I am about being a bridge between people and equal access to the resources, employment, services, and opportunities they require to be self-determining. I would encourage social work students to identify your distaste for policy and embrace it. At the very least you may be able to identify a social issue or marginalized population that you feel passionate about giving voice to. If a skeptical individual such as myself can be converted to a policy geek in just four short months, anything is possible!

Illustration 5.1

To: Senate Committee on Health Care, Human Services, and Rural Health Policy

From: Elaine Charpentier Philippi
            Pacific University Social Work Undergraduate Student
            Member, National Association of Social Workers

Date: May 16, 2011

Re: Testimony in Favor of HJM 12

Chair Monnes Anderson and Members of the Committee:

My name is Elaine Charpentier Philippi, and I am an undergraduate student of Social Work and a member of the National Association of Social Workers. I am also a mom to three children. After receiving my bachelor's and master's degrees in social work, I plan on having a career focused on improving the lives of vulnerable children in Oregon. Today, I ask for your support of HJM 12, a bill that would urge our federal lawmakers to convene a White House Conference on Children.

The White House Conference on Children and Youth Act focuses on a myriad of child welfare issues. Included are actions for prevention and intervention in abuse and neglect, and increasing the number of foster children that are successfully and permanently placed through kinship care, adoptions, and reunification. It addresses issues like poverty and substance abuse, health and mental health care access, and the over-representation of minority populations served in child and youth systems.

Nationally, rates of child abuse and neglect, homelessness, and mental and physical health risks for children and youth are increasing exponentially. The current economic crisis is having a significant impact on the issues that impact our children and youth—it is also widening the margin of families that enter the system. Children and youth represent some of the largest populations of the homeless, the hungry, and the abused. Child abuse is costly on many levels—none of us are immune to this. In our global world we can no longer look at the issues plaguing our children and youth as someone else's problem.

In May of last year, msnbc.com ran an article reporting that the numbers of children hospitalized for shaken baby syndrome had risen since the onset of the recession. The article was based on research led by University of Pittsburgh's Medical Center/brain injury specialist, Dr. Rachel P. Berger.

Nineteen month-old Leonard McIntire is named as one of the cases in the study. Leonard was reportedly bitten, beaten, and shaken by the mother's boyfriend. After he was taken into custody, the boyfriend admitted punching Leonard and shaking him violently. Leonard's injuries included a broken left arm and ligature marks on his neck. After five days on a ventilator, Leonard died.

Dr. Berger called our current fiscal and social climate the "perfect storm: increased stress, increased poverty and yet . . . social services [are] being cut." Understandably these cuts are largely the result of dramatic economic and budget reductions faced by many states. Obviously, there are no easy answers.

A quote from Lilian Katz says it best: "Each of us must come to care about everyone else's children. We must recognize that the welfare of our children is intimately linked to the welfare of all other people's children. After all, when one of our children needs life-saving surgery, someone else's child will perform it. If one of our children is harmed by violence, someone else's child will be responsible for the violent act. The good life for our own children can be secured only if a good life is also secured for all other people's children."

The White House Conference on Children would give child welfare advocates and professionals from all over the country the opportunity to review the best practices research pertaining to the prevention of child abuse and neglect and to make recommendations. This conference would help us to shine a spotlight on the needs of vulnerable children.

Thank you for hearing HJM 12 today. Today, I urge you to support HJM 12 and the White House Conference on Children and Youth Act.

Illustration 5.2

Source: Shaken baby injuries rose in recession, at: http://www.msnbc.msn.com/id/36859272/ns /health-kids_and_parenting

Educational Outreach

One way to build support for a candidate, ballot measure, or piece of legislation is to plan and organize events in your community in order to educate people and to persuade them to support your position on the issue. Examples of this kind of outreach to the public can include town hall meetings, house parties, and community forums. Of course, these days with the increasing use of technology as a communication tool, many advocacy organizations are using **social media** (Facebook, Twitter, email action alerts) in order to educate others and mobilize them to act.

Political Dissent/Visibility

Some involved in advocacy work differentiate between "inside the system" tactics and "outside the system" tactics—sometimes referred to as **direct action**, **civil disobedience** or **political dissent** (e.g., rallies, protests, pickets, boycotts, marches, sit-ins/stand-ins, street theater, and demonstrations). Some social workers are more comfortable engaging as citizen lobbyists by understanding and using the system to forward an issue. However, when certain issues are being ignored by elected officials, sometimes activists will plan a direct action (e.g., being forcibly removed or arrested, organized march in the street) in order to attract media attention (i.e., visibility) and to pressure lawmakers to take action. Other types of direct action can demonstrate large-scale support for the issue and can be used to supplement other advocacy activities. In recent years, the United States has seen large rallies in Washington, DC, and across the country on a range of issues including those of concern to the Tea Party movement, the need for immigration reform, calls to end the war in Iraq, and the Occupy Wall Street movement. Chapter 8 on the DREAM Act profiles some youth activists engaging in some very interesting strategies involving political dissent that were similar to those used by previous social movements (e.g., Civil Rights movement).

It is critical to understand the full ramifications of direct action when making strategic decisions about how extreme the action will be. Before this tactic is used, many considerations should be discussed: Is this the right tactic, or would the organization be better off using other methods of communication? Does it have the right people at the table to ensure that the action is well organized? Will the action bring more support from the public? Will it be well attended? Will it attract a good deal of media attention? How can the organization ensure that it will be a peaceful protest? What message is the action going to convey, and who are the best people to convey that message? And most importantly, how can the organization make it fun for the activists who attend?

How Do I Find the Time to Volunteer?

A common feeling among practicing social workers is that they want to be more active politically in order to meet the ethical obligation of advocating for the clients they serve, but it is very challenging to find the time. This is understandable, and every social worker needs to find a method that works for him or her based on his or her life and work circumstances. There are times in people's lives when they have more time than others to devote to political advocacy. Sometimes people have only the time to contact a legislator by email or phone to convey a message about a particular bill that is under consideration, whereas at other times, they have the time to testify at a public hearing or attend a political rally.

III. CAREER OPTIONS IN THE POLITICAL ARENA

There are numerous jobs and career paths one could take as a social worker interested in policy practice.

There are numerous jobs and career paths one could take as a social worker interested in policy practice. Today, those with MSWs are serving in the U.S. Congress, state legislatures, city councils, and school boards across the country. They are also spearheading large-scale government programs, small non-profits, and advocacy organizations. Senior positions may include executive director, development director, public affairs manager, and political director. Entry-level positions may include volunteer coordinator, grassroots organizer, government relations coordinator, event coordinator, or researcher.

Executive Director of an Advocacy Organization

As the chief executive, the executive director has a number of responsibilities, and the role will vary depending on the budget and overall staff size of an organization. Generally, the executive director will be responsible for fund-raising, board development, program and policy, communications, and fiscal and staff management. Executive directors usually report to a board of directors.

Policy Staff (Related Titles: Policy Director/ Policy Associate/Policy Analyst)

Many organizations, large and small, have full-time political directors on staff. This is particularly true for organizations with associated PACs. The political director is often responsible for all aspects of an organization's electoral program, which may include interviewing and endorsing candidates, targeting races, and determining how to best use an organization's resources to advance electoral goals. In some organizations, especially in western states, this may include addressing ballot measures that impact the organization or issue area.

Policy staff positions often focus on research, writing, and various aspects of program development. Policy research is used in advocating for policy, rule, or law changes. It may be used in presenting testimony to a decision-making body or with the media to try to hold decision makers accountable or raise the visibility of an issue. Staff in these kinds of positions will often write policy briefs or develop "report cards" that grade legislators or states on their level of support for various issues (e.g., funding for child welfare or education). It is not unusual for policy researchers to be found working in government agencies as well as advocacy nonprofits.

Social Worker Spotlight: Cathy Kaufmann, MSW

More than 80,000 Oregon Children to Receive Health Insurance

Cathy Kaufmann was in sales briefly after graduating college, but quickly knew she wanted to do more with her life and career. She joined the staff of a nonprofit in Portland, Oregon, and went to work improving literacy for children. However, it wasn't long before Cathy realized she wanted to have a greater impact on social policies affecting children and their families. "We were conducting meaningful research showing that our literacy program was working, but it was just a band aid and not a long-term solution to the problem," said Kaufmann. So, while maintaining her position as a project coordinator, Kaufmann entered the MSW program at Portland State University. "I knew from the beginning of the program that I was interested in solving problems and advocacy was the solution. I wasn't personally interested in direct service." In her first year of the program, Kaufmann's field placement was with the state's most populated county working on poverty issues. During her second year, she held a placement at the Juvenile Rights Project (JRP). The organization is dedicated to improving the lives of vulnerable children and families through legal representation and advocacy in the courts, legislature, schools, and community. At JRP, Kaufmann worked for the "School Works Program," advocating for educational access for formerly incarcerated youth and foster children. Upon completing her degree, Kaufmann worked for Portland State University, conducting research on child welfare. She again realized that although research is important, the reports she worked on would quickly gather dust on a shelf. Kaufmann wanted more direct advocacy work and found it at Children First for Oregon, the state's most respected advocacy organization committed to improving the lives of Oregon's vulnerable children and families. Kaufmann found her calling at Children First, starting as a policy associate and was quickly elevated to policy and communications director. It was at Children First that Kaufmann saw all the pieces come together: "Issue expertise, strategic advocacy, targeted communications, direct lobbying and grassroots organizing combined to make a significant difference on policy issues."

For more than 10 years, the priority issue at Children First was the expansion of health insurance for children. The organization had built an extensive coalition (the Healthy Kids Coalition), and Kaufmann, among others, lobbied for the policy change in the state legislature. However, when the legislation failed to pass due to a

(continued)

lockdown by House Republicans, the Healthy Kids coalition worked to get the Oregon legislature to refer the issue directly to the ballot.

With the measure to appear on the ballot in less than 5 months, Kaufmann got "loaned" by Children First to serve as the campaign's communication director. Measure 50 would raise state tobacco taxes to pay for the Healthy Kids program. Many aspects of Kaufmann's experience and skills were put to the test during the campaign. However, it proved impossible to overcome a four-to-one spending deferential. The Yes on Healthy Kids PAC spent $3.7 million, and the tobacco industry answered by spending $12.1 million (this was the costliest measure in the state's history). Voters rejected the measure by 59%–41%.

Despite the defeat at the ballot, Kaufmann and the coalition went back to work and ultimately secured a legislative win when the governor prioritized spending for the Healthy Kids program and came up with an alternative funding scheme during the 2009 legislature.

Immediately following the passage of the legislation, Kaufmann was recruited by the director of the state's Department of Human Services to oversee the Office of Healthy Kids. As the program's administrator, Kaufmann has a staff of 17 and a budget of $13 million. "In my position I am responsible for running the outreach, education and marketing programs associated with getting 80,000 Oregon children enrolled in health insurance. I see the impact of my work daily." Health and Human Services (HHS) Secretary Kathleen Sebelius has cited Cathy's program as a model for outreach and marketing.

"The work is certainly not always glamorous, I know each and every day that I am making a difference. Whether your interest is macro or clinical, it is imperative to engage in political advocacy," Kaufmann says.

Illustration 5.3

Public Affairs Director or Public Affairs Staff

The Public Affairs Director is ultimately responsible for managing the flow of information from the organization to various audiences, stakeholders, and the general public (also referred to as Public Relations). A public affairs director may be responsible for serving as an organization's lobbyist. In addition, the public affairs director may have duties related to media and message development, strategic planning, coalition building, publications, and internal communications.

Campaign Staff

Most political campaigns require campaign staff, and the size will vary. A statewide issue campaign requires more staff than a legislative race. Following are some of the more common paid positions on a campaign:

Campaign Director
A campaign director is responsible for implementing all aspects of a campaign plan, crafting the campaign plan, and ensuring that the resources are there to fully implement it.

Fund-Raising Director
A fund-raising director is responsible for raising the funds. This may include major donor solicitation, direct mail, telemarketing, and online fund-raising. In addition, a fund-raising director will work with allied organizations to secure PAC donations.

Political Director

A political director is responsible for coalition building, coalition communications, and securing endorsements.

Field Director

A field director is often responsible for overseeing all aspects of the voter contact program. This includes voter identification, voter persuasion, and GOTV.

Lobbyist (Contract vs. Staff)

Lobbyists are responsible for developing legislation and getting it introduced and passed, as well as anticipating/addressing legislation in opposition to the organization and planning and organizing for its defeat. Lobbyists are usually either "contract" or "in-house" depending on the size of the organization and its needs. A contract lobbyist usually works alone or as part of a firm and has contracts with a number of organizations. A staff lobbyist works "in-house" and may have other duties related to the overall public affairs program.

An experienced lobbyist with a lot of access to decision makers can command a high salary, which might be challenging for an advocacy nonprofit to afford to have on staff. Hiring such a person on contract for a portion of his or her time gives a nonprofit a way to hire someone with experience and clout to work on its issues. Hiring a less experienced staff lobbyist ensures no conflicts of interest and the full focus of that staff person on the needs and concerns of the organization. There is no right or wrong answer regarding contract or staff but rather meeting the needs of the organization.

Legislative Staff

Most elected officials have staff who help them carry out many of the day-to-day tasks involved in legislative work. Positions may include chief of staff, legislative aide/assistant, policy liaison, and administrator. The chief of staff generally is responsible for the day-to-day management of an elected official's office and during campaign season may shift roles and become the candidate's campaign director. A chief of staff often represents the elected official at events or other functions. A legislative aide is often responsible for maintaining communication with an elected official's constituency, which includes in-person meetings as well as written communication. One article reports that legislative casework is performed in many state and federal legislative offices, and that social workers at the BSW and MSW levels are well suited for this type of work (Ortiz, Wirz, Semion, & Rodriguez, 2004). Nancy Walker is a MSW who works as a legislative director for a Texas state representative (see her story in Illustration 5.3).

Consider Running for Office

Too few people consider entering politics as a candidate. There are many good reasons for not running (e.g., often low pay, constantly campaigning, and opening self and family up to attacks). But what better way to effect change than to be

Social Worker Spotlight: Nancy Walker, MSSW

Legislative Director for Texas State Representative Elliott Naishtat

Nancy Walker received her master of science in social work degree from the University of Texas at Austin in 1999. Despite having little experience in the legislative arena, she completed her senior year practicum with State Representative Elliott Naishtat, a state legislator with degrees in social work and law. Before receiving her bachelor's degree in social work, Nancy worked as a licensed chemical dependency counselor, and over time, she began questioning who was making the decisions that were hampering the continuity of care of her patients (e.g., lack of community resources, funding cuts for programs serving her clients) and found out that many of these decisions were made at the state capitol in Austin.

When she began her practicum in Rep. Naishtat's office, she was not sure she would be successful due to her lack of previous experience, but according to her, "I was hooked from day one!" She had a strong desire to learn everything about the legislative process and was able to focus on human services issues such as affordable housing for seniors and those with mental illness. Nancy learned that her social work skills were put to good use in this environment. Before long, she was learning how to assess a problem and gather information about the problem from a variety of perspectives, how to research and read laws/proposals, and how to write succinct bill analyses.

After graduating with her MSSW, Nancy was hired to work in Rep. Naishtat's office. In her current position as his legislative director, she helps him to develop his legislative package and is able to work on issues that she is passionate about that fall under the umbrella of health and human services (e.g., policies affecting children and families, mental health, disabilities, poverty, and housing). Ms. Walker works with advocacy organizations and assists them in developing policy proposals, responds to calls from constituents, does drop-in visits to government offices to ensure that the system is working properly, and lobbies other legislators in order to move Rep. Naishtat's legislation forward. She also gets a lot of satisfaction from supervising social work students who do their practicum in Naishtat's office and "watch the light bulbs go on."

Nancy loves every part of her job and states, "If a social worker is interested in the ultimate setting to have impact at the macro level, they should definitely consider a job with a legislator at the state or federal level!" The best part of her job is having the opportunity to have a positive impact on the lives of individuals and families who do not have much influence politically. One of Nancy's favorite wins was helping to pass a bill that created a "Texans conquer cancer" specialty license plate. Texas drivers pay a fee for this plate, and the money funds a grant that nonprofit organizations can apply for in order to provide needed yet unfunded services to individuals and families affected by cancer. Every time she's driving down the road and sees a car with that license plate, it gives her a secret thrill.

Illustration 5.4

in a position to legislate it? There are social workers all across the country who hold elected office at various levels of government, including Capitol Hill. In fact, there are currently seven social workers serving in the 112th U.S. Congress (see Figure 5.6). In 2011, Senator Barbara Mikulski (pictured here) became the longest serving female senator in history; she was first elected to office in 1987. Please see photo of Congresswoman Barbara Lee (D-CA) in the opening chapter photograph.

Representative Susan A. Davis (D-CA)	www.house.gov/susandavis/
Representative Luis V. Gutierrez (D-IL)	http://luisgutierrez.house.gov/
Representative Barbara Lee (D-CA)	http://lee.house.gov/
Senator Barbara Mikulski (D-MD)	http://mikulski.senate.gov/
Representative Allyson Y. Schwartz (D-PA)	http://schwartz.house.gov/
Senator Debbie Stabenow (D-MI)	http://stabenow.senate.gov/
Representative Edolphus "Ed" Towns (D-NY)	http://www.house.gov/towns/

Figure 5.6
Social Workers in the 112th U.S. Congress.

Section 6 of the NASW *Code of Ethics* states that "social workers should engage in social and political action that seeks to ensure that all people have equal access to the resources, employment, services, and opportunities they require to meet their basic human needs and to develop fully. Social workers should be aware of the impact of the political arena on practice and should advocate for changes in policy and legislation to improve social conditions in order to meet basic human needs and promote social justice." The code says that social workers have an ethical duty to engage in political action, but it does not tell social workers what they need to do exactly in order to meet this ethical standard. Thus, individual social workers have the flexibility to decide how to best accomplish this. As this chapter demonstrates, there is a wide array of options available based on one's interests, skills, and abilities.

Critical Thinking

Practice Behavior Example: Use critical thinking augmented by creativity and curiosity.

Critical Thinking Question: How do you think the United States and its priorities might be different if more social workers held political office?

Official photo of Congresswoman Barbara Mikulski.

The following questions will test your knowledge of the content found within this chapter. For additional assessment, including licensing-exam type questions on applying chapter content to practice behaviors, visit **MySearchLab**.

1. According to the American National Election Studies (2008), what percentage of Americans feel that government is run for the benefit of all people?
   a. 10%
   b. 17%
   c. 29%
   d. 37%

2. According to research by the Center for Information and Research on Civic Learning and Engagement (2006) at Tufts University, what percentage of young people aged 15–25 are civically and politically disengaged?
   a. One-quarter
   b. One-third
   c. One-half
   d. Two-thirds

3. Which of the following explanations for social workers' ambivalence toward political involvement is false?
   a. Social work training does not provide them with the confidence and skills needed.
   b. They fear breaking legal codes that restrict the political activities of social workers.
   c. They are not interested in social/political change.
   d. They feel politics is corrupt and they want nothing to do with it.

4. The following social worker is in the U.S. Congress:
   a. Barbara Mikulski
   b. Barbara Boxer
   c. Susan Collins
   d. Diane Feinstein

5. Which of the following basic principles of grassroots fundraising is false?
   a. Asking people to give, regardless of their ability
   b. Asking people to give, who have a belief in the issue or cause
   c. Asking people to give, who have a personal connection to you
   d. Asking people to give, who have a personal connection to your organization

6. You are a social worker who works with low-income single mothers in your community, and you would like to talk with your state legislator about your clients' barriers to employment, particularly the lack of affordable day care. Which of the following strategies would make the most impact?
   a. Sending an email
   b. Mailing a personal letter
   c. Making a phone call to the legislator's office
   d. Arranging in-person visit

7. Visit the "Advocacy" section of NASW's website to learn more about legislative issues of interest to the social work profession. What was most interesting or surprising to you in terms of the issues that are prioritized? Is there an issue of interest to you that was not mentioned?

Reinforce what you learned in this chapter by studying videos, cases, documents, and more available at **www.MySearchLab.com**.

Watch and Review

Watch these Videos

* Collaborate with colleagues and clients for effective policy action in community organization

Read and Review

Read these Cases/Documents

Δ Community to community

Explore and Assess

Explore these Assets

* Electoral College, The (interactive case study)
* Interactive Case Study: You Are a Lobbyist
* Interactive Case Study: You Are a State Legislator
* Interactive Case Study: You Are an Informed Voter Helping Your Classmates Decide How to Vote

Research these Topics

Ways to get engaged in policy change efforts as a student

How social work professionals can volunteer their time

Careers in the political or legislative arena

Assess Your Knowledge

Go to **MySearchLab** to test your knowledge of key topics in this chapter with topic-specific quizzes. Conclude your assessment by completing the chapter exam.

---

* = CSWE Core Competency Asset   Δ = Case Study

6

Health Care Policies and Programs

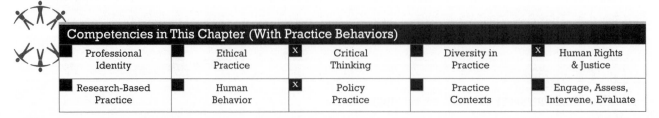

Competencies in This Chapter (With Practice Behaviors)				
■ Professional Identity	■ Ethical Practice	X Critical Thinking	■ Diversity in Practice	X Human Rights & Justice
■ Research-Based Practice	■ Human Behavior	X Policy Practice	■ Practice Contexts	■ Engage, Assess, Intervene, Evaluate

> The enjoyment of the highest attainable standard of health is one of the fundamental rights of every human being without the distinction of race, religion, political belief, economic or social condition.
>
> —*World Health Organization Constitution*

The debate over **universal health care** in the United States is an interesting history lesson. A number of Democratic U.S. presidents were unsuccessful in their attempts to enact a national health care program beginning with President Theodore Roosevelt. President Franklin Delano Roosevelt (FDR) was unable to include health care in the Social Security Act of 1935 due to heavy political opposition, particularly from the American Medical Association (AMA). President Truman, FDR's successor, proposed a single insurance system that would cover all Americans, but this also failed due to opposition from Republicans, Southern Democrats who were leery of federal intervention into state matters (e.g., segregation), and a vigorous public campaign against "socialized medicine" by the AMA. In the 1960s, major progress was made when President Lyndon B. Johnson and a heavily Democratic Congress passed legislation to create the **Medicaid** and **Medicare** programs as part of Johnson's "Great Society" agenda, despite opposition from the AMA. Truman was by Johnson's side when the legislation was signed into law. These programs provide comprehensive medical coverage for people over 65, as well as the poor, blind, and disabled. Yet, this still left millions of Americans without coverage.

In 1971, Senator Edward Kennedy proposed single-payer health care legislation, and this marked the beginning of his career-long effort to reform the nation's health care system. However, it would take three decades until another U.S. president, Bill Clinton, would take up the cause of health care reform. President Clinton appointed the First Lady, Hillary Clinton, to head up this effort, but it was a spectacular failure. Some observers blame the administration for using a flawed closed-door process and emerging with a plan that was too complicated for many to understand. Others point to the successful efforts of powerful special interests, most notably the Health Insurance Association of America (HIAA) and the pharmaceutical industry, which worked with conservative lawmakers to preserve the status quo and mobilized to defeat this effort. In Congress, this effort was led by then speaker of the House, Newt Gingrich. The now infamous "Harry and Louise" commercials were aired by the HIAA to scare the American public away from the Clinton health plan.

After the Clinton health plan stalled in Congress, child welfare advocates were cheered when in 1997 President Clinton signed legislation creating the State Children's Health Insurance Program (S-CHIP) (with bipartisan support) so that more children in the United States would have access to health coverage. Because little progress was being made at the federal level, over a decade later, a number of states and localities passed legislation in efforts to provide universal coverage to their citizens including Massachusetts, Vermont, and San Francisco. Vermont became the first state in the nation to establish a single-payer health care plan when Governor Peter Shumlin signed this health care bill into law on May 26, 2011. Since the beginning, the battle has raged on between conservatives who argue that the provision of medical services should be left in the marketplace (where doctors, drug companies, and other providers are free to establish the price of health care goods and services) and progressives who believe that health care is a basic human right and is too important to be left to the uncertainties of the market.

Since the beginning, the battle has raged on between conservatives who argue that the provision of medical services should be left in the marketplace and progressives who believe that health care is a basic human right.

The National Association of Social Workers views health care as a right and supports a national health care system that provides individuals with universal access to a full range of health and mental health care throughout all stages of life. Additionally, it supports a health care policy that ensures that health care services are delivered equitably (National Association of Social Workers, 2009).

WHAT IS THE PROBLEM?

The U.S. system of medical care is quite complicated and includes a number of pathways through which Americans can have health insurance, from both the private and public sectors. The various options include private insurance (employer-based or self-contracted) or coverage provided through one of many government programs such as **Medicare**, **Medicaid**, the **VA health care system**, or the **State Children's Health Insurance Program (S-CHIP)**. According to the U.S. Census Bureau, in 2010, the vast majority of Americans were covered by private health insurance (195.9 million), while 95 million were covered by government health insurance. The majority of Americans (55.3%) were covered by employment-based health insurance. The number of people without health insurance was 49.9 million (DeNavas-Walt, Proctor, & Smith, 2011).

Despite the fact that Americans have some of the best doctors, treatment, and medical technology in the world, there is a rather long list of problems with the current system that have been identified by experts and advocacy groups:

- According to the U.S. Census Bureau, in 2008, there were 46.3 million uninsured people in the United States, including 7.3 million children. The majority of people without insurance are caught in the middle because they cannot afford private insurance, but their income is too high to qualify for many government programs (DeNavas-Walt, Proctor, & Smith, 2009).
- According to a report from the Commonwealth Fund, 29 million Americans were "**underinsured**" in 2010, up 80% from 2003. This means their health care coverage does not adequately protect them from high medical expenses (Schoen, Doty, Robertson, & Collins, 2011).
- The number of employers offering health coverage has fallen significantly in recent years.
- A 2009 Harvard study published in the *American Journal of Public Health* reported that 45,000 people die every year in the United States due to lack of health insurance (Wilper, Woolhandler, Lasser, McCormick, Bor, & Himmelstein, 2009).
- Government research shows that there is a widening gap in life expectancy when comparing the affluent to those with low socioeconomic status. In 1998–2000, people in the most affluent group could expect to live 4.5 years longer than people in the most deprived group. However, a deeper look at the data reveals that the difference between affluent White women and poor Black men was more than 14 years. The reasons for this disparity are varied but can be explained in part by the fact that lower-income people are less likely to have health insurance (Singh & Siahpush, 2006).
- Medical bills are a major cause of bankruptcy in the United States.
- Insurance companies have been allowed to exclude people for various **preexisting conditions**.
- Health insurance premiums and deductibles have increased significantly in recent years, making insurance unaffordable for many families.

- In 2000, the World Health Organization ranked the United States 37th in the world on measures of medical outcomes (France and Italy were 1st and 2nd). When compared to other developed countries, the United States does not fare well when it comes to life expectancy, rates of infant mortality, and other measures of health.
- A study published in the journal *Health Affairs* reported that the United States has the highest rate of preventable deaths when compared to 19 other industrialized nations (Nolte & McKee, 2008).
- The United States has the most expensive health care system in the world despite the fact that millions of Americans do not have health coverage. In 2010, health care was a $2.6 trillion industry, and health care spending accounted for 17.9% of the nation's GDP. As of 2009, health spending was roughly 90% higher than in many other industrialized nations (Kaiser Family Foundation, 2012).
- Very powerful special interests have contributed vast amounts of money to elected leaders in Washington, DC, which has prevented the United States from achieving meaningful health care reform for more than eight decades.

Human Rights & Justice

Practice Behavior Example: Understand the forms and mechanisms of oppression and discrimination.

Critical Thinking Question: The failures and problems of the U.S. health care system have not been a secret. Despite all of the many flaws, why do you think the United States has been unable to achieve having a universal health care system?

OVERVIEW OF MAJOR GOVERNMENT-FUNDED HEALTH CARE PROGRAMS IN THE UNITED STATES

Medicaid

The Medicaid program was established in 1965 during the Johnson administration and was a major achievement in providing health insurance to America's poorest individuals and families. It is also the largest single funding source for people with AIDS, for those living in nursing homes, and for those with developmental disabilities who live in a facility. There are five groups eligible for services: children, pregnant women, parents with dependent children, people with severe disabilities, and seniors. About half of Medicaid beneficiaries are children. Under health care reform passed by President Obama, beginning in 2014, nearly everyone under age 65 with an income up to 133% of the federal poverty level will be eligible. The federal government and the states share the costs of Medicaid. Medicaid covers roughly 60 million low-income Americans, and in 2008, Medicaid spending totaled about $339 billion (Kaiser Family Foundation, 2010).

Medicare

The Medicare program was also created in 1965 during the Johnson administration. Medicare is a health insurance program for people aged 65 and older regardless of their income and/or medical history. In addition to serving seniors, the program also serves people under age 65 with permanent disabilities and those diagnosed with end-stage renal disease and ALS (Lou Gehrig's disease). Medicare has a complicated structure and is organized into four parts: Parts

A, B, C, and D. This program covers about 47 million Americans, but this will continue to grow as more baby boomers start to reach the age of 65. Medicare is financed by a combination of general revenues, payroll taxes, and beneficiary premiums. Medicare spending was $519 billion in 2010 and is expected to rise to $929 billion by 2020 (Kaiser Family Foundation, 2010). This is an example of a single-payer health care system because the government is the sole payer.

CHIP

The Children's Health Insurance Program (CHIP) (originally called S-CHIP; the S was for "State") was created to cover uninsured children who are not eligible for Medicaid. In 2009, CHIP was reauthorized by the 111th Congress and was signed into law by President Obama. The reauthorization expanded funding by $33 billion in federal funds with an aim to increase enrollment from 7 million to 11 million children. This is an important policy goal because it is estimated that two-thirds of children are eligible for Medicaid or CHIP, but are not enrolled. States are now required to include dental services. The federal government and states share the costs of CHIP, but federal funds are capped.

VA System

The Veterans Affairs (VA) health care system is set up to provide a full range of outpatient and inpatient services to the veterans of the U.S. military. In the United States, there are almost 800 outpatient clinics and 152 VA hospitals. According to the Department of Veterans Affairs, in fiscal year 2010, the VA spent $42 million in medical care costs. This is an example of socialized medicine because the health care services are provided, and paid for, by the government.

WHAT IS SINGLE-PAYER HEALTH CARE?

For those working in the area of health care policy, a number of important questions need to be considered: How should health care resources be distributed? Should access to health care be based on one's income? Should it be linked to one's employment? Should quality and accessibility of health care vary state by state? Is health care a right or a privilege? Do Americans want a "health care system" or a "health care industry"? The health care debate can get rather confusing at times because many terms get thrown around, such as universal health care, single-payer health care, and socialized medicine.

When people talk about universal health care, they are referring to a system of care in which everyone is guaranteed health care coverage.

When people talk about **universal health care**, they are referring to a system of care in which everyone is guaranteed health care coverage. The United States is virtually alone in the Western industrialized world in not making this assurance to its citizens. In **single-payer** health care systems, there is one payer, which is typically the government. The advantage to this is that administrative costs are very low because it is much more efficient to process claims when there is only one payer versus hundreds of insurance companies. It would be incorrect to call this **socialized medicine** however, if the health care services are being provided in the private sector.

For example, Canada has a single-payer health care system because the government is the payer; however, health care services are delivered by the private sector so it would not be considered socialized medicine. This is similar to the Medicare program in the United States. Canada's government is able to keep the costs of health care low because it is able to negotiate prices with hospitals, pharmaceutical companies, and other providers. It would be more accurate to call Britain's health care system "socialized medicine" because Britain's government is not only the payer of health care services but also the provider of those services. Its system is similar to the VA system in the United States. Hospitals are run by the government, and doctors are government employees. Physicians for a National Health Program (PNHP) define *single-payer health care* as, "A system in which a single public or quasi-public agency organizes health financing, but delivery of care remains largely private. Under a single-payer health care system, all Americans would be covered for all medically necessary services" (n.d.). Single-payer health care is sometimes called Universal Health Insurance or Improved Medicare for All.

Proponents of single-payer health care believe that health insurance companies are a major source of the problem because they operate from a profit motive and are ultimately concerned about the bottom line. As evidence, critics point to the fact that insurance companies routinely deny coverage to people with preexisting conditions, find creative ways to deny medical procedures that are recommended by a patient's physician, and increase the costs of premiums, making insurance unaffordable for many families. Doctors often feel frustrated that they cannot make medical decisions without the approval of a HMO (health maintenance organization) bureaucrat.

There is certainly much debate over which kind of health care system is the best option. Ideally, health care systems would provide high quality services to every citizen at a reasonable cost. Critics of the health care systems in Europe and Scandinavian countries point out that these countries have to ration services in order to cover everyone, and that as a result, there are waiting lists for certain medical and surgical procedures. However, critics of the U.S. healthcare system are quick to point out that health care services are rationed in the United States as well, because health care services are provided for some citizens, whereas others go without.

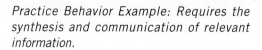

Critical Thinking

Practice Behavior Example: Requires the synthesis and communication of relevant information.

Critical Thinking Question: What are the differences and connections between universal health care, single-payer health care, and socialized medicine? Practice telling a friend to ensure that you can articulate these concepts well.

THE MAD AS HELL DOCTORS TOUR

There were many Americans who were hopeful that with the election of Barack Obama, the United States would finally be able to make universal health care a reality. However, when the debate over health care reform in Congress heated up, single-payer proponents were extremely disappointed when they learned that a single-payer system of health care would not be one of the options under consideration. In fact, Democratic U.S. Senator Max Baucus, chairman of the Senate Finance Committee, did not invite any representatives from groups advocating for single-payer health care to the series of meetings held before his committee where health care reform was discussed. He had 13 protesters (doctors, nurses, and activists) removed by Capitol police for demanding that single-payer advocates be given a seat at the table. They were arrested and soon became known as the *Baucus 13*.

After much pressure, Baucus later agreed to have a meeting with five prominent single-payer advocates. At the meeting were Dr. David Himmelstein, associate professor of medicine at Harvard Medical School and cofounder of PNHP; Dr. Marcia Angell, senior lecturer, Harvard Medical School, and former editor-in-chief of the *New England Journal of Medicine*; Dr. Oliver Fein, associate dean, Cornell Weill Medical School and president of PNHP; Rose Ann DeMoro, executive director of the California Nurses Association; and Geri Jenkins, president of California Nurses Association, each of whom pleaded his or her case for allowing single-payer health care to be considered and debated (see Figure 6.1 to learn more about the California Nurse's Association and the PNHP). Baucus admitted that he made a mistake for not leaving single-payer health care on the table, despite the fact that he did not believe that it was politically feasible. He agreed to use the power of his office to have the charges dropped against the Baucus 13.

In August 2009, Mad as Hell Doctors was formed by media expert Adam Klugman, campaign organizer Gary Jelenik, and a group of five Oregon physicians who are members of PNHP. They decided that something drastic was needed to bring attention to single-payer health care, which was being excluded by lawmakers in Washington, DC. Their strategy was to embark on a 3-week road trip through the heartland of America, and they would call it the *Mad as Hell Doctors Tour*. They would get their message out to the public through education, advocacy, and entertainment. Their Winnebago (see picture), which was decorated with the name of their cause, was used to carry

---

California Nurses Association (www.calnurses.org) Founded in 1903, the California Nurses Association/National Nurses Organizing Committee/AFL-CIO is an organization of registered nurses with more than 86,000 members in hospitals, clinics, and home health agencies in all 50 states. CNA/NNOC is also a founding member of the 150,000-member National Nurses United, which in 2009 united CNA/NNOC, the United American Nurses, and the Massachusetts Nurses Association to create the largest union and professional association of nurses in U.S. history.

CNA/NNOC activities have included advocating for guaranteed health care by expanding and updating Medicare to cover all Americans, negotiating collective bargaining contracts for RNs in the nation, and fighting for regulatory protections for patients and nurses.

Physicians for a National Health Program (www.pnhp.org) PNHP is the only physician organization in the country dedicated to a single issue—the implementation of a universal, comprehensive single-payer national health care program. It began advocating for reform of the U.S. health care system in 1987 and today has more than 17,000 members. The organization has done this by educating physicians and other health professionals about the benefits of a single-payer health care system, publishing scholarly research articles and educating the public by speaking at community forums and town hall meetings, and through interviews in the media.

Mad as Hell Doctors (www.madashelldoctors.com) In 2009, the Mad as Hell doctors drove a Winnebago across the country organizing town hall meetings and rallies in 30 towns and cities in 15 states to educate the public and stakeholders about the benefits of a single-payer health care system.

Figure 6.1
Activist Spotlight.

Winnebago.

them across the country so they could speak at single-payer rallies and town halls in churches, union halls, universities, public parks, and arts centers.

The Goal and the Strategy

The Mad as Hell Doctors Tour was run by a few paid people with expertise in political campaigns, along with many people who volunteered their time to this cause. Adam Klugman was hired to do the media work that involved designing the logo, formulating the initial concept and messaging of the campaign, and putting together the campaign's website. Gary Jelenik was hired as the campaign organizer and was responsible for planning the nuts and bolts of the road tour, which involved contacting people in the various cities they would visit, putting together a "ground crew" in those cities, and planning the events. There was a third person who was paid to staff the phones and help with setup. The goal of the campaign would be to educate the public about single-payer health care system (via political rallies and media coverage), strengthen linkages between organizations interested in advocating for single-payer health care, and try to propel single-payer health care onto the national agenda. There was a 6–8 week planning period before kicking off the road tour.

The Rallies

The heart of this campaign was the organized rallies and town hall meetings. All in all, the doctors made stops in 30 towns and cities in 15 states. The kick-off event was held in Portland, Oregon, and the final stop was in Washington, DC, where the doctors hoped to have a meeting with President Obama. The tour started with five

Advocacy Tip

When embarking on a policy change effort, having paid staff with expertise in working with the media and designing a website can be instrumental to winning.

Advocacy Tip

Deciding whether (and when) to organize a rally is a strategic decision that must be carefully considered. If carefully planned and organized, a rally can be an effective way to get media attention and mobilize supporters, **but** you have to be able to turn people out.

- People attending the rally were filmed talking about why they are upset about the current health care system, and this was projected on a screen for all to see;
- The physicians were introduced at the beginning of the rally, and each one spoke from his or her experience for a couple of minutes about why they were "mad as Hell";
- An excerpt of a video was shown to educate the audience about single-payer health care (produced by Dr. Paul Hochfeld);
- Mad as Hell Minutes: Anyone at the rally could talk for one minute to tell his or her story and to explain why he or she was "mad as Hell." These were all filmed and posted on the Mad as Hell Doctors website;
- Sometimes there was musical entertainment, such as singing by the "Mad as Hell Nurses" at the rally in Portland, Oregon;
- At the end of the rally, attendees were asked to engage in some sort of action. They were asked to contact the White House and ask the White House officials to meet with the Mad as Hell Doctors. The White House later blocked emails sent from the Mad as Hell Doctors website so people had to send emails from other email boxes. Attendees were asked to sign a petition at the rally. Finally, they were asked to contribute money to the Mad as Hell Doctors Tour to support their road tour;
- There was a table at the rallies that had literature, campaign materials for sale (buttons, T-shirts, etc.), and white ribbons that could be tied near government buildings to represent people who die every year due to lack of health insurance.

physicians who made the entire trip, and they were joined by four other physicians who were able to travel various segments of the trip. There were also a few critical people who volunteered their time to work as support crew, such as social work professor Bill Whitaker (see Dr. Whitaker's personal account of his experience on the Mad as Hell Doctors Tour at the end of this chapter). See also photo of Dr. Whitaker in action in the opening chapter photo. Their Winnebago, affectionately nicknamed "Winnie," was very useful in generating interest and enthusiasm as they traveled across the country. Over time, they refined the format of the rallies, which typically went as follows:

Messaging

Because health care reform is a rather complicated topic, it is important to be able to break the issue down into key messages that will resonate with the people one is trying to influence. On the tour, the doctors developed a working definition of *single-payer health care*, which was, "A system of payment that redirects all current health care monies, both public and private, into a single public fund that covers everyone." Other key messages are listed under the Advocacy Tip box in the following page.

Funding

As you can imagine, the Mad as Hell Doctors tour required funds in order for it to be successful. The physicians funded much of this effort, and this

A significant amount of time in issue campaigns is spent on messaging or "framing" the issue. Your message must be persuasive and resonate with those you are trying to influence. This is much easier said than done!

- "Single payer is the fiscally conservative approach to universal coverage, the only affordable approach for the long haul."
- "We need a single risk pool—everyone in, nobody out."
- "Stop insurance company 'cherry picking'—limiting insurance to the most healthy and denying coverage to those most likely to need medical care."
- "The current health care funding system is broken and cannot be repaired incrementally."
- "Under single payer, health care delivery (physicians, hospitals, etc.) remains as is. Only health care funding is carried out by the government."
- "Single-payer is essentially an improved Medicare for All system."
- "Thirty percent of all health care dollars go to insurance company overhead and profits."
- "Under a single-payer system, current levels of health care expenditures would be enough to provide universal coverage at no additional cost."
- "The U.S. is the only industrialized country lacking universal, publicly funded health care."
- "The U.S. spends nearly twice as much per capita on health care, leaves many millions uncovered, and has poorer health outcomes than any other industrialized country."

fund was supplemented by generous donations from people passionate about this cause. The funding was used to pay for work performed by the three paid staff members, the Winnebago, and gas, meals, and motel stays along the way. People who donated $500 or more were made an honorary "Mad as Hell Doctor."

Media Coverage

The Mad as Hell doctors were disappointed that they did not seem to get as much national media coverage as the "anti-groups" such as the Tea Party protesters. However, they were successful in getting a lot of coverage in local media (radio, television, and newspaper), and they did get some coverage on national news programs such as MSNBC's *Countdown with Keith Olbermann* (for a sample of one of these interviews, visit http://www.youtube.com/watch?v=I_hmiLzBEFw). On the tour, each physician averaged 3–4 media interviews per day. Finally, the Mad as Hell Doctors made a documentary film showcasing their travel experience across the country, which can be viewed on their website.

Social Media

The Mad as Hell Doctors had a professional website developed, and followers were able to visit the website to learn about their progress as they made their way across the country. They also communicated with their "fans" on Facebook.

Tactics Used by Mad as Hell Doctors	
☑ Coalition building	☐ Direct lobbying (in-person lobby visits; sometimes by a professional lobbyist)
☑ Earned media (letters to the editor; actions that lead to media coverage)	☑ Grassroots lobbying (e.g., urging people to call, write, email legislators)
☐ Paid media (paying for tv/radio ads)	☑ Educational outreach (town halls; house parties; community forums)
☑ Visibility (rallies; marches)	☑ Online advocacy (using social media)
☐ Political dissent (e.g., civil disobedience; protest)	☐ Paid communication (paid staff who call voters; materials mailed out)
☐ Providing testimony in a legislative committee hearing	☑ Fund-raising activities

Policy Practice

Practice Behavior Example: Collaborate with colleagues and clients for effective policy action.

Critical Thinking Question: Take some time to critically evaluate the tactics and strategies used by the single-payer advocates. What worked well? How effective was their messaging? If you were working on this campaign, what skills, ideas, and suggestions would you offer?

Was the Mad as Hell Doctors Tour a Success?

In the end, the Mad as Hell Doctors did not win their battle. Single-payer health care never made it on the political agenda and was not taken seriously as an option by lawmakers in Washington, DC. However, advocates cannot get discouraged and have to come to terms with the fact that significant progress can take a long time when working on causes that represent a major change to the status quo. Even though the doctors did not ultimately win this round, progress was made. The White House would not agree to meet with the doctors; however, their final rally in Washington, DC, included a rousing speech by Congressman Dennis Kucinich, a single-payer supporter. A single-payer bill (H.R. 676) introduced in the 111th Congress sponsored by Representative John Conyers (D-MI) had 87 cosponsors. Members of the Mad as Hell Doctors Tour were able to educate thousands of Americans who turned out to attend their rallies or heard their message in various media outlets.

This was also the beginning of a new organization, Mad as Hell Doctors, which has a website and future plans to continue to press for a single-payer health care system in the United States, along with other coalition partners such as the California Nurses Association and Physicians for a National Health Program. They are copying Canada's success by using a state-level strategy. Canada started out by having single-payer health care in one province, and when it was shown to be successful, it spread to the rest of the country. In 2010, Mad as Hell Doctors had another road tour, but this time they focused solely on California where they hope to get the state to pass a single-payer health care bill.

Practice Activity 6.1

There were a lot of Mad as Hell doctors and Mad as Hell nurses involved in this effort, along with a very dedicated social work professor. If more social workers were involved, what could they add to this effort? Visit their website to learn about their current activities: http://madashelldoctors.com.

HEALTH INSURANCE REFORM UNDER PRESIDENT OBAMA

President Clinton's health care failure was a stinging loss for the Democratic Party, and Democrats would not seriously revisit the issue until the election of President Obama who made health care reform one of his campaign promises. In 2008, health care spending topped $2.3 trillion, and an estimated 46 million Americans lacked health care coverage. Many thought that health care reform would be a relatively quick and painless process because the government was now controlled by a popular, new Democratic president and a heavily Democratic U.S. Congress. Also, Americans were increasingly disillusioned with their employer-based, HMO health care system. Obama promised that a bill would be signed by summer, but the road to health care reform under the new president was a rocky one. Defeat seemed eminent at several points along the way as Americans became increasingly confused and frustrated with the process.

After a long and tenuous 15-month political battle, the **Patient Protection and Affordable Care Act** was signed into law by President Obama. The new law made some significant changes to the U.S. health care system but left many Americans disappointed. It was too radical for many Tea Party activists who feared that this was just the first step toward a "government takeover of health care" and was not radical enough for single-payer activists who were stunned to find that the new law would not even include a public option, the compromised alternative to single-payer health care. The Congressional Budget Office estimates that the bill would provide coverage to 32 million uninsured people, but would still leave 23 million uninsured in 2019, thus falling short of the goal of ensuring that all Americans have health insurance coverage. The new law preserved the private insurance system and left many spectators around the world wondering why the United States remains the only industrialized country that does not ensure health care coverage for all of its citizens. Here are some of the highlights of the road to health care reform under President Obama:

> After a long and tenuous 15-month political battle, the Patient Protection and Affordable Care Act was signed into law by President Obama.

- In February 2009, President Obama laid out eight principles of health care reform: protect families' financial health, make health coverage affordable, aim for universality, provide portability of coverage, guarantee choice, invest in prevention and wellness, improve patient safety and quality care, and maintain long-term fiscal sustainability.
- As Democratic lawmakers in Washington set out to draft legislation to reform the nation's health care system, there were a number of areas of consensus, for example, the practice of health insurance companies denying coverage to those with preexisting conditions must end. Also, most agreed that the escalating costs of health care and health insurance must be addressed and that health care reform has to be paid for so that it does not add to the exploding federal deficit. There was also a consensus among Democrats on a number of areas such as requiring American citizens to have health insurance or pay a penalty, requiring businesses to offer health insurance to their employees or pay a penalty, and paying for health care, in part, by raising taxes on the rich.
- However, large-scale social change is never easy, so there were a number of sticking points. The largest bone of contention among Democrats concerned whether reform should involve the creation of a new government insurance plan or "**public option**." Democrats were divided between

conservative Democrats who opposed the public option and liberal law-makers who embraced a government insurance plan that would be able to compete with private insurance. Health insurance agencies and Republican lawmakers were unanimous in their opposition to the public option. Opponents of the public option were criticized for being in the pocket of the health insurance industry or for being too scared to oppose insurance providers because this motion was not successful during the reform effort under President Clinton.

- There was also a fairly significant debate over **abortion,** which threatened to derail health care reform efforts. Pro-life Democrats threatened to vote against any health care bill that did not include restrictions on abortion. Michigan Representative Bart Stupak introduced an amendment, later named the "Stupak amendment," which would impose tight restrictions on abortions that could be offered through a new government-run insurance plan and through private insurance that is bought using government subsidies. However, this amendment was not included in the final bill to the dismay of pro-life supporters.

- The first major task was to get lawmakers to reach consensus on a bill in each chamber. In the U.S. House of Representatives, bills from three committees had to be melded into a consensus bill that would win a House majority. The bill included new restrictions to abortion coverage. The bill passed in the House on November 7, 2009, with a vote of 220 to 215. Only one Republican voted for it.

- It took a little longer to get a bill passed in the U.S. Senate due to disagreement over the public option from conservative Democrats such as Ben Nelson, Blanche Lincoln, and Mary Landrieu. Two bills emerged from two separate Senate committees, the Senate Health, Education, Labor, and Pensions Committee and the Senate Finance Committee, which was more conservative and middle of the road and rejected the public option to compete with private insurers. Despite Senator Harry Reid's advocacy for the public option, the Senate passed a compromise bill on December 24, 2009, without the public option; a compromise to allow people aged 55–64 to buy into Medicare was also unsuccessful. The bill passed with a vote of 60 to 39 after 25 straight days of debate.

- While all of this activity was going on inside closed door meetings and committee meetings on Capitol Hill, there was a lot of discontentment being expressed both inside and outside the Beltway. On the left, liberals were revolting and some were advocating the defeat of the health care bill because it had been too compromised in their view. Single-payer activists could not believe that the public option was off the table and that the new president stated he could support a "nonprofit health care cooperative" as an alternative. Meanwhile, crowds of Tea Party activists were disrupting town hall meetings by demonstrating, shouting down members of Congress and hanging them, and Obama, in effigy. They were adamantly opposed to increased taxes and a larger role for government.

- Republican lawmakers were uniformly opposed to "ObamaCare" and were focusing on the cost and scope of the new bill and talking to seniors about cuts to Medicare and end-of-life planning services included in the legislation, which they renamed "death panels." After being criticized for not offering any of their own ideas, they offered their own plan in November 2009 (see the Conservative Response to Health Care Reform section).

- The final step in the process was to reconcile House and Senate versions of the bill. The process was almost derailed again with the special election of Republican Senator Scott Brown who filled the Senate seat that was held by Ted Kennedy for over 50 years. The Democrats would no longer have the 60 votes they needed to overcome a Republican filibuster.

- However, in February 2010, President Obama seemed to find new momentum as he seized his last opportunity to pass a historic health care bill. Some wondered if this was too little too late. He announced plans to hold a televised, bipartisan, half-day health summit where leaders on both sides of the aisle were encouraged to air their concerns and find areas of agreement. Obama vowed to listen to all ideas, from Republicans as well as Democrats.

- Then Anthem Blue Cross announced that premiums for its insurance policies would be raised anywhere between 25% and 39%. Obama took advantage of this opportunity and made an example out of Anthem in his talks and speeches. Obama then laid out a detailed White House plan for expanding health care to the uninsured that bridges elements of the House and Senate bills. In March, he sold his plan to the public by giving speeches and attending political rallies. The White House focused on lining up the votes it needed and pressured Democrats to get on board.

- On March 21, 2010, the House passed the Senate bill with not one single Republican vote. This was historic in modern history for a major piece of legislation to pass without a single Republican vote. In order to get the votes of a handful of anti-abortion Democrats, President Obama agreed to issue an executive order after the passage of the bill reaffirming that it will be consistent with current laws that restrict the use of federal funds for abortion. Obama signed the Patient Protection and Affordable Care Act into law two days later surrounded by House and Senate lawmakers, the wife of deceased Senator Edward Kennedy (a longtime champion of U.S. health care reform), and individuals who have suffered due to lack of health insurance.

THE CONSERVATIVE RESPONSE TO HEALTH CARE REFORM ("OBAMACARE")

President Obama's hope that health care reform could be a bipartisan effort was completely dashed when it became clear that Republicans and Democrats have very different ideas regarding how the nation's health care system should be reformed. Once again, it became clear how polarized and politicized things are inside the Beltway. Republicans complained that they were being shut out of the process and that the Democratic plan was a "government takeover of health care." Democrats portrayed Republicans as the "party of no" and countered that many Republican ideas were included in the health reform legislation.

In November 2009, Republicans offered their own health care plan, which involved limiting damages in medical malpractice lawsuits, allowing small businesses to join together to buy insurance exempt from most state regulation, and rewarding states for reducing the number of uninsured. It had similar components to the Democratic legislation in that it would allow young adults to stay on their parents' health plans at least through age 24 (compared with age 26 under the Democrats' bill) and would prohibit insurers from imposing annual or lifetime limits on spending for covered benefits.

However, there were also some key differences. It differed from the Democratic plan in that it did not require citizens to have health insurance or employers to offer it and would not expand any of the current government programs such as Medicaid. It would not provide subsidies to individuals to help them purchase insurance, nor would it impose any new taxes. Finally, the Republican bill would not prohibit health insurance companies from denying coverage to people due to a preexisting condition. When the new bill was signed into law by President Obama, Democrats lauded it as major reform that was historic, whereas House Republican leader John Boehner stated, "This is a somber day for the American people. By signing this bill, President Obama is abandoning our founding principle that government governs best when it governs closest to the people" (Stolberg & Pear, 2010).

THE PATIENT PROTECTION AND AFFORDABLE CARE ACT

Although some lauded the new health care reform law as historic, groundbreaking legislation, there were many critics on both sides of the aisle.

This new law (now commonly referred to as the Affordable Care Act) is very complicated and will take some time before lawmakers at the state and federal level are able to fully implement it. The bill was over 2,000 pages long and was supported only by Democratic lawmakers, despite Obama's wish for bipartisan support. Although some lauded the new health care reform law as historic, groundbreaking legislation, there were critics on both sides of the aisle. Many liberals did not feel the bill went far enough and was too compromised; in their view, the new bill was health "insurance" reform, not health "care" reform. Conservatives on the other hand saw this new effort as a slippery slope toward a government takeover of the health care system. Here are some important features of the new law:

- The health reform legislation requires that all individuals have health insurance beginning in 2014, or else face paying a tax penalty.
- The poorest Americans will be covered under a Medicaid expansion.
- Those with low and middle income who do not have access to affordable coverage through their jobs will be able to purchase coverage with federal subsidies through new "American Health Benefit Exchanges."
- Beginning in 2014, employers are not mandated to provide health benefits; however, businesses with more than 50 employees, whose employees receive insurance subsidies, will pay penalties. Small businesses will be able to access more plans through a separate exchange.
- Tax credits to small employers with no more than 25 employees and average annual wages of less than $50,000 that purchase health insurance for employees will be provided.
- Health plans will not be allowed to deny coverage to people for any reason, including a preexisting condition (this takes effect in 2010 for children and in 2014 for adults).
- Assistance for Medicare beneficiaries with high drug costs will be provided (helps to close the "doughnut hole").
- The legislation will include a focus on prevention by covering proven preventive services, providing grants for up to 5 years to small employers that establish wellness programs (starting in 2011), and requiring chain restaurants and food sold from vending machines to disclose the nutritional content of each item (starting in 2011).
- Investments in community health centers, school-based health centers, and various strategies to improve the health care workforce, including social workers, are included.

• Young adults will now have the option of being covered under their parents' plan, up to age 26 (starting in 2010).

The final bill did not include the public option, but some Democrats vowed to get this passed in a separate bill in the future. However, as is common in many controversial legislative battles, this was not the end of the story for the Affordable Care Act, and its future was uncertain. Twenty-six states, and a few individuals, joined together to challenge the constitutionality of the new law, in particular the mandate that all Americans must obtain insurance coverage or pay a financial penalty. Ultimately, the Supreme Court would have to rule on whether the federal government can compel individuals not engaged in commerce to buy a product (i.e., health insurance) from private companies. The Court heard oral arguments from attorneys on both sides in March 2012, and the final ruling came down on June 28, 2012.

On June 28th, Americans anxiously tuned in to various media outlets to learn how the U.S. Supreme Court would rule on President Obama's healthcare reform law, the centerpiece of his presidency that he took great risk to pass. Many political pundits asserted that if the Supreme Court were to rule against Obama, this could doom his chances for a second presidential term. Many expected at least part of the new law to be overturned in light of the conservative bent to the high court. However, to the shock of many Americans, the U.S. Supreme Court upheld Obama's health care reform law in a 5-4 decision, with Chief Justice John Roberts joining with Court's four more liberal justices. The court ruled that the law's mandate that most Americans obtain insurance or pay a penalty was authorized by Congress's power to levy taxes.

In the majority opinion, Chief Justice Roberts wrote, "The Affordable Care Act's requirement that certain individuals pay a financial penalty for not obtaining health insurance may reasonably be characterized as a tax. Because the Constitution permits such a tax, it is not our role to forbid it, or to pass upon its wisdom or fairness" (Liptak, New York Times, June 28, 2012). President Obama who was clearly relieved at the outcome stated, "Whatever the politics, today's decision was a victory for people all over this country whose lives are more secure because of this law (Liptak, New York Times, June 28, 2012).

The only downside to the ruling from the perspective of the Obama administration was the Court's ruling by 7 of the Justices that Congress had exceeded its constitutional authority by forcing states into participating in the expansion of the Medicaid program by threatening them with the loss of existing federal payments. Thus, states will now have the option of whether to expand their Medicaid program to include more state residents. A piece in the New York Times was glowing despite acknowledging that the debate over the role of government was far from over in the U.S.:

> For Barack Obama who staked his presidency on a once-in-a-generation reshaping of the social welfare system, the Supreme Court's health care ruling is not just political vindication. It is a personal reprieve, leaving intact his hopes of joining the ranks of Franklin D. Roosevelt, Lyndon B. Johnson and Ronald Reagan as presidents who fundamentally altered the course of the country (Landler, New York Times, June 28, 2012).

CHAPTER 6 PRACTICE TEST

The following questions will test your knowledge of the content found within this chapter. For additional assessment, including licensing-exam type questions on applying chapter content to practice behaviors, visit **MySearchLab**.

1. According to the U.S. Census Bureau, in 2008, there were _____ million uninsured people in the United States.
   a. 14
   b. 28
   c. 46
   d. 64

2. What is the main similarity between Canada's health care system, the health care system in the United Kingdom, the VA system in the United States, and the Medicare system in the United States?
   a. They are all single-payer systems.
   b. They are all examples of socialized medicine.
   c. They are all examples of universal health care.
   d. They all rely on private health insurance.

3. Which of the following statements about the problems in the U.S. health care system is false?
   a. The United States has a high rate of preventable deaths compared to other industrialized nations.
   b. The United States has the most expensive health care system in the world.
   c. Insurance companies have been allowed to exclude people for preexisting conditions.
   d. There is a significant gap in life expectancy in the United States, but there are no apparent racial disparities.

4. You are working with a low-income family, and the parents want your help finding health care coverage for their children. They are struggling financially, but are not eligible for many government programs that serve those at the bottom of the income ladder. Which program is likely the best fit to help this family?
   a. Medicaid
   b. CHIP
   c. Medicare
   d. The VA system

5. Which of the following is true about the new health care reform bill signed into law by President Obama?
   a. It included a "public option" that would compete with private insurance companies.
   b. It preserved the private insurance system.
   c. Private insurance companies are still allowed to deny coverage to those with preexisting conditions.
   d. It does not require citizens to have health insurance.

6. The health care system that is set up to serve primarily senior citizens who are retired is:
   a. CHIP
   b. VA system
   c. Medicaid
   d. Medicare

7. After reading this chapter about different views about health care, different types of systems of health care, and an overview of the U.S. health care system, how do you feel about the new health care reform law passed by President Obama? Many progressives feel it did not go far enough, and many conservatives feel it went too far. Others argue that the passage of this legislation was a remarkable achievement because no president since Johnson has been able to pass legislation making major changes to the way health care works in the United States. What do you think? What kind of system would you advocate for as a social worker?

Reinforce what you learned in this chapter by studying videos, cases, documents, and more available at **www.MySearchLab.com**.

Watch and Review

Watch these Videos

* The 2010 Health Care Legislation (2010)
* Vaccines: Mandatory Protection (2007)

Read and Review

Read these Cases/Documents

Δ What's Medically Wrong With This?

Δ A Community Coalition

Explore and Assess

Explore these Assets

Interactive Case Study: Comparing Health Systems

Research these Topics

Overview of Major Government-Funded Health Care Programs in the United states

What Is Single-Payer Health Care?

The Patient Protection and Affordable Care Act

Assess Your Knowledge

Go to **MySearchLab** to test your knowledge of key topics in this chapter with topic-specific quizzes. Conclude your assessment by completing the chapter exam.

---

* = CSWE Core Competency Asset   Δ = Case Study

On the Road with the Mad as Hell Doctors' Health Care-a-Van*

by

Bill Whitaker, PhD., ACSW

On September 8th, as the health care debate raged in Congress, a group of five doctors from Oregon embarked on an historic road trip through the heartland of America, arriving on September 30th at the doors of Congress and the White House. Other doctors, nurses, social workers and concerned citizens joined our caravan for varying lengths of time.

Our mission was to promote single-payer health insurance as a fiscally conservative, affordable way to provide universal health care to the 47 million Americans who are currently uninsured; to improve coverage for the many millions more of us who currently have catastrophic insurance at best; and to help every insured American cope with declining benefits accompanied by increasingly high premiums, deductibles and co-pays.

Through our Health Care-A-Van we educated Americans about the advantages of single risk pool, single-payer health care and recorded the stories of countless individuals and families whose lives have been shattered by lack of access to affordable health care.

> Our proposal is simple. The United States needs single-payer health care, a system of payment that redirects all current health care monies, both public and private, into a single public fund that covers everyone.

A single-payer system is built on a single risk pool with "everybody in and nobody out." We believe a single-payer health care system is the only means to lasting, substantive health care reform for the United States.

"I'm mad as hell and I'm not going to take it any more!" This refrain was heard over and over again as the Mad as Hell Doctors' Health Care-A-Van traveled through state capitals, major cities and rural communities in fifteen states. Enthusiastic crowds greeted us at rallies and town halls in 30 cities large and small. More than 6,000 persons attended the 46 rallies and town halls we held in churches and union halls, in universities, public parks and arts centers.

Our journey took us from Sequim, Washington, to Portland to Seattle and on to Spokane, Bozeman, Idaho Falls, Pocatello, Salt Lake City, Fort Collins, Denver, Des Moines, Mankato, Minneapolis/St. Paul, Madison, Gary, Bloomington, Nashville, Louisville, Xenia, Yellow Springs, Detroit, Chicago, Toledo, Pt. Clinton, Cleveland and Pittsburgh before arriving at a rally at Lafayette Park across from the White House on September 30.

We began our rallies and town meetings by distinguishing between anger and rage. Anger is a normal human feeling, a healthy feeling which can be channeled productively to generate change and work for social justice. Anger is what the Mad As Hell Doctors expressed and attempted to harness with the tour. Rage is the type of feeling fostered by those funding Tea Party attempts to disrupt public discourse and to prevent others from exercising their freedom of speech.

We explained that we support the full expression of all points of view whether or not they agree with us. Each of our events included a series of "mad as hell minutes" in which any person could say anything uninterrupted for

*Courtesy of Dr. William Whitaker.

60 seconds. Perhaps as a consequence we encountered no organized disruption. There was only one organized opposing demonstration.

In the mad as hell minutes we heard heartbreaking story after story of the crushing impacts of the lack of health insurance on human lives. In one case, a man was fired from his job in a small firm when his wife was diagnosed with MS—if he had been permitted to continue employment, health insurance would have been too costly for anyone who worked there. We heard repeatedly about bankruptcies resulting from medical expenses. We heard about couples being advised to divorce so one member could be insured or to avoid total loss of family assets through medical bills.

A woman, a doctor from Spokane, spoke for many: "I'm mad because medicine should be a human enterprise, not a commercial enterprise, because we don't have access to health care for all, because there are unneeded disparities in health outcomes between poor and rich, between blacks and whites." A veteran put it this way: "I'm mad as hell because I have excellent socialized medicine from the Veteran's Administration but not everyone has access like I do."

Some of the most moving stories will be included in a full-length documentary of our campaign.

We asked President Obama to do two things: 1) meet with us so we could share with him what we have learned in our travels, and 2) appoint a White Ribbon Commission consisting of public health experts and health care professionals—but no health insurance or pharmaceutical corporation representatives—to compare health care systems throughout the world and to develop a uniquely American system that will provide access to health care for every American. We posted our requests on our website and asked supporters to contact President Obama in support of our requests.

Several days into the trip we received a phone call from a White House staffer. "When," he asked, "are you going to take that request off your website? We are receiving so many emails that our mailbox is being flooded." Our reply was straight forward. "We'll remove the request when President Obama agrees to meet with us." The White House responded by blocking emails from our site. We asked our supporters to cut and paste the request into their own email addresses. Emails continued to flood the White House.

President Obama has not yet met with the Mad As Hell Doctors. From our perspective he has missed the opportunity to make history by bringing us health care reform we can believe in.

This is disappointing but not surprising. The systematic exclusion of full and fair consideration of single risk pool, single-payer options in congressional deliberations on health insurance reform demonstrates the near strangle-hold of corporate interests on Congress. Billions of dollars in profits are at stake. It is no surprise that health insurance and pharmaceutical special interests are employing six full-time health insurance lobbyists for every member of Congress and are spending more than 1.4 million dollars daily to prevent even the most modest reform of the system. If we follow the money trail, it is increasingly clear that we do have the best Congress that money can buy.

As organizers we know that breaking the hold of corporate greed on Congress is a daunting task. But it is essential for progressive change. It will require mobilization of the growing outrage we encountered throughout the nation.

Might a "White Ribbon Campaign" help spark the continuation of the civil rights movement? Dr. Martin Luther King, Jr. put it this way some 40 years ago: "Of all the forms of inequality, injustice in healthcare is the most shocking and inhumane." His words continue to resound today.

In communities throughout the nation concerned and angry citizens are placing flowers and lighting candles at city halls and in front of health insurance company offices—mourning the 45,000 persons who die needlessly in the United States each year from lack of health insurance. They are tying white ribbons to symbolize the hope for enactment of single-payer health care legislation that will prevent these unnecessary deaths. And increasingly, protestors are putting their bodies on the line, being arrested for civil disobedience. Perhaps an aroused citizenry can even reclaim the democratic structure of the United States.

* * * * *

Bill Whitaker is Professor Emeritus of social welfare at the Boise State University School of Social Work. He lives in La Grande, Oregon, where he is active in local and state issues and politics, single-payer advocacy and work to mitigate the effects of global warming on climate change. He may be contacted at wwhitak@boisestate.edu or 541-663-1358.

Full information about Mad as Hell Doctors is found on www .madashelldoctors.com. A short video about the MAHD Health Care-a-Van is found on www.madashelldoctorsvideo.com. For comprehensive information about single-payer health programs, see www.PNHP.org.

7

Mental Health Advocacy

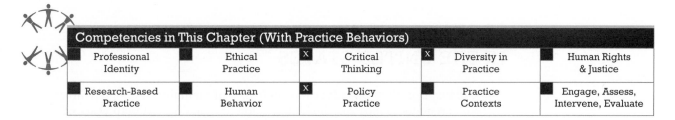

Competencies in This Chapter (With Practice Behaviors)				
Professional Identity	Ethical Practice	x Critical Thinking	x Diversity in Practice	Human Rights & Justice
Research-Based Practice	Human Behavior	x Policy Practice	Practice Contexts	Engage, Assess, Intervene, Evaluate

> Everyday language tends to encourage a misperception that
> *mental health* or *mental illness* is unrelated to *physical health* or
> *physical illness*. In fact, the two are inseparable.
>
> —*The Surgeon General's Report*
> *on Mental Health, 1999*

For many decades, mental health advocates have fought tirelessly for a system of care that is less fragmented and one in which affected individuals have access to quality care. Unfortunately, the United States has a long history of stigmatizing mental disorders and providing dehumanizing and degrading care to the mentally ill. It is somewhat surprising that there is so much stigma surrounding mental illness because according to the National Institute of Mental Health (NIMH), about one in four adults suffer from a diagnosable mental disorder in a given year (this represented 57.7 million people in 2004) (Kessler, Chiu, Demler, & Walters, 2005).

MENTAL ILLNESS

Mental illness generally refers collectively to all mental disorders that can be diagnosed in the *Diagnostic and Statistical Manual of Mental Disorders* published by the American Psychiatric Association (APA). Mental disorders are health conditions that are characterized by alterations in thinking, mood, or behavior (or some combination of these three) associated with impaired functioning and/or distress. Examples of mental disorders include mood disorders (e.g., depression, bipolar disorder), anxiety disorders (e.g., post-traumatic stress disorder [PTSD], social phobia, obsessive-compulsive disorder), autism, attention deficit hyperactivity disorder (ADHD), schizophrenia, and eating disorders. Collectively, anxiety disorders are the most common type of disorder experienced by Americans.

Mental disorders are often viewed on a continuum from mild to severe with **serious mental illness** being defined as a serious functional impairment that substantially interferes with or limits one or more major life activities. According to data reported by the NIMH, about 6% of the population (or 1 in 17) suffer from serious mental illness (Kessler, Chiu, Demler, & Walters, 2005). Due to the tireless efforts of advocates in the United States, such as Clifford Beers and Dorothea Dix, it gradually became less acceptable to warehouse the mentally ill in prison or to allow inhumane treatment in overcrowded state mental hospitals. The legislative priorities of mental health advocates over the years have grown extensively but have included issues such as access to quality care, sufficient funding for mental health treatment in the public health sector, concerns over the criminalization of the mentally ill, ensuring that veterans are adequately served, funding programs that assist with employment and housing, and mental health parity, the focus of this chapter.

TIME LINE OF MENTAL HEALTH ADVOCACY IN THE UNITED STATES

- **1840s,** Dorothea Dix advocates on behalf of mentally ill people who are incarcerated, many of whom are beaten and chained. Her 40 years of dedicated advocacy work leads to the establishment of 32 state hospitals for the mentally ill.

- **1909**, Clifford Beers founds the National Mental Health Association after publishing an autobiography titled *A Mind That Found Itself*, which detailed his negative experience in a Connecticut mental institution. (Visit http://www.pbs.org/wgbh/amex/nash/timeline/index.html, which includes a historical time line of treatments for mental illness).
- **1946**, President Truman signs the National Mental Health Act calling for a national institute of mental health to conduct research on mental illness.
- **1949**, NIMH is formally established.
- **1962**, author Ken Kesey publishes *One Flew Over the Cuckoo's Nest*, which becomes a best seller and later gets made into a Hollywood film starring Jack Nicholson.
- **Mid-1960s**, the deinstitutionalization movement in the United States begins, which results in the removal of hundreds of thousands of patients from mental institutions. The goal was to serve patients in community facilities and mental health centers; however, many become homeless due to inadequate funding and infrastructure.
- **1963**, the Mental Retardation Facilities and Community Mental Health Centers Construction Act is passed.
- **1979**, the National Alliance for the Mentally Ill (NAMI) is founded.
- **1986**, the National Alliance for Research on Schizophrenia and Depression is formed.
- **1986**, Congress passes the State Comprehensive Mental Health Services Plan Act.
- **1996**, the first federal Mental Health Parity Act is passed and signed into law by President Clinton (this law is very compromised and does not solve the parity problem).
- **2008**, federal Mental Health Parity legislation is passed, championed by late Senator Paul Wellstone and Senator Pete Domenici, which significantly improves the 1996 law.

Lawmakers, and the American public, are sometimes forced to focus on the failings of the mental health system in the United States when examples of untreated mental health disorders result in unspeakable tragedy. Some high profile examples include the 2001 case of Andrea Yates (who drowned her five children in a bathtub after suffering from severe postpartum depression and psychosis) and the 2007 school shooting at Virginia Tech by a college student who killed over 30 of his fellow students and several faculty members before turning the gun on himself. In order for mental health advocates to make progress politically, it has been necessary to address the stigma surrounding mental disorders by spending significant time and resources focused on public education. Another strategy has been to join forces with legislators who have firsthand experience with mental illness in their family.

OVERVIEW OF THE U.S. MENTAL HEALTH CARE SYSTEM

The U.S. mental health care system is often described as a fragmented, loosely coordinated system of care. There are four major sectors of this system in which clients may be served:

- **The specialty mental health sector**, which consists of mental health professionals such as psychiatrists,

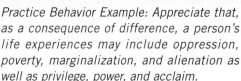
Diversity in Practice

Practice Behavior Example: Appreciate that, as a consequence of difference, a person's life experiences may include oppression, poverty, marginalization, and alienation as well as privilege, power, and acclaim.

Critical Thinking Question: Much progress has been made, but stigma is still a societal problem when it comes to mental health disorders. What could be done to decrease stigma? What kind of media campaign would be effective in changing attitudes/ misconceptions?

psychologists, and psychiatric nurses and social workers who are trained to treat those with mental disorders.

- **The general medical care sector**, which consists of health care professionals such as physicians, nurse practitioners, and social workers in medical settings.
- **Human service organizations**, such as nonprofit organizations, school-based counseling services, residential programs, criminal justice settings, and faith-based organizations.
- **The voluntary support sector**, which consists of self-help groups such as 12-step programs and peer counselors. This is often where people with mental illness and their family members assist others dealing with the same problem.

The mental health service system can also be categorized by whether services are provided by the public sector or the private sector. Services provided by the public sector include services directly operated by government agencies (e.g., state and county mental hospitals) and services financed with government resources (e.g., Medicaid and Medicare). It is important to note that publicly financed services may be provided by private organizations. In contrast, services provided by the private sector include those directly operated by nongovernmental agencies and services that are financed with private resources (e.g., employer-provided insurance).

There are a variety of ways that people pay for their care. Some access treatment through private health insurance provided by their employer. Others access care through funding provided by the government. State and local government is the major payer of public mental health services. But since the mid-1960s, the role of the federal government has increased through the Medicare and Medicaid programs as well as special programs for adults with serious mental illness and children with serious emotional disability. However, historically, mental health care services have been viewed as the stepchild of the health care industry, and as a result, treatment has been inaccessible to many patients. According to data reported by the NIMH, between 36% and 41% of those diagnosed with a mental disorder are receiving treatment, and much fewer are receiving adequate treatment (Wang, Lane, Olfson, Pincus, Wells, & Kessler, 2005).

MENTAL HEALTH PARITY

Simply put, mental health parity is the principle that health insurance plans should include equal coverage for medical care and mental health care, when policies cover both.

One of the biggest legislative battles in the field of mental health has been the fight to get leaders in Washington, DC, to pass a strong federal bill to address discrimination against those with mental health problems who require treatment. Simply put, **mental health parity** is the principle that health insurance plans should include equal coverage for medical care and mental health care, when policies cover both. For social workers, this is not a radical idea because there is an overwhelming body of research that shows that mental illnesses have biological causes and are diseases of the brain. The National Association of Social Workers (NASW) has been an ardent supporter of mental health parity legislation, and its position has been formalized in its book of policy statements, *Social Work Speaks*. In a 1999 report on mental health, U.S. Surgeon General David Satcher stated that one of the most important contributions of mental health research is the extent to which it has debunked the misconception that there is a division between "mental" health and "physical" health (U.S. Department of Health and Human Services, 1999).

However, for decades, it has been legal for insurers to provide less coverage for mental health care than for the treatment of conditions such as heart disease, diabetes, or cancer. Many were often not aware of this inequity until a family member required treatment for severe depression, schizophrenia, or substance abuse, and were shocked to discover that their insurance plan provided limited mental health coverage, which was quickly exhausted. Most plans limited the number of outpatient visits and hospital days covered for those with a mental disorder. Mental health benefits were also typically more costly and involved higher co-pays.

HOW THE PAUL WELLSTONE AND PETE DOMENICI MENTAL HEALTH PARITY AND ADDICTION EQUALITY ACT OF 2008 WAS PASSED INTO LAW

Efforts to pass mental health parity legislation at the state and federal level began in the early 1990s, and a strong federal bill was not passed until 2008. Legislation seeking social change often involves taking on powerful special interests with significant financial resources. This story has a long and winding path. But as you will see, this legislation would not have been successfully passed into law without the ongoing efforts of committed mental health advocacy organizations. These kinds of settings are ideal for social workers who have a desire to work for change in the legislative arena at the local and national level.

> **This legislation would not have been successfully passed into law without the ongoing efforts of committed mental health advocacy organizations.**

PHASE I: FIRST PARITY LAW IS PASSED (SMALL STEP FORWARD)

Policy change efforts are much more likely to achieve success when they are spearheaded by organizations with sufficient funding and resources to devote to the issue. It is also crucial to have lobbyists and professional staff with knowledge and expertise in how to work with lawmakers and key stakeholders to get legislation passed. Two nonprofit organizations worked tirelessly to get a strong mental health parity bill passed: NAMI and Mental Health America (formerly the National Mental Health Association) (see Figure 7.1). Andrew Sperling, lobbyist for NAMI, was a key player in this effort.

As described in Chapter 5, when working on a policy change effort it is important to find legislators who will passionately take up and champion your cause. There were two legislators who were key in this effort: **Republican Senator Pete Domenici** who had a daughter with schizophrenia and **Democratic Senator Paul Wellstone** who had a brother with severe mental illness. Senator Wellstone also worked with a female constituent who had a 22-year-old daughter with anorexia who later committed suicide. The family's insurance company, Blue Cross and Blue Shield of Minnesota, denied some coverage for her daughter's condition and later settled with the family. In a separate settlement with the state of Minnesota, Blue Cross and Blue Shield agreed to cover more mental health claims. The first serious effort to get a federal bill passed

---

National Alliance on Mental Illness (www.nami.org)

Started in 1979, NAMI is one of the most prominent mental health advocacy organizations in the United States. The organization describes itself as a grassroots organization made up of families, friends, and other individuals who seek to improve the lives of those affected by mental illness through awareness, education, and advocacy. NAMI has more than 1,200 local affiliates spanning all 50 states.

Mental Health America (www.mentalhealthamerica.net)

Mental Health America is another leading national organization that advocates on behalf of those with mental and substance use conditions. It has over 300 affiliates in 41 states and the District of Columbia. Visit its website to learn more about the important work it carries out on an annual basis.

Figure 7.1
Advocacy Spotlight.

Advocacy Tip (Agenda Setting)

Find legislators who have a personal connection to the issue to help champion your bill. It will take time to do the background research needed on various legislators, but this is definitely time well spent.

occurred in 1996 under President Bill Clinton. Wellstone and Domenici introduced legislation requiring parity for mental health and substance abuse. The primary opponents were insurance companies and businesses who argued that expanding coverage for mental health conditions would be too costly.

The first blow came when the bill (which was offered as an amendment to another piece of legislation) was dropped during final negotiations due to heavy opposition and lobbying from health insurers. As a result, 150 NAMI members protested across the street from the White House, which was not good for President Clinton because it was a reelection year. Less than two months later, Congress passed an extremely compromised mental health parity bill, and President Clinton signed it into law on September 22, 1996. Advocates were less than enthusiastic because the new law was such a small step in the right direction and did not result in true parity. The new law prevented employers with more than 50 employees from imposing more restrictive annual or lifetime dollar limits on these services than they do on medical or surgical care. However, the legislation:

- allowed insurers to limit the number of outpatient visits and hospital days covered for mental health services;
- did not include substance abuse;
- did not address parity regarding co-pays, deductibles, and out-of-pocket maximums; and
- allowed employers and health plans to waive the parity requirement if the cost of compliance exceeded 1%.

Advocacy Tip

Deciding whether (and when) to organize a protest is a strategic decision that must be carefully considered. If carefully planned and organized, this can be a good way to get media attention, mobilize supporters, and apply political pressure.

By the end of 1996, eight states had passed some form of mental health parity legislation. It would take another 12 years before a strong mental health parity bill was passed by the U.S. Congress. On June 7, 1999, President Clinton signed an executive order directing the Office of Personnel Management (OPM) to require all health plans in the Federal Employee Health Benefits Program (FEHBP) to meet a standard of equitable coverage for mental health and substance abuse benefits.

On May 18, 2000, a public hearing was held before the U.S. Senate Committee on Health, Education, Labor, and Pensions. See testimony provided by Jacqueline Shannon, a mother of a child with schizophrenia and then-executive director of the NAMI, at the end of this chapter.

PHASE II: STAGNATION DUE TO POLITICAL OPPOSITION FROM THE REPUBLICAN PARTY

> ### Advocacy Tip
>
> **P**roviding written and/or in-person oral testimony at a committee hearing is a fantastic way for social workers to influence legislation in a very direct way. Helping clients do this can be even more powerful. Get to know the protocol in your state or locality and get coached by an experienced person the first time around.

On March 15, 2001, Senators Domenici and Wellstone introduced parity legislation requiring parity for all DSM-IV diagnoses. However, according to another champion of the federal mental health parity bill, Republican Representative Jim Ramstad, little progress was made during the next 10 years of a Republican-controlled Congress. Ramstad, a recovered alcoholic, sponsored the bill in the House of Representatives for years despite opposition from his own party. According to Ramstad, "I couldn't get a hearing, let alone a vote" (Minnesota Public Radio, 2008).

> ### Critical Thinking
>
> *Practice Behavior Example: Demonstrate effective oral and written communication in working with individuals, families, groups, organizations, communities, and colleagues.*
>
> **Critical Thinking Question:** How would you grade Jim McNulty's speech at the rally in the U.S. Capitol in support of mental health parity? What are the strengths of this speech, in your view?

However, things started looking up when the Democrats took over the Senate in 2001 and when President Bush voiced his support for mental health parity during a speech at the University of New Mexico in 2002 (Bush had signed a state mental health parity bill when he was Governor of Texas). Bush stated, "Senator Domenici and I share this commitment. Health plans should not be allowed to apply unfair treatment limitations or financial requirements on mental health benefits" (National Public Radio, 2007). On June 6, 2002, a political rally was held in support of mental health parity in Washington, DC. Senators Paul Wellstone (D-MN) and Pete Domenici (R-NM) and Representatives Marge Roukema (R-NJ) and Patrick Kennedy (D-RI) spoke at the rally, as well as former NAMI President Jim McNulty who detailed his history with mental illness and barriers to getting treatment (see his remarks next).

However, soon there were a couple of serious setbacks. The legislation moved to the back burner after the September 11th attacks and then Senator Paul Wellstone, one of the bill's champions, was killed in a plane crash just before election day in 2002. Senator Wellstone's son, David Wellstone, continued to lobby Congress for mental health parity in the years following his father's death. A very interesting development occurred in 2004 when Senators Pete Domenici and Edward Kennedy invited insurers and business leaders to work with mental health advocates on drafting the legislation. Because they could see growing bipartisan support for the legislation, the insurance and business lobbies realized it was in their interest to come to the table. "It was an incredible process," said E. Neil Trautwein, a vice president of the National Retail Federation. "We built the bill piece by piece from the ground up" (*New York Times*, October 5, 2008).

Depressed teenage girl.

Pass Parity Now:*

Statement of Jim McNulty, President, National Alliance for the Mentally Ill at U.S. Capitol Rally

My name is Jim McNulty. I am president of the National Board of Directors of the National Alliance for the Mentally Ill (NAMI). I also suffer from bipolar disorder (manic depression). I am on the podium today because I am living proof of the profound, positive effects that parity has for people with mental illnesses.

In 1987, when I was first diagnosed, my health insurance plan provided virtually no coverage for treatment of mental illness. I desperately needed psychiatric medications and therapy, but my insurance wouldn't pay for them. I was forced to seek treatment from my primary care physician, who knew nothing about treating manic depression. The negative consequences on my life were traumatic and extreme. I lost my job, my home, and my family. Were it not for the kindness of friends, I would have become homeless.

I can't even begin to explain how devastating the consequences were. And if it happened to me, it can happen to anyone. I had been a successful businessperson. I was an elected Alderman. A family man. All of these roles and identities were lost, because I could not get the treatment I needed for what was a medical illness—as much as diabetes, heart disease or cancer. Had it affected any other part of my body, my insurance would have covered the treatment I needed. But because my illness affected my brain, I was discriminated against. I was denied. I could not get my treatment covered.

Then, in 1994, Rhode Island enacted one of the first parity laws in the nation. Finally, I was able to see a psychiatrist for medication prescription and regular monitoring. I also was able to see a therapist for help in coping with the profound losses I had suffered and the changes that were needed because of my illness. The results of good treatment were rapid. I recovered from the depths of despair. I started a business as a computer consultant. Most importantly, I started to get involved in helping others with similar problems.

I initiated local self-help groups for people with bipolar disorder. I became active in NAMI Rhode Island and the Manic-Depressive and Depressive Association of Rhode Island. In 1999, the Governor of Rhode Island appointed me to the Governor's Council on Mental Health, a statutory body that advises the executive branch of Rhode Island on mental health issues. This past year, as a consumer, a person with a mental illness, I was proud to be elected national board president of NAMI—the nation's voice on mental illness.

I am telling you this not because I want to try to impress anyone with lofty titles. Instead it is to make a point. I could be anyone. There are literally tens of thousands of people with mental illnesses in this country who lead highly productive lives and many more who could if they had access to treatment through adequate insurance coverage.

This year, Congress has the opportunity to follow the recommendations of the Office of the U.S. Surgeon General to end discrimination against mental illnesses in insurance coverage. The cost is modest and outweighed by the benefits. They include decreased hospitalizations or emergency costs and increased productivity. As a society, we already know this. Thirty-four states have passed parity laws and the experiences in those states have demonstrated that parity is cost-effective. Now it's time to cover those Americans who aren't already covered by these laws.

In the last 20 years, scientific progress in understanding and treating mental illness has been phenomenal. Today, we have the ability to diagnose and treat people with schizophrenia, bipolar disorder, major depression, and severe anxiety disorders as accurately and effectively as other illnesses. People with mental illnesses, their families, and advocates know that **treatment works, but only if we can get it**.

I am humbled and moved as I look out today and see so many people like me rallying for parity. After this rally, we will visit our Representatives to remind them how important parity is and that **it is a priority that must be enacted into law this year**. President Bush has recognized this fact and pledged his support. Now, it's time for Congress to recognize it too by passing the Domenici-Wellstone mental health parity bill.

No more excuses. No more games. No more backroom deals. Insurance discrimination kills. Parity saves lives. Give Americans the coverage that Members of Congress and other federal workers already have. Invest in recoveries like my own. Invest in our return to productivity. Invest in America's future.

*Courtesy of Jim McNulty/National Alliance for the Mentally Ill.

PHASE III: TRUE PARITY IS FINALLY ACHIEVED

When the Democrats took control of Congress in 2007, they were able to put mental health parity on the fast track. When it was introduced in the 110th Congress, it had 57 cosponsors in the Senate (S.558) and 274 cosponsors in the House (H.R.1424). On March 24, 2007, the *New York Times* published an editorial calling on the House and Senate to pass the legislation stating it "would be a boon to the millions of Americans who suffer from mental illness or addiction and find it hard to afford treatment. It should also reduce the high productivity losses from depressed or stressed workers."

A number of legislators were key in getting the bill through Congress including both Senators from the state of Minnesota (Republican Senator Norm Coleman and Democratic Senator Amy Klobuchar), as well as Senator Edward Kennedy (D-MA), his son Representative Patrick Kennedy (D-RI) who had suffered from addiction and mental health problems, Republican Senator Mike Enzi, and Democratic Senator Chris Dodd. Other prominent individuals who promoted passage of the legislation included Tipper Gore, and former first ladies Betty Ford and Roslyn Carter.

In early 2007, Representatives Patrick Kennedy and Jim Ramstad participated in a series of forums that were held in major cities across the county in order to gather testimony from citizens affected by mental illness and addiction as well as business leaders and mental health experts. The "Equity Campaign Tour" was sponsored by the NAMI and Mental Health America (see following press statement).

Policy Practice

Practice Behavior Example: Know the history and current structures of social policies and services, the role of policy in service delivery, and the role of practice in policy development.

Critical Thinking Question: Why did it take so long to get a strong mental health parity bill passed by the U.S. Congress? What were the biggest barriers to overcome?

Congressmen Kennedy and Ramstad Embark on Nationwide Tour to Promote Mental Health Parity Bill

The Campaign to Insure Mental Health and Addiction Equity

FOR IMMEDIATE RELEASE January 12, 2007

WASHINGTON—Congressmen Patrick J. Kennedy (D-RI) and Jim Ramstad (R-MN) are embarking on a nationwide tour, traveling to forums taking place in major cities all across the country. The national tour entitled, "The Campaign to Insure Mental Health and Addiction Equity," will hear testimony from ordinary American citizens whose lives have been touched by mental illness and addiction.

The first forum in the series is scheduled for Tuesday, January 16, 2006, at the Rhode Island State House. Members of the public, employers, mental health advocates, and health care professionals will share personal stories pertaining to their experience negotiating the health care system as it relates to mental health. The sessions will also include the leadership of all three commercial insurers in Rhode Island. The testimony will be used to help facilitate a comprehensive debate over equal access to health care for mental health and addiction treatment.

The Congressmen are preparing to reintroduce federal legislation aimed at ensuring that health plans offer fair coverage for mental health and addiction care. The bill, called the Paul Wellstone Mental Health and Addiction Equity Act

"Our goal is to compile testimony from Americans across the country in an effort to pass the most responsible and comprehensive federal equity bill possible," said Congressman Kennedy. *"Americans with these physiological diseases of the brain pay their premiums like everyone else and their insurance should be there when they need it, like it is for everyone else. Every family in America has, in some way, come face to face with the burden of these diseases and the difficulty in getting care. We pay enormously, as individuals and as a society, the costs of leaving these diseases untreated. It's time for action."*

"The American people should not be forced to wait any longer for Congress to knock down the barriers to treatment for mental illness and chemical addiction," said Congressman Ramstad. *"Congress must hear their call and pass the Paul Wellstone Mental Health and Addiction Equity Act."*

"Every day that we allow insurance discrimination against mental illnesses is another day 82 Americans will die of suicide," said Kennedy. *"It's another day that American business will lose $85 million in lost productivity to depression alone. It's another day that thousands of children will be in state custody instead of home with their parents. It's another night on the streets for 200,000 homeless Americans living with mental illness and addictions. We cannot afford the status quo."*

after the late Senator who championed the cause, had majority support in past Congresses but was blocked from consideration by House leadership. The new House Leaders have promised Congressmen Kennedy and Ramstad that they will bring the bill up for a vote.

Additional forums are being organized across the country by Mental Health America (formerly the National Mental Health Association) and the National Alliance for the Mentally Ill (NAMI). Congressmen Kennedy and Ramstad will join other Members of Congress at scheduled forums in Minnesota, Maryland, Los Angeles, and Washington State leading up to Congressional hearings in Washington, D.C.

The Paul Wellstone Mental Health and Addiction Equity Act expands the Mental Health Parity Act of 1996 by requiring group health plans to offer benefits for mental health and addiction on the same terms as care for other diseases. The legislation closes the loopholes that allow plans to charge higher copayments, coinsurance, deductibles, and maximum out-of-pocket limits and impose lower day and visit limits on mental health addiction care.

According to the Government Accountability Office, nearly 90 percent of plans impose such financial limitations and treatment restrictions on mental health and addiction care despite voluminous scientific research documenting the biological, genetic, and chemical nature of these diseases, and the effectiveness of treatment. The bill applies to group health plans of 50 or more people.

The legislation is modeled after the Federal Employees Health Benefit Program, which covers Members of Congress and other federal workers and dependents and which implemented parity in 2001. According to an exhaustive study published earlier this year by the Department of Health and Human Services, the federal employees' parity policy was implemented with "little or no increase in total MH/SA [mental health/substance abuse] spending."

A majority of respondents to a Mental Health America survey indicated that they would support equity legislation even if it meant a $1 per month increase to their premiums. The Congressional Budget Office has estimated that such legislation will increase health care costs by far less than that amount.

Forum Schedule:

Jan. 16 Providence, RI, District of Rep. Patrick Kennedy
Jan. 22 Minneapolis, MN, District of Rep. Jim Ramstad
Jan 29 Rockville, MD, District of Rep. Chris Van Hollen
Feb. 10 Los Angeles, CA, District of Rep. Grace Napolitano
Feb. 17 Vancouver, WA, District of Rep. Brian Baird

*dates pending in many other locations

The Senate passed a mental health parity bill in September 2007, and the House passed a different version of that bill in March 2008. There were some interesting tensions that emerged because many advocates, including Rep. Patrick Kennedy, felt that the House bill was a stronger piece of legislation. His father, Senator Edward Kennedy, however, felt that the Senate bill would have more success passing because it included a number of compromises that had the support of insurance and business lobbies who helped write the legislation along with mental health advocates. The standoff ended when sponsors of the House bill agreed to drop a provision that required insurers to cover treatment for *any* condition listed in the *Diagnostic and Statistical Manual of Mental Disorders.*

> **Advocacy Tip**
>
> Legislators work with advocates behind the scenes and consult with them when making difficult decisions regarding when (and if) to make political compromises in order to get legislation passed.

The Paul Wellstone and Pete Domenici Mental Health Parity and Addiction Equality Act of 2008 was attached to the $700 billion Wall Street bailout bill and was signed into law by President Bush on October 3, 2008. After its passage, Senator Edward Kennedy stated, "Congress has finally agreed to end the senseless discrimination in health insurance coverage that plagues persons living with mental illness for so long" (Minnesota Public Radio, 2008). Mental Health America's president and CEO hailed the new law as "a great civil rights victory" for the millions of Americans with mental disorders who have been unable to gain access to treatment (Mental Health America, 2008).

> **The Paul Wellstone and Pete Domenici Mental Health Parity and Addiction Equality Act of 2008 was attached to the $700 billion Wall Street bailout bill and was signed into law by President Bush on October 3, 2008.**

The new mental health parity legislation outlaws health insurance discrimination by requiring insurance companies to treat mental health on an equal basis with physical illnesses, when policies cover both. It is important to understand that the act does not mandate coverage of a particular service or diagnosis; but whatever is covered must be on parity with medical coverage (except to the extent that a state parity law requires broader coverage). Specifically, it prohibits group health plans that offer coverage for mental health and substance-use conditions from imposing treatment limitations and financial requirements on those benefits that are stricter than for medical and surgical benefits. Beginning January 1, 2010, parity included the following categories of coverage:

- Co-pays
- Deductibles
- Inpatient hospital days
- Number of outpatient visits

A managed care company can refuse to pay for care on the grounds that it is not medically necessary, but the new law will require the company to disclose its reason for denying any particular claim for mental health treatment. According to federal officials, the new law will improve coverage for 113 million people and will increase premiums by only an average of about two-tenths of 1%. Businesses with fewer than 50 employees are exempt. A separate bill passed 3 months earlier eliminated discriminatory co-payments in Medicare.

The Strategy

Many lessons can be learned from the successful effort to get mental health parity legislation passed by federal lawmakers in Washington, DC. Lesson one is that some policy change efforts turn into rather lengthy battles. Major changes to the system often require many years of hard work on behalf of dedicated individuals and organizations. In this case, various strategies were used

> **Major changes to the system often require many years of hard work on behalf of dedicated individuals and organizations.**

in order to raise awareness of this issue and to create the political pressure needed for passage:

- Individuals and organizations who lobbied federal lawmakers for years, including paid lobbyists with expertise in mental health as well as friends and relatives of people with mental illness and addiction, including those directly affected;
- The impassioned and aggressive support of a number of key legislators, most of whom were personally affected by the issue (Sen. Pete Domenici [R-NM]; Sen. Edward M. Kennedy [D-MA]; Sen. Paul Wellstone [D-MN]; Rep. Patrick Kennedy [D-RI]; and Rep. Jim Ramstad [R-MN]);
- The work of prominent advocacy organizations such as NAMI and the National Mental Health Association (now named Mental Health America) that urged their own members and members of the public to contact their legislators. They also did a lot of work in the area of public education and awareness (dispelling the myths) by posting information on their website and getting information out through various media outlets;
- Well-attended political rallies held in Washington, DC, with people who were able to speak eloquently on the issue;
- Framing the issue as discrimination: "Health insurance plans should include equal coverage for medical care and mental health care, when policies cover both";
- Sitting at the table with the opposition in order to find common ground and areas of compromise was key. Negotiating with business leaders and demonstrating to employers that state parity laws, as well as the health insurance program for federal employees, have not broken the bank;
- The Equity Campaign Tour, which was a series of community forums that were held in major cities across the country in order to gather testimony from citizens affected by mental illness and addiction as well as business leaders and mental health experts;
- Providing testimony to Congress. To see the appropriate format for written testimony, please see following example from former NAMI president, Jackie Shannon.

Policy Practice

Practice Behavior Example: Collaborate with colleagues and clients for effective policy action.

Critical Thinking Question: What strategies/tactics, used by mental health advocates in order to secure passage of the Mental Health Parity Act, were most effective in your view? What lessons can be learned from their experience?

Tactics Used by Mental Health Advocates to Get This Act Passed Into Law

✔ Coalition building	✔ Direct lobbying (in-person lobby visits; sometimes by a professional lobbyist)
✔ Earned media (letters to the editor; actions that lead to media coverage)	✔ Grassroots lobbying (e.g., urging people to call, write, and email legislators)
☐ Paid media (paying for TV/radio ads)	✔ Educational outreach (town halls; house parties; community forums)
✔ Visibility (rallies; marches)	✔ Online advocacy (using social media)
✔ Political dissent (e.g., civil disobedience; protest)	☐ Paid communication (paid staff who call voters; materials mailed out)
✔ Providing testimony in a legislative committee hearing	☐ Fund-raising activities

LOOKING TO THE FUTURE: THE CRIMINALIZATION OF THE MENTALLY ILL

An issue that is getting increased attention in the United States concerns the growing number of inmates in the nation's jails and prisons, who are mentally ill. According to a recent report by National Public Radio (NPR), more Americans receive mental health treatment in prisons and jails than in mental health facilities. This is a result of the closing of state-run hospitals by the government. As a result, prisons and jails are "the new asylums," as explained in a PBS Frontline television special (see http://www.pbs.org/wgbh /pages/frontline/shows/asylums/ to watch the full program online). According to NPR, the three largest inpatient psychiatric facilities in the country are jails: Los Angeles County Jail, Rikers Island Jail in New York City, and Cook County Jail in Illinois. Jails and prisons are not set up to treat those with mental illness but they have been forced to adapt because this is often the only option for many with mental illness who are unstable and in need of treatment. Despite all of the progress that was made by social crusaders such as Dorothea Dix, it seems that the United States has taken a huge step backward regarding how it cares for the nation's mentally ill. However, there has been one positive development. In recent years, the United States has witnessed the development of mental health courts that are set up to serve mentally ill individuals who have become involved with the criminal justice system. The criminalization of the mentally ill will be an important policy issue for mental health advocates in the coming years.

Source: http://www.npr.org/2011/09/04/140167676/nations-jails-struggle-with-mentally-ill-prisoners

CHAPTER 7 PRACTICE TEST

The following questions will test your knowledge of the content found within this chapter. For additional assessment, including licensing-exam type questions on applying chapter content to practice behaviors, visit **MySearchLab**.

1. Mental health parity means that:
   a. health insurance companies are required to offer coverage for mental health treatment.
   b. health insurance plans should include equal coverage for medical care and mental health care, when policies cover both.
   c. companies are not allowed to discriminate against employees who suffer from mental illness.
   d. mental health providers must provide quality treatment to those they serve.

2. According to the NIMH, roughly _____ of adults in the United States suffer from a diagnosable mental disorder in a given year.
   a. 5%
   b. 15%
   c. 25%
   d. 35%

3. Which of the following was true about the first parity bill that was passed by the U.S. Congress?
   a. Included substance abuse
   b. Addressed parity regarding co-pays, deductibles, and out-of-pocket maximums
   c. Insurers not allowed to limit the number of outpatient visits and hospital days covered for mental health services
   d. Prevented employers from imposing more restrictive annual or lifetime dollar limits on mental health services than they do on medical care

4. You are working with a family who needs help accessing mental health services for a 45-year-old father who has been suffering from an addiction to alcohol as well as severe depression. Due to the new parity law, you would advise them of the following:
   a. Insurers are now obligated to include mental health coverage in their health care plans for employees.
   b. The new parity law specifically excludes substance abuse conditions.
   c. The new law does not take effect until 2014.
   d. Insurance plans that include mental health coverage are required to be on parity with medical coverage in the areas of co-pays, deductibles, inpatient days, and outpatient visits.

5. Which of the following statements about the fight for mental health parity is false?
   a. Money was raised in order to fund television and radio ads promoting mental health parity legislation.
   b. Advocates found legislative champions who were personally affected by the issue.
   c. Advocates worked with the opposition to craft the legislation.
   d. Political rallies and community forums were used to allow affected individuals to tell their stories.

6. In 1949, the _____ was established in order to conduct research on mental illness.
   a. National Association of Social Workers (NASW)
   b. National Institute of Mental Health (NIMH)
   c. American Psychological Association (APA)
   d. National Alliance on Mental Illness (NAMI)

7. Review the Activist Spotlight in Chapter 2 that profiles social reformer Dorothea Dix. Do some Internet research on Dix to learn more about her advocacy efforts. How was she able to make such significant progress on behalf of the mentally ill?

Reinforce what you learned in this chapter by studying videos, cases, documents, and more available at **www.MySearchLab.com**.

Watch and Review

Watch these Videos

* Hidden Addictions (Nightline, October 14, 2009)

Read and Review

Read these Cases/Documents

Δ Mental Health Services Consumers

Δ The Chronically Mentally Ill Young Adult

Explore and Assess

Explore these Assets

* Website: Counseling Today
* Website: National Alliance on Mental Illness
* Website: National Institute on Mental Health

Research these Topics

Mental Health Advocacy in the United States

What Is Mental Health Parity?

How the Paul Wellstone and Pete Domenici Mental Health Parity and Addiction Equality Act Was Passed Into Law

Assess Your Knowledge

Go to **MySearchLab** to test your knowledge of key topics in this chapter with topic-specific quizzes. Conclude your assessment by completing the chapter exam.

---

* = CSWE Core Competency Asset   Δ = Case Study

NAMI President Jackie Shannon Gives
Testimony on Mental Health Parity

On May 18, the Senate Health, Education, Labor, and Pensions Committee held a hearing on mental illness parity focusing on implementation of the Mental Health Parity Act of 1996 as well as legislative proposals at the federal level that would expand previous efforts to full parity.

Statement of Jacqueline Shannon, President, National Alliance for the Mentally Ill (NAMI)

Regarding Mental Health Parity

For the Committee on Health, Education, Labor, and Pensions, United States Senate

MAY 18, 2000

Chairman Jeffords, Senator Kennedy and members of the Committee, I am Jacqueline Shannon of San Angelo, Texas, President of the National Alliance for the Mentally Ill (NAMI). In addition to serving as NAMI's president, I am also the mother of Greg Shannon. Greg was diagnosed with schizophrenia in 1985, during his senior year in college. For the past 15 years, Greg and our entire family have struggled with his illness. We have experienced discrimination in health insurance first-hand. Our health insurance had a lifetime maximum benefit for mental illness of six thousand dollars. Greg exhausted this benefit during his first hospitalization.

For the past decade, insurance parity has remained NAMI's top legislative priority. As the nation's largest organization representing individuals with serious brain disorders and their families, 210,000 members and 1,200 affiliates, we know why a minimum standard for parity in insurance coverage is desperately needed. Our members—individuals with mental illnesses and their families—know first-hand what it means to face discrimination in health insurance.

NAMI members understand what it is like to exhaust their coverage with a single hospital stay, to be forced to pay higher deductibles and co-payments, to run through unfair limits on inpatient days and outpatient visits. What makes these discriminatory limits so unjust is that they apply only to illnesses of the brain and not to any other organ or system of the body. As I will discuss in greater detail in my testimony, NAMI believes strongly that insurance parity for the treatment of severe mental illness is at its core an issue of discrimination. We believe that mental illnesses are brain disorders, and that treatment for these illnesses are just as (if not more) effective than for other diseases. We therefore believe that health plans should not be allowed to impose limits and conditions in insurance plans that do not apply to all other diseases. In short, we are not asking for special treatment, merely the coverage that any of us expect when we need treatment.

1. Mental Illnesses Are Brain Disorders

A mental illness is, more accurately, a brain disorder; and brain disorders—like epilepsy—are biologically based medical problems. The newest medical technology can take "pictures" that show differences between brains with disorders and normal brains. In any given year, about five million American adults suffer from an acute episode of one of five serious brain disorders: schizophrenia, bipolar disorder (manic depression), severe depression, obsessive-compulsive disorder, and severe anxiety disorders. Even many of America's children—more than three million—suffer from these disorders.

Untreated, disorders of the brain profoundly disrupt a person's ability to think, feel, and relate to others and to his or her environment. Despite age-old myths and misinformation, "mental illnesses" are not caused by bad character, poor child rearing, or an individual's behavior.

Brain disorders are shrouded in stigma and discrimination. For centuries they have been misunderstood, feared, hidden, and often ignored by science. Only in the last few decades has the first real hope for people with mental illnesses surfaced, and that hope has grown from pioneering research that found both a biological basis for brain disorders and treatments that work. NAMI's efforts to combat discrimination and stigma received a major boost in December 1999 with the release of the U.S. Surgeon General's Report on Mental Health. This historic report documents the scientific evidence that treatment is effective and concludes that there is no justification for health plans to cover treatment for serious brain disorders such as schizophrenia and bipolar disorder differently from any other disease.

2. Treatment Works

As the Surgeon General documented, science has proven that severe mental illnesses are treatable. The current success rate for treating schizophrenia is 60 percent. The success rate for treating manic depression is 65 percent, and for major depression it is 80 percent. By contrast, treatment efficacy rates for interventions such as angioplasty (41 percent) and atherectomy (52 percent) are lower. Mental illnesses can now be diagnosed and treated as precisely and effectively as other medical disorders. Tragically, the stigma associated with these illnesses too often prevents people from seeking the treatment that science has proven is effective. More importantly, the fact that health insurance plans have historically imposed limitations and conditions on coverage for treatment for severe mental illness compounds this stigma.

3. Discrimination Is Wrong

Discrimination in health insurance takes many forms. The most common techniques to avoid fair coverage of mental illness treatment are: higher cost-sharing requirements for outpatient visits and prescriptions, fewer allowed inpatient days and outpatient visits, and greater annual and lifetime dollar limits. The use of these discriminatory limits and conditions has been well documented.

Numerous studies compiled prior to the enactment of parity laws (including surveys of plans by the U.S. Bureau of Labor Statistics) found that 85 percent of all plans limit inpatient care and more than 98 percent limit outpatient care. In 1991–92, the BLS Employee Benefit Survey also found that one-half of plans were restricting hospitalization to 30 to 60 days. More than 70 percent of plans were found to have limited either the dollar value of outpatient benefits or the actual number of visits. These surveys also found that arbitrary limits were often unrelated to actual treatment needs. While the federal Mental Health Parity Act (MHPA) and the 31 state parity laws are changing this discrimination, clearly a legacy of discrimination still exists in the private health insurance market.

Mr. Chairman, while these studies are persuasive, the experience of Bonnie Putnam of Florence, South Carolina, more clearly articulates what NAMI members go through every day to get coverage for the treatment they need. Every year, we at NAMI receive hundreds of these personal stories that demonstrate how health insurance plans discriminate against individuals with severe mental illness and their families.

Bonnie is from Florence, South Carolina, and has been diagnosed with major depression since 1979. Even though she has worked for the same company for more than 25 years, she is on the verge of having to leave her job because she cannot afford to pay for the treatment she needs on her own, the very treatment that keeps her well enough to work. Her employer qualifies for the small-business exemption under the MHPA. South Carolina's parity law is of little benefit to Bonnie because it still allows her health plan to strictly limit coverage for outpatient medication and therapy—limits she long ago exceeded. Passage of South Carolina's law actually made things worse for Bonnie since her health plan responded by further limiting outpatient coverage. Bonnie Putnam needs true parity.

4. The 1996 Mental Health Parity Act Was an Important Step Forward

The first major step toward ending discrimination in health insurance came in 1996 when President Clinton signed the federal Mental Health Parity Act (P.L. 104-204) into law. With the leadership of Senators Pete Domenici (R-NM) and Paul Wellstone (D-MN), this landmark law establishes a standard of parity for annual and lifetime dollar limits only. The law applies only to employers that offer mental health benefits; i.e., it does not mandate such coverage. More important, the MHPA allows many cost-shifting mechanisms, such as adjusting limits on mental illness inpatient days, prescription drugs, outpatient visits, raising co-insurance and deductibles, and modifying the definition of medical necessity.

As the General Accounting Office (GAO) noted in their testimony before this Committee, lower limits for inpatient and outpatient mental illness treatments have continued and, in some cases actually expanded to help keep costs down. However, it is important to note that the MHPA does apply to both fully insured state-regulated health plans and self-insured plans that are exempt from state laws under the Employee Retirement Income Security Act (ERISA), which are regulated by the Department of Labor. Existing state parity laws are not preempted by the MHPA (i.e., a state law requiring more comprehensive coverage is not weakened by the federal law, nor does it preclude a state from enacting stronger parity legislation, which many have). Other critical limitations in the MHPA include a small-business exemption (for firms with 50 or fewer employees) and an increased cost exemption for employers that can demonstrate a one percent or more rise in costs due to parity implementation will be allowed to exempt themselves from the law.

NAMI is encouraged by the GAO findings presented at this hearing that 86 percent of surveyed health plans are complying with the MHPA. While it is alarming that 14 percent of the surveyed plans are not in compliance, we view this as a lack of effort on the part of state insurance commissioners, the Health Care Financing Administration (HCFA), and the Pension and Welfare Benefits Administration (PWBA) to educate employers about the new law. Likewise, as the GAO noted, compliance is based largely on a complaint-driven process, that places responsibility on aggrieved plan participants to come forward—which often fails because of the stigma associated with mental illness. To ensure greater compliance with the MHPA and all future federal parity efforts, NAMI urges Congress to push HCFA and PWBA to do more to educate employers and health plans about their responsibilities under the law and to randomly audit representative samples of large, medium, and small employers for compliance.

Mr. Chairman, it is interesting to note that while the opponents of the MHPA attempted to vastly expand the scope of this increased cost exemption during regulatory implementation of the MHPA, relatively few employers have used it. NAMI believes that this is due in part to accountability measures included in the regulations (by retrospective examination of claims data, disclosure to employees when a firm seeks an exemption, etc.). However, the fact that fewer than ten employers have sought the one-percent cost exemption is more than likely due to the fact that parity is affordable and costs simply have not gone up because of it.

5. 31 States and FEHBP Have Adopted Parity

As is often the case, states have taken the lead ahead of Congress in ending insurance discrimination. The original idea behind parity was modeled on legislation in the 1960s that prohibited cancer exclusions in insurance coverage. Mental health parity was first successful with state employees in Texas, then in Maine, New Hampshire, Rhode Island, and Maryland. By the early 1990s, parity laws had been passed in six states. Although these laws do not apply to ERISA self-insured companies, they give employees some protection and they serve to statistically validate the fact that parity is affordable. After enactment of the federal MHPA in 1996, we saw the passage of nine more state parity laws in 1997 and seven (unfortunately three were vetoed) in 1998. In 1999, 11 more states enacted parity laws, bringing the total number of states with such laws to 28. With the addition of California, now more than half the population lives in States that require non-discriminatory coverage.

Already in 2000, Kentucky, Massachusetts, and New Mexico have passed parity laws, which brings the total to 31 states. Clearly, the trend to pass state parity legislation is picking up momentum. Even today, NAMI affiliates are continuing to seek out legislative leaders to sponsor State parity bills of all types with the ultimate goal of ending all insurance discrimination against those who suffer from mental illnesses. NAMI will continue to provide documentation of the experiences of the states that passed parity laws in the early 1990s and other evidence of the affordability of parity and the effectiveness of treatment. NAMI will seek coverage equal to that of other medical conditions covered in each policy written, and we will not turn away from this effort until the discrimination has ceased.

Even though Congress has not acted to expand the modest protections in the Mental Health Parity Act since its passage nearly four years ago, the Clinton Administration has moved to expand the scope of parity. In June of 1999, as part of the historic White House Conference on Mental Health, the President announced that the Federal Employees Health Benefits Program (FEHBP) would require parity beginning in January 2001. FEHBP is the largest health insurance program in the nation, covering 9.5 million federal employees, retirees, and their families.

6. Parity Is Affordable

One of the principal lessons learned from the experience in the states that have enacted parity laws—as well as from preliminary estimates by the Office of Personnel Management (OPM) for FEHBP—is that parity is unquestionably affordable. This affordability is especially evident under the laws that focus the parity requirement on a categorical list of severe diagnoses.

As has been made clear at this hearing, the cost of paying for health insurance parity for mental illness unfortunately remains a hotly debated issue. This is disturbing to us at NAMI since overwhelming evidence from multiple studies controversy demonstrates the minimal cost impact resulting from parity. As the GAO found in its report on MHPA implementation, only 3 percent of surveyed plan administrators found that their insurance costs went up as a result of compliance. For the record, I would like to briefly summarize just a few of these studies—most of them from independent sources with no stake in the policy debate over parity—that have provided data in recent years:

- Background Report: Effects of the Mental Health Parity Act of 1996 (March 30, 1999)—Issued by the Substance Abuse and Mental Health Services Administration (SAMHSA), results of this national survey showed that 86 percent of employers who made changes in health plans to comply with the 1996 federal law did not make any compensatory reductions in other benefits because the cost of compliance was minimal or nonexistent.
- Parity in Financing Mental Health Services: Managed Care Effects on Cost, Access & Quality (July 15, 1998)—The second in a series of reports to Congress issued by the National Advisory Mental Health Council found that full parity costs less than one percent of annual health care costs. When implemented in conjunction with managed care, parity can reduce costs by 30 to 50 percent.
- Rand Corporation Study (November 12, 1997)—This study found that equalizing annual limits (typically $25,000)—a key provision of the Mental Health Parity Act of 1996—will increase costs by only about $1 per employee per year under managed care. An even more comprehensive change required by some state laws (i.e., removing limits on inpatient days and outpatient visits) will increase costs by less then $7 per enrollee per year. The main beneficiaries of parity were found to be families with children who, under current conditions, are more likely than adult users to quickly exceed their annual benefit limits and go uninsured for the remainder of the year.
- Mercer Study (October 23, 1997)—The findings of this study indicated that 85 percent of American companies are either in compliance with the federal law or plan to comply with the Mental Health Parity Act of 1996 by January 1, 1998. Seven out of ten of those same employers agree that mental health parity is a reasonable national policy goal and that parity is important to their employees.
- National Advisory Mental Health Council's Interim Report on Parity Costs (April 29, 1997)—This report found that the introduction of parity in combination with managed care results in, at worst, very modest cost increases. In fact, lowered costs and lower premiums were reported within the first year of parity. Maryland reported a 0.2 percent decrease after the implementation of full parity at the state level. Rhode Island reported a less than 1 percent (0.33 percent)

increase of total plan costs under state parity. Texas experienced a 47.9 percent decrease in costs for state employees enrolled in its managed care plan under parity.

- Lewin Study (April 8, 1997)—In this survey of New Hampshire insurance providers, no cost increases were reported as a result of a state law requiring health insurance parity for severe mental illnesses.

7. Let's Finish the Job—S. 796

As I noted above, the combined effect of the MHPA, the 31 state laws, and parity for FEHBP participants, while substantial and historic, still leave too many individuals with mental illness behind. Parity has become a reality in our country, but discrimination persists—particularly for individuals in ERISA self-insured plans and in cost-sharing requirements that apply only to mental illness treatment.

NAMI believes strongly that S. 796, the Mental Health Equitable Treatment Act, is needed to address these gaps in parity and finish the job of ending discrimination for persons living with the most severe and disabling forms of mental illness. NAMI's consumer and family membership is extremely grateful for the leadership of Senators Domenici and Wellstone in seeking to once and for all end discrimination.

The Mental Health Equitable Treatment Act requires that limitations on the coverage of benefits for "severe biologically based mental illnesses" may not be imposed unless comparable limitations are imposed on medical and surgical benefits. This provision provides full insurance parity for treatment for people with severe mental illnesses and effectively removes all inequitable limits on co-pays, deductibles, inpatient days, and outpatient visits.

S. 796 targets specific adult and childhood mental illnesses and defines the term *"severe biologically based mental illnesses"* as illnesses determined by medical science in conjunction with the Diagnostic and Statistical Manual of Mental Disorders (DSM IV) to be severe and biologically based. These illnesses are listed in the bill as: schizophrenia, bipolar disorder (manic depression), major depression, obsessive-compulsive disorder, panic disorder, post-traumatic stress disorder, autism and other severe and disabling mental disorders such as anorexia nervosa and attention deficit/hyperactivity disorder.

S. 796 also prohibits unequal limits on the number of covered inpatient days and outpatient visits for people seeking treatment for all mental illnesses. Under this provision, the number of covered inpatient days and outpatient visits for mental illnesses must be equal with covered medical/surgical inpatient days and outpatient visits.

Other key features of S. 796 include a small-business exemption for firms with 25 or fewer employees. This change from the 1996 MHPA (its small-employer exemption is 50 or fewer workers) will result in an additional 15 million workers and their families being covered by parity. S. 796 also eliminates the existing expiration provision in the MHPA that sunsets its requirements on October 1, 2001. In addition, S. 796 eliminates the "one percent" cost exemption in the MHPA mentioned above.

S. 796 is core to NAMI's vision of ensuring that the next generation of individuals with mental illness and their families will not have to live out their lives on disability or in public institutions, unable to get the very care that would give them back productive lives. Insurance discrimination enforces the invalid message that mental illnesses are "untreatable" and "hopeless." As I have noted above, parity is both affordable and cost-effective. With parity as envisioned in S. 796, businesses in fact stand to gain: from reduced absenteeism, reduced health care costs for physical ailments related to mental illnesses, increased employee morale, and increased productivity overall.

Mr. Chairman, I would like to make one additional point about S. 796 as it relates to a very important new law that Congress enacted last year—the Ticket to Work and Work Incentives Improvement Act (TWWIIA) (P.L. 106-170). First, on behalf of NAMI's consumer and family membership I would like to thank you, Chairman Jeffords, and you, Senator Kennedy, for the outstanding bipartisan leadership you showed in moving this legislation through the Senate last year by wide bipartisan margins. We are extremely grateful for your efforts on the critical issue of extending health insurance coverage for adults with severe disabilities who can, and in fact, want to work. In the coming years, thousands of adults with severe mental illnesses will be able to leave the Social Security rolls for the workforce, without fear of losing coverage under Medicare and Medicaid.

How does parity relate to TWWIIA? Just as with the "pre-disability" Medicaid state demonstration in the new law, NAMI believes that parity is integral to establishing state and federal policies that prevent people from ever having to quit their job and go into poverty to get the medical care they need. If working adults with severe mental illnesses have adequate and non-discriminatory health care coverage, they will be able to access the treatment they need earlier in the course of their illness and perhaps need less treatment over their lifetimes. Likewise parity will ensure that they can retain access to coverage for the treatment they need to maintain functioning and stay in a job. For NAMI, parity as envisioned in S. 796 is an extension of TWWIIA and its goal of shifting disability in our nation to foster, rather than inhibit, employment, productivity and independence.

Finally, Chairman Jeffords, I would like to respond on the record to the observations made by Ken Libertoff, Ph.D., of the Vermont Mental Health Coalition earlier in this hearing. In his testimony, Dr. Libertoff characterized S. 796 as inadequate for meeting the needs of children and adolescents with mental illnesses. He also stated that this important legislation is a "step sideways" in ending insurance discrimination. NAMI would like to take issue with his unfair and inaccurate observations about S. 796.

First, it should be noted that S. 796 includes full parity for every major severe mental disorder in children and adolescents, including early onset bipolar disorder, major depression, obsessive-compulsive disorder, panic disorder, autism, and other severe and disabling mental disorders such as anorexia nervosa and attention-deficit/hyperactivity disorder. In addition, the bill includes full parity for adolescents experiencing the onset of schizophrenia—a process that can commonly exhaust coverage for many families with a single hospitalization. More important, this legislation contains protections that will permit adding to the list of diagnoses for which full parity is required as medical science accumulates more evidence about which childhood disorders are biologically based (thereby to be covered under full parity). Thus, the provisions in S. 796 will keep pace with scientific advances in knowledge about child and adolescent disorders and their treatments. NAMI strongly supports S. 796 as a major step forward for children and adolescents with mental illnesses and their families.

Finally, as a response to the allegation that S. 796 is a "step sideways," NAMI notes how clear it is quickly becoming that, in seeking to end discrimination, Congress and the states have an obligation to first address the needs of those most profoundly and directly affected by inadequate coverage. Given the broad scope of mental health disorders as defined by the DSM IV, NAMI emphasizes that it is the severe diagnoses listed in this legislation as those to be included in the full parity requirement that cause people to exhaust the coverage in their health plans. It is these diagnoses that result in families having to borrow, go into debt, take out second mortgages, file for bankruptcy, quit jobs and relinquish custody of their children to qualify for public benefits that—when all else fails—give them access to treatment.

In NAMI's view, it is these families and individuals that have historically shouldered the burden of severe mental illness in our country. In NAMI's view, it is these families and individuals that Congress and the President should place foremost in their priorities while moving forward in the debate over mental illness parity. Clearly, S. 796 is a profound, life-saving, and historic step for these families and individuals touched by mental illness.

Conclusion

Chairman Jeffords and Senator Kennedy, thank you for the opportunity to share NAMI's views on this important issue. We look forward to working with you and all members of this Committee to ensure that the Senate acts on S. 796 this year.

8

From Civil Rights to Immigrant Rights

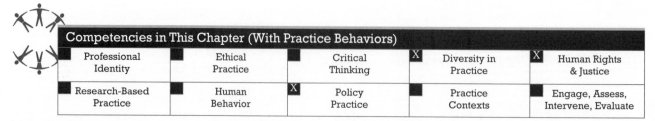

Competencies in This Chapter (With Practice Behaviors)				
Professional Identity	Ethical Practice	Critical Thinking	X Diversity in Practice	X Human Rights & Justice
Research-Based Practice	Human Behavior	X Policy Practice	Practice Contexts	Engage, Assess, Intervene, Evaluate

No human being is illegal.

—Elie Wiesel, Nobel laureate, author,
and Holocaust survivor

Despite the fact that it has cherished ideals that include freedom, the right of citizens to pursue happiness, and the value that all men are created equal, the United States has often faced great difficulty living up to the principles of tolerance, equality, and inclusion. Historically, women, ethnic minorities, gays and lesbians, newly arriving immigrants, and people with disabilities have been systematically shut out of participating in the public sphere. These groups have endured discrimination and violence at the hands of those in power who sought to keep them marginalized by denying them access to the vote, education, equality in the workplace, and other basic human rights. Significant progress has been made by each of these groups who over time rose up, banded together in social movements, and demanded social justice by challenging the power structure and status quo. Although each of these social movements has its own unique story, disenfranchised groups share many common experiences as can be seen in Table 8.1.

The subjugation of these groups was achieved at least in part by policies that were passed and codified into law by local, state, and federal lawmakers, including the executive branch, as well as Supreme Court decisions. It is often assumed that legislation is passed in order to solve a pressing social problem in a constructive way. However, it is important to keep in mind that legislation can be harmful to vulnerable groups in society as the following examples demonstrate:

- Indian Removal Act (1830)
- Laws allowing slavery
- Dred Scott Supreme Court ruling (1857) that slaves were not U.S. citizens and were not protected by the U.S. Constitution
- Women and African Americans legally barred from voting
- Laws restricting the immigration of certain groups such as the Chinese Exclusion Act (1882)
- *Plessy v. Ferguson* (1896) Supreme Court ruling that state laws enforcing racial segregation were constitutional
- Operation Wetback (1954), a program of the INS (Immigration and Naturalization Service) to remove illegal Mexican immigrants from the United States
- Jim Crow laws in the South that enforced racial segregation (see Figure 8.1 for examples of state laws)
- The internment of Japanese Americans during World War II
- Laws making birth control illegal
- Sodomy laws
- Laws banning gays/lesbians from joining the military
- Laws defining marriage as a union of a man and a woman (e.g., Defense of Marriage Act)

LAWS AND COURT CASES OUTLAWING DISCRIMINATION

A critical component in creating a just and equal society for all citizens has included the use of the legal system and the passage of legislation in order to

Table 8.1   Discrimination: Women, African Americans, and Gay Men and Lesbians

	Women	African Americans	Gay Men and Lesbians
Legal Discrimination	Once barred from voting; Civil Rights Act of 1964 outlawed discrimination based on sex	Once barred from voting; Jim Crow laws; no federal protection against racial discrimination until the Civil Rights Act of 1964	No federal law prohibiting employment discrimination due to sexual orientation
Violence	Domestic violence and sexual assault	Violence and hate crimes (lynchings, bombings, mob violence)	Hate crimes; sexual orientation was not included in federal hate crimes legislation until 2009
Segregation	Historically, women were not allowed in certain settings (universities, politics, men's clubs, military schools, etc.)	Segregation in schools and many other settings: buses, restaurants, separate restrooms, and separate drinking fountains	"Don't ask don't tell" policy in the military; gays must often segregate themselves because it is not socially acceptable for them to show physical affection in public (e.g., gay bars and clubs)
Hurtful and Degrading Stereotypes	Viewed as "less than" and not as intelligent as men	Viewed as "less than" and not as intelligent as Whites	Viewed as "abnormal" or deviant
Family	Women could not divorce or own property; birth control was illegal; abortion continues to be debated	During slavery, denied the opportunity to marry and have families; many states had laws forbidding Blacks and Whites to marry	Denied the opportunity to marry; a number of states do not allow gays to adopt; sodomy laws that made sex acts between men illegal (outlawed in 2003 by Supreme Court)
Religion	Bible is/was used to argue the traditional role of women in society and that women are subservient to men	Bible was used to justify slavery and to argue that Whites and Blacks should not be allowed to marry	Bible is used to argue that gays should not marry and that sexual acts between same-sex couples are immoral and forbidden by God
Representation	Underrepresented in U.S. Congress; no female president	Underrepresented in U.S. Congress	Underrepresented in U.S. Congress
Income	Feminization of poverty; wage gap; glass ceiling	Disproportionate number of Blacks living in poverty; serious wealth disparities	No federal protection from discrimination in the workplace
The Role of Social Movements	Women's movement	Civil Rights Movement	Gay rights movement

Alabama

Health Care
No person or corporation shall require any white female nurse to nurse in wards or rooms in hospitals, either public or private, in which negro men are placed.

Public Facilities
It shall be unlawful for a negro and white person to play together or in company with each other at any game of pool or billiards.

It shall be unlawful to conduct a restaurant or other place for the serving of food in the city, at which white and colored people are served in the same room, unless such white and colored persons are effectually separated by a solid partition extending from the floor upward to a distance of seven feet or higher, and unless a separate entrance from the street is provided for each compartment.

Florida

Marriage/Cohabitation
All marriages between a white person and a negro, or between a white person and a person of negro descent to the fourth generation inclusive, are hereby forever prohibited.

Any negro man and white woman, or any white man and negro woman, who are not married to each other, who shall habitually live in and occupy in the nighttime the same room shall each be punished by imprisonment not exceeding twelve months, or by fine not exceeding five hundred dollars.

Education
The schools for white children and the schools for negro children shall be conducted separately.

Georgia

Public Facilities
No colored barber shall serve as a barber [to] white women or girls.
The officer in charge shall not bury, or allow to be buried, any colored persons upon ground set apart or used for the burial of white persons.

All persons licensed to conduct a restaurant shall serve either white people exclusively or colored people exclusively and shall not sell to the two races within the same room or serve the two races anywhere under the same license.

It shall be unlawful for colored people to frequent any park owned or maintained by the city for the benefit, use and enjoyment of white persons...and unlawful for any white person to frequent any park owned or maintained by the city for the use and benefit of colored persons.

Mississippi

Free Speech
Any person . . . who shall be guilty of printing, publishing or circulating printed, typewritten or written matter urging or presenting for public acceptance or general information, arguments or suggestions in favor of social equality or of intermarriage between whites and negroes, shall be guilty of a misdemeanor and subject to fine of not exceeding five hundred dollars or imprisonment not exceeding six months or both.

Hospital Entrances
There shall be maintained by the governing authorities of every hospital maintained by the state for treatment of white and colored patients separate entrances for white and colored patients and visitors, and such entrances shall be used by the race only for which they are prepared.

Texas

Education
The County Board of Education shall provide schools of two kinds; those for white children and those for colored children.

North Carolina

Textbooks
Books shall not be interchangeable between the white and colored schools, but shall continue to be used by the race first using them.

Figure 8.1
Examples of Jim Crow Laws in Selected States.

Source: National Park Service, U.S. Department of the Interior (n.d.). Retrieved from www.nps.gov/malu /forteachers/jim_crow_laws.htm

outlaw discrimination and to redress the harmful effects of past discrimination. Examples are:

- President Lincoln's Emancipation Proclamation (1863)
- 13th Amendment to the U.S. Constitution that abolished slavery (1865)
- 14th Amendment to the U.S. Constitution (1868) that granted citizenship to all persons born or naturalized in the United States, including former slaves recently freed. It also forbids states from denying any person "life, liberty or property, without due process of law" and includes the now famous Equal Protection Clause.
- 15th Amendment to the U.S. Constitution that granted African American men the right to vote
- 19th Amendment to the U.S. Constitution that granted women the right to vote
- *Brown v. Board of Education* (1954)
- Equal Pay Act of 1963 and the Lilly Ledbetter Fair Pay Act (2009)
- Civil Rights Act of 1964
- Voting Rights Act of 1965
- Affirmative action policies
- Age Discrimination in Employment Act of 1967
- Pregnancy Discrimination Act of 1978
- Americans With Disabilities Act (1990)
- Same-sex marriage laws in Massachusetts, Connecticut, Iowa, New Hampshire, Vermont, New York, and the District of Columbia
- Hate crimes legislation, including the recently enacted Matthew Shepard and James Byrd, Jr. Hate Crimes Prevention Act (2009). (See Illustration 8.1 to learn about the role of Matthew Shepard's Mom, Judy, in getting this bill passed into law.)

Today, according to federal law, it is illegal to discriminate against individuals in the workplace based on race, religion, sex, national origin, age, and disability; however, these federal protections do not include sexual orientation or gender identity. For years, the HRC has been advocating for the passage of the **Employment Non-Discrimination Act (ENDA)**, which would protect LGBT

Activist Spotlight: Judy Shepard

Shortly after her son, University of Wyoming student, Matthew Shepard died after being beaten by two men for being gay in October 1998, **Judy Shepard** became a gay rights activist and made it her mission to expand federal hate crimes legislation to include sexual orientation. She and her husband Dennis founded the Matthew Shepard Foundation, and Judy became the foundation's executive director. For the next 11 years, Judy would work alongside the Human Rights Campaign (HRC) to get a bill passed into law by lobbying legislators and participating in marches and rallies in Washington, DC.

The bill stalled in Congress until 2009, after which the momentum started to build. Judy met with President Obama in May 2009, and he promised to help her pass the act. The bill finally passed in the 111th Congress by a vote of 249 to 175 in the House and 63 to 28 in the Senate, when it was attached to a Department of Defense authorization bill. The new law expanded hate crimes legislation to include gender, sexual orientation, gender identity, and disability. The **Matthew Shepard and James Byrd, Jr. Hate Crimes Prevention Act** was signed into law by President Obama on October 28, 2009. The act was named after Matthew and James Byrd, Jr., an African American man who was dragged to his death by three white men in Jasper, Texas, in 1998.

Illustration 8.1

(lesbian, gay, bisexual, and transgender) individuals from employment discrimination; it has yet to pass. In recent years, there has been a move away from affirmative action policies (which have always been quite controversial) in lieu of policies that promote equal opportunity for low-income and oppressed groups by providing funding for programs that invest in human capital and address structural barriers (e.g., improving substandard schools, job creation strategies, neighborhood/community revitalization, affordable housing, individual development accounts, micro-enterprise programs, living wage campaigns).

IMMIGRATION

From the beginning, the United States has had an uneasy and somewhat contradictory relationship with immigrants. On the one hand, this country often touts itself as "a nation of immigrants." In 1964, John F. Kennedy published a book by this very name. Indeed, every citizen of the United States is a descendent of immigrants except those who descended from Native Americans. Many people around the world long to come to the United States for a better life, for job opportunities, and in order to pursue the American Dream. And large business sectors have taken advantage of the benefit immigrants provide in the form of cheap labor. On the other hand, some Americans fear and resent newly arriving immigrants. Some even resort to vigilante violence so that many immigrants fear for their physical safety.

From the beginning of America's founding, each new generation of immigrants has had to face racism and discrimination and hear complaints that the newly arrived immigrants are taking jobs away from other low-wage earners and keeping wages low, do not share American values, and are a drain on public resources. As soon as immigrants arrive, they are expected to quickly assimilate and to learn to speak English. According to the U.S. Census Bureau, in 2009, there were 38.5 million foreign-born residents, representing one in eight residents. Over one-half were from Latin America (53%), 28% were from Asia, 13% from Europe, 4% from Africa, and 3% from other regions (Grieco & Trevelyan, 2010).

> From the beginning, the United States has had an uneasy and somewhat contradictory relationship with immigrants.

All countries have to deal with the issue of how to handle immigration. Government officials must decide who can come in, in what numbers, and under which circumstances. Some countries are fairly welcoming, whereas others take great care to preserve their country's homogeneity when it comes to race, religion, and culture. In the United States, the pendulum swings back and forth between immigration policies that restrict immigration (e.g., Chinese Exclusion Act, Emergency Quota Act of 1921, Immigration Act of 1924, Operation Wetback in the 1950s) and policies that ease quota restrictions (e.g., Immigration and Nationality Act of 1965, Refugee Act of 1980, Immigration Act of 1990).

One tragic chapter in U.S. history is the treatment of **migrant farmworkers**. Before Mexican laborers were used to support American agriculture, it was the Chinese and then the Japanese who worked as field hands in California. Then the **Bracero Program** was created during World War II to import temporary guest workers into the United States from Mexico in order to meet the growing demand for agriculture laborers. Under this program, which operated for over 20 years, more than 4 million farmworkers from Mexico came to work in the fields in the United States. However, these farmworkers had few rights and were often mistreated and exploited. They were not allowed to unionize or demand fair pay or safe working conditions. When their contracts expired, they were forced to return to Mexico. However, out of this struggle, a famous civil rights activist named **Cesar Chavez** was born. Chavez was a cofounder of the National Farm Workers Association, which later became the United Farm Workers (UFW). He became an inspiration to many around the world as he used nonviolent strategies (e.g., strikes and boycotts such as "no grapes" or "uvas no") and inspirational rhetoric in order to demand basic human rights for farmworkers.

ILLEGAL IMMIGRATION

After the 9/11 attacks in 2001, the issue of illegal immigration rose to the top of the political agenda as concerns over homeland security were heightened. After 9/11, a number of bills were passed into law to address homeland and border security such as the controversial **USA Patriot Act**, the **Enhanced Border Security and Visa Entry Reform Act of 2002**, the **Homeland Security Act of 2002**, and the **Secure Fence Act of 2006**, which authorized the construction of a 700-mile fence along the southern border. In addition, a new program called **Secure Communities** was started by President George Bush and greatly expanded by the Obama administration.

The Secure Communities program requires local and state law enforcement to do an automatic check of immigration status for anyone who has been arrested and to report what they find to Immigration and Customs Enforcement (ICE). The goal of the program was to remove those arrested for serious violent crimes, but the program has recently come under criticism for deporting undocumented immigrants for minor offenses (some with no criminal record) and separating families. This is particularly concerning to those who point out that coming to the United States illegally is a civil violation, not a crime. Supporters of the program argue that this program is an important tool that has resulted in the deportation of violent criminals. A growing number of states have become disenchanted with the program, and Governor Pat Quinn has stated that Illinois is pulling out of the program, setting up a showdown with the Obama administration whose position is that participation in Secure Communities is mandatory.

Diversity in Practice

Practice Behavior Example: Gain sufficient self-awareness to eliminate the influence of personal biases and values in working with diverse groups.

Critical Thinking Question: Why do you think people come to the United States without going through the normal legal channels of becoming a legal resident or citizen? How do you feel about those who are in the country illegally?

There is a delicate balance between immigration policy and policies focused on homeland security. For example, lawmakers must find a way to pass laws that keep the country safe while at the same time strive to create sensible immigration policies that allow foreigners to immigrate to the United States. Those on both sides of the political spectrum agree that there is a problem and that the immigration system is in need of reform. According to a 2010 report from the Office of Immigration Statistics at the Department of Homeland Security, there were roughly 10.8 million people living in the United States in January 2009 who were undocumented or without legal status. The report estimates that 8.5 million of the total 10.8 million were from the North American region and 6.7 million were from Mexico. The next leading sources were El Salvador (530,000), Guatemala (480,000), Honduras (320,000), and the Philippines (270,000) (Hoefer, Rytina, & Baker, 2010).

ADVOCATES OF COMPREHENSIVE IMMIGRATION REFORM

In the United States, there is a significant divide over how to address the problems with U.S. immigration policy. On one side are many Democrats and pro-business conservatives who have come together in advocating for **comprehensive**

immigration reform that would create a path to citizenship for the roughly 11 million undocumented immigrants currently residing in the United States. Efforts to pass comprehensive immigration reform have failed in Congress since 2004 when President Bush proposed a guest worker program that would provide legal status to undocumented workers, angering conservatives in his own party who labeled it an "amnesty" program. Bipartisan legislative proposals to pass comprehensive immigration reform in 2006 and 2007 were also unsuccessful due to heavy political opposition from legislators who were against any process that would give undocumented immigrants the opportunity to become American citizens.

This failure of efforts was widely viewed as a political failure of President Bush who had made it one of his priorities to pass comprehensive immigration reform. In early 2008, the Bush administration unveiled a new philosophy that focused on cracking down on illegal immigration. This new strategy included increasing fines for businesses that hire undocumented immigrants, creating a "virtual fence" along the Mexican border, extending the construction of the "real" fence along the border, and stepping up federal prosecutions against those who cross the border illegally. In reaction to this new strategy, the *New York Times* published an editorial on March 4, 2008, titled "Border Insecurity" and argued that the fence is a symbol of a conflicted nation's effort to literally wall itself off after being unable to resolve the problem intelligently.

On June 23, 2009, 23 Latino organizations, including the National Council of La Raza (NCLR), sent a letter to President Obama urging him to act on immigration reform. NCLR, a prominent national civil rights organization, argues that the United States has a history of exploiting immigrants for their labor but then not affording them any legal protections. NCLR points out that undocumented workers contribute to the economy, pay more taxes than they receive in benefits, deal with family separation, and are vulnerable to crime and exploitation by unscrupulous employers. In fact, many die each year as they attempt to cross the Mexico-U.S. border. According to NCLR, the current immigration system is broken, is full of bureaucratic obstacles, and is a lengthy, expensive process. NCLR explains that federal law provides only 5,000 permanent visas each year to "unskilled" workers, a category that covers most of today's necessary workers. Temporary work visas and family-based avenues for entry are also extremely restrictive, and it is not unusual for a Mexican resident to wait 7 to 9 years for a visa ("Five facts about undocumented workers in the United States," 2008).

At the end of 2009, an immigration bill was introduced in the U.S. House by Representative Luis V. Gutierrez. The bill would create a path to citizenship for undocumented immigrants, enhance border security, and penalize employers who hire those without legal status. President Obama has vowed to make immigration reform a priority of his administration, but so far, the country has seen little movement on this divisive issue.

OPPONENTS OF COMPREHENSIVE IMMIGRATION REFORM

The Republican Party has been split on this issue between (a) pro-business conservatives who have joined Democrats in supporting comprehensive immigration and (b) social conservatives who advocate for a policy that would treat undocumented individuals as criminals who have broken the law and should be penalized and deported. Opponents of comprehensive immigration reform believe that creating a path to citizenship for those residing in the United States equates to amnesty and argue that it is unfair to grant legal status to those who came here illegally when others are waiting in line and going through the appropriate legal channels. In this context, amnesty would mean that the government would allow undocumented individuals to become citizens without any form of punishment or penalty. The last time this was carried out on any widespread scale by the federal government was under President Ronald Reagan in 1986 when the Immigration Reform and Control Act of 1986 was passed. This act granted amnesty to roughly 3 million undocumented immigrants.

Opponents of immigration reform are joined by groups such as the **Minuteman Project** (armed volunteers who patrol the Arizona border); the **Federation for American Immigration Reform (FAIR)**, which advocates ending illegal immigration and significantly reducing legal immigration; **NumbersUSA**; and popular news anchor Lou Dobbs who is an outspoken critic of "illegal aliens" and aired frequent features on the subject when he worked for CNN. Sheriff Richard Jones of Butler County, Ohio, received some national press when he put up a sign outside of the jail that said, "Illegal aliens here" with an arrow pointing to the jailhouse (www.butlersheriff.org/illegals/). Sheriff Jones stated, "I wanted to let the federal government know that if they couldn't find any illegals, I've got some right here in my jail" (Preston, 2006). Those opposing a comprehensive approach to solving the immigration problem were able to effectively derail bipartisan legislative efforts in 2006 and 2007.

Human Rights & Justice

Practice Behavior Example: Understand that each person, regardless of position in society, has basic human rights, such as freedom, safety, privacy, an adequate standard of living, health care, and education.

Critical Thinking Question: Many use the term *illegal alien* to describe those living in the United States without citizenship. Some feel that this term is offensive and prefer to use the terms *undocumented* or *individuals without legal status*. Is it fair to call them criminals when they have committed a civil violation and not a crime?

WHAT NOW?

In the meantime, people across the country have been extremely frustrated with Washington's inability to come together to pass an immigration bill. Immigrants have taken to the streets to rally for reform at the same time that lawmakers at the state and local level have passed legislation of their own. More than 30 towns nationwide have enacted laws in recent years to crack down on illegal immigration by instituting fines and/or jail sentences to those who knowingly rent apartments to undocumented immigrants or give them a job. Many of these towns later reconsidered these laws when their local economy suffered after the departure of those without legal status. Farmers in states such as Colorado, Alabama, and Georgia have reported to the media that they have no workers to work their farms after the state cracked down on illegal immigration. They claim that American workers are not willing to do this form of manual labor. Some states are so desperate for farmworkers that they have turned to their state department of corrections in order to gain access to prison labor. And the nation was riveted by news reports in Arizona, which passed a controversial law in 2010 using a new strategy in its attempt to crack down on illegal immigration.

ARIZONA'S SUPPORT OUR LAW ENFORCEMENT AND SAFE NEIGHBORHOODS ACT (SB 1070)

Arizona has been at the center of the immigration debate because many undocumented immigrants attempt to cross from Mexico into the United States through the Arizona desert; many of them do not survive this treacherous journey. In 2005, then-Governor Janet Napolitano issued a state of emergency declaration after significant increases of drug smuggling and violence were witnessed along the border. Due to the failure of the federal government to pass legislation, Arizona decided to take things into its own hands. In 2008, a new law went into effect to crack down on employers who hire undocumented workers. Soon Sheriff Joe Arpaio of Maricopa County made national news with his controversial tactics of conducting sweeps through Latino neighborhoods without any evidence of criminal activity and segregating these detained inmates in a separate area of his Tent City jail.

When Governor Jan Brewer signed one of the country's most stringent immigration bills into law in April of 2010, many Americans cheered although many others were outraged. The goal of the bill was to identify, prosecute, and deport illegal immigrants, and the bill gave broad new powers to law enforcement to question, and later detain, anyone *suspected* of being in the country illegally. SB (Senate Bill) 1070 requires immigrants to carry their alien registration documents at all times. Failure to carry immigration documents would now be a crime. It also targets those who hire those without legal status or knowingly transport them.

An April 17, 2010, editorial in the *New York Times* called SB 1070 a "mean spirited bill that would do little to stop illegal immigration," and critics asserted it would lead to harassment and racial profiling of Latinos ("Arizona goes over the edge," 2010). The National Association of Social Workers (NASW) came out with a strong statement voicing its opposition as well arguing that the Arizona law goes against the profession's core values of human rights and social justice, will criminalize immigrants, threatens the civil liberties of citizens and immigrants, and increases discrimination and racial profiling because it permits police to apprehend individuals based on their appearance ("Arizona laws decried," 2010).

Over Memorial Day weekend, thousands of protesters marched to oppose the new law. Many civil rights groups called for an economic boycott of the state, and even the Phoenix Suns basketball team entered the political fray by wearing jerseys that said "Los Suns" to show their opposition to the new law. President Obama called the new Arizona law "misguided," and on July 6, 2010, the Justice Department brought a lawsuit against the state of Arizona arguing that only the federal government can set or enforce immigration policy. Later that month, a federal judge blocked the most controversial parts of the new law from going into effect until the legal suit has been resolved. In April 2011, a federal appeals court ruled against Arizona, upholding the lower court's ruling that the state had overstepped its authority. One year later, U.S. Supreme Court was hearing oral arguments from Paul D. Clement representing Arizona, and Solicitor General Donald B. Verrilli Jr. representing the federal government. While SB 1070 was being debated in the courts, Arizona State Senator Russell Pearce, the architect of SB 1070, put together a national coalition of Republican lawmakers from 15 states called State Legislators for Legal Immigration. The coalition's goal is to change the way the 14th Amendment is interpreted and stop granting citizenship to babies born in the United States to parents without legal status.

On June 25, 2012 the Supreme Court struck down several key parts of SB 1070 and agreed with the Obama administration that it is the role of the federal government, and not state officials, to make immigration policy. But the court upheld the most controversial part of SB 1070 (the "show me your papers" provision), which requires police officers to check the immigration status of people they detain and suspect to be in the country illegally. However, the court stated that the courts would be closely watching the implementation of this practice, a clear warning that law enforcement would need to be careful not to abuse the law and engage in racial profiling. The mixed decision had both sides claiming victory with both President Obama and Governor Brewer stating that they were pleased with the outcome.

WHAT IS THE DREAM ACT?

The DREAM Act would provide a path to citizenship to undocumented youth who were brought to the United States as minors by their parents, have grown up here, and consider the United States their home.

The goal of most immigration advocates would be to get a comprehensive immigration bill passed into law that would provide a path to citizenship for the roughly 11 million individuals residing in the United States with no legal status. However, because this has proven very difficult politically, some of these advocates support the Development, Relief, and Education of Alien Minors (DREAM) Act (S. 729/H.R. 1751), a policy that would result in incremental change, or a small, yet significant step in the right direction. The **DREAM Act** would provide a path to citizenship to undocumented youth who were brought to the United States as minors by their parents, have grown up here, and consider the United States their home. Proponents of the DREAM Act emphasize that these children did not break the law and should not be penalized as such. There is precedence for this type of policy since the U.S. Supreme Court ruled in 1982 that K-12 schools cannot deny public education to undocumented students (see Illustration 8.2).

It is estimated that there are 2 million undocumented children in the United States and roughly 65,000 graduate from high school every year. Because they do not have "papers," they cannot obtain a driver's license, get a job, or qualify for federal student loans in order to attend college. The specific requirements in order to qualify for the DREAM Act are as follows:

- Must have entered the United States at age 15 or younger;
- Must have been present in the United States for at least 5 consecutive years prior to enactment of the bill;

Plyler v. Doe

In 1975, Texas amended its education statute to prohibit state education funding for children who were not legal residents of the United States. The new law also allowed school districts to deny enrollment to these students. As a result, the Tyler Independent School District began charging $1,000 a year in tuition for these undocumented children. Attorney Larry Daves agreed to represent a few of the families who could no longer afford to attend school in Tyler ISD in a lawsuit titled *Plyler v. Doe*, a case that would make it all the way to the U.S. Supreme Court. On June 15, 1982, in a 5 to 4 decision, the U.S. Supreme Court struck down the Texas law stating that it was a violation of the Equal Protection Clause of the 14th Amendment, which guarantees that "no state shall deny to any person within its jurisdiction the equal protection of the laws." This set a precedent in the United States that public schools (K-12) cannot deny education to undocumented students.

Texas later became the first state in the nation to allow undocumented students to pay in-state college tuition. Thirteen other states have followed, including California, Illinois, Washington State, New York, and most recently Connecticut and Maryland. And in 2011, Illinois became the first state in the nation to pass legislation that would create a private scholarship fund for children of undocumented parents.

Illustration 8.2

- Must have graduated from a U.S. high school, or have obtained a GED, or have been accepted into an institution of higher education (i.e., college/university);
- Must be between the ages of 12 and 35 at the time of application;
- Must have good moral character; and
- Students would not qualify if they had committed a crime or were deemed to be a security risk.

Qualified students would be given a temporary legal status for 6 years, and they would be able to drive, work, and attend school. They would be eligible for federal work study and student loans (but not grants). At the end of the conditional period, permanent resident status would be given to those who maintained good moral character and completed at least 2 years of college or 2 years of military service. The DREAM Act would also eliminate a federal provision that penalizes states that provide in-state tuition without regard to immigration status. The DREAM Act is sponsored by a bipartisan group of legislators in the U.S. House and Senate.

WHO SUPPORTS THE DREAM ACT?

The DREAM Act has wide support including the following:

- Numerous newspaper editorial boards including the *New York Times*, the *Los Angeles Times*, and *the Washington Post*.
- Educators including the Secretary of Education Arnie Duncan, the National Education Association, and over 100 university presidents and higher education associations (e.g., American Association of State Colleges and Universities, American Association of Community Colleges, National PTA).
- Over 100 national organizations and child advocacy groups such as the Children's Defense Fund, NASW, and Voices for America's Children.
- Faith communities (e.g., American Jewish Committee, Episcopal Church, United Methodist Church, U.S. Catholic Conference of Bishops).
- Unions and civil rights organizations (e.g., Service Employees International Union [SEIU], American Federation of Teachers, American Federation of Labor and Congress of Industrial Organizations, NAACP Legal Defense Fund).
- Elected officials and military leaders such as Robert Gates, Colin Powell, and Mayor Michael Bloomberg.
- Businesses such as Microsoft and the U.S. Hispanic Chamber of Commerce.

For a full list, please visit: www.nilc.org/immlawpolicy/DREAM/crescendo-of-pro-DREAM-2010-09-29.pdf

WHO OPPOSES THE DREAM ACT?

The same groups that oppose comprehensive immigration reform (such as the Federation for American Immigration Reform) do not support the DREAM Act because they view it as giving amnesty to "illegal aliens." The DREAM Act is supported by the majority of Democrats and opposed by the majority of social

Practice Activity 8.1

1. Visit the websites of the National Immigration Law Center, the Immigration Policy Center, dreamactivist.org, and the National Council of La Raza to read more about these organizations and the information they have posted about the DREAM Act. What are their arguments in support of the DREAM Act?

2. Visit the Federation for American Immigration Reform to read its opposition to the DREAM Act. What are its arguments against the act?

3. In your view, who makes the more compelling case?

conservatives and Republicans (though a handful of each have gone against the position of their party). Some Republicans have flip-flopped on the issue, such as Senator John McCain who used to be a cosponsor on the bill, but now opposes it, most likely due to heavy political opposition from his supporters and members of his party who have grown more conservative in recent years.

WHAT STRATEGIES HAVE BEEN USED TO GET IT PASSED INTO LAW?

The most fascinating part of this story is that the individuals who have been driving the passage of this bill are the undocumented youth affected by this problem.

A version of the DREAM Act was first proposed in 2001; thus advocates have been fighting for this legislation for a long time. The most fascinating part of this story is that the individuals who have been driving the passage of this bill are the undocumented youth affected by this problem. They have become courageous youth activists and have honed their skills in leadership and advocacy. In the beginning, advocates of the DREAM Act engaged in the more traditional tactics such as lobbying legislators, encouraging others to contact legislators to urge passage of the bill, and getting resolutions passed by local government. However, over time, these youth activists began employing tactics used by other famous social movements (e.g., Civil Rights Movement) and engaging in various activities that would garner national and local media attention.

The tactics used by advocates of the DREAM Act have included the following:

- Political rallies and marches, including those held in the nation's capitol where youth wear their caps and gowns and perform a mock graduation ceremony;

Advocacy Reflection

Activities involving **political dissent** can include protests, consumer boycotts, strikes, sit-ins, marches, and civil disobedience (i.e., refusal to obey a law that is immoral or unjust). What is your comfort level with these kinds of political activities? Would you be willing to be arrested for an issue you care deeply about?

- In September of 2009, United We Dream's hosting of over 100 coordinated events in 26 states to bring greater awareness of the plight of undocumented students and the need for the DREAM Act;
- Screenings of the documentary film *Papers* held in every state in various communities across the country (more on this film in a separate section);
- Hundreds of thousands of calls, emails, and faxes in support of the DREAM Act to Congress;
- Press conferences;
- Spanish language television and radio stations urging people to call their senator;

- Letters and petitions urging legislators to support the DREAM Act, such as the 1,500 letters that were delivered to the office of Senator Scott Brown (R-MA);
- "Coming out" events where youth publicly reveal their undocumented status;
- Walking across the country; four students from Miami Dade College walked from Miami to Washington, DC, and called their campaign the Trail of Dreams (http://trail2010.org/);
- Hunger strikes, such as a November 2010 hunger strike by students at the University of Texas at San Antonio, who belong to a student organization called DREAM Act Now.
- Peaceful sit-ins at various federal legislators' offices, which have resulted in the arrest of a number of these youth activists (see Illustration 8.3, Social Worker Spotlight, for Isabel Castillo's story of getting arrested);
- Support the DREAM Act mobilized by 108 national organizations and 179 local/state organizations through a sign-on letter; and
- United We Dream's Education Not Deportation (END) campaign focusing on preventing the deportation of the young people that the DREAM Act is designed to assist (www.unitedwedream.org). The campaign's activities entail educating lawmakers, public campaigns, and legal advocacy. The organization works in partnership with organizations such as the Immigrant Legal Resource Center, National Immigration Law Center, and SEIU.

Many of these stories have been featured on local and national news stations such as CNN and MSNBC and in newspapers, including the piece by the *New York Times* Magazine titled, "Coming out illegal," published on October 21, 2010.

This movement has also been built with the help of the Internet and social media such as Facebook and Twitter, which have allowed undocumented youth from all over the country to connect with each other. Youth activists have used YouTube to tell their stories and have started websites such as **Dreamactivist .org** in order to communicate with each other and to educate the public about this issue. Finally, they have built relationships with organizations across the country in order to build a more powerful coalition, for example: Dreamactivist.org, United We Dream Network, Immigrant Youth Justice League, New York State Youth Leadership Council, MEChA, Orange County Dream Team, Students Working for Equal Rights (S.W.E.R), The Dream Is Coming, National Council of La Raza, Campus Progress (part of the Center for American Progress), the United States Student Association (USSA), and a number of faith-based organizations and labor groups. This list is not exhaustive because it is not possible to list the countless

Advocacy Tip

For the DREAM Act activists, **social media** (e.g., Facebook and Twitter) was an important organizing tool. It was crucial in helping them to share information with each other, mobilize support, and to plan and organize their events.

Policy Practice

Practice Behavior Example: Collaborate with colleagues and clients for effective policy action.

Critical Thinking Question: Take some time to critically evaluate the tactics and strategies used by the DREAM Act youth activists. What did they do well? What could they have done differently? If you were working on this campaign, what skills, ideas, and suggestions would you offer?

Isabel Castillo, BSW (DREAM act activist).

Tactics Used to Get the DREAM Act Passed Into Law

- ☑ Coalition building

- ☑ Earned media (letters to the editor, actions that lead to media coverage)

- ☐ Paid media (paying for TV/radio ads)

- ☑ Visibility (rallies, marches)

- ☑ Political dissent (e.g., civil disobedience, protest)

- ☑ Providing testimony in a legislative committee hearing

- ☑ Direct lobbying (in-person lobby visits, sometimes by a professional lobbyist)

- ☑ Grassroots lobbying (e.g., urging people to call, write, and email legislators)

- ☑ Educational outreach (town halls, house parties, community forums)

- ☑ Online advocacy (using social media)

- ☐ Paid communication (paid staff who call voters, materials mailed out)

- ☐ Fund-raising activities

Social Worker Spotlight: Isabel Castillo, BSW

Isabel Castillo graduated with her BSW from Eastern Mennonite University in Virginia in 2007; however, because she is undocumented, she is not able to secure employment and work as a social worker. She was brought to the United States from Mexico when she was 6 years old by her parents who went to work in the poultry industry in Virginia. Her parents instilled in her the value of education because they wanted her to have a better life than they had. As a result, Isabel excelled in school and graduated high school with a 4.0 GPA. However, she soon learned that she would not be able to attend college because she had no Social Security number and would not be eligible to apply for federal loans to help her pay for her college education.

She was overjoyed to learn that Eastern Mennonite accepted undocumented students, and she graduated 3½ years later with her social work degree, after struggling to pay for her tuition each semester (e.g., by working and getting help from her community). She would like to earn her MSW, but finances are currently a barrier. She has now become a DREAM Act activist because this is her only hope for a viable future and the opportunity to use her degree and work as a social work professional.

Isabel's activism began when she attended a conference in Washington, DC, where she met other "Dreamers." She immediately realized that she needed to start organizing in her home state of Virginia. In October 2009, she helped found a local organization, Dream Activist Virginia, which can be found on Facebook. The activists meet weekly and strategize about how to raise awareness and build support for the DREAM Act. They write letters and lobby legislators. They were able to get a resolution passed by the Harrisonburg City Council and organized the first immigrant rights rally in Harrisonburg. Isabel regularly shares her story by speaking at churches and schools, and to community groups and has been interviewed by radio and newspaper journalists.

Perhaps the most exciting activity she participated in was a peaceful protest outside of Senator Harry Reid's office where she was arrested by Capitol Police after being there for 5 hours. Though Reid has been a supporter of the DREAM Act, Isabel and her fellow Dreamers were frustrated with him for not providing the leadership needed to really move the act forward. On this same day, other Dreamers were arrested for participating in a peaceful sit-in at Senator John McCain's office. The judge and prosecutor were very sympathetic to their stories; yet the Dreamers were still found guilty of "unlawful entry" with a punishment of one year on probation and a $50 fine.

When asked whether she is scared that her activism will result in her deportation, Isabel states, "This is not about me anymore, it's about thousands of students. I am part of a movement." She goes on to explain, "This is home to me. I have grown up here. I am American in every sense of the word except on paper."

In May 2011, Isabel received an honorary doctorate from the University of San Francisco.

Illustration 8.3

number of national and local groups that are involved across the country. The NASW also supports the DREAM Act and issued an action alert to its members asking them to contact their representatives to explain that social workers support policies that provide children of immigrants with access to higher education and policies that do not punish children for their parents' actions ("Provide legal, earned pathway to citizenship," NASW).

PAPERS: STORIES OF UNDOCUMENTED YOUTH (THE MOVIE)

This movie is unique because two dedicated advocates/allies/filmmakers embarked on the making of a documentary about the DREAM Act to enable undocumented youth to tell their stories and to help build support for the legislation. *Papers: Stories of Undocumented Youth* is a 90-minute film that was directed by Anne Galisky and produced by Rebecca Shine, both of Graham Street Productions. Galisky has a masters degree in history and has conducted research on the Japanese internment during World War II. Shine has a lot of experience working with nonprofits, schools, and public agencies in the areas of economic development, social services, mentoring, and youth leadership. Both have a passion for advocacy and issues of social and economic justice.

However, perhaps the most interesting part of this movie is that filmmakers Galisky and Shine decided to train and engage a youth crew who would collaborate with them in the making of this film. Galisky explains, "While Rebecca and I were certainly leaders in putting the film together, it would not be the same film without the intensive participation of the youth crew. Their involvement is what makes this film different, both the production and the distribution of it. It is not just a film *about* undocumented youth, it was made *with* undocumented youth. I am convinced that this is what makes the film fresh and honest and why it appeals to young people. I see our role as facilitating the youth telling their own stories. We could have not have made this film without them" (Personal communication, n.d.).

Shine and Galisky knew the value of including the youth, who were affected by this issue, in every phase of the filmmaking process including preproduction, fund-raising, filming, marketing, and distribution. Their first planning meeting with youth occurred in January 2008, and just over a year and a half later the film premiered in September 2009. After working with many of these youth activists, the filmmakers have witnessed firsthand the youths' growth and development as they have gained valuable skills in advocacy, public policy, and community organizing. These young adults have learned what it means to be part of a movement that is larger than themselves. In the view of Galisky and Shine, many of them will become the future leaders of tomorrow.

Papers has been screened in every U.S. state, including a screening on Capitol Hill. Five main characters are profiled in the film to show the diversity of their experiences and backgrounds despite the common problem they all share. Two are Mexican American, one is Guatemalan American, one is Korean American, and one is Jamaican American (Juan Carlos, Monica, Yo Sub, Simone, and Jorge). Elected officials and leaders from various human rights organizations are also interviewed in this film, which puts the DREAM Act into the larger context of the historic struggle for immigrant rights in the United States.

Practice Activity 8.2

If your university library has a copy of *Papers*, watch this film in order to critique how well it (a) informs people about the issue and (b) whether it is a good vehicle to get others to act. The DREAM Act is an example of a policy in which those who are directly impacted by the issue are among those lobbying for the change. Sometimes social workers advocate for others in the legislative arena, but it is often much more powerful when we can help others tell their own stories in this environment. Think about your own interest in social work—how might you empower your clients to advocate for themselves politically?

INTERVIEW with *Papers*

Director, Anne Galisky, and Producer, Rebecca Shine*
September 2010

(Source: *Papers* press materials)

Q: What first drew you to this story?

A: About 6 years ago, we both began tutoring and mentoring immigrant youth who were at risk of dropping out of high school in Portland, Oregon. Even though we knew a lot about challenges facing at-risk youth, we were dismayed by the extra obstacles that stood in the way of some of these young people because of their lack of "papers." That in turn made us painfully aware of the bigger picture: how much our nation is losing by keeping laws in place that bar millions of children from pursuing their dreams and realizing their potential.

Most of all, we grew to love each of these young people and began wondering how we could help them fight the injustice of their circumstances. We came to believe that making a film would be a great way to help other people meet these extraordinary youth, understand their stories, and hopefully begin to relate to them in a new way. As the idea grew, our group of willing participants grew and evolved into a crew that came to be called El Grupo Juvenil, young people from across the United States who wanted to help undocumented youth tell their own stories to a national audience.

Then, in the fall of 2007, two things happened. First, the DREAM Act failed to overcome a filibuster in the Senate. Second, Oregon's governor, Ted Kulongoski issued an executive order changing state law to require that all applicants for state IDs or drivers licenses have Social Security numbers. Both of these events took a terrible toll on the immigrant youth we worked with, and gave us the impetus to start the production of *Papers*.

Q: Why don't you show the other side of the debate?

A: We spend the first 3 minutes of the film without dialogue, showing images from both pro-immigrant and anti-immigrant marches and rallies to remind audiences of the extremely polarized and vitriolic debate that surrounds these young people every day. We also interviewed over 150 people from across the country who were both in favor of and against immigration reform and conducted many interviews at the Democratic and Republican National Conventions in the summer of 2008.

However, as we continued to film, we realized how rare it is to hear directly from undocumented students and how common it is to hear anti-immigrant and anti-immigration-reform voices, so we decided to emphasize the students' stories first and foremost. There's no arguing with someone's personal experience, and this is the story that is so often overlooked—how do undocumented immigrant youth feel and what do they think about their situation? Politicians, teachers, and community leaders provide the historical, cultural, and political context to the youths' stories.

Q: How did you find the students? Isn't it dangerous for them to appear in the film?

A: We interviewed dozens of undocumented youth across the country. Some we already knew from our work as mentors and advocates, and others were introduced to us as we traveled. Still others heard about the project and contacted us to share their stories. Over the course of a year we identified the five main characters, each of whom was willing to

*http://www.papersthemovie.com

sacrifice anonymity to appear on film, had come from different countries under widely varying circumstances, and who had unique personalities, dreams and struggles.

Each of the main characters, Monica, Yo Sub, Juan Carlos, Simone, and Jorge, had the awareness that telling their stories would encourage other people to become more public about who they are. And we have seen that this is in fact true: at many screenings of the film across the country, young people are "stepping out of the shadows" and, sometimes for the first time, declaring their immigration status openly.

And yes, it does pose risks to publicly declare your undocumented status, so we were very careful to respect each of the students' choices about their level of exposure. Simone, for example, made the choice to only show her eyes in order to protect her safety and privacy. Her choice demonstrates the fear that millions of kids currently live with every day, and emphasizes the huge risk a handful of them are taking by telling their stories.

Despite a recent *New York Times* article about the Obama administration not prioritizing the deportation of undocumented students, no one knows when the political winds could shift and each of the students is still legally at risk of arrest, detention and deportation at any time.

Q: What is happening in the lives of your main characters today?

A: Jorge recently completed a 14-day hunger strike in front of Sen. Diane Feinstein's Los Angeles office, the latest step in his overall choice to be more public about his immigration status. His personal hope is to convince a filibuster-proof majority in the Senate to support the DREAM Act and then he will move on to pursue a graduate degree in African American literature.

Monica lives with her husband and works in elder care. Her family remains split between the United States and Guatemala while her father's 19-year-long asylum case is still pending.

Juan Carlos struggles with his limited choices now that he has graduated from high school. He feels that his dreams are on hold until the DREAM Act passes so he advocates for its passage while continuing to try to be a role model for young people in his community.

Simone finished her associates degree and wants desperately to contribute to the country she calls home. She worries about her little brother and tries

to keep up his hopes so that he will think that it is worthwhile to stay in school.

Yo Sub is getting ready to start his second year of college and is majoring in economics. He loves college life and is thriving academically as could be expected of someone who graduated high school with a 4.5 GPA. What happens after graduation will depend on whether the DREAM Act or comprehensive immigration reform passes by then.

Q: What has changed in the DREAM Act movement since the film's release?

A: The good news is that momentum is building behind the DREAM Act, and it is becoming better known and more widely supported. Dreamers have begun to deliberately draw inspiration from the Civil Rights Movement and the gay rights movement, both in terms of messaging and tactics, which has added a historical dimension to their work that not only adds a great deal strategically, but inspires them and others to see themselves in that proud, and ultimately triumphant, historical context.

They are taking some enormous risks like conducting hunger strikes in New York and Los Angeles, walking from Miami to Washington, DC, taking part in civil disobedience actions including staging sit-ins at Congressional offices and marching on Capitol Hill. Mostly, they are going public and telling their stories and the American people are starting to listen. President Obama is in support of the DREAM Act and Senate Majority leader Harry Reid has expressed a willingness to bring the DREAM Act forward this fall. Even in an era of rare bipartisan cooperation, both Democrats and Republicans are cosponsors and proponents of this legislation.

Someday soon we hope to look back on this as an extraordinary time in the history of the immigrant rights movement. We are thrilled to have been able to both chronicle the movement and to support its expansion and public support through *Papers*.

Q: You make strong connections between the LGBT rights movement and the immigration rights movement in the film. Can you explain how they are linked?

A: One of the main characters in *Papers*, Jorge, is both undocumented and queer. He likens his experience to living at two borders at the same time. In fact, as we were working on the film, we found that a large proportion of the young people who are leading the movement and going public about their status as undocumented (they call it "coming out") also identify as queer or LGBTQ.

(contiuned)

They realize that there is extraordinary power in their stories and in telling the truth. The boldness of it inspires us. By coming out as undocumented, they risk arrest, detention, and deportation. By coming out as queer, they risk being ostracized from their families, their churches, their cultures of origin and their communities. But in talking with these courageous young people, it is obvious that they are not going to stop being public about who they are. In some ways the most vulnerable, they are also the most brave. They, more than anyone, know the power of "coming out" and recognize that going public is the way to change peoples' hearts and minds.

Q: El Grupo Juvenil is mentioned in the film's credits and on your site. Who are they and what role did they play in *Papers*?

A: El Grupo Juvenil is the *Papers* youth crew. This group of young people was integral to every aspect of the film's production and distribution and includes over 750 participants nationwide. These youth come from a wide variety of neighborhoods, races, ethnicities, religions, and abilities, and vary in immigration status and sexual orientation. We wanted to make a film about undocumented youth but also wanted to include as many of them, and other youth who care about them, in every step of creating the film, and El Grupo Juvenil was our answer.

The group began with the youth we were mentoring and tutoring and soon grew like wildfire into a national network that will have lasting value far beyond helping with the film. Participants developed their leadership capacities, learned public policy advocacy, presented at local, regional and national conferences, and designed and led workshops for middle school

and high school students. Some of the group's leaders have now appeared on CNN and Univision, on radio and in newspapers. They were honored in May at a Congressional reception at the U.S. Capitol.

Q: Once the DREAM Act becomes law, why should people buy and watch *Papers*?

A: *Papers* is timeless and universal because it is ultimately about overcoming obstacles, especially those that seem insurmountable. No matter who you are, struggle is a major element of the human experience and something we all relate to. Who knows, it might even be more inspiring after DREAM becomes law—everyone loves to see others succeed despite impossible odds because it gives us faith we can do the same. This film directly chronicles five incredible young people facing that challenge, but represents 2 million more such stories.

Q: What's next for Graham Street Productions?

A: Well, we are still very busy with *Papers* this year. The film is coming out on DVD on September 14th, just in time for back-to-school—a period that is extremely hopeful and fun for most families, but that means the beginning of a crisis for the 65,000 undocumented high school seniors who will graduate this year—and we are hoping that will kick off another amazing round of screenings and discussions around the nation.

Anne has continued to film the DREAM Act movement and exploring what to do with that additional footage while also looking forward to starting another yet-to-be-announced film project. Rebecca is working closely with El Grupo Juvenil to expand their youth organizing work in 2011.

Filmmakers Shine and Galisky believe that documentary films can be a powerful vehicle for social and political change because of the power they have to move people, touch the audience on an emotional level, and raise consciousness. In their view, people would prefer to learn about an issue by experiencing a movie or piece of art. They made a film that was not meant for people to watch alone. It was important for them to make a film that did not make people feel depressed afterward, but rather empowered to act because their film profiles a problem that has a straightforward solution. After the film was made, the film was purchased by individuals and local grassroots organizations across the country where screenings of the film were planned and organized. The majority of the screenings were organized by high school students, college students, and educators. The typical format was as follows:

- Organize screenings in the community so that community members can watch the film together.

- Invite community leaders and elected officials to attend.
- After the film, include a Q&A session and engage the audience in a conversation.
- It was fairly common for the groups that hosted the screening to give action items to audience members after the film, based on what they wanted to mobilize people to do.
- After the screening, people were often moved to act because the stories of these youth are so compelling.

WHAT IS THE CURRENT STATUS OF THE DREAM ACT?

Despite the fact that the bill had 134 cosponsors in the House and 40 cosponsors in the Senate, the DREAM Act failed to pass in the remaining months of the lame duck 111th Congress. It fell 5 votes short of the 60 votes needed to overcome a Republican-led filibuster in the Senate. The vote was largely along party lines although three Republicans went against their party and voted to advance the legislation, whereas five Democrats went against their party and voted no. For DREAM Act activists, it was a heartbreaking defeat; however, it was the closest the DREAM Act ever came to passage in the U.S. Congress. Afterward, President Obama expressed his disappointment over the defeat of this legislation. When it was reintroduced in the 112th Congress in 2011, this marked more than 10 years of advocacy efforts on behalf of the DREAM Act.

However, it is important to keep in mind that not all young people will be eligible for the DREAM Act; so for undocumented youth, a comprehensive immigration bill that provides a path to citizenship for all undocumented immigrants will be necessary. Despite President Obama's support for the DREAM Act and comprehensive immigration reform, pro-immigration organizations and advocates have been disappointed with his lack of leadership on this issue and with his administration's support of programs, such as Secure Communities (fingerprinting those in custody to identify deportable immigrants), which have resulted in record numbers of deportations, surpassing that of the Bush years.

An interesting development occurred on June 15, 2012, when President Obama announced a major policy change with regard to young undocumented youth residing in the United States. Making the announcement to reporters in the Rose Garden, Obama explained, "They are Americans in their heart, in their minds, in every single way but one: on paper" (*New York Times*, 2012). White House officials explained that the timing for the policy shift coincided with the 30th anniversary of the *Plyler v. Doe* Supreme Court decision (see Illustration 8.2).

Under the change, the Department of Homeland Security will no longer initiate the deportation of undocumented immigrants who had come to the United States before age 16, have lived in the United States for at least five years, and are in school, are high school graduates, or have served in the military. They must be under 30 and have no criminal record.

Filmmakers Shine and Galisky believe that documentary films can be a powerful vehicle for social and political change because of the power they have to move people, touch the audience on an emotional level, and raise consciousness.

Policy Practice

Practice Behavior Example: Analyze, formulate, and advocate for policies that advance social well-being.

Critical Thinking Question: In your opinion, would it be better to work for comprehensive immigration reform (large-scale change) or for a policy that would result in smaller, more incremental change, such as the DREAM Act? What are the pros and cons of each approach?

However, it is important to note that the new policy is a temporary measure and is not a path to permanent citizenship as laid out in the Dream Act legislation. For immigrants who come forward and qualify, Homeland Security officials have the authority to grant deferred action, a reprieve that will have to be renewed every two years. Under current law, this status allows immigrants to apply for work permits. This means that young undocumented immigrants will be able to work legally and obtain driver's licenses as well as other documents they have lacked earlier. This policy has been estimated to benefit anywhere from 800,000 to 1.4 million youth without legal status (*New York Times*, 2012).

Reactions to the new policy varied, with many Republicans angered that the president circumvented Congress, while many of the affected youth were elated. "People are just breaking down and crying for joy when they find out what the president did," said Lorella Praeli, a leader of the United We Dream Network, the largest coalition of undocumented immigrant students (*New York Times*, 2012). The president received praise from many Democratic lawmakers and a number of immigrant and civil rights organizations, many of whom pointed out, however, that this is not a long-term solution, and Congress will ultimately need to act. Even President Obama acknowledged this in his remarks when he stated, "This is not a path to citizenship. It is not a permanent fix" (*New York Times*, 2012). Representative Steve King, (R-Iowa), an outspoken critic of illegal immigration, vowed to bring a lawsuit against the president in order to stop the new measure.

The following questions will test your knowledge of the content found within this chapter. For additional assessment, including licensing-exam type questions on applying chapter content to practice behaviors, visit **MySearchLab**.

1. The following group is still not afforded protection from the federal government when it comes to workplace discrimination:

   a. women

   b. older adults

   c. sexual minorities

   d. ethnic minorities

2. According to the U.S. Census Bureau (2009), roughly _____ people in the United States were born in a foreign country.

   a. one in three

   b. one in four

   c. one in six

   d. one in eight

3. Which of the following is false regarding Arizona's controversial immigration bill (SB 1070) that was passed into law?

   a. The NASW did not take an official position on the new law.

   b. It allows law enforcement to question or detain anyone suspected of being in the country illegally.

   c. It was opposed by the Obama administration as well as the Phoenix Suns basketball team.

   d. The *New York Times* wrote that the new law will lead to racial profiling and harassment of Latinos.

4. You are a school social worker and work in a school with a high population of Latino children, some of whom are undocumented. One of the teachers has contacted you and is concerned because she heard on a news report that a state lawmaker would like to pass a new law requiring schools to check the citizenship status of all children who are enrolled. You would tell her the following:

   a. She should be very concerned because eight other states have recently passed similar legislation.

   b. The law of the land is that public schools have the right to deny public education to undocumented students.

   c. This would be unconstitutional due to the 1982 U.S. Supreme Court ruling, *Plyler v. Doe*.

   d. This is a concern because each state has the right to set its own policies in this regard.

5. Who would be eligible for the DREAM Act?

   a. Those who entered the United States before age 18

   b. Those who have lived in the United States for at least 3 consecutive years

   c. Those with a criminal record for only minor offenses

   d. Those who have grown up in the United States and consider the United States their home

6. Those opposing comprehensive immigration reform include:

   a. social conservatives

   b. pro-business conservatives

   c. Democrats

   d. President George W. Bush

7. Documentary films are often used to educate the public and to raise consciousness about a social problem. What do you think about the idea of using documentary films as a strategy to help to pass legislation and create social/political change? How might social workers work in collaboration with documentary filmmakers to tell important stories?

Reinforce what you learned in this chapter by studying videos, cases, documents, and more available at **www.MySearchLab.com**.

Watch and Review

Watch these Videos

* Social and Economic Justice: Understanding Forms of Oppression and Discrimination
* Photographing the Civil Rights Movement
* The Real ID (2008)
* Rev. Martin Luther King Jr.'s Speech

Read and Review

Read these Cases/Documents

* Cesar Chavez, from "He Showed Us the Way" (1978)
* The Gay Liberation Front, Come Out (1970)
* Undocumented Mexicans
* John Lewis, Address at the March on Washington (1963)
* Fannie Lou Hammer, Voting Rights in Mississippi (1962–64)

Explore and Assess

Explore these Assets

* Interactive Case Study: Civil Rights Movement
* Interactive Case Study: Comparing Civil Rights
* Interactive Case Study: Women's Struggle for Equality
* Interactive Case Study: The Mexican American Civil Rights Movement
* Interactive Case Study: The Struggle for Equal Protection

Research these Topics

Laws and Court Cases Outlawing Discrimination

The Heated Debate Over Illegal Immigration Policies

What Is the DREAM Act?

Assess Your Knowledge

Go to **MySearchLab** to test your knowledge of key topics in this chapter with topic-specific quizzes. Conclude your assessment by completing the chapter exam.

* = CSWE Core Competency Asset   Δ = Case Study

9

Child Welfare and Children's Rights

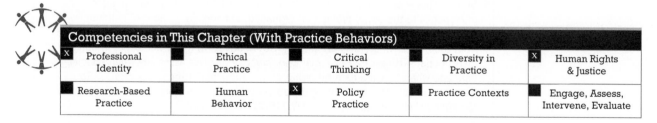

Competencies in This Chapter (With Practice Behaviors)				
x Professional Identity	Ethical Practice	Critical Thinking	Diversity in Practice	x Human Rights & Justice
Research-Based Practice	Human Behavior	x Policy Practice	Practice Contexts	Engage, Assess, Intervene, Evaluate

If our American way of life fails the child, it fails us all.

—*Pearl S. Buck*

The idea that children should have certain rights and need special protection based on their vulnerable status is not a controversial idea to most social workers. Even though the United States has experienced thriving social movements on behalf of ethnic minorities, the poor, women, older adults, and people with disabilities, a social movement for children has not occurred perhaps because children cannot vote, are dependent upon adults for their care and protection, and cannot mobilize on their own behalf in the same way that adults can. Thus, children, more than many other vulnerable groups, depend on committed adults who will advocate for them in the public sphere.

CHILD MALTREATMENT IN THE UNITED STATES

It is shocking that there was a Society for the Prevention of Cruelty to Animals (SPCA) in the United States before there was a Society for the Prevention of Cruelty to Children (SPCC).

Child maltreatment is not a new social problem. Historically, children have been viewed as the property of their parents, and too many have been victims of abuse, neglect, and exploitation at the hands of adults, both inside and outside of the family. The government has also failed children at times by allowing millions of them to be without health care coverage, not outlawing child labor until the 1920s, and looking the other way when they are abused by powerful people (e.g., priests, football coaches) and institutions designed to protect them. To child welfare advocates, it is shocking that there was a Society for the Prevention of Cruelty to Animals (SPCA) in the United States before there was a Society for the Prevention of Cruelty to Children (SPCC). Illustration 9.1 describes the Orphan Train movement, an effort to place homeless "street" children into the homes of families living in rural America. This laid the groundwork for the American foster care system.

The Orphan Trains

In 1853, minister Charles Loring Brace founded the Children's Aid Society to assist the thousands of orphaned, abandoned, and unwanted children living on the streets of New York City. Horrified by the living conditions of these children, Brace believed that they needed to get out of their harmful environment and could have better lives with kind, Christian families in the country who were in need of farm labor. Between 1854 and 1929, more than 100,000 children were put on a train and sent to various states in the United States to be placed with rural families, many of them farming families. Some children were lucky to be placed with loving families whereas others were mistreated and wanted only for farm labor.

The "orphan trains" were a precursor to the foster care system in the United States. This is one example of a child welfare practice or policy that emerged in response to the social problem of orphaned, abandoned, or abused children. Modern child welfare policies allow children in certain circumstances to be removed from their home where they are placed with relatives, in foster homes, or in other institutional settings. Part of social work practice involves assessing when policies help and when they are harmful. What do you think about the orphan trains? To learn more about this fascinating period of child welfare history, watch *American Experience: The Orphan Trains* on DVD (PBS Home Video).

Illustration 9.1

Each state operates a child welfare system that is responsible for investigating reports of child maltreatment, which consists of both abuse and neglect. **Abuse** includes physical abuse, sexual abuse, and psychological abuse. **Neglect** involves failing to provide a child with needed food, clothing, shelter, medical care, or supervision to the extent that there is a serious risk to the child's health and safety. Many states also include abandonment and parental substance abuse in their definition of *child maltreatment.* In fiscal year 2010, child protective services (CPS) agencies across the country received an estimated 3.3 million reports of suspected child abuse and neglect, representing more than 5.9 million children (U.S. Department of Health and Human Services, 2011). Sometimes, reports do not receive a CPS response because the situation does not fall under the state's rules for investigation, or the case is not given a high priority and the state lacks the resources to follow up on every report.

In 2010, 61% of reports were screened in and 90% of those received an investigation. Of the 1.7 million reports that received a CPS investigation, 22% were **substantiated**. (i.e., evidence of maltreatment was found) or indicated (i.e., there was reason to suspect maltreatment). This means that approximately 754,000 children were identified as victims of child abuse or neglect in 2010 (however, this is a duplicate count meaning that some children were victims more than once; the nonduplicate child count was 695,000). The other 70% to 80% of reports were not substantiated because CPS investigations found either no evidence, or insufficient evidence, to indicate that the children in these cases were maltreated.

Children younger than 1 year had the highest rate of victimization, and more than one-third were under age 4. Victimization was split relatively equally between the sexes. More than 75% of substantiated child victims (78.3%) suffered neglect, 17.6% suffered physical abuse, 9.2% suffered sexual abuse, 8.1% suffered from psychological maltreatment, and 2.4% were medically neglected. These percentages sum to more than 100% because a child may have suffered more than one type of maltreatment. In addition, 10.3% of victims experienced such "other" types of maltreatment as abandonment, threats of harm to the child, or congenital drug addiction. A nationally estimated 1,560 children died from abuse and neglect.

CHILD WELFARE LEGISLATION

Child welfare policies govern how the United States responds to children who are maltreated by their parents and caregivers in an effort to keep children safe and free from abuse and neglect. These policies are often fraught with controversy because they involve the government's intrusion into the family home, a place most Americans view as sacred. State child protection systems find themselves in a no-win situation because many Americans believe they do not go far enough in protecting the nation's children from abuse and neglect, whereas others believe they are overly intrusive into the private lives of families. Throughout most of American history, children were considered the property of their parents and it was not the role of the government to intervene. Societal attitudes slowly began changing after the "discovery" of parental child abuse by pediatric radiologists in the 1940s and when Dr. Henry Kempe and colleagues coined the term *battered child syndrome* in 1962 to describe children who had suffered from serious physical abuse. Since then, child welfare advocates have grappled over whether child welfare policies should focus primarily on preserving the family or protecting the child, or whether it is possible to do both.

First White House Conference on Children, 1909
Social Security Act of 1935
Child Abuse Prevention and Treatment Act, 1974
Indian Child Welfare Act, 1978
Adoption Assistance and Child Welfare Act of 1980
Multi-Ethnic Placement Act, 1994
Inter-Ethnic Placement Provisions Act, 1996
Adoption and Safe Families Act, 1997
Foster Care Independence Act, 1999
Texas is the first state to pass Safe Haven or "Baby Moses" law, 1999
Fostering Connections to Success and Increasing Adoptions Act, 2008

Figure 9.1

Significant U.S. Child Welfare Legislation.

The federal government's initial involvement in the welfare of children began with the first White House Conference on Children in 1909 and the establishment of the Children's Bureau in 1912. The Social Security Act of 1935 authorized the first federal funding for child welfare services and allowed states to develop local agencies and programs. However, it is hard to believe that a fully funded, formalized child welfare system was not in place in the United States until the 1970s when the **Child Abuse Prevention and Treatment Act** was passed (sponsored by Senator Walter Mondale), and significant levels of federal dollars were dedicated to aiding states in the investigation and treatment of child abuse. This was a huge step forward, and since then many important pieces of legislation have been passed over the years in an attempt to better address the needs of vulnerable children, particularly those in state foster care (see Figure 9.1). Child welfare policies have focused on many aspects of child welfare practice including prevention of child abuse and neglect, foster care, adoption, kinship care, and foster youth emancipating from the foster care system when they reach adulthood.

The United States has also seen the development of a number of prominent child welfare advocacy organizations, such as the **Child Welfare League of America (CWLA)** and the **Children's Defense Fund**, whose mission is to advocate on behalf of children (see Figure 9.2). However, despite this progress, state child protection systems continue to be underfunded and understaffed, creating a revolving

Child Welfare Advocacy Organizations

Two of America's leading child welfare advocacy organizations are the **Child Welfare League of America** and the **Children's Defense Fund**. **Every Child Matters** is a newer organization that is also at the forefront in fighting to make children one of the nation's priorities. For social workers interested in the macro side of child welfare, organizations like this at the state or national level will be of interest.

Visit the websites of each of these organizations in order to learn more about their missions, their public policy issues of interest, and their current legislative agenda. What was most surprising to you about the work of these organizations? Next, do some research online to find out about child welfare advocacy organizations in your city or state. How many exist?

Figure 9.2

Advocacy Spotlight.

Practice Activity 9.1

In 2008, a new law, the Fostering Connections to Success and Increasing Adoptions Act, was passed by the U.S. Congress. It has been lauded as the most important piece of child welfare legislation in more than a decade by experts such as the CWLA because it was intended to make important improvements to the child welfare system. Do some research on this act. What are the major components of this legislation?

door for caseworkers who burn out too soon. The qualifications of child protection caseworkers are also cause for concern because many states do not require a social work or related degree. According to the CWLA, less than one-third of staff in state child welfare agencies have a formal social work education (CWLA, 2002).

Figure 9.1 shows a number of important pieces of legislation that have been passed into law to address the needs of children and families served by state child welfare systems in the United States. A number of them have been quite controversial. For example, in response to the concern over the disproportionate number of children in foster care who are ethnic minorities, Congress passed the **Multi-Ethnic Placement Act (MEPA)** in 1994, which prohibited states from delaying or denying adoption and foster placements on the basis of race or ethnicity, but allowed states to consider race as one of many factors in making placement decisions. Then in 1996, the Inter-Ethnic Placement Provisions Act made it illegal for states to include race as a factor at all. Some child welfare professionals agree with these policies and believe that adoption should be a color-blind process in which race is not a major factor when making placement decisions. In other words, they are not concerned over the practice of placing Latino or African American children into the homes of Caucasian families. However, other professionals disagree and believe that children of color are better off when they are placed with families, and live in communities, that match and can preserve their cultural background.

Child welfare professionals were similarly divided over one provision of the **Adoptions and Safe Families Act** (1997) that significantly shortened the time line when child welfare officials are required to file a petition to terminate parental rights. Supporters of this provision felt this was important so that children do not languish in the foster care system waiting for their parents to get rehabilitated. Others disagreed and argued that parents with serious substance abuse problems, for example, cannot possibly recover successfully within this more stringent time frame. In child welfare policies, there are often competing values at play such as the rights of children versus the rights of parents. This values debate can be clearly seen when examining the UN Convention on the Rights of the Child, which is the focus of the rest of this chapter.

WHAT IS THE UN CONVENTION ON THE RIGHTS OF THE CHILD?

Social workers are committed to improving the welfare of children in the United States and around the world; however, most have never heard of the United Nations Convention on the Rights of the Child (CRC) despite the fact that the National Association of Social Workers (NASW) supports its passage. The CRC is a human rights treaty that outlines the rights that every child should be entitled to regardless of national boundaries (see Figure 9.3). The CRC is widely recognized as the first legally binding international instrument

The CRC is a human rights treaty that outlines the rights that every child should be entitled to regardless of national boundaries.

(193 countries have ratified this treaty and
only 2 have not: The United States and Somalia)

Children have the right to:

Nondiscrimination
Survive and develop healthily
A legally registered name
A nationality
Know and be cared for by their parents
An identity
Live with their parents unless it is bad for them
Move between different countries to visit their parents
Say what they think should happen and have their opinions taken into account
Freedom of expression
Freedom of thought, conscience, and religion
Freedom of association
Right to privacy
Have access to information that is important to their health and well-being (mass media)
Protection from all forms of violence
Special protection if they are a refugee
Be cared for by people who respect their ethnic group, religion, culture, and language
Special care and support if they have disabilities
Good quality health care
Help from the government if they are poor or in need
Adequate standard of living
An education (special focus on girls)
Relax and play
Be protected from child labor that is harmful and exploitative
Be protected from drugs
Be protected from sexual exploitation and abuse
Not be abducted, sold, or trafficked
Not be punished in a cruel or harmful way
Protected from war; not be forced to take part in a war or join the armed forces
Receive special help to recover from abuse and neglect
Fair treatment in a justice system that respects their rights; minimum age set below
which children cannot be held criminally responsible.
Full text of the CRC can be found at: http://www.2.ohchr.org/english/law/crc.htm

Figure 9.3

Summary of the UN Convention on the Rights of the Child.

Source: © United Nations High Commissioner for Human Rights.

that incorporates the full range of human rights (civil, cultural, economic, political, and social) into a single text. The convention includes basic standards that individual nations agree to pursue on behalf of children, including providing assistance to parents as they fulfill their childrearing responsibilities. These standards rest on the convention's four underlying themes:

- the right to **survival**;
- the right to **develop** to the fullest potential;
- the right to **protection** from abuse, neglect, and exploitation; and
- the right to **participate** in family, cultural, and social life.

The CRC calls on governments to develop and implement policies and programs that ensure all children will grow up in supportive family and community environments. States that are a party to the convention are obliged to develop and implement policies and programs that promote and protect children's best interests.

INTERNATIONAL HUMAN RIGHTS TREATIES

The CRC is just one example of a body of international law that is designed to protect human rights for individuals and groups of people around the world. Early examples that mark the beginning of human rights include the American Bill of Rights adopted in 1791 and the Universal Declaration of Human Rights of 1948. Other examples include the Convention on the Elimination of all Forms of Racial Discrimination, the Convention Against Torture, and the Convention on the Elimination of all Forms of Discrimination Against Women. For a complete list of international human rights instruments, please visit http://www2.ohchr.org/english/law/ housed at the UN website.

The purpose of **international human rights treaties** is to persuade nations around the world to commit to protect the rights of various vulnerable populations. Nations that ratify these treaties are asked to make a commitment to abide by them, to set goals and benchmarks, and to measure progress over time. Some critics argue that international treaties are not very effective because enforcement is weak and there are often no real consequences for violating them. Supporters disagree and believe that these treaties can be an effective mechanism in requiring nations to focus on the needs of oppressed populations, which are often ignored. They point to a number of examples in which nations have made concerted efforts to improve their domestic laws as a result of ratifying an international treaty.

Countries that are a party to the United Nations must decide whether they will ratify these international human rights treaties, which commits them to ensuring that their own domestic laws are compatible with the treaties. The United States has ratified a number of these treaties (e.g., the Convention on the Prevention and Punishment of the Crime of Genocide, the Convention on the Elimination of all Forms of Racial Discrimination, the Convention Against Torture) but has not yet ratified others (e.g., the Convention on the Elimination of all Forms of Discrimination Against Women, the Convention on the Rights of the Child). It is noteworthy that 193 counties have ratified the CRC, making it the most widely ratified treaty. Figure 9.4 describes the steps involved with ratifying an international treaty.

Human Rights & Justice

Practice Behavior Example: Recognize the global interconnections of oppression and be knowledgeable about theories of justice and strategies to promote human and civil rights.

Critical Thinking Question: Some critics have alleged that international social work is a neglected area of practice in the United States. Should social workers learn more about global issues facing people in other countries, or should they focus mainly on social problems at home?

1. Signing by the president
2. Transmittal to the U.S. Senate by the president
3. Referral to the Senate Committee on Foreign Relations
4. Senate Committee recommends approval to ratify (may include reservations, which modify U.S. obligations without changing the treaty language)
5. Two-thirds of Senate approves ratification of treaty
6. Ratification by the president

Figure 9.4

Steps Involved in Ratifying an International Treaty.

THE CONTROVERSY OVER THE CRC IN THE UNITED STATES

Starting in 1979, over a 10-year period, child welfare experts from around the world (government and nongovernmental organizations, or NGOs) worked on drafting the language of the CRC. They wanted to set forth basic standards that nations would agree to pursue on behalf of children in their country and to create a human rights treaty that outlines the basic rights and protections of children, no matter which country they live in. The CRC was adopted by the UN General Assembly in 1989 and was instituted in international law in 1990. In the early 1990s, several attempts were made in the U.S. Congress to ratify the CRC; however, these attempts were ultimately unsuccessful. In 1990, resolutions were adopted in the U.S. House and Senate; however, President George H. W. Bush failed to sign or pursue ratification of the CRC due to concerns about the CRC's impact on state and federal laws, U.S. sovereignty, and parental rights.

In 1994, another CRC resolution was introduced in the Senate by Senator Bill Bradley (D-NJ), along with 54 cosponsors. The following year, the White House issued a press release stating that President Clinton would sign the CRC and send it to the Senate for advice and consent to ratification. On February 16, 1995, Madeleine Albright signed the CRC on behalf of the United States. However, it soon faced political opposition from the Right. Jesse Helms exclaimed that as long as he was chairman of the Senate Committee on Foreign Relations, he would do everything he could to prevent the CRC from being given a hearing. He went as far as introducing a separate resolution (S. RES. 133), in the 104th Congress, along with 26 cosponsors, urging the president not to support the CRC because it is "incompatible with the God given right and responsibility of parents to raise their children" and because "the United States Constitution is the ultimate guarantor or rights and privileges to every American, including children" (S. RES 133, 1995). The strong opposition from several members of Congress prevented the Clinton administration from moving forward. The George W. Bush administration opposed the CRC and argued that it conflicted with U.S. laws regarding family rights and privacy.

Even though the CRC has widespread support from child welfare experts and advocates, there are some who view it as extremely controversial. It has been described by the Home School Legal Defense Association (HSLDA) as "the most dangerous attack on parental rights ever." According to the HSLDA, the CRC would "undermine families by granting to children a list of radical rights. . . . These new radical rights would include the right to privacy, the right to freedom of thought and association, and the right to freedom of expression" (2002). Groups such as Focus on the Family and the Christian Coalition have joined the HSLDA in working to defeat passage of the CRC.

In 2002, the United States decided to ratify the two optional protocols in lieu of ratifying the entire CRC. These two protocols are the Optional Protocol on the Sale of Children, Child Prostitution, and Child Pornography, which protects the rights and interests of children affected by these issues, and the Optional Protocol on the Involvement of Children in Armed Conflict, which states that children under age 18 should not be recruited or required to enter the armed forces. As of 2012, the CRC has been ratified by all UN member countries except the United States and Somalia.

As of 2010, the CRC has been ratified by 193 countries who are a party to the United Nations; only the United States and Somalia have not.

WHAT IS THE PROBLEM THAT THE CRC IS ADDRESSING?

It is not a surprise to most social workers that there is much room for improvement when it comes to measures of child well-being in the United States and around the world. Because children are not a strong voting bloc and rely on adults for their care and protection, their needs are often neglected, and problems facing children are often not prioritized by policy makers. Living conditions of children in developing countries are cause for serious concern; however, many Americans would be surprised to learn about the numerous challenges facing children in the United States, the richest country in the world.

Poverty and Hunger

According to researchers from the National Center for Children in Poverty (NCCP), children are overrepresented among the nation's poor (Addy & White, 2012). In 2010, they were 24% of the population yet comprised 34% of all Americans living in poverty. They are over twice as likely as adults aged 65 and older to live in poor families. Among all children under 18, 44% (31.9 million) live in low-income families and approximately one in every five (15.5 million) live in poor families. The poverty rate for children has worsened in recent years. Data reported by NCCP shows that the number of children living in poverty increased by 17% between 2005 and 2010. Black, American Indian, and Hispanic children are disproportionately poor. Together, they represent 38% of all children but more than one-half (54%) of low-income children. They are more than twice as likely to live in a low-income family compared to White and Asian children. In 2010:

- 31% of Asian children (1.0 million) lived in low-income families.
- 31% of White children (12.1 million) lived in low-income families.
- 63% of American Indian children (0.4 million) lived in low-income families.
- 63% of Hispanic children (10.7 million) lived in low-income families.
- 64% of Black children (6.5 million) lived in low-income families.

The United States ranks highest in levels of child poverty when compared to 17 wealthy industrialized countries. The United States has been criticized for not doing more to decrease child poverty through government spending on family and social benefits. For example, countries like Finland, Norway, Sweden, and France are able to reduce their child poverty rates substantially through government spending (Mishel, Bernstein, & Shierholz, 2008/2009).

Child Abuse and Neglect

A primary measure of child well-being is the prevalence of child abuse and/or neglect in a society. A previous section "Child Maltreatment in the United States" provides an overview of this social problem in the United States, including the latest child abuse statistics.

Human Rights & Justice

Practice Behavior Example: Understand that each person, regardless of position in society, has basic human rights, such as freedom, safety, privacy, an adequate standard of living, health care, and education.

Critical Thinking Question: After learning about the UN Convention on the Rights of the Child, what is your opinion? Should the United States ratify this treaty? Why or why not?

Infant Mortality

Infant mortality refers to children who die before the age of 1. According to a 2007 UN report, the United States ranks 33rd in the world on this measure of child well-being. The latest report shows the infant mortality rate of the United States at 6.6 deaths per 1,000 live births compared to Japan's 3.2, Sweden's 3.3, France's 4.4, and Canada's 5.1. Many are quite surprised to learn that the richest country in the world ranks so poorly on measures of infant mortality compared to other Western, industrialized countries. According to experts, a significant risk factor is the high number of preterm births, which has increased rapidly in the United States in recent years.

Health

According to the National Center for Children in Poverty, 17% of poor children lack health insurance, whereas 10% of all children (poor and nonpoor) lack health insurance. In the 10 most populated states, the percentage of poor children who lack health insurance ranges from 9% in Michigan to 31% in Florida (Wight, Chau, & Aratani, 2010). Again, the United States is an outlier when it comes to this measure of child well-being because virtually every other Western, industrialized country provides health insurance for children.

WHY HAS THE UNITED STATES FAILED TO RATIFY THE CRC?

Many who first learn about the CRC immediately want to understand why the United States has failed to ratify this human rights treaty for children when 193 nations around the world have done so. The first answer is that there is a rather lengthy review process in the United States, and the U.S. government typically considers one international treaty at a time. For example, the **Convention on the Prevention and Punishment of the Crime of Genocide** took more than 30 years to be ratified in the United States, and the **Convention on the Elimination of All Forms of Racial Discrimination (CERD)** was ratified 28 years after being signed by President Johnson. If the treaty is controversial (or depicted as such), it can become politicized, which often lengthens the process even more.

    Widespread misconceptions about the CRC's intent and potential impact have created obstacles to moving the CRC ahead expeditiously. For example, opponents of the CRC have pitted children's rights against parents' rights and have argued that if the United States ratifies the CRC, children will be able to get an abortion without their parents' consent, the government will tell parents how they should raise their children, schools would be required to distribute contraceptives, and children will be allowed to choose their own religion and sue their parents. Supporters of the CRC have tried to correct these misconceptions and explain that the CRC includes language that speaks of the pivotal role that parents play in their children's lives. For example, in emphasizing the primacy and importance of the role and authority of parents, the treaty calls for governments to respect the responsibilities, rights, and duties of parents to provide direction and guidance to their children. However, these misconceptions have resulted in opposition to the treaty within the U.S. Senate and in some sectors of the general public.

Finally, some policy makers do not like the idea of ratifying international treaties and believe that doing so threatens U.S. national and state sovereignty. In other words, they do not like the idea that an international treaty could supersede national, state, and local laws. There are a number of areas where the CRC may conflict with U.S. laws and philosophy, particularly in the areas of ensuring that all children have access to health care as well as laws that govern juvenile justice and education.

THE EMERGENCE OF THE CAMPAIGN FOR U.S. RATIFICATION OF THE CRC

As a result of this stalemate, child welfare advocates in the United States had to figure out a plan to move the CRC forward. Through the leadership of the CWLA, a core group of advocates convened the first meeting of the Campaign for U.S. Ratification of the CRC in August 2002. Participants focused on efforts needed to build a national coalition. Then in 2003, representatives from more than 50 U.S. nongovernmental organizations met in Washington, DC, for a 2-day strategy session titled, "Moving the CRC Forward in the United States." Out of this effort, the Campaign for U.S. Ratification of the CRC was born. One of the cochairs of the campaign is social worker Martin Scherr.

> **Advocacy Tip**
>
> **Coalition building** is an advocacy strategy that can be very useful because it demonstrates "power in numbers" and allows groups to share their resources and expertise.

Today, the campaign hosts a professional website full of information about the CRC (http://childrightscampaign.org) and has over 200 members made up of academics, attorneys, child and human rights advocates, educators, members of religious and faith-based communities, physicians, social workers, representatives from nongovernmental organizations, students, and other concerned citizens (see Figure 9.5).

Early on, the focus of the campaign was to educate the public and raise awareness of the CRC because most Americans are unaware of this human rights treaty for children. A series of events were planned for this purpose. In the spring of 2006, the CRC campaign convened its first national summit, "Convention on the Rights of the Child: Mobilizing Communities for Ratification," on the campus of American University in Washington, DC. This event was attended by over 300 individuals, including 100 youth from 29 states, Puerto Rico, and 11 countries. Professionals working in the civil and human rights, educational, legal, medical, religious, and social services fields were present at the summit alongside youth from Covenant House, Homeschoolers UN Club, High School for Human Rights (Brooklyn, NY), and the Children's Theater Company. Participants took part in and attended

---

The sole mission of the campaign is to work towards the ratification of the CRC in the United States. Its efforts include mobilizing a diverse network of supporters, educating the public about the CRC in order to build support in communities across the country, and advocating for the CRC directly with federal lawmakers. Visit its website at: www.childrightscampaign.org

---

Figure 9.5

Campaign for U.S. Ratification of the UN Convention on the Rights of the Child.

Sometimes organizations will organize a **congressional briefing** in order to educate lawmakers and/or members of their staff about a particular issue. Some briefings have even involved showing a compelling documentary film.

various workshops, panels, plenary sessions, and artistic presentations designed to educate individuals on the CRC, implications of U.S. ratification, best practice models for advancing children's rights, and how to organize efforts at the local, state, and national levels.

Next, the campaign cohosted a U.S. Senate Briefing on Juvenile Justice in April 2007 along with the following sponsors: Georgetown University's Center for Juvenile Justice Reform and Systems Integration, the Children and Family Justice Center at Northwestern University School of Law, the Juvenile Justice Initiative of Illinois, and the National Juvenile Justice Network. Speakers included individuals from the UN Committee on the Rights of the Child, the Center for Children's Law and Policy, the University of Chicago Law School, and Georgetown University.

In celebration of Universal Children's Day and the CRC's 18th Anniversary, local and state CRC briefing days were convened at universities across the country in November, 2007. Over 800 individuals attended these events, which were held in the following cities: Atlanta, Boston, Denver, Hartford, Honolulu, Los Angeles, New Orleans, New York City, Suffern (suburban NYC), and Washington, DC. Participants included academics, legal and health care professionals, social workers, representatives from child advocacy and humanitarian organizations, students, elected officials, and members of the media. Topics discussed ranged from education, health, juvenile justice, poverty, and welfare to the historical importance of the treaty and the need for and impact of U.S. ratification.

In commemoration of the 19th anniversary of the adoption of the Convention on the Rights of the Child by the UN General Assembly, the campaign convened its second U.S. Senate Briefing, "Children's Health Issues and the Convention on the Rights of the Child." This initiative was cohosted by the American Academy of Pediatrics (AAP), American Psychological Association (APA), and CWLA. The briefing was moderated by an attorney with the American Bar Association Center on Children and the Law.

The next major event for the campaign included organizing a national symposium on June 1–2, 2009, in Washington, DC, at the Georgetown University Law Center. This event was cosponsored by the Georgetown University Law Center's Juvenile Justice Clinic. The focus of the symposium, "The Convention on the Rights of the Child: Why It Is Time to Ratify," was to look at the convention through the lens of its impact on U.S. children. The symposium brought together a multidisciplinary group of experts representing the fields of child and human development, education, health/medicine, law, psychology, public policy, and social work.

Practice Activity 9.2

Visit the website of the campaign (childrights-campaign.org), and review campaign materials and other information on the website. Having a good website is crucial for most advocacy organizations and campaigns in order to get their message out and educate the public. What do you like about the campaign's website? What would make this website more effective, in your opinion?

WHAT IS THE CURRENT STATUS OF THE CRC IN THE UNITED STATES?

In order for the United States to ratify an international treaty, the president must send it to the U.S. Senate, and two-thirds of the Senate must consent—that is, 67 "yes" votes. Thus, it needs to have the support of the president and two-thirds of the Senate. The campaign for the CRC was hopeful that this might be possible with the election of President Obama in 2009. The campaign is currently using the following strategies to try to get the United States to ratify the CRC:

- Actively lobbying members of the U.S. Senate;
- Using the campaign website to inform the public about the CRC (www .childrightscampaign.org). Its website has a whole host of campaign materials under "resources" tab that people can use to educate others about the CRC, including an information packet, a one-page summary, myths and facts on the CRC, a campaign brochure, campaign flyers, key points on the CRC, fact sheets, and more.
- Getting people and organizations to become members of the campaign and to join its email listserv; this is a great example of coalition building!
- Encouraging members to engage in community outreach and education;
- Encouraging members to write letters to the editor and op-eds in area newspapers (see newspaper op-ed example below);
- Encouraging members to write their U.S. Senators;
- Encouraging members to enact state and local resolutions; and
- Assisting members in doing these various activities (e.g., writing letters; passing resolutions) by posting an advocacy toolkit on its website, which people can download (includes a number of templates so that people do not have to reinvent the wheel).

Policy Practice

Practice Behavior Example: Collaborate with colleagues and clients for effective policy action.

Critical Thinking Question: Take some time to critically evaluate the tactics and strategies used by the campaign. Looking at the tactics checklist, which unchecked items would you propose tackling if you were working on this campaign? Which unchecked items do you think would be most helpful in helping this campaign reach its goals?

Example of Newspaper Op-ed

It is time to make children a national priority in the United States

Each April, the president proclaims National Child Abuse Prevention Month. This month, President Barack Obama will uphold this tradition, presenting us with an opportunity to reflect on the well-being of children in our state and what we can do to protect children from abuse, neglect, and sexual exploitation.

This month, we should pause to consider why the richest country in the world:

- Had 754,000 victims of child abuse or neglect in 2010.
- Passively accepts the fact that 19% of children live in families that are officially poor.

- Ranks highest in levels of child poverty when compared to 17 wealthy industrialized countries.
- Ranks 33rd in the world in infant mortality (i.e., children who die before the age of 1).

Child maltreatment in the United States is not a new social problem. Federal and state governments have often failed children by allowing millions of them to forgo health care coverage and attend highly segregated, substandard schools, and by looking the other way when they are abused by powerful people and institutions. It's hard to believe that our nation had a Society for the Prevention of Cruelty to Animals before

(continued)

a Society for the Prevention of Cruelty to Children. A fully funded, formalized child welfare system was not in place in the United States until the 1970s, when the Child Abuse Prevention and Treatment Act was passed and significant levels of federal dollars were dedicated to aiding states in the investigation and treatment of child abuse. It's easy to feel overwhelmed by the problem of child abuse in light of recent horror stories in our state, including a 3-year-old who was beaten and starved to death; a 12-year-old who was raped by her father, who videotaped the abuse; a man who forced his 13-year-old relative to have sex with men in order to support his drug habit; and a 16-year-old who died from an untreated urinary tract blockage because his parents believe in "faith healing." But there are a few concrete steps that could be taken that would make a huge difference in the lives of the nation's children:

- Obama should convene a White House conference on children; no such conference has been held since 1970.
- The U.S. Senate should take steps to ratify the U.N. Convention on the Rights of the Child; the United States is one of only two countries in the world that has not ratified this celebrated human rights treaty for children.
- Raise the salaries of our nation's child-protection caseworkers and mandate that they have a social work or related degree. This is a stressful, demanding occupation that requires extensive knowledge and skills in risk assessment and intervention methods. Abused children deserve to have a highly qualified caseworker.

Call or write your U.S. Senators and tell them that you're tired of politicians who pay lip service to "family values," echoing that "children are our future," while the share of federal and state spending on children continues to plummet. Urge them to prioritize the needs of children by advocating for a White House Conference on Children and the ratification of the U.N. Convention on the Rights of the Child. Urge them to make child welfare prevention a serious priority in this country by funding proven strategies such as early childhood education and home visiting programs. Remind them that in the words of former author and activist Pearl S. Buck, "If our American way of life fails the child, it fails us all."

Tactics Used to Get the CRC Ratified

- ☑ Coalition building

- ☑ Earned media (letters to the editor, actions that lead to media coverage)

- ☐ Paid media (paying for TV/radio ads)

- ☐ Visibility (rallies, marches)

- ☐ Political dissent (e.g., civil disobedience, protest)

- ☐ Providing testimony in a legislative committee hearing

- ☑ Direct lobbying (in-person lobby visits; sometimes by a professional lobbyist)

- ☑ Grassroots lobbying (e.g., urging people to call, write, and email legislators)

- ☑ Educational outreach (town halls, house parties, community forums)

- ☐ Online advocacy (using social media)

- ☐ Paid communication (paid staff who call voters, materials mailed out)

- ☐ Fund-raising activities

President Obama has indicated his overall support for the objectives of the CRC and has stated that his administration would conduct a legal review of the treaty. At her confirmation hearing, Susan Rice, the U.S. permanent representative to the United Nations, reiterated this commitment to reviewing the CRC but did not indicate how long this process would take.

CASE EXAMPLE: SOCIAL WORK STUDENTS AT PACIFIC UNIVERSITY, OREGON. THINK GLOBALLY, ACT LOCALLY

During the Spring of 2008, social work undergraduate students, in a course titled "Macro Social Work," embarked on a class project with the goal of increasing awareness of the CRC in the greater Portland, Oregon, area. Students broke out into three groups. One group focused on community education by creating a MySpace page, canvassing in the community and handing out literature, and getting an op-ed published in a community newspaper. One group organized a forum at Portland State University and invited community members and child welfare professionals who were likely to be interested in this topic. The third group set out to get a resolution passed by the Portland City Council.

> **Advocacy Tip**
>
> One strategy that can be used to pressure federal lawmakers to pass a piece of legislation is to **pass a resolution** at the state or local level urging the U.S. Congress to pass said legislation (see case example).

The first step in getting a resolution passed was finding a Portland City Council member who would be interested in sponsoring the resolution. Students did some research on the city council members and found out that there was a connection between the university and one of the council members because there were two Pacific University alumni who work in the council's office. Students then contacted the office of council member Randy Leonard and arranged a meeting with one of his staff members to discuss the resolution.

At this meeting, students brought materials on the CRC to share with the staff member and gave a brief overview of the issue. Students explained how similar resolutions have been passed in other cities and states in the United States. Students then requested that Commissioner Leonard sponsor this resolution. The students later heard from Commissioner Leonard's office that he had agreed to sponsor the resolution.

The next step was writing the resolution and crafting language that would be most appropriate for this local city resolution. Luckily, the Campaign for the Ratification of the CRC had a sample resolution that cities and states could use as a template and then tailor to their own needs. Students used this template but included some facts and figures related to the welfare of children in Portland, Oregon. Students stayed in good communication with Commissioner Leonard's office throughout the process and sent them the resolution after the students agreed on a final version. Students were then told when they were scheduled to speak to the Portland City Council.

It was agreed that two students would address the Portland City Council because they were most comfortable doing public speaking. However, ahead of time, these students prepared their remarks and practiced. Everything went very smoothly on the day the students addressed the city council. They read their prepared remarks and answered a couple of questions from the city council members, and then the council voted unanimously to pass the resolution. A photo of two students testifying before the Portland City Council and a copy of the resolution that passed (Figure 9.6) are provided here.

RESOLUTION No.   3 6 6 0 4

Urge the United States Congress to pass binding legislation that ratifies the United Nations Convention on the Rights of the Child. (Resolution)

WHEREAS, In Oregon children are still 5% more likely to live below the poverty line than the general population, a trend that has existed for over eight years; and

WHEREAS, In a recent United Nations study of the 21 wealthiest nations, the United States ranged 20th in child welfare; and

WHEREAS, Globally, an average of 26,000 children under the age of five die every day, mostly due to preventable causes; and

WHEREAS, After almost twenty years the United States remains one of the two countries still needed to ratify the United Nations Convention on the Rights of the Child; and

WHEREAS, Portland has already adopted a Bill of Rights for Children and this resolution would be the first step in expanding these rights to all children; and

WHEREAS, Oregon's Congressional delegation should unite in support of the binding legislation proposed by the United Nations Convention on the Rights of the Child to help ensure the mental, physical, and emotional prosperity of all children everywhere.

NOW, THEREFORE BE IT RESOLVED, that the Council of the City of Portland, on behalf of the people of Portland, urges the United States Congress to ratify the United Nations Convention on the Rights of the Child; and

BE IT FURTHER RESOLVED, that a suitable copy of this resolution shall be sent to George W. Bush, President of the United States, and the members of the Oregon Congressional delegation.

Adopted by the Council: **Gary Blackmer**
                        MAY 1 4 2008   Auditor of the City of Portland
                                              By:

Commissioner Randy Leonard
Mayor Tom Potter, Commissioner Sam
Adams, Commissioner Dan Saltzman
Sara Petrocine :sp   Deputy
May 6, 2008

Figure 9.6

STATE-LEVEL CHILD WELFARE ADVOCACY EFFORTS

The CRC is a great example of a policy at the international level that can effect positive change for children. But there are countless examples of legislation that get passed at the state and local level that are aimed at improving the lives of children served by the child welfare system. Large government bureaucracies are designed to provide stability and, by the same token, resist sudden changes. Because of this tendency to re-sist change, large systems often need to be helped (or forced) to change their practices so that they are able to operate in the best interests of the

Social work students from Pacific University Oregon, Jean Laschever and Celeste Goulding, testifying before the Portland City Council, May 2008.

individuals they serve. Nongovernmental or nonprofit advocacy organizations are crucial to ensuring that this happens, and one way they do this is by passing legislation.

For 35 years, the Juvenile Rights Project (JRP) has advocated for children in the foster care system in Oregon. In 2010, JRP changed its name to Youth, Rights & Justice, Attorneys at Law. According to its mission statement, "Youth, Rights & Justice" is dedicated to improving the lives of vulnerable children and families through legal representation and advocacy in the courts, legislature, schools and community. Their executive director is Mark McKechnie who has a master's degree in social work (see Illustration 9.2).

Large systems often need to be helped (or forced) to change their practices so that they are able to operate in the best interests of the individuals they serve.

Because Youth, Rights, and Justice's mission is to advocate for foster youth, in recent years it has focused on a couple of issues that were causing problems for these youth served by the state child welfare system: (a) the fact that foster youth change schools so often, which hampers their success in school; and (b) the problem of relative caregivers not being given the same financial support that foster parents receive. Two recent legislative wins for JRP are discussed next.

Educational Stability of Foster Youth

JRP drafted and successfully lobbied for the passage of House Bill 3075, which focused on addressing the problem of foster youth changing schools multiple times, the result of multiple foster care moves. JRP had observed how

Illustration 9.2

disruptive this was for foster children and how this instability led to poor educational outcomes. HB 3075:

1. Amended ORS 339.133, Oregon's school district residency requirements, to permit a child in foster care to remain in the school he or she attended prior to placement in foster care, or prior to a move between foster homes, if it is in the child's best interest as determined by the juvenile court.

2. Requires the placing agency (the state child welfare agency) to provide transportation for the child when the court determines he or she should attend the school he or she attended prior to placement. School districts were not required by this legislation to provide transportation across district lines.

3. Requires a preference to place a child in a foster home that can maintain his or her educational stability in addition to the existing statutory preference for placement with a relative.

4. Requires schools to request and send the records of a new student more quickly when the student is in foster care (5 days to request and 5 days to send versus the current requirement of 10 days to request and 10 days to send).

Supporting Relative Caregivers of Children in Foster Care

Before the passage of Senate Bill 282, many relative foster parents in Oregon were denied foster care support payments because the statute in Oregon defined foster care as being provided by someone who had no blood or legal relationship to the child. The state law meant that only relatives caring for children eligible for federal foster care support under Title IV-E would receive basic financial support for the child's room, board, and clothing. SB 282 eliminated this distinction so that Oregon would be allowed to follow best practices and the latest research, which finds that children placed with relatives fare better than other foster children on a number of key measures. Kinship care offers children more stability and preserves their connection to their family, culture, and community.

SB 414 was a companion bill to SB 282, and included a number of revised policies to improve services to children and families served by the Department of Human Services (DHS) such as: (a) requiring DHS to make diligent efforts to place children with relatives and to place siblings in foster care together in the same foster homes whenever possible; (b) encouraging frequent, quality visitation between children and their parents and allowing the juvenile court to order specific visitation plans; and (c) encouraging other research-based child welfare practices such as consistent contact between children and their caseworkers, and a heightened focus on the educational needs of children in foster care.

Professional Identity

Practice Behavior Example: Commit themselves to the profession's enhancement and to their own professional conduct and growth.

Critical Thinking Question: What is your opinion on the usefulness of international treaties like the CRC? Should social workers be engaged in doing policy work on the international stage, or would they have more impact on the local level?

FINAL THOUGHTS

In summary, this chapter demonstrates that in every social work field of practice, there are opportunities to impact the legislative process at multiple levels from the local level to the international level. Some social workers prefer to work locally, whereas others enjoy working on the national or international stage. This is good news for social workers because it provides an array of opportunities to choose from in their ongoing work to effect positive change on behalf of the individuals and families that they serve.

The following questions will test your knowledge of the content found within this chapter. For additional assessment, including licensing-exam type questions on applying chapter content to practice behaviors, visit **MySearchLab**.

1. According to the Child Welfare League of America (CWLA), less than _____ of staff in state child welfare agencies have a formal social work education.

   a. one-quarter

   b. one-third

   c. one-half

   d. three-quarters

2. The two countries that have not ratified the UN Convention on the Rights of the Child are:

   a. the United States and Ghana

   b. Iran and China

   c. the United States and Afghanistan

   d. the United States and Somalia

3. For the United States to ratify an international treaty, it requires:

   a. the approval of the president and two-thirds of the U.S. Senate

   b. a bill to pass in the U.S. Senate and House of Representatives

   c. the approval of the U.S. Supreme Court

   d. the approval of the president by executive order

4. Which of the following statements is true about the UN Convention on the Rights of the Child?

   a. It states that children's rights should be paramount in comparison to parents' rights.

   b. It is unusual that it has taken so long to get ratified compared to other human rights treaties.

   c. Most Americans are very familiar with the UN Convention on the Rights of the Child.

   d. It outlines basic human rights a child should have regardless of what country he or she resides in.

5. According to data from the U.S. Children's Bureau, the most common type of child maltreatment is:

   a. physical abuse

   b. sexual abuse

   c. neglect

   d. psychological abuse

6. After learning about the story of the U.S. Campaign to Ratify the CRC and its political tactics, what is at the heart of its strategy?

   a. Political dissent

   b. Paid media

   c. Coalition building

   d. Direct lobbying

7. There are a number of bills pending in Congress that are designed to improve the well-being of children in the United States. Do research on one of these bills to find out the goals and specifics of the legislation: The White House Conference on Children; the Education Begins at Home Act and/or Early Support for Families Act; the Improving Nutrition for America's Children Act of 2010.

Reinforce what you learned in this chapter by studying videos, cases, documents, and more available at **www.MySearchLab.com**.

Watch and Review

Watch these Videos

* Grandmothers Raising Grandchildren

Read and Review

Read these Cases/Documents

Δ The Impact of Childhood Trauma on Development

Δ Crisis and Kinship in Foster Care

* Keating-Owen Child Labor Act of 1916

* United Nations Universal Declaration of Human Rights (1948)

Explore and Assess

Explore these Assets

* Website: Child Abuse Prevention Network
* Website: Children's Defense Fund
* Website: Children's Rights
* Website: Child Welfare League of America

Research these Topics

Child Welfare Legislation

International Human Rights Treaties

What Is the UN Convention on the Rights of the Child?

Assess Your Knowledge

Go to **MySearchLab** to test your knowledge of key topics in this chapter with topic-specific quizzes. Conclude your assessment by completing the chapter exam.

---

* = CSWE Core Competency Asset Δ = Case Study

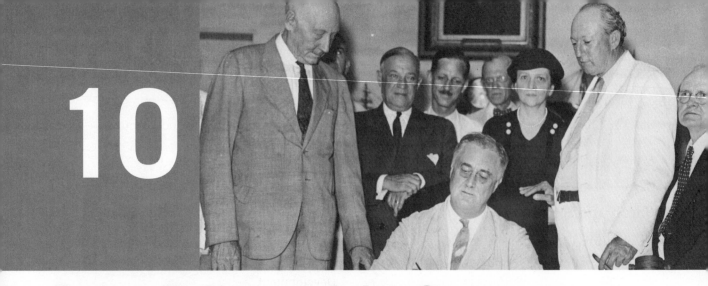

10

Aging Policy and the Controversy Over End-of-Life Policies

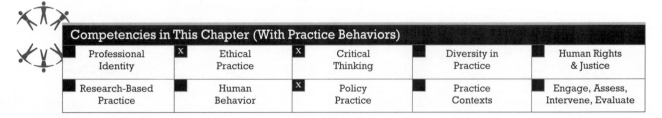

Competencies in This Chapter (With Practice Behaviors)				
Professional Identity	X Ethical Practice	X Critical Thinking	Diversity in Practice	Human Rights & Justice
■ Research-Based Practice	■ Human Behavior	X Policy Practice	■ Practice Contexts	Engage, Assess, Intervene, Evaluate

Death is not the greatest of evils; it is worse to want to die, and not be able to.

—*Sophocles, Greek playwright*

Social workers who work in the field of aging know firsthand the many challenges faced by individuals as they grow older and leave the workforce. However, in contrast to children, seniors are a strong and organized voting bloc with the ability to mobilize and advocate for themselves in the social and political spheres. According to the Administration on Aging, in 2009, the number of adults age 65 and older was 39.6 million; this represented almost 13% of the population, or one in eight Americans. However, the proportion of older adults in the United States will continue to grow in the coming years as the baby boomers begin to retire en masse. Current estimates indicate that by 2030, older adults will total 72.1 million, almost twice their number in 2008 (Administration on Aging, 2010). This is one of the most pressing social issues because "**the graying of America**" will soon begin to stress federal programs that are set up to meet the needs of older Americans. Policy makers need to carefully consider whether current programs will be able to meet the needs of these new retirees, and social workers certainly have an important role to play in these policy discussions.

POLICIES AFFECTING OLDER ADULTS

Potential problems facing older adults include lack of income security and poverty; deteriorating health, including mental health; the need for affordable housing and caregiver support; elder abuse; discrimination in the workplace; and issues of death and dying, which is the focus of this chapter. Each of these is an opportunity for advocates to help address the needs of older adults in the legislative arena. According to the Administration on Aging (2010), almost 3.4 million older adults (8.9%) were below the poverty level in 2009 and another 2.1 million or 5.4% were classified as "near-poor." See Figure 10.1 for examples of important U.S. legislation affecting older adults, including the founding of advocacy organizations such as the American Association of Retired Persons (AARP) and the Gray Panthers.

Social Security Act of 1935

American Association of Retired Persons founded, 1958

First White House Conference on Aging, 1961

Medicare and Medicaid established as part of Social Security Act, 1965

Older Americans Act (1965), passed by Congress to help each state develop a comprehensive and coordinated network that would provide services, opportunities, and protections for older Americans to help them maintain health and independence in their homes and to be able to continue to function as a part of their community. Established Administration on Aging.

Age Discrimination in Employment Act, 1967

Gray Panthers founded by Maggie Kuhn, 1970

Oregon's Death with Dignity Act, 1994

Washington State's Death with Dignity Act, 2008

Figure 10.1
Advocacy Organizations and Significant Legislation Affecting Older Adults.

In most states, **elder abuse** must be reported to the authorities by law, and elder abuse allegations are investigated similar to child abuse allegations. The primary difference is that older adults have more decision-making power in adult protective services cases, whereas in child protection cases, the "best interests of the child" are decided by the caseworkers and other legal officials. According to the National Center on Elder Abuse (2005), between 1 and 2 million older adults have been injured, exploited, or mistreated by someone on whom they depended for care or protection. However, it explains that this data has severe limitations because elder abuse is greatly underreported and no national data are collected. The National Center on Elder Abuse defines seven different types of elder abuse: physical abuse, sexual abuse, emotional abuse, financial exploitation, neglect, abandonment, and self-neglect. Neglect is the most common form of elder maltreatment in domestic settings (versus abuse that occurs in institutional settings) (National Center on Elder Abuse, n.d.).

THE SOCIAL SECURITY PROGRAM

Perhaps the most significant piece of legislation impacting the lives of older adults is the Social Security Act of 1935, which created the Social Security system in the United States.

Perhaps the most significant piece of legislation impacting the lives of older adults is the **Social Security Act of 1935**, which created the Social Security system in the United States. The opening chapter photo shows President Franklin Delano Roosevelt signing the Social Security Act into law, and social worker Frances Perkins, one of the architects of the Act, is standing behind him. The Social Security program is a federal entitlement program and is the largest government program in the world. According to the Congressional Budget Office (CBO), in 2010, 54 million people received Social Security benefits, totaling $706 billion dollars, which is one-fifth of the federal budget. The actual name of the program is the Old Age, Survivors, and Disability Insurance (OASDI) program. The Social Security system is actually made up of two programs: Old Age Survivors Insurance (OASI), which serves retired workers and their spouses and children (69% of recipients) as well as survivors of deceased workers (12% of recipients); and Disability Insurance (DI), which provides benefits to disabled workers and their spouses and children (19% of recipients) (Congressional Budget Office, 2010).

The philosophy of the program centers around the idea of an "**intergenerational compact**" whereby current workers in the workforce contribute to a program that funds the retirement of former workers who are now retired. The "old age" part of Social Security is a social insurance program that insures people against their own poverty after they leave the workforce. The program is funded through the payroll tax (Federal Insurance Contributions Act, or FICA tax), which is split evenly between employer and employee, and the money goes into the Social Security Trust Fund where it earns interest. When a person retires, his or her benefits are in proportion to his or her contribution. Retirement benefit calculations are based on one's average earnings during a lifetime of work under the Social Security system. For most current and future retirees, one's 35 highest years of earnings are averaged. According to the Social Security Administration, the average monthly payment at the beginning of 2011 was $1,172.00 a month, whereas the maximum payment for a worker retiring at age 66 in 2011 was $2,366.00 a month.

The Social Security system has been touted as one of the country's most effective social welfare programs for many reasons. Because Social Security is the major source of income for a majority of retirees, it successfully keeps millions of older adults above the poverty line. The poverty rate for older adults has lowered from about 40% to 10% over the past 50 years. It is a very efficient program because it costs less than one cent per dollar to administer the program. It helps the unemployment rate because when older adults leave the workforce, there are more jobs for younger workers, and it helps the economy because senior citizens remain viable consumers. Finally, it takes the financial burden away from the children and grandchildren who otherwise would be responsible for the financial support of their aging parents and/or grandparents. There is no stigma due to collecting Social Security because all Americans participate and benefit from this social program. Finally, the program adjusts for inflation, and the benefits are portable from job to job.

Social security was meant to be part of a three-legged stool (personal savings, pension, and Social Security) that Americans relied on after retirement, but for many reasons, most people rely on Social Security as a major source of income after leaving the workforce. Americans are also living much longer than they did when the program was first devised during the 1930s. Increasingly, Americans have been hearing about the "crisis" of the Social Security system due to the impending retirement of millions of baby boomers, which will cause great financial stress to the Social Security system. The trust fund is adequate when there is enough money in the fund at the beginning of the year to pay out all of the benefits owed for that year. Since the beginning of the program, this has not been a problem; in fact, in most years, there have been significant surpluses in the trust fund. In 2007 for example, OASDI had a balance of $2 trillion and owed $495 billion in benefits. For this reason, the U.S. government often borrows money from the Social Security Trust Fund when it is running a deficit. But projections estimate that the trust fund will bankrupt in the coming years because there will be too few workers in the workforce compared to those who are retired, which is referred to as the dependency ratio. The **dependency ratio** is the ratio of workers to beneficiaries. For example, in 1950, there were 16 workers for every 1 person on Social Security, and today the ratio is 3 to 1. Estimates show that this ratio will shrink to 2 to 1 by 2032.

Unless something is done, in the not too distant future the trust fund will not have enough funds to pay out to its beneficiaries. The CBO (2010) projects that the DI trust fund will be exhausted in 2018 and the OASI trust fund will be exhausted in 2042. Thus, policymakers are going to have to make some tough choices in order to keep the Social Security program solvent, some of which will be more popular than others with Americans. Potential options include: decreasing benefits for retirees, raising the retirement age, raising the payroll tax, eliminating the earning ceiling, which taxes only the first $110,100 that individuals make (this means that for someone earning $2 million a year, only his or her first $110,100 is taxed), and cutting wealthier Americans off from collecting at all (i.e., creating a means test). Some conservatives have advocated privatizing the Social Security system, but this has not been popular with a majority of Americans who are fearful about a program that relies on investments in the stock market. Thus, there are a number of ways to save the Social Security program, but strong leadership will be needed to find the right solution.

END-OF-LIFE POLICIES

When many people think about working for social change, they often visualize grassroots movements that are low in financial resources but high in passion and "people" resources. Many social workers have been a part of one of these efforts at the local or national level. However, some policy change efforts are well financed, and social workers may be hired to work on a professional campaign that is charged with getting a policy passed into law. This requires a skill-set that involves the ability to (a) frame an issue in a way that resonates with lawmakers and the public and (b) communicate that message effectively and persuasively. This chapter will profile a successful policy change effort by a professional campaign. It will also provide an opportunity for readers to examine their own values and beliefs in relation to an issue that is quite controversial and complex.

Some political issues are much more controversial than others. In recent years, conversations about **end-of-life care** have entered the national discourse, and this topic is being discussed more frequently than ever before, perhaps due to the impending retirement of millions of baby boomers. *End-of-life care* is a broad term that encompasses a range of issues such as living wills, advance directives, pain management (also referred to as palliative care), hospice care, do-not-resuscitate orders, who can make decisions for those who lack decision-making capacity (i.e., durable power of attorney), and how to help people live out their final years with dignity.

Americans saw firsthand how heated this issue can be when it emerged as a hot topic during the debate over health care reform under President Obama. A provision of the massive healthcare bill would have required the Medicare program to reimburse healthcare practitioners when consulting with patients on end-of-life care. Sarah Palin took to Facebook and referred to this provision as "death panels" made up of government bureaucrats who would have the power to decide who should live and who should die. Although the myth that the provision would encourage euthanasia was debunked by a number of reputable fact-check sites and news organizations, it caught on like wildfire and was soon used by some on the Right to scare older adults in their efforts to denounce the new health care reform legislation. Due to the controversy, Democrats were forced to drop the provision from the healthcare bill, but the Obama administration later achieved the same goal through a new Medicare regulation that went into effect on January 1, 2011.

THE DEATH WITH DIGNITY ACT

The **Death with Dignity Act** is a good example of an issue that divides Americans who have different views about whether people should have the right to end their life with a physician's assistance when they have a terminal or debilitating illness. Oregon and Washington State are the only two states in the United States to have passed physician-assisted suicide laws (though Montana's Supreme Court recently decriminalized it in that state). These state laws are part of a larger **right-to-die movement** that advocates on behalf of an individual's right to die with dignity and to make his or her own end-of-life decisions. The debate not only concerns what the laws should be but also concerns what terminology should be used. Many right-to-die activists prefer the terms *physician-assisted death*, *physician aid in dying*, or *hastened death* over *physician-assisted suicide*, which they see as a politically loaded term used by the opposition. Opponents of these laws include the American Medical Association (AMA), the Catholic church, pro-life

Policy Practice

Practice Behavior Example: Collaborate with colleagues and clients for effective policy action.

Critical Thinking Question: Framing is an important component of policy practice. Do you agree with right-to-die activists that *physician aid in dying* should be used instead of *physician-assisted suicide*? Is *suicide* an accurate descriptor, or is this language too polarizing?

Christian organizations, and disability advocacy groups. Assisted suicide is legal in a few other countries such as Belgium, Luxembourg, the Netherlands, and Switzerland, but this debate is far from over in the United States.

What Was the Impetus Behind the Death with Dignity Act?

The aid-in-dying movement is a fascinating story of a diverse range of committed individuals determined to change U.S. laws that govern whether, and under what circumstances, an individual has the right to end his or her life with the assistance of a medical professional. A number of organizations were formed to further their cause such as the Hemlock Society, Compassion in Dying, Compassion & Choices, and the Death with Dignity National Center (Figure 10.2). Members of these organizations typically include citizens who are directly affected by this issue, scholars, and medical and legal experts. Right-to-die activist Dr. Jack Kevorkian and former Washington governor Booth Gardner are examples of prominent citizens who have become the public face of this issue in recent years. A right-to-die bill was first introduced in the Florida legislature in 1967, and the Hemlock Society was formed in 1980. Oregon passed the Death with Dignity Act in 1994, and it took until 2008 for another state (Washington) to join Oregon. This is yet another example of how some policy change efforts take a long time to achieve a legislative victory. Thus, advocates often have to be patient and work year after year to raise awareness until attitudes change and a tipping point is reached.

The aid-in-dying movement is a fascinating story of a diverse range of committed individuals determined to change U.S. laws that govern whether, and under what circumstances, an individual has the right to end his or her life with the assistance of a medical professional.

What Is the Death with Dignity Act?

Two U.S. states have a Death with Dignity Act. Oregon was the first state to pass such a law, and Washington State based its law on Oregon's statute because it is considered model legislation. The law allows terminally ill patients to obtain a prescription from their physician for a lethal dose of medication. The medication must be self-administered. People unable to use the law include those with debilitating illnesses that are not terminal, such as Parkinson's disease, anyone deemed not mentally competent to make this decision, and those who are unable to self-administer the medication (e.g., those with paralysis).

To use the Oregon law, a patient must be: 18 years of age or older, an Oregon resident, able to make and communicate their own health care decisions, and diagnosed with a terminal illness with 6 months or less to live. A patient must provide the attending physician proof of Oregon residency. There is no minimum residency requirement. The attending physician must decide whether these criteria have been met.

The two organizations below work to allow people to make their own decisions regarding their end-of-life care, including policies that allow individuals under certain circumstances to hasten their own death. Please visit their websites to learn more.

The Death with Dignity National Center   www.deathwithdignity.org

Compassion & Choices   www.compassionandchoices.org

Figure 10.2

Advocacy Spotlight: End of Life.

The Oregon law requires that the patient:

- make two verbal requests—separated by 15 days—to the physician,
- make a written request to the attending physician, and the request is witnessed by two individuals who are not primary caregivers or family members,
- is able to rescind the verbal and written requests at any time, and
- is able to self-administer the prescription (lethal dose of medication is ingested).

The law further requires that:

- The attending physician must be Oregon-licensed.
- The physician's diagnosis must include terminal illness, with 6 months or less to live.
- The diagnosis must be certified by a consulting physician, who must also certify that the patient is mentally competent to make and communicate health care decisions.
- If either physician determines that the patient's judgment is impaired, the patient must be referred for a psychological examination.
- The attending physician must inform the patient of alternatives, including palliative care, hospice, and pain management options.
- The attending physician must request that the patient notify his or her next of kin of the prescription request.

The Oregon Department of Human Services (DHS) enforces compliance with the law. Physicians are required by law to report all lethal prescriptions to DHS. Physicians and patients who comply with the law are protected from criminal prosecution. The use of the Death with Dignity Act cannot affect the status of a patient's health or life insurance policies. Physicians and health care systems are not obligated to participate in Oregon's Death with Dignity Act.

One of the criticisms of the act was that people from other states would move to Oregon to use the law to hasten their death. This same accusation gets leveled at countries like Switzerland where the term **suicide tourism** has been coined to describe the phenomenon of people who visit countries where assisted suicide is legal in order to take advantage of an assisted suicide law. However, this does not seem to be the case in Oregon. According to DHS, 596 terminally ill patients used the Oregon law to hasten their own deaths between 1998 and 2011. Characteristics reveal that most patients were White (98%), had cancer (81%), and were between the ages of 55 and 84. Fifty-three percent were male. The majority of patients (95%) died at home and most (90%) were enrolled in hospice care. Only 8% were referred for a mental health evaluation. The most frequently mentioned end-of-life concerns were losing autonomy (91%), less able to engage in activities making life enjoyable (88%), loss of dignity (83%), and losing control of bodily functions (54%). The time from ingestion to death ranged from 1 minute to 104 hours, and the median was 25 minutes. In 2011, a total of 71 Oregon patients used the law to hasten their deaths. A total of 114 prescriptions for lethal medications were written that year.

The Controversy Over the Death with Dignity Act

Earlier in this book, the role of values in the political process was discussed, and the fact that many of the positions that people take on various political issues stem from their personal values or belief system. This is particularly true when it comes to the debate over physician-assisted suicide. This debate has religious overtones because much of the opposition comes from the Catholic Church and various pro-life organizations that oppose the Death with Dignity Act on moral grounds. The opposition of the Catholic Church is clearly explained in the catechism of the Catholic Church (#2277), which condemns "an act or omission which, of itself or by intention, causes death in order to eliminate suffering." Many Catholic Church leaders remind their flock that human life is sacred and of the commandment "Thou shall not kill." The Catholic Church poured large sums of money into the 2008 Death with Dignity campaign in Washington State in its efforts to defeat the measure.

Despite the fact that many physicians support this act, the medical establishment does not. Some physicians believe that assisted suicide violates the Hippocratic oath. The state medical associations in most states oppose physician-assisted suicide as does the AMA. During the debate over the Death with Dignity Act in Washington State in 2008, the president of the Washington State Medical Association stated that physician-assisted suicide is dangerous and "fundamentally incompatible with the role of physicians as healers" (Washington State Medical Association, 2008).

Another argument that is used to oppose the Death with Dignity Act is that the law will be abused by doctors and healthcare workers, and that individuals from certain vulnerable or oppressed groups will be disproportionately targeted. In particular, concerns have been raised about patients with mental health conditions such as clinical depression, and groups who may be more prone to ending their life in order to avoid being a burden to their families such as women and those with serious disabilities. The overriding fear is that certain lives are deemed as less valuable or worthy than others. Many **disability rights groups** have entered the fray in opposing the Death with Dignity Act and efforts in other states to pass assisted suicide laws. One such group is a national organization called Not Dead Yet (Figure 10.3).

Proponents of the Death with Dignity Act are just as passionate as the opposition. Most activists believe it is cruel and inhumane to let people suffer a slow, painful death. They often frame the issue as "death with dignity" because many have the experience of witnessing the passing of a loved one who was not allowed to die in a dignified manner. After the passage of the Death with Dignity Act in Washington, president of Compassion & Choices, Barbara Coombs Lee, exclaimed that the new law was "a turning point on the path to human liberty." She went on to say, "No terminal Washingtonian will ever have to shoot themselves or use other violent means again. We hope someday

> This debate has religious overtones because much of the opposition comes from the Catholic church and various pro-life organizations that oppose the Death with Dignity Act on moral grounds.

Critical Thinking

Practice Behavior Example: Requires the synthesis and communication of relevant information.

Critical Thinking Question: Summarize why many disability rights groups are opposed to legislation like the Death with Dignity Act. Do you agree with their position? Why or why not?

The organization *Not Dead Yet* strongly opposes legalized assisted suicide and the euthanasia movement. It was founded in 1996, shortly after physician Jack Kevorkian was acquitted in the assisted suicides of two women. It takes credit for helping to put Kevorkian behind bars in 1999. In 2003–2005, alongside other national disability rights groups, it fought to save Terri Schiavo and opposed her guardian's "right to starve and dehydrate her to death."

Figure 10.3

About *Not Dead Yet.*

to be able to say the same for patients in the other 48 states" (Compassion & Choices, 2008).

Advocates also believe that it should be an individual's right or choice to determine when life has become too unbearable and to end his or her suffering. They cite freedom of religion and decry the fact that certain religious institutions would force their beliefs onto others who do not share those same beliefs. However, like any social movement, not every member has the same opinions and perspective, and a small number of members have views that would be considered "on the fringe." The right-to-die movement is a broad movement, and the Death with Dignity movement is a subset of this movement. For instance, some advocates do not believe the Oregon and Washington laws go far enough and believe that people who are depressed should also be able to end their life with assistance. Others, such as the **Final Exit Network**, support the idea that it is a basic human right to end one's life when that individual's quality of life has been seriously threatened (e.g., individual does not have to be diagnosed with a terminal illness). They believe this is an individual choice that should not be restricted by "the law, clergy, medical profession, even friends and relatives no matter how well intentioned" (visit www .finalexitnetwork.org).

Advocates believe that it should be an individual's right or choice to determine when life has become too unbearable and to end his or her suffering.

When visiting the websites of the various right-to-die organizations, you will find personal testimonies of those with a terminal illness who are desperate for the right to hasten their death, as well as family members who have had to witness the prolonged suffering of a loved one. Compassion & Choices issued a press release about the first patient in Washington State, Linda Fleming, to use the Death with Dignity Act. Fleming, age 66, had a terminal illness and explained,

> The pain became unbearable, and it was only going to get worse. I am a very spiritual person, and it was very important to me to be conscious, clear-minded, and alert at the time of my death. The powerful pain medications were making it difficult to maintain the state of mind I wanted to have at my death. And I knew I would have to increase them. I am grateful that the Death with Dignity law provides me the choice of a death that fits my own personal beliefs." (Compassion & Choices, 2009)

The right to-die movement is also full of physicians, scholars, and church leaders who believe strongly in a patient's right to die with the aid of a physician. Perhaps the most famous and controversial right-to-die activist is **Dr. Jack Kevorkian** who served 8 years in prison for euthanizing a patient (see Dr. Kevorkian's picture and story). His detractors have called him "Doctor Death." He believes that the U.S. government's opposition to physician-assisted suicide is tyrannical. Dr. Kevorkian is critical of the Death with Dignity Act, a law that in his view does not go far enough because it would exclude people who cannot administer the legal drugs themselves. Many right-to-die activists view Dr. Kevorkian as a renegade and are quick to point out that he would be prosecuted under the Death with Dignity Act because he violated many of the safeguards and protocols of this law.

Former Washington governor Booth Gardner made statements that he views the Death with Dignity Act as a first step because he would be unable to take advantage of the law but cannot because he has Parkinson's disease, a debilitating disease that is not terminal. Some in this movement, such as Derek Humphry, look forward to the day when the Death with Dignity laws include more people who in his view are deserving of assisted dying, such as the law

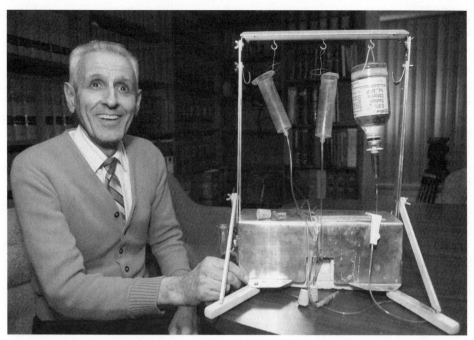

Dr. Jack Kevorkian poses with his "suicide machine" in Michigan, Feb. 6, 1991.

in the Netherlands that permits lethal prescriptions for those whose suffering is unbearable. Humphry is an important and influential person in the right-to-die movement because he was the founder of the Hemlock Society in 1980 and has published many books on the topic including the controversial and best-selling book, *Final Exit*, published in 1991.

Dr. Jack Kevorkian

Most Americans know the name Dr. Kevorkian. He is either famous or infamous, depending on one's viewpoint. Dr. Kevorkian was the first doctor in the United States to become known for his advocacy of a patient's right to die. He steadfastly believes that it is a physician's role to help people live, but also to help them die when it is their wish or desire. In his heyday, he was on the cover of major magazines like *Time Magazine*, interviewed by journalists such as Barbara Walters, and featured on news programs like *60 Minutes*. Over the course of his career, he helped 130 patients hasten their death and was tried in court several times for these actions. His medical license was revoked as well. He was always acquitted of the charges in court until he helped Thomas Youk, a patient who was suffering from Lou Gehrig's Disease. In each of Kevorkian's cases, the patients administered the medication themselves, but with Youk, Kevorkian administered the lethal injection himself (with the consent of the patient and the patient's family). He then went on *60 Minutes* where the footage of Youk's hastened death was shown on national television. He was quickly charged with first-degree murder, yet the jury found him guilty of second-degree homicide. The judge sentenced Kevorkian to serve 10–25 years in prison, but he was released after 8 years for good behavior. Upon his release, he vowed to stop his practice of physician-assisted suicide and to instead work toward the decriminalization of assisted suicide in the United States. In 2008, Kevorkian ran for the U.S. Congress in Michigan as an independent but did not win the election. An HBO movie about his life called *You Don't Know Jack* aired in 2010 with Oscar-winning actor Al Pacino playing the title role.

Illustration 10.1

I n your opinion, how should a social worker handle the following situation: Martha is a social worker in a medical clinic in Washington State where the Death with Dignity Act is law. She has a terminally ill male client who wants her help to begin the process of learning about this law and making a decision on whether or not he would like to use it to hasten his own death. The patient would like Martha's support throughout this process

because he does not have many friends and his relationships with his grown children are strained. However, due to her religious beliefs, Martha does not agree with assisted suicide and she feels very strongly about this. As a professional social worker, what are Martha's ethical obligations to her patient in this scenario? Because her personal and professional values are in conflict, how can she best sort this out?

HOW THE DEATH WITH DIGNITY ACT BECAME LAW

Some policies consist of minor tweaks or changes to existing laws. The Death with Dignity Act, however, is an example of what one might refer to as landmark legislation or a groundbreaking policy change effort. This act has the power to radically change the way society thinks about and responds to terminally ill people who wish to hasten their death with the aid of a health professional. These kinds of change efforts can take many decades before progress is made in order to change public opinion and build a movement that is able to take on more powerful interests. When the time is right, a number of possible strategies must be considered. Should social workers and advocates try to get a bill passed at the federal level? Should they try to get a bill passed at the state level? Would it make sense to use the judicial system by filing a lawsuit? How about a ballot measure and letting the voters decide? Which approach is most feasible?

Oregon's Death with Dignity Act (ODWDA)

The story begins in Oregon, in the early 1990s, when the first Death with Dignity Act was developed by a group of Oregonians with a strong interest in changing the law. Oregonians were able to learn from the experiences of two other states that lost their battles, Washington State in 1991 and California in 1992. In these two states, voters were voting on whether to allow euthanasia by lethal injection. In Washington, the initiative failed by a margin of 46% to 54%, and in California, it failed by the same exact margin. Oregon did two things differently, which seemed to make the difference. First, the Death with Dignity Act that was crafted prohibited lethal injection and active euthanasia and only allowed the patient to self-administer the lethal medication with many safeguards in place. (Figure 10.4 describes the difference between euthanasia and assisted suicide.) This had the advantage of silencing many of the critics' arguments. Secondly, Oregonians learned that in order to defeat the well-financed opposition, it would be necessary to run a professional campaign. A grassroots effort would not cut it.

The campaign was able to gather the signatures needed to get the issue on the ballot so that the voters in Oregon could decide the outcome. A **ballot initiative** is a process that allows citizens to draft legislation, place it on a

It depends on *who* performs the last act.

Euthanasia: a third party performs the act, which hastens the patient's death (e.g., patient given a lethal injection)

Assisted suicide: the person who dies hastens his or her own death (e.g., swallows an overdose of drugs)

Figure 10.4

What Is the Difference Between Euthanasia and Assisted Suicide?

ballot, and submit it to the voters to decide instead of being adopted by a state legislature. A predetermined number of signatures are needed to qualify a measure for the ballot, and the number needed varies by state. Measure 16 established the Death with Dignity Act in Oregon in November 1994 when it was approved by a narrow margin of 51% to 49%. However, that was

Advocacy Tip

A **ballot measure** is a good strategy to use when the policy is not likely to pass by the state legislature but when the public is behind it.

just the beginning of the story as opponents tried to repeal the ODWDA using a number of strategies over the next several years (Death with Dignity National Center).

- November 1994, Oregon voters approved Measure 16 by a slim margin (51% to 49%) establishing the Death with Dignity Act.*
- In December 1994, *Lee v. State of Oregon* became the ODWDA's first legal challenge. The plaintiffs in the case were doctors and patients who contended that the Oregon law violated the Constitution's First and Fourteenth Amendments. (*Lee v. State of Oregon* eventually made its way to the U.S. Supreme Court, which refused to hear the case.)
- In 1995, District Judge Hogan ruled that ODWDA violates the U.S. Constitution's Equal Protection Clause. The ruling was immediately appealed to the U.S. Circuit Court of Appeals.
- In 1997, a three-judge panel of the Ninth Circuit Appeals Court dismissed the district court's challenge to Oregon's Death with Dignity Act.
- In 1997, in two related rulings, *Vacco v. Quill* and *Washington v. Glucksberg*, the U.S. Supreme Court ruled that assisted suicide is not a constitutional right. However, according to the Court, the issue would be best addressed in the "laboratory of the states," which are free to prohibit or legalize physician-assisted dying.
- In 1997, the Oregon state legislature sent Measure 51 to voters in an attempt to repeal the Death with Dignity Act, but it was defeated by voters (60% voted against it).
- In 1997, Drug Enforcement Administration (DEA) chief Thomas Constantine stated that Oregon physicians participating under the law's guidelines would be in violation of the Controlled Substances Act.
- In 1998, Attorney General Reno issued a reversal of the DEA's position, saying that the Department of Justice would not prosecute physicians who had assisted their patients' deaths in compliance with the Oregon law.

*Death with Dignity National Center.

- In 1998, the Death with Dignity Act is implemented. During the first year of its implementation, 15 patients died after taking lethal medication.
- In 1998, congressional opponents to physician-assisted dying introduced the Lethal Drug Abuse Prevention Act (HR 4006/S 2151), designed to overturn the Oregon law. However, it did not pass due to opposition from President Clinton, healthcare organizations, and congressional legislators.
- In 1999, the U.S. House of Representatives passed the Pain Relief Promotion Act to bar physicians from prescribing medications as allowed by the ODWDA. However, it did not pass because it never made it to the floor of the U.S. Senate for a full vote.
- In 2001, U.S. Attorney General John Ashcroft attempted to block the ODWDA by authorizing DEA agents to investigate and prosecute doctors who prescribe federally controlled drugs to help terminally ill patients die.
- Over the next several years, Ashcroft's case was heard in various court cases and was eventually appealed all the way to the U.S. Supreme Court.
- On January 17, 2006, the Supreme Court voted 6 to 3 to uphold an Oregon physician-assisted suicide law in the case *Gonzales v. Oregon* (formerly *Oregon v. Ashcroft*), ruling that former attorney general John Ashcroft overstepped his authority in seeking to punish doctors who prescribed drugs to help terminally ill patients end their lives. In the decision, the Supreme Court ruled that the Oregon law has superseded federal authority to regulate physicians and that the Bush administration improperly attempted to use the Controlled Substances Act to prosecute Oregon physicians who assist in patient suicides.
- In 2006, U.S. Senator Sam Brownback introduced the Assisted Suicide Prevention Act, which would prohibit doctors from prescribing federally controlled substances for the purpose of physician-assisted suicide. Oregon Senator Ron Wyden announced that he will block the bill indefinitely through a legislative hold. The bill was eventually withdrawn.
- Five-hundred and ninety-six terminally ill patients have used the Oregon law to hasten their own deaths between 1998 and 2011.
- In 2011, HBO aired a documentary film titled *How to Die in Oregon*, winner of the 2011 Sundance Film Festival U.S. Documentary Grand Jury Award.

Washington State's Death with Dignity Act

In November 2008, Washington became the second state in the United States to pass a Death with Dignity Act. However, it was a long road to get there. The Washington law was modeled on the Oregon law because Oregon law was deemed to be model aid-in-dying legislation. The ballot measure in 2008 won by a sizeable margin, with 58% voting to approve and 42% opposed. An important lesson to be learned is that most successful policy change efforts are not achieved by individuals, but rather by an organized effort or coalition of individuals and groups working together.

Social Worker Spotlight: Peg Sandeen, MSW

Peg Sandeen, MSW, is the executive director of the Death with Dignity National Center in Portland, Oregon, a policy organization that advocates for expanded end-of-life options in the form of Death with Dignity legislation.

Sandeen has been a policy-level social worker her entire career, starting out as an intern in the Iowa House of Representatives during the final year of her master's degree. She was a multiclient lobbyist in the Iowa Statehouse for two years, working to strengthen domestic violence and sexual assault laws, as well as to promote civil rights protections for individuals from the lesbian, gay, bisexual, and transgender (LGBT) community.

In her professional capacities, as well as through personal loss, Sandeen has felt firsthand how legal and medical interaction affects people's lives in both positive and negative ways. As a result, her scholarly and professional efforts have increasingly focused on health-related ethical concerns, particularly end-of-life decisions, privacy issues, and mental health.

At the AIDS Project of Central Iowa, she was a public policy specialist (and later executive director) advocating at both the state and federal levels to achieve funding for HIV prevention and care services. As a result of her exploration of ethical, legal, and medical issues related to HIV care in social work, Sandeen was named a 2002 Price Fellow in HIV Prevention Leadership by the Centers for Disease Control and Prevention.

As a volunteer, she helped to found two LGBT-oriented groups, the Iowa Coalition for Human Rights and the Queer Youth Alliance, and she worked for the Bridges Project of the American Friends Service Committee as a research volunteer.

In her position at the Death with Dignity National Center, she led the organization through the complexities of a public opinion campaign during the U.S. Supreme Court case *Gonzales v. Oregon*. More recently, she was a member of the political strategy team that successfully worked to pass a Death with Dignity ballot initiative in the state of Washington. Her current work includes legislative and ballot initiative activities in New England.

Sandeen is currently a doctoral candidate in social work and social research at Portland State University.

Illustration 10.2

How the Washington State Death with Dignity Act Was Passed

In April 2005, the Death with Dignity National Center decided to pursue a ballot initiative in Washington State for the 2008 election. According to Eli Stutsman, one of the chief architects of the Oregon and Washington laws, "Political success demands a well framed message delivered by well chosen messengers against a well defined opponent" (Quill & Battin, 2004, p. 259). He believes that initiatives failed in other states (despite popular support) because supporters failed to run an effective, professional political campaign. The moral of the story is that if you want to win, you must organize and raise money even if public opinion is on your side. Paid media are necessary to beat a wealthy opponent. Some policy change campaigns are grassroots "outside the system" efforts; however, the Death with Dignity movement is an example of a professional campaign that was operating within the system in order to achieve a win. Various phases of the successful effort are described here.

I. A Coalition Was Formed

In February 2006, a coalition was formed, and it had its first official meeting. The coalition included the Death with Dignity National Center, Compassion & Choices, Compassion & Choices of Washington, and Dignity 2000, which was formed by former Washington governor Booth Gardner. Each of these four groups had three representatives for a total of 12 coalition members. Putting a coalition together takes a lot of time and energy and is not an easy feat. Gardner was a key person in this effort because he had name recognition and was able to put a public face on the issue due to his Parkinson's disease diagnosis. He helped the coalition early on by conducting focus groups to ensure that Oregon's law is the best policy for Washington.

Advocacy Tip

Coalition building is an advocacy strategy that can be very useful because it allows groups to share their resources and expertise. Having famous and/or influential people in your coalition can also be useful.

II. Official Campaign Was Launched

At the end of 2007, the campaign became official. The campaign was named It's My Decision Committee, and a campaign office was opened in Seattle. The Oregon Death with Dignity Political Action Fund donated $200,000 in seed money to jump-start the campaign. All of the money was raised by donors. One of the tricky parts to raising money in the early phase of a campaign is doing this under the radar without alerting the opposition. In February 2008, the campaign was renamed Yes on I-1000 (I-1000 was the name of the ballot measure that Washington voters would vote on). In May 2008, a campaign manager was hired.

III. The Death with Dignity Act Was Certified for the Ballot

The lead author of ODWDA drafted the Washington Death with Dignity Act. Over 3,600 volunteers assisted in the gathering of signatures. However, in order to gather the number of signatures needed, it was necessary for the campaign to hire paid signature gatherers, which cost the campaign roughly a quarter of a million dollars. In July 2008, Booth Gardner turned in 320,000 signatures to the secretary of state's office (100,000 more than was needed), and the proposed act was officially certified for the November 2008 ballot. The Coalition Against Assisted Suicide challenged the language of the ballot title and wanted it to include the phrase "physician-assisted suicide." Judge Wickham ruled against this challenge and explained that according to the statute, the language used should be as neutral as possible. In the ruling, the judge stated that the term is too broad and politically loaded. The language that was on the actual ballot can be seen in Figure 10.5.

IV. Money Was Raised

In September 2008, Gardner donated $300,000 to the campaign, making him the campaign's single largest donor. The Oregon Death with Dignity Political Action Fund donated $615,000 to the campaign, which was the largest check from a single organization. By the end of October 2008, the campaign raised a total of $4.8 million, far outspending the opposition.

BALLOT TITLE

Statement of Subject: Initiative Measure No. 1000 concerns allowing certain terminally ill competent adults to obtain lethal prescriptions.

Concise Description: This measure would permit terminally ill, competent, adult Washington residents, who are medically predicted to have six months or less to live, to request and self-administer lethal medication prescribed by a physician.

Should this measure be enacted into law?   Yes [] No []

BALLOT MEASURE SUMMARY

This measure would permit terminally ill, competent, adult Washington residents medically predicted to die within six months, to request and self-administer lethal medication prescribed by a physician. The measure requires two oral and one written request, two physicians to diagnose the patient and determine the patient is competent, a waiting period, and physician verification of an informed patient decision. Physicians, patients and others acting in good faith compliance would have criminal and civil immunity.

Figure 10.5
A Ballot Title.

V. Allies Lent Their Support and Endorsed the Campaign

Organizations that publicly supported Yes on I-1000 included the American Medical Student Association, the American Medical Women's Association, the Lifelong AIDS Association, the American Civil Liberties Union, the National Women's Law Center, the Washington Chapter of the National Association of Social Workers, and the Washington State Public Health Association. The position paper of the Washington State Chapter of NASW is presented in Figure 10.6.

VI. Media Campaign and the Importance of Framing the Issue

In June 2008, the Yes on I-1000 campaign hired a political consulting firm based in Tennessee to coordinate and produce all of its media efforts. It is often said that an issue is lost or won in the last 6 weeks of the campaign. During this phase, the campaign manager, pollster, and media firm work very closely in order to run an effective media campaign. Many activities are performed in order to get the campaign's message out to voters, including door knocking, radio spots, making presentations to various audiences across the state, and meeting with opinion leaders such as mayors and newspaper editorial boards in order to win endorsements. However, nothing is more effective in getting your message out than running television commercials in major metropolitan markets. The campaign ran a number of television spots in the last weeks of the campaign, which cost

Advocacy Tip: Media

Raising enough money to be able to run ads on radio and/or television means that your message will be able to reach thousands of people. This can be the difference between winning and losing an issue campaign.

Support the Death with Dignity initiative to legalize the option of assisted death for terminally ill, mentally competent adults.

ISSUE

End-of-life care has improved with the expansion of hospice programs, which are justifiably recognized as expert in the provision of palliative care to terminally ill people. However there are those who reach a point where they want an additional service not offered by hospice; they want assisted death. They want to control the manner and timing of their deaths, and they want the option whether or not they use it. Most of Dr. Kevorkian's patients were in hospice programs, and 86% of those who have used the Oregonian Death with Dignity Act were hospice patients. LAC priorities for the 2008 legislative agenda include "legislative issues related to civil rights." The option of hastened death may be regarded as the ultimate civil right.

BACKGROUND

The Hemlock Society of Washington State was founded in 1988 to promote end-of-life options for terminally ill, qualified adults. In 1990, it cosponsored a Death with Dignity initiative campaign to legalize physician-assisted death. NASW/Washington State was one of the first organizations to endorse this initiative, followed by several special-interest social work groups. In 1991, it was on the ballot and narrowly failed, 46%–54%. However the extensive support for this issue led to practice changes by oncologists and other physicians caring for the dying.

Following this effort, Oregon passed a similar law in 1994 with some modifications. It was subjected to a series of attacks by then-attorney general John Ashcroft but has been operating in exemplary fashion since 1997. Over 9 years of implementation, only 292 people have used prescriptions to hasten death, although 455 requested prescriptions. Their primary concerns were loss of autonomy (96%), decreasing ability to participate in meaningful activities (96%), and loss of dignity (76%). Less than 50% were concerned about pain control.

The Washington Hemlock Society changed its name and subsequently merged with a sister right-to-die organization to become Compassion & Choices of WA. Its mission includes advocating for "excellent end-of-life care, . . . and, for terminally ill, competent adults, aid in dying to avoid intolerable suffering."

This issue has always involved social workers and attracted their support. Social workers were members and officers of the National Hemlock Board since its formation in the 80s and continue to take leadership positions in Washington. Many if not most Washington NASW members work in medical settings, and many are involved in end-of-life care. Oregonian social workers play a key role in the practice of their law, promoting client self-determination and working with patients and their families to ensure that all other options have been explored.

Opposition to hastened death comes primarily from the religious right and anti pro-choice groups. Opposition from the hospice administration does not seem to represent their staff; the social workers and nurses providing direct care are generally supportive.

ACTION

Support for the Death with Dignity initiative is modeled on the Oregon law and will be launched in January 2008. Endorsement is by the Board of Washington/NASW following the recommendation of LAC, with publicity through currents. Education about this issue is imparted through classroom teaching, conferences, mailings, with specific reference to the role of the social worker following the successful passage of the law.

Figure 10.6

NASW/Washington Chapter, 2008 Legislative Session Position Paper.

Source: http://www.nasw-wa.org/associations/8192/files/DeathwithDignityPaper08.pdf

around \$650,000. Links to these commercials can be found at: http://www
.youtube.com/watch?v=sXZSyXB1IX4 (features a doctor whose mother
used the Oregon law to hasten her death); http://www.youtube.com/watch?
v=T-DwFmZP0Lw (responds to the No on I-1000 commercial featuring actor
Martin Sheen); and http://www.youtube.com/watch?v=sOr4rYiNsTo (features former Oregon governor Barbara Roberts).

Framing is critical in terms of communicating with the target audience
and persuading others to your side of the issue. This has to be very carefully
considered, and often focus groups and polling are used to find out the best
way to frame an issue so that the message resonates with the public. The individuals delivering the message are also key. It would not have been effective if
only right-to-die activists delivered the message. In the commercials, doctors,
nurses, and surviving family members were featured. In Washington, the issue
was framed in the following ways:

- The law is compassionate to allow terminally ill
  patients to end their suffering.
- It is based on the Oregon law, which has been proven
  safe and effective.
- There are many safeguards in place, and public
  oversight, to ensure a high standard of care (e.g.,
  competency and age requirements; written request
  by patient; two physicians' approval; waiting period; informed decision; and witness, residency
  requirement).
- The law is NOT euthanasia or mercy killing; it is
  self-administered by the patient.
- It is for people with a terminal illness only—not for
  people with chronic illness.
- The other side (e.g., the Catholic Church) is lying and
  making distortions.

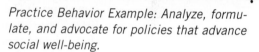

Policy Practice

*Practice Behavior Example: Analyze, formu-
late, and advocate for policies that advance
social well-being.*

Critical Thinking Question: What tactics
were most critical in passing Washington
State's Death with Dignity Act in your view?
What do you think about the use of voter
ballot initiatives in changing the laws of a
state versus laws that get passed by a state
legislature? What are the pros and cons of
this approach?

Tactics Used to Get the Death with Dignity Ballot Measure Passed Into Law

☑ Coalition building	☐ Direct lobbying (in-person lobby visits, sometimes by a professional lobbyist)
☑ Earned media (letters to the editor, actions that lead to media coverage)	☐ Grassroots lobbying (e.g., urging people to call, write, and email legislators)
☑ Paid media (paying for TV/radio ads)	☐ Educational outreach (town halls, house parties, community forums)
☐ Visibility (rallies, marches)	☐ Online advocacy (using social media)
☐ Political dissent (e.g., civil disobedience, protest)	☑ Paid communication (paid staff who call voters, materials mailed out)
☐ Providing testimony in a legislative committee hearing	☑ Fund-raising activities

The Opposition

Major opposition to Yes on I-1000 came from the **Coalition Against Assisted Suicide** (www.noassistedsuicide.com/supporters.html). This coalition consisted of a range of individuals who are opposed to assisted suicide, including doctors, nurses, hospice workers, disability rights advocates, pro-life Christian organizations, and politicians from both major parties, including the current governor of Washington, Christine Gregoire. However, the largest block of opposition came from the Catholic Church, which was also the largest financial contributor. Money was raised from Catholic parishes, dioceses, and organizations from all over the country. Initiative opponents raised and spent $1.6 million in their efforts to defeat the ballot measure. The biggest donors included Catholic groups such as the Knights of Columbus, the Washington State Catholic Conference, the Seattle Archdiocese, and the Catholic Health Association. The Washington Medical Association was also strongly opposed to I-1000 (see quote from the association's president in Figure 10.7).

The No on I-1000 campaign also had a famous face in actor Martin Sheen, known for his role as the U.S. president in the television drama *The West Wing*, and films such as *Apocalypse Now*. Sheen, whose politics usually lean Left, is a staunch Catholic. He was featured in television ads opposing I-1000 (see http://www.youtube.com/watch?v=zGLaZmOZFxo). In the ad, Sheen states that the law would endanger the poor, the disabled, and those suffering from depression. He goes on to say that "people who are ill need real medical care and compassion, not lethal drugs." Eileen Geller, campaign coordinator for the Coalition Against Assisted Suicide, says that her group will look at various options to continue the fight against the measure.

MONTANA BECOMES THE THIRD STATE TO DECRIMINALIZE PHYSICIAN-ASSISTED SUICIDE

On December 31, 2009, Montana's Supreme Court ruled in a 4 to 3 decision that doctors who help terminally ill patients hasten their death cannot be prosecuted. However, it avoided the question of whether physician-assisted

> We believe physician-assisted suicide is fundamentally incompatible with the role of physicians as healers. Patients put their trust in physicians, and that bond of trust would be irrevocably harmed by the provisions of this dangerous initiative. . . . The initiative is a dangerous distraction from symptom-directed end-of-life care that provides comfort for dying patients and their families. Our focus should remain on caring for terminally ill patients and should never shift toward helping them kill themselves.

Figure 10.7

Brian P. Wicks, MD, President, Washington State Medical Association.

Source: http://www.noassistedsuicide.com/supporters.html

suicide is a right guaranteed under the state's constitution. This makes Montana the third state in the United States to allow the practice of physician-assisted suicide. The ruling on the case was brought by the advocacy group Compassion & Choices and was filed on behalf of Robert Baxter of Billings (diagnosed with leukemia) and four physicians. Montana's state solicitor reacted by asserting that this is an issue that should be decided by the voters and state lawmakers, not by seven supreme court judges. Opponents of the decision vowed to turn to Montana's state legislature to make efforts to pass a bill that would overturn this ruling. However, in February 2011, one such attempt failed when SB 116 was voted down 7 to 5 in Montana's Senate Judiciary Committee.

Ethical Practice

Practice Behavior Example: Recognize and manage personal values in a way that allows professional values to guide practice.

Critical Thinking Question: What are your personal values and beliefs in regard to assisted suicide? Would you have a difficult time assisting terminally ill patients with making end-of-life decisions?

NEXT STEPS FOR THE DEATH WITH DIGNITY MOVEMENT

The success in Washington was a big win for the Death with Dignity movement. The Death with Dignity National Center will continue to make efforts to get the Death with Dignity Act passed in other states in the United States. Because the movement has limited resources for these campaigns, it does careful research to select states where it is sure to win. Part of this research includes public opinion polling and assessing factors such as cost, demographic profile, geography, and leadership in said state.

The following questions will test your knowledge of the content found within this chapter. For additional assessment, including licensing-exam type questions on applying chapter content to practice behaviors, visit **MySearchLab**.

1. Which of the following is true about the Social Security program in the United States?
   a. It is an inefficient and poorly run program.
   b. People who collect Social Security are stigmatized because it is a means-tested program.
   c. It keeps millions of seniors above the poverty line.
   d. It is funded by a range of taxes, including sales tax.

2. Which states have legalized physician-assisted suicide?
   a. Oregon and Washington State
   b. Oregon and Washington, DC
   c. California and Washington State
   d. California and Oregon

3. Which of the following cases would be eligible under the Death with Dignity Act?
   a. A 70-year-old man with paralysis diagnosed with Lou Gehrig's disease
   b. A 50-year-old woman diagnosed with terminal brain cancer who has less than 3 months to live according to two physicians
   c. A 63-year-old man who is suffering greatly from Parkinson's disease, a nonterminal illness
   d. An 80-year-old woman who has been diagnosed with terminal cancer and has 13 months to live

4. Which of the following statements about the campaign to pass the Death with Dignity Act is false?

   a. The campaign was successful in getting a ballot initiative passed in two states.
   b. The campaign was successful in getting a bill passed by the state legislature in two states.
   c. The campaign raised money in order to run a professional media campaign.
   d. The campaign used coalition building as a strategy in order to win.

5. According to this chapter, the largest block of funding from those opposing the Death with Dignity Act came from:
   a. the Mormon Church
   b. the health care industry, including the AMA
   c. pro-life politicians
   d. the Catholic Church

6. The dependency ratio is an important concept that helps explain the future financial stress to the Social Security system. This refers to:
   a. the ratio of children to adults in the United States
   b. the ratio of employees to employers in the United States
   c. the ratio of workers to people collecting Social Security
   d. the ratio of employed workers to unemployed workers in the United States

7. The Washington Chapter of the National Association of Social Workers supported the Death with Dignity Act in that state. Do you think this should be an issue of concern for the social work profession? Is it relevant to the work that social workers do? Why or why not?

Reinforce what you learned in this chapter by studying videos, cases, documents, and more available at **www.MySearchLab.com**.

Watch and Review

Watch these Videos

* * Recognizing Personal Values
* * Managing Personal Values: The Code of Ethics
* * America's Aging Population

Read and Review

Read these Cases/Documents

* Δ Elderly People
* Δ Residents' Rights to Intimacy in an Assisted Living Residence
* Δ End-of-Life Decisions in an Intensive Care Unit

Explore and Assess

Explore these Assets

* * Website: AARP
* * Website: Administration on Aging
* * Website: National Institute on Aging

Research these Topics

Policies Affecting Older Adults

The Role of "Values" in Policies That Involve Issues of Life and Death

What Is the Death with Dignity Act?

Assess Your Knowledge

Go to **MySearchLab** to test your knowledge of key topics in this chapter with topic-specific quizzes. Conclude your assessment by completing the chapter exam.

---

* = CSWE Core Competency Asset   Δ = Case Study

11

Using the Judicial System to Effect Change

with Maura Roche

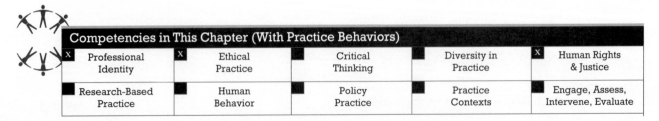

Competencies in This Chapter (With Practice Behaviors)				
x Professional Identity	x Ethical Practice	Critical Thinking	Diversity in Practice	x Human Rights & Justice
Research-Based Practice	Human Behavior	Policy Practice	Practice Contexts	Engage, Assess, Intervene, Evaluate

> Let us realize the arc of the moral universe is long,
> but it bends toward justice.
>
> —*Dr. Martin Luther King, Jr.*

Using the legislative process is a common and useful strategy for creating needed change on behalf of vulnerable and/or oppressed groups in the United States. Indeed, the bulk of this book is dedicated to exploring this aspect of macro-level change efforts. However, there are times when the court system can be used as a vehicle for social change when people are not being treated equally under the law. Thus, it is important to understand when it makes sense to use the legislative system for change and when it makes sense to utilize the courts. Social workers engaged in policy practice must be familiar with the court system because sometimes legislation that is passed into law by policy makers is challenged in the courts when some individual or group tries to argue that it is unconstitutional. Additionally, as the case examples in this chapter show, lawsuits can be used to advance social justice by protecting the constitutional rights of various groups of people. Court cases have focused on a wide variety of hot-button social issues over the years including LGBT (lesbian, gay, bisexual, and transgender) rights, abortion, gender discrimination, capital punishment, immigrant rights, and broader issues of racial justice.

Lawsuits can be used to advance social justice by protecting the constitutional rights of various groups of people.

One of the most famous U.S. Supreme Court cases is ***Brown v. Board of Education*** (1954). The plaintiffs believed that allowing racially segregated schools was a violation of the Equal Protection Clause of the Fourteenth Amendment of the Constitution. Thurgood Marshall (pictured above) successfully argued this landmark case against the Board of Education of the City of Topeka, Kansas, before the U.S. Supreme Court. The Court was unanimous in its ruling, and Chief Justice Earl Warren wrote in his opinion that separate educational facilities are inherently unequal. In 1967, Thurgood Marshall was nominated to the U.S. Supreme Court by President Lyndon Johnson, where he served until 1991. This case was extremely significant to the cause of racial justice in the United States and laid the groundwork for outlawing racial segregation in all public facilities in the United States. This is just one example of many in which a court case has been used as a vehicle for advancing social justice. Another famous U.S. Supreme court case was **Loving v. Virginia** (1967) in which the court struck down a Virginia law that prohibited interracial marriages, ruling that it was a violation of the 14th amendment.

SOCIAL WORK AND LEGAL PRACTICE

Some social workers are interested in working in a legal setting where litigation is a strategy used to reform systems of care that serve vulnerable individuals. Social workers are often hired by legal advocacy organizations engaged in litigation because they are skilled in performing many of the activities involved in legal work including research, mediation, and casework. Attorneys bring their legal expertise, whereas social workers bring years of experience working with a specific population. Social workers with experience in traditional social work roles (e.g., therapist, case manager) often can serve as in-house experts on substantive issues. Some social workers with a strong passion for working in the legal arena choose to combine their social work education with a law degree, or get additional legal training, though this is not always necessary. There are even some graduate programs in the United States in which students can earn a joint MSW and law degree. **Mediation** is a growing area of specialization for social workers in the United States and is used in many legal systems to try to get the parties to resolve their conflict and reach an agreement so that the case does not have to go to trial. Social workers who are trained in mediation learn how to be a neutral third party in order to help resolve a legal dispute.

Social workers have the ability to build trust with the clients whom the advocacy organization is there to represent and to gather important case information from them, which is needed to build a solid legal case. For example, a social worker who has spent 10–15 years working with foster youth is ideally suited to interview foster youth to gather information about their experiences of being served by the state foster care system. Social workers have strong communication and interviewing skills and are trained to be sensitive and ethical when working with vulnerable populations. Social workers may also review the social science research and summarize the findings on evidence-based practices as the legal advocacy organization prepares various legal documents to explain and support its positions. When the case goes to court, social workers can be called to provide testimony as expert witnesses.

However, not all cases end up going to court because sometimes the threat of a lawsuit can provide the impetus for an agency to change its practices. In these instances, a settlement may be reached by the legal parties. After a settlement is reached, social workers may be tasked with monitoring the settlement to ensure that the agency is doing what it agreed to, and they may also provide training to the staff in the organization to help them improve the identified problem areas that were the focus of the lawsuit. This can involve making site visits, reviewing case files, and conducting interviews with staff, community partners, and clients. Often the social worker will write reports detailing the agency's progress and may even make additional recommendations for improvement.

Finally, social workers may also work with federal, state, or local lawmakers to provide the funding needed for an agency to make the changes it needs to make. For example, in state child welfare organizations, caseworkers often have unmanageable caseloads, which may prevent them from providing quality care to the youth and families whom they serve. Thus, the advocacy organization may be able to convince lawmakers to appropriate additional funding to the child welfare agency in order to hire additional caseworkers and bring caseloads down.

Many advocacy groups across the country use the judicial system to combat injustice when it is deemed an appropriate strategy by legal experts. The **three branches of government** in the United States, the executive, legislative, and judicial, have a vital role to play and together create a system of checks and balances. The **legislative branch** is charged with making laws, but it is the role of the **judicial branch** to determine whether those laws are constitutional when challenged through litigation. Lawsuits can also be used by advocacy organizations to make a case that the constitutional rights of a particular group are being violated, as shown in the following two case examples.

Professional Identity

Practice Behavior Example: Serve as representatives of the profession, its mission, and its core values.

Critical Thinking Question: What social work knowledge, values, and skills do you think lend themselves well to a social work career in the legal arena? Can you see yourself doing mediation work or testifying as an expert witness?

DISABILITY ADVOCATES VERSUS THE STATE OF NEW YORK

In 2003, a nonprofit advocacy group called Disability Advocates (see Figure 11.1) filed a federal lawsuit against the state of New York alleging that the state violated the Americans with Disabilities Act by warehousing thousands of mentally ill

Started in 1989, Disability Advocates, Inc. fights to protect the rights of persons with mental and physical disabilities through litigation, policy advocacy, coalition building, public information, and technical support for other advocates for people with disabilities in New York. Visit its website at http://disability-advocates.org /advocacy.html to learn more about their programs and services.

Figure 11.1

Disability Advocates, Inc.

people in New York City in privately run, adult homes where they were isolated and forced to live in squalid conditions. Lawyers in this case were inspired by a landmark legal settlement in the 1970s against the Willowbrook State School that housed over 6,000 children and adults with mental retardation and developmental disabilities. A series of newspaper articles and television reports (by journalist Geraldo Rivera) documented horrifying living conditions, including unspeakable abuse and neglect of residents. As a result, the state was required to move thousands of residents into small community residences, and the school eventually closed.

The adult home model was developed in the 1960s and 1970s after efforts were made to deinstitutionalize the mentally ill, and many large psychiatric hospitals run by the state were shut down. The idea was to serve patients in smaller, less restrictive housing where they would be integrated into the community and provided with supervision and mental health services. However, this did not turn out to be the case. At the time, there were 380 adult homes in New York, including 44 in New York City housing approximately 4,300 mentally ill people. The lawsuit was filed after an expose by the *New York Times* describing the conditions of these facilities and uncovering an array of horror stories:

- Adult homes were run by businesspeople who were motivated by financial profit and had no mental health training. The direct care staff who were charged with dispensing medication were unqualified, low-wage workers (some barely literate); they provided little supervision and were understaffed.
- There were reports of horrible nightmarish stories of residents who died by committing suicide (e.g., overdosing, hanging themselves, jumping out of a window); by being murdered by an unstable resident; by overheating during a heat wave because many rooms had no air-conditioning; and from medical neglect.
- Some of these adult homes were larger and more institutionalized than some state-run psychiatric hospitals in the nation.
- Homes where mentally ill residents (most of them poor and many of them Black and Hispanic) are segregated from the community.
- Medicaid and Medicare fraud, including the practice of forcing residents to obtain unnecessary medical treatment, such as eye surgery, so that administrators would benefit financially.
- New York State had over 30 years of inspection records documenting filthy rooms and patients and fraudulent record keeping and billing practices, yet did nothing to hold these private operators accountable and failed to make significant changes to this system of care.

According to one advocate who spent a decade visiting these adult homes, "They are seen as dollar signs, as property, and not as human beings"

(*New York Times*, 2002). A lawyer in the case stated, "The shameful fact in New York State is that adult homes are the dumping ground for a wide range of individuals whose real problem is lack of access to housing, not mental illness" (*New York Times*, 2003).

In September 2009, a federal judge sided with the plaintiffs and ruled that the state of New York discriminated against thousands of mentally ill people by allowing them to reside in these privately run, segregated adult homes where they received substandard care. The court held that the state violated the Americans with Disabilities Act since these adult homes did not allow residents to be in the most integrated setting possible. In March 2010, the same judge ordered the state to develop supported housing units (at least 1,500 per year for 3 years) where residents can receive mental health and social services in their own apartments and homes. However, two years later there was a serious setback when an appeals court vacated these previous court decisions on a legal technicality. However, there was good news again in May 2012 when Governor Cuomo Mr. Cuomo stated that he would work to win passage of legislation overhauling how the state responds to the abuse and neglect of vulnerable state residents. The Governor is proposing to create an agency dedicated to investigating problems with the care of nearly one million vulnerable New Yorkers, including those with developmental disabilities, mental illnesses, traumatic brain injuries, and other conditions. It would have a special prosecutor and be granted subpoena power and the authority to convene grand juries. Other legal advocacy wins by Disability Advocates include a settlement with the New York State Department of Correctional Services and the Office of Mental Health, which agreed to improve psychiatric treatment for state prisoners with mental illness as well as an agreement with Hoyts Cinemas Corp. to modify its movie theaters to make them wheelchair accessible.

THE FIGHT OVER MARRIAGE EQUALITY IN CALIFORNIA (PROPOSITION 8)

Marriage equality has been a major hot-button political issue in recent years. To gay rights advocates, it is the civil rights issue of our time, whereas religious opponents believe it goes against the traditional view of marriage between one man and one woman (see Figure 11.2 for more on LGBT advocacy organizations). Currently, six states and the District of Columbia issue marriage licenses to same-sex couples: New York, Connecticut, Iowa, Massachusetts, New Hampshire, and Vermont. Like in many states, the story of marriage for same-sex couples in California has been a long and winding road full of twists and turns and includes battles at the ballot box and the courthouse (see Figure 11.3).

The organizations below are well-known advocacy groups that work to achieve equality for LGBT individuals. Visit their websites to learn more about their mission and advocacy work.

Human Rights Campaign	www.hrc.org
The National Gay and Lesbian Task Force	www.thetaskforce.org
Marriage Equality USA	www.marriageequality.org

Figure 11.2
Advocacy Spotlight: LGBT Equality.

1. **March 2000**, California voters approve Proposition 22 changing California statute to read that only marriage between one man and one woman is valid or recognized in California.
2. **May 2008**, California Supreme Court overturns ban on marriage for same-sex couples.
3. **November 2008**, California voters approve Proposition 8 amending the state constitution to define marriage as between one man and one woman.
4. **March 2009**, California Supreme Court rules that Proposition 8 is valid and constitutional.
5. A **federal lawsuit is filed** challenging the constitutionality of Proposition 8. The California Governor and Attorney General refuse to defend the law and anti-gay activists come into the lawsuit as third-party.
6. **August 2010**, a federal district court (trial court) judge (Vaughn R. Walker) rules Proposition 8 unconstitutional.
7. **February 2012**, a federal appeals court upholds the lower court's ruling that Proposition 8 violated the constitutional rights of gay men and lesbians in California.
8. Both sides in the case have stated their intention to take the case all the way to the U.S. Supreme Court.
9. **May 2012**, President Obama publicly voices support for same-sex marriage for the first time as President.

Figure 11.3

Timeline of Recent Marriage Equality Battle in California.

California made national news on May 15, 2008, when the California State Supreme Court ruled in *In re Marriage Cases* that limiting marriage to opposite-sex couples violates the state constitutional rights of same-sex couples and cannot be used to prevent same-sex couples from marrying. This ruling struck down a ballot initiative passed in 2000 (Proposition 22) in which a majority of Californians voted to change California statute so that only marriages between a man and a woman would be recognized. Various organizations and individuals filed 30 amicus briefs urging the court to reject state laws denying marriage equality to same-sex couples. The National Association of Social Workers (NASW) filed an 87-page brief along with the American Psychological Association (APA), California Psychological Association, and American Psychiatric Association (see summary of this brief in Figure 11.4). Approximately 18,000 same-sex couples were married in California after this court ruling.

Well before the May 2008 state supreme court ruling, opponents of marriage equality were already planning to get Proposition 8 (Prop 8) on the California ballot. The last time they had an initiative on the ballot (Proposition 22), the California statute was amended, but this time they wanted a ballot measure that would amend the state constitution, a tougher standard, making it more difficult to overturn in the future and ineligible for a state-based constitutional challenge. Prop 8, officially titled "Eliminates Right of Same-Sex Couples to Marry," would amend the California state constitution so that only marriage between a man and a woman would be valid or recognized in the state of California. Supporters of Prop 8 gathered roughly 1.1 million signatures, far more than the 694,354 valid signatures needed to qualify the measure for the ballot.

The contest over Prop 8 was extremely heated. Supporters and donors of Prop 8 included the Knights of Columbus (Catholic organization), National Organization for Marriage, Focus on the Family, Mormon Church leaders, evangelical minister Rick Warren, and presidential candidate John McCain.

Submitted by: The National Association of Social Workers, American Psychological Association, California Psychological Association, and American Psychiatric Association.

Brief filed: September 2007

Amici, the nation's and state's leading associations of mental health professionals, and behavioral scientists present this brief to provide the court with a comprehensive and balanced review of the scientific and professional literature pertinent to the issues before the court. In preparing this brief, amici have been guided solely by criteria relating to the scientific rigor and reliability of studies and literature, not by whether a given study supports or undermines a particular conclusion.

Homosexuality is neither a disorder nor a disease, but rather a normal variant of human sexual orientation. The vast majority of gay and lesbian individuals lead happy, healthy, well-adjusted, and productive lives.

Many gay and lesbian people are in a committed same-sex relationship. In their essential, psychological respects, these relationships are equivalent to heterosexual relationships.

The institution of marriage affords individuals a variety of benefits that have a favorable impact on their physical and psychological well-being.

A large number of children are currently being raised by lesbians and gay men, both in same-sex couples and as single parents. Empirical research has consistently shown that lesbian and gay parents do not differ from heterosexuals in their parenting skills, and their children do not show any deficits compared to children raised by heterosexual parents.

State policies that bar same-sex couples from marrying are based solely on sexual orientation. As such, they are both a consequence of the stigma historically attached to homosexuality, and a structural manifestation of that stigma. By allowing same-sex couples to marry, the court would end the anti-gay stigma imposed by the state of California through its ban on marriage rights for same-sex couples. In addition, allowing same-sex couples to marry would give them access to the social support that already facilitates and strengthens heterosexual marriages, with all of the psychological and physical health benefits associated with that support. In addition, if their parents are allowed to marry, the children of same-sex couples will benefit not only from the legal stability and other familial benefits that marriage provides, but also from elimination of state-sponsored stigmatization of their families.

Figure 11.4

Summary of Argument (*In re Marriage Cases*).

Courtesy of Elizabeth J. Clark, National Association of Social Workers, Washington, DC.

Source: http://www.socialworkers.org/assets/secured/documents/ldf/briefDocuments/In%20re%20Marriage%20Cases%20California.pdf

Opponents of Prop 8 included a number of gay rights organizations including the Human Rights Campaign and Equality California, California Teachers Association, presidential candidate Barack Obama, and a whole host of Hollywood celebrities. On November 4, 2008, Prop 8 was passed by 52% of California voters, making same-sex marriage illegal in California once again. Protests erupted around the country, and the battle returned once again to the courts.

In *Strauss v. Horton* (a consolidation of three lawsuits), the California State Supreme Court ruled that Prop 8 was constitutional but that the 18,000 marriages performed before it went into effect would remain legal. However, supporters of marriage for same-sex couples were not surprised by this ruling and quickly went to the next level and filed a lawsuit (*Perry v. Schwarzenegger*) in federal court challenging the constitutionality of Prop 8. The Prop 8 challenge was financed by the American Foundation for Equal Rights, a nonprofit advocacy group. The two high-profile attorneys who were hired to argue the case, David Boies and Theodore B. Olson, were previous opponents in *Bush v. Gore,* which ruled in favor of George W. Bush over the results of the 2000 presidential election. However, these former foes (one a well-known conservative) would team up to argue that Prop 8 violates the constitutional guarantee of equal protection and due process.

After the trial that lasted two and a half weeks, attorney Boies said testimony from the plaintiffs had established three major points: "That marriage is a fundamental right, that depriving gay people of that right caused harm, and that there was no societal benefit to denying gays and lesbians the right to marry" (*New York Times*, 2010). The other side argued that Californians have the right to establish marriage as between a man and a woman, and they did so when they approved Prop 8.

California made national news again on August 4, 2010, when federal judge Vaughn R. Walker overturned the ban on marriage for same-sex couples saying it discriminates against gay men and women. In his written opinion that was 136 pages long, Judge Walker wrote that Prop 8 "fails to advance any rational basis in singling out gay men and lesbians for denial of a marriage license" and "does nothing more than enshrine in the California Constitution the notion that opposite-sex couples are superior to same-sex couples" (CNN, 2010). The case next advanced to the Ninth Circuit Court of Appeals and on February 7, 2012, this three-member panel upheld the lower court's ruling that Proposition 8 violated the constitutional rights of gay men and lesbians in California. In the decision, Judge Stephen R. Reinhardt wrote, "Although the Constitution permits communities to enact most laws they believe to be desirable, it requires that there be at least a legitimate reason for the passage of a law that treats different classes of people differently." He added, "Proposition 8 serves no purpose, and has no effect, other than to lessen the status and human dignity of gay men and lesbians in California" (*New York Times*, 2012). Attorneys on both sides of the case have stated their intention to take the case all the way to the U.S. Supreme Court in order to have the issue settled once and for all in the United States. However, it is not clear whether the high court will agree to hear it.

CHILDREN'S RIGHTS: WORKING TO REFORM THE NATION'S FAILING CHILD WELFARE SYSTEMS

The previous stories in this chapter are examples of lawsuits that were filed to address discrimination against a particular group. However, lawsuits (often class action lawsuits) can also be used in an attempt to reform large systems that are failing the people they serve. Children's Rights is an advocacy organization based in New York City whose goal is to reform failing child welfare systems in the United States that are not operating in the best interests of the children and families they serve. The kinds of problems it is typically attempting to remedy include, but are not limited to, failing to respond to reports of child abuse/neglect quickly enough, high rates of abuse and/or neglect of children in foster homes, failure to properly monitor children in foster homes, children in foster care who bounce from one foster home to another, caseworkers who are poorly trained and have dangerously high caseloads, and not moving foster youth into permanent living arrangements in a timely manner.

Lawsuits (often class action lawsuits) can also be used in an attempt to reform large systems that are failing the people they serve.

> Children's Rights is a national advocacy group that works on behalf of abused and neglected children to reform failing child welfare systems in the United States. They have been doing this work for more than a decade and have used legal action to force improvements in child welfare systems in more than a dozen states.
>
> Visit their website online to learn more about their work: www.childrensrights.org

Figure 11.5

Children's Rights (New York City).

In recent years, Children's Rights (see Figure 11.5) has won legal victories in roughly 13 states and the District of Columbia. Its legal process typically includes the following steps:

- Filing a class action lawsuit on behalf of children in foster care in a specific state.
- Using court orders to negotiate with the state for the purpose of developing detailed reform plans designed to improve the way the child welfare system operates.
- Monitoring progress to ensure that the changes that were agreed to actually take place.
- If not, returning to court.

A settlement agreement reached with the state of New Jersey is detailed in Figure 11.6.

> Children's Rights filed a class action lawsuit in 1999 on behalf of more than 11,000 children in New Jersey's child welfare system. In 2003—following the much publicized death of Faheem Williams and the discovery of his two starving siblings, children known to the state's Division of Youth and Family Services (DYFS)—a landmark settlement agreement mandating sweeping reforms was reached, but initially yielded few results.
>
> In October of 2005, the independent panel monitoring the reform effort found that New Jersey was making "seriously inadequate progress" toward implementing the court-ordered improvements. After negotiations to expedite the reforms ended unsuccessfully, Children's Rights filed a contempt motion against the state and requested that newly elected Governor Jon Corzine be appointed receiver of the child welfare system. In January of 2006, after Governor Corzine announced the creation of a new cabinet-level children's agency, Children's Rights put the contempt motion on hold and began negotiations with the new administration.
>
> Since then, New Jersey has made significant progress in implementing the first phase of the massive reform effort. DYFS is recruiting and licensing more foster parents; caseworkers are better trained and have more manageable caseloads; and in 2007, New Jersey broke its own record for the most adoptions finalized in one year. However, significant challenges lie ahead, including recent changes in DYFS leadership, as the state moves toward Phase II, which began in January of 2009. Children's Rights will remain in place as a watchdog until all of the court-ordered reforms are fully implemented.

Figure 11.6

Children's Rights, New Jersey (*Charlie and Nadine H. v. Corzine*).

Source: www.childrensrights.org/reform-campaigns/legal-cases/new-jersey-charlie-and-nadine-h-v-corzine/

There is some debate over whether lawsuits are an effective mechanism for changing systems of care. According to Gerald Rosenberg, a law professor at the University of Chicago,

> The problem that litigators face is that courts lack power. If a court says to a governor or the administrator, you must do X, the court has no means to enforce that. Often, what is at stake is financial resources, and if the state is unwilling to reorder its budget priorities, there's often very little that can be done." (National Public Radio, 2007)

However, attorneys and advocates at Children's Rights disagree. Although they agree that change is often not as rapid as they would like, they point to significant and concrete changes to state child welfare systems as a result of the legal settlements they reach with the state. Examples of improvements in various states have included:

- the creation of a statewide hotline for reporting child abuse and neglect
- responding better to reports of abuse and neglect within required time frames
- significantly cutting rates of abuse of children in state custody
- the closure of facilities found to provide inadequate care to children
- improving the quality of child abuse investigations and other child welfare practices
- improving placements of children in foster care (e.g., fewer placement changes, fewer placed in institutionalized settings, placed with siblings, better meeting their educational and mental health needs, more regular visits by their caseworkers, and increasing number of foster homes as well as reimbursement for foster parents)
- ensuring that children in foster care have effective legal representation
- moving children to a permanent living arrangement (e.g., adoption) more quickly so they do not languish in the foster care system
- a number of changes needed to improve the quality of caseworkers (e.g., higher qualifications, more training, reduced caseloads)
- increased funding for child welfare systems in order to make needed reforms.

Children's Rights currently has active class action lawsuits in Massachusetts, Oklahoma, and Rhode Island. To watch a short video about the work of this organization, visit http://www.youtube.com/watch?v=sCCChz7X5Z4.

Ethical Practice

Practice Behavior Example: Obligation to conduct themselves ethically and engage in ethical decision making.

Critical Thinking Question: Work in the court system can be very heated and contentious. What is your comfort level doing work that involves a lot of conflict? How can social workers work successfully in this arena while upholding social work values and ethics?

NASW's LEGAL DEFENSE FUND

The NASW Legal Defense Fund is used to weigh in on legal cases on issues of importance to the social work profession (see Figure 11.7). NASW does this through the filing of amicus curiae briefs. NASW and its chapters file amicus curiae (friend of the court) briefs in 10 to 12 appellate cases each year. **Amicus briefs** are filed by an individual/organization who is not a party to the case, but has a strong interest in the case, and has expertise to share with the court. It is an effort to weigh in and to influence the opinion of the presiding judge. It is vital that an amicus brief provide a strong and reasoned argument and

The NASW Legal Defense Fund was established to advocate on behalf of the social work profession on issues of particular importance to the social work profession in legal cases reflecting the application of NASW Policy Statements (see *Social Work Speaks*, NASW, 2009). Through the filing of *amicus curiae* briefs, NASW provides the courts with knowledge of social work research and social policy considerations relevant to the courts' deliberations on matters that affect a wide array of individuals and populations.

Figure 11.7
NASW Legal Defense Fund.

be written very persuasively. Earlier in this chapter, NASW's involvement in *In Re Marriage Cases*, a California court case involving marriage for same-sex couples, was detailed (see Figure 11.3). Following are a few more examples of court cases in which NASW has filed an amicus brief on issues ranging from psychotherapist-patient privilege to adoption by same-sex couples.

Jaffee v. Redmond (1996)

This Supreme Court case is important to social workers because this ruling reinforced the protection of psychotherapist-patient privilege by keeping private psychotherapy records out of the courtroom. The Supreme Court ruled 7 to 2 that federal courts must allow psychotherapists and other mental health professionals to refuse to disclose patient records in judicial proceedings, similar to the lawyer-client and marital privileges that the federal courts have recognized for years. In this particular case, Redmond was a police officer who had killed a man in the line of duty. When it was discovered that Redmond had received counseling from a licensed clinical social worker, records from her therapy sessions were subpoenaed as evidence. However, the clinical social worker refused to produce the notes or answer any questions about her sessions with Redmond.

Justice John Paul Stevens wrote the decision and explained that without psychotherapist-patient privilege, confidential conversations between psychotherapists and their patients would be compromised. Justice Stevens said the privilege would apply to clinical social workers as well as to psychiatrists and psychologists because the reasons for having the privilege apply with equal force to all the professions. This ruling was very significant for the social work profession because the ruling recognized that "psychotherapist-patient privilege" is a doctrine that applies to clinical social workers and their clients as well as to any psychiatrist or psychologist and patient. Thus, it treated the mental health records of licensed social workers similar to those of psychiatrists and psychologists. It also clarified the importance of mental health records and ruled that clinical notes and client communications are distinct from other types of confidential communications and worthy of special protection.

In re Matter of Adoption of X.X.G. and N.R.G. (2010)

A Florida appeals court ruled that the state's ban on adoption by same-sex couples violates the state constitution's guarantee of equal protection of the law, which NASW also asserted in its amicus brief filed with the court. According to NASW, "Rather than protecting children . . . Florida's ban does just the opposite—it profoundly harms them by denying them a permanent adoptive family" (NASW News, 2010, p. 5). The brief was joined by a number of other child welfare advocacy groups such as the Child Welfare League of America, the Center for Adoption Policy, the North American Council on Adoptable Children, and Florida's chapter of the American Academy of Pediatrics.

Graham v. Florida (2010)

NASW and the NASW Florida Chapter joined with the APA in filing an amicus brief in *Graham v. Florida*, a case challenging the imposition of a life without parole sentence for a crime committed while the defendant was a 16-year-old juvenile. The amicus brief pointed out to the Court research findings on adolescent brain development, indicating the neurological changes that occur well into the early 20s. Due to the significant differences between the adult brain and the adolescent brain, the APA and NASW argued that juveniles have a "lesser capacity for mature judgment," are "more vulnerable to negative external influences," and their "unformed identity makes it less likely that their offenses evince a fixed bad character and more likely that they will reform" (NASW).

The Supreme Court issued a decision on May 17, 2010, holding that a sentence of life without parole for a crime committed by a juvenile violates the Eighth Amendment's prohibition on cruel and unusual punishment. This judgment follows a series of Supreme Court decisions in the past two decades in which the Court has recognized the unique status of juveniles.

Kennedy v. Louisiana (2008)

NASW officially opposes the death penalty and has been involved in a number of court cases arguing this position. In 2008, the Supreme Court decided *Kennedy v. Louisiana*, which involved an appeal to the U.S. Supreme Court, challenging the imposition of the death penalty for the rape of a minor in Louisiana. NASW's brief, which was joined by several sexual assault treatment organizations, argued that, among other things, the death penalty would create an incentive for perpetrators to kill their victims in order to silence the only witness to these private crimes, is likely to increase the trauma to the victim due to repeated court testimony in death penalty cases, and would deter reporting by family members. The Court relied on NASW's brief in reaching its conclusions, citing it in the formal opinion written by Justice Kennedy (NASW).

In June 2008, the U.S. Supreme Court issued a precedent-setting 5–4 decision, reversing the Supreme Court of Louisiana, and holding that the imposition of the death penalty for the rape of a minor violates the Eighth Amendment's prohibition against cruel and unusual punishment. Upon request for a rehearing, the Court slightly modified its opinion on October 1, 2008, and upheld the ban on capital punishment for rape of a minor as a matter of constitutional law.

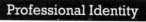
Professional Identity

Practice Behavior Example: Know the profession's history.

Critical Thinking Question: NASW gets involved with and takes strong positions in court cases involving controversial issues such as same-sex marriage, adoption by same-sex couples, and the death penalty. Do you agree with its stances on these issues? Why or why not?

OVERVIEW OF THE U.S. JUDICIAL SYSTEM

Sometimes a lawsuit is the best strategy to employ in order to change a particular policy or practice. Judges are in the branch of government most insulated from politics (although not entirely), and therefore it is often said that the courts are at liberty to apply the Constitution in a way that protects the minority from the tyranny of the majority. Sometimes a court case involves one

> **It is often said that the courts are at liberty to apply the Constitution in a way that protects the minority from the tyranny of the majority.**

American Bar Association, Center on Children and the Law (children)
American Civil Liberties Union (civil rights, freedom of speech)
Annie E. Casey Foundation (children)
Children's Rights Council (children)
Disability Advocates, Inc.
Disability Rights and Education & Defense Fund (disability)
Lambda Legal Defense Fund (LGBT rights)
Latino Justice (race-based discrimination)
Mental Health America (mental illness)
NAACP (race-based discrimination)
National Alliance for the Mentally Ill (mental illness)
National Center for Lesbian Rights (LGBT rights)
National Center for Youth Law (children)
National Disability Rights Network (disability rights)
National Legal Resources Center (aging)
The Bazelon Center (mental illness)
The Legal Aid Society (criminal/juvenile, civil, law reform, domestic violence)
Womenslaw.org (domestic violence)

Figure 11.8
Select Legal Resources.

client, and other times it may involve a "class" of clients like the examples earlier in this chapter (e.g., children in foster care, mentally ill individuals served in institutions). Figure 11.8 includes a lengthy list of legal resources, including the well-known American Civil Liberties Union (ACLU) and Legal Aid Society.

FEDERAL JUDICIARY

The United States Supreme Court

The U.S. Supreme Court is the highest court in the land and therefore the court of last resort—there is no higher court to file appeal. It is made up of nine members (chief justice and eight associates) who are appointed for life by a U.S. president and confirmed by the U.S. Senate. Its task is to ensure that state and federal laws, lower court decisions, and state constitutions are not in conflict with the U.S. Constitution. A limited number of cases come to the Supreme Court on appeal from federal courts of appeals and state supreme courts, and the Supreme Court can decide to accept or reject a particular case.

The Federal Circuit Courts of Appeals

There are 12 regional circuits, and each of those has a court of appeals that hears cases from the federal district courts below them. These courts are made up of judges from the region. Cases from a circuit court of appeals can be appealed to the U.S. Supreme Court.

The Federal District Courts

There are 94 district courts throughout the United States and territories. These are trial courts, and both civil and criminal matters are tried in federal district court. Often these courts empanel juries who decide many of these cases.

Facade of US Supreme court in Washington DC on sunny day.

State Supreme Courts, State Appeals Courts, and State Courts

The three levels of courts at the state level somewhat mirror the federal system with trial courts, (district, county, or municipal), a court of appeals, and a supreme court.

State Supreme Courts

Every state has a court of last resort and for most states it is a supreme court (except Maryland and New York whose highest court is the court of appeals), and the justices are usually elected rather than appointed. Most state supreme courts have five to nine justices, and the chief justice may be elected by his or her peers or be based solely on seniority. Only the U.S. Supreme Court may overturn the decisions made by state supreme courts.

State Court of Appeals

Most, but not all, states have an appeals court, Nevada being an exception with no such court, which is an intermediary between the trial court and the supreme court. Utah's supreme court is the arbiter of cases going to the court of appeals. The structure and function of these courts varies somewhat from state to state. Most states have a website for their judiciary, and this can be a helpful tool in learning about the specifics where you live.

State Trial Courts and Specialty Courts

While all states have trial level courts, they vary widely. Some are district courts established by county, and some are municipal. A few states have "chancery courts" and others

Human Rights & Justice

Practice Behavior Example: Engage in practices that advance social and economic justice.

Critical Thinking Question: Based on what you read in this chapter, do you think lawsuits are an effective way to reform large systems of care in the United States (e.g., child welfare system, criminal justice system) and to advance social justice, or do you think there are more effective ways to do this?

have "courts of equity," which in modern times hold little distinction from "courts of law." In addition, there are specialty courts like drug courts, mental health courts, or juvenile courts that preside over a very narrow range of cases. Most states have a state government or state court website on which you can find more information about courts in your state.

FINAL THOUGHTS

The legal arena can be an exciting place for social workers to practice.

The legal arena can be an exciting place for social workers to practice. There are many fields of social work practice where social workers commonly come into contact with the court system such as child welfare, juvenile justice, and when working with clients experiencing addiction and/or mental illness. Social workers working in the field of criminal justice with youth and adults are concerned about the disproportionate rates of incarceration for racial and ethnic minorities in the system, the incarceration of the mentally ill and mentally retarded, the often inhumane treatment of prisoners, scarce state and federal resources that are spent on prisons and the "War on Drugs" in lieu of education and social services, and some systems in the United States that treat children and youth as adults. Social workers are also concerned about people being wrongfully convicted as well as fairness in sentencing. See Figure 11.9 for information on two legal advocacy organizations that are doing important work in these areas.

Social workers advocate for community-based prevention services, alternatives to incarceration such as diversion programs for nonviolent offenders, and enhanced funding for substance abuse treatment and mental health. The death penalty is a controversial issue in the United States and divides social workers as well. However, NASW has taken a formal position opposing **capital punishment** stating that it is at odds with social work values and is a violation of human rights. It is important for social workers to have a working knowledge of the U.S. court system because it can be used as a vehicle for social change. As shown in this chapter, litigation can be used to reform large systems of care and to protect the constitutional rights of groups of people.

The Sentencing Project (www.sentencingproject.org)

The Sentencing Project is a national organization that advocates for reforms of the criminal justice system so that it is fair and effective. It is concerned about inequities in the system and is concerned that "the U.S. is the world's leader in incarceration, that one in three young black men is under control of the criminal justice system, that five million Americans can't vote because of felony convictions, and that thousands of women and children have lost welfare, education and housing benefits as the result of convictions for minor drug offenses." They also promote alternatives to incarceration.

The Innocence Project (www.innocenseproject.org)

The Innocence Project (founded in 1992) is a nonprofit legal clinic affiliated with the Benjamin N. Cardozo School of Law at Yeshiva University. The project is a national litigation and public policy organization dedicated to exonerating wrongfully convicted people through DNA testing and reforming the criminal justice system to prevent future injustice. It operates as a clinic where law students handle casework while supervised by a team of attorneys and clinic staff.

Figure 11.9
Legal Advocacy Spotlight.

CHAPTER 11 PRACTICE TEST

The following questions will test your knowledge of the content found within this chapter. For additional assessment, including licensing-exam type questions on applying chapter content to practice behaviors, visit **MySearchLab**.

1. _____ is a specialized area of legal practice where a neutral third party helps two or more legal parties resolve their legal dispute to avoid a court case.
   a. Legal advocacy
   b. Expert testimony
   c. Legal counseling
   d. Mediation

2. Which of the following statements best explains the relationship between the various branches of government?
   a. The judicial branch is charged with making laws, but it is the role of the legislative branch to determine whether those laws are constitutional.
   b. The legislative branch is charged with making laws, but it is the role of the judicial branch to determine whether those laws are constitutional.
   c. The legislative branch is charged with making laws, but it is the role of the executive branch to determine whether those laws are constitutional.
   d. The executive branch is charged with making laws, but it is the role of the legislative branch to determine whether those laws are constitutional.

3. In *Disability Advocates v. the State of New York*, Disability Advocates filed a federal lawsuit against the state of New York alleging that it violated the:
   a. Americans with Disabilities Act
   b. constitutional guarantee of equal protection

c. constitutional guarantee of due process
d. Civil Rights Act

4. The attorneys challenging Prop 8 in California argued that it violates the:
   a. Civil Rights Act
   b. Defense of Marriage Act
   c. constitutional guarantee of equal protection and due process
   d. constitutional guarantee of the right to pursue happiness

5. There are _____ members of the U.S. Supreme Court, each of whom are appointed for life.
   a. 6
   b. 7
   c. 9
   d. 10

6. A legal advocacy organization in Florida files a lawsuit against an adoption agency that will not place children for adoption into the homes of gay and/or lesbian couples. This is an example of using a lawsuit for the following purpose:
   a. protecting a group's constitutional rights
   b. attempting to reform a large system of care
   c. raising awareness of an issue with the general public
   d. in order to sue for damages

7. Some social workers may be uncomfortable with the idea of suing certain systems of care such as child welfare systems because they know that child welfare systems face many challenges such as lack of adequate funding to carry out their work successfully. This approach also may not feel very strengths-based. Should these be reasons not to use lawsuits as a means to advance social justice for marginalized groups? Why or why not?

Reinforce what you learned in this chapter by studying videos, cases, documents, and more available at **www.MySearchLab.com**.

Watch and **Review**

Watch these **Videos**

* Court Rules on Hazelton's Immigration Laws (2010)
* Funeral Protesters Push the Limit of Free Speech (2007)
* Proposition 8
* Supreme Court: No Race-Based Admissions (2007)

Read and **Review**

Read these **Cases/Documents**

* *Brown v. Board of Education of Topeka, Kansas* (1954)
* *Plessy v. Ferguson* (1896)
* *Roe v. Wade* (1973)

Explore and **Assess**

Explore these **Assets**

* Interactive Case Study: You Are a Supreme Court Justice Deciding a Free Speech Case

Research these **Topics**

Overview of the U.S. Judicial System

Lawsuits as a Vehicle for Social Change and Social Justice

Social Work Profession's Role in Legal Advocacy

Assess Your Knowledge

Go to **MySearchLab** to test your knowledge of key topics in this chapter with topic-specific quizzes. Conclude your assessment by completing the chapter exam.

---

* = CSWE Core Competency Asset   Δ = Case Study

12

The Politics of Economics

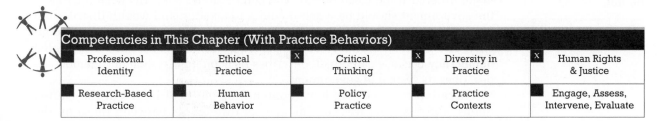

Competencies in This Chapter (With Practice Behaviors)

Professional Identity	Ethical Practice	X Critical Thinking	X Diversity in Practice	X Human Rights & Justice
Research-Based Practice	Human Behavior	Policy Practice	Practice Contexts	Engage, Assess, Intervene, Evaluate

> In this world nothing can be said to be certain, except death and taxes.
>
> —*Benjamin Franklin, 1789*

> Like slavery and apartheid, poverty is not natural. It is man-made and it can be overcome and eradicated by the actions of human beings.
>
> —*Nelson Mandela*

> NASW supports a national economic policy that . . . recognizes that a nation's well-being derives not only from an economic balance sheet, but also from the well-being of its members.
>
> —*NASW, Social Work Speaks, 2009, p. 260*

Although many political debates are focused on social issues, some of the biggest political battles involve how Americans should spend their state and federal resources (i.e., taxpayer money). Indeed, a significant portion of political action by social workers involves trying to convince local, state, and federal government to commit more public dollars to safety net programs as well as programs that invest in human and social capital. By better understanding government budgets, social workers can learn what Americans prioritize as a society and where advocacy efforts are needed in order to ensure that vital social services are available to individuals and families in need. One of the primary tasks of advocacy groups is to be at the table explaining to lawmakers why more resources are needed to address a whole host of social problems from child welfare, to poverty and homelessness, to mental health. Often there is stiff competition between various interest groups that are trying to get a bigger piece of the funding pie. However, getting increased funding has become increasingly challenging in recent years due to the current economic recession and record deficits at all levels of government. This requires great skill and creativity.

POLITICAL ECONOMY

Social work practitioners who have a basic working knowledge of economic issues and budgeting will be much more effective than those who do not.

Social work students are not always thrilled to have to learn about economics, but social work practitioners who have a basic working knowledge of economic issues and budgeting will be much more effective than those who do not. Anyone who is heavily involved with politics and legislation understands the important connection between a country's political and economic system. **Political economy** is the study of this interrelationship and seeks to understand (a) how government passes laws and policies that affect a society's allocation of resources and (b) how a society's economic system impacts the kinds of laws and policies that get passed by government. The strong connection between politics and economics cannot be overstated, and one of the major differences between liberals and conservatives concerns what the role of the government should be when it comes to taxation and wealth distribution (see Figure 12.1). Some universities offer degree programs in political economy. The political economy of the United States is often termed a **capitalist democracy** because capitalism describes its economic system and democracy describes its system of government.

Taxation is one of the most contentious political issues in the United States, and there are distinct ideological differences between those on the Left and those on the Right, which often seem almost impossible to bridge.

	Conservatism	Liberalism
View of the Free Market	Free market economy is the best mechanism for distributing a fair share of societal resources; competition is at the heart of free market economics.	The market is not equipped to meet basic needs; it produces an unequal distribution of income, resources, and life chances; and it fails to account for discriminatory barriers that stand in people's way.
Taxes	Lower taxes for corporations and the rich because this will allow businesses to expand and hire more workers. Conservatives embrace supply side economics which argues that the govern-ment should not meddle with the free market; oppose excessive government regulation.	Tax the wealthy and corporations to fund programs for the middle class and the poor. Liberals embrace Keynesian economics, which argues that the government must intervene into the affairs of the market in order to address its inadequacies and to ensure low unemployment; support policies that use taxation as a mechanism for redistributing wealth in society.

Figure 12.1

Conservativism Versus Liberalism: view of taxes and the free market.

The Tea Party movement has made this one of its key issues, and its stance is that taxes take people's freedom away from them. Its position is that citizens should be allowed to keep the money that they earn and should not be heavily taxed. Those on the Left maintain that taxes are necessary in order to ensure a level playing field and to fund important social programs that contribute to the greater public good.

There are two dominant, and somewhat opposing, economic ideologies that have had great influence in the United States: Keynesian economics (also called demand side economics) and free market economics (also called supply side economics). The father of **free market economics** is economist Milton Friedman whose theories have been embraced by conservatives and U.S. presidents such as Ronald Reagan. The basic idea behind this economic school of thought is that the government should not meddle in the affairs of the free market, and that the market works best when it is left to operate freely. Supporters advocate low taxes and minimal government regulation and argue that high taxes on corporations prevent companies from being able to invest, expand their business, and hire more workers. Supply-siders also support the privatization of social services and other governmental functions because, in their view, money spent on public welfare is money that could be spent in the private sector. They argue that economic growth is better than public welfare because it provides people with a job and a way to make a living (instead of making people dependent on government services). Opponents of supply side economics have derisively labeled it "trickle down economics" because it is predicated on the belief that letting wealthy people keep more of their money (via low taxation) will trickle down to benefit the rest of society.

Critics of supply side economics dispute the contention that the free market can be left to its own devices and have referred to ardent supporters of this economic philosophy as "free market fundamentalists." **Keynesian economics**, which is named after the economist John Maynard Keynes, is the economic philosophy embraced by those on the Left. Supporters of this school of economic thought believe that there are times when the government must take an active role in addressing the inadequacies of the free market, particularly during economic recessions when people lose confidence in the system and save their cash instead of spending and/or investing. This model guided the economic policies of President Roosevelt in the aftermath of the Great Depression, and to some extent the policies of President Obama who came into office facing a serious economic recession. Keynesian economic philosophy posits that there are a range of options for spurring demand and ensuring that the economy can provide near-full employment: increasing or decreasing taxes, overseeing the transfer of public goods or services, printing more money, spending money on public works projects, and subsidizing demand via the provision of welfare entitlements. According to Keynes, social welfare spending boosts the economy because it increases people's spending capacity and increases productivity as social welfare programs are investments in human capital (e.g., provides people with education, training, skills).

REVENUES ("TAXES 101")

To begin learning about the U.S. federal budget, first we will examine **revenues**, or how money comes into the government. Sometimes social workers are in the position of advocating for increased revenue (i.e., taxes) to pay for a variety of social welfare programs. This is often a hard sell to politicians who know this is not a popular stance with many constituents in their home districts who would prefer not to pay higher taxes. So, what is the purpose of taxation? Many discussions and debates surrounding taxation gloss over this question. Generally speaking, taxes provide the revenue needed to address the public good, and they are a major source of funding for many public programs. Taxes support the following (though this list is not exhaustive):

- public safety (police, child protection)
- public education, including higher education (teachers, state colleges, financial aid)
- infrastructure (roads, bridges)
- funding for the arts
- public broadcasting
- national defense and homeland security
- research (e.g., science and technology)
- health care (e.g., Medicare, Medicaid, public hospitals)
- public housing
- environmental protection
- consumer protection (e.g., food safety)
- Social Security program
- income support programs (e.g., TANF [Temporary Assistance for Needy Families], WIC Program, Supplemental Nutrition Assistance Program)
- public libraries
- post office

PROGRESSIVE VERSUS REGRESSIVE TAXATION

It is important for social workers to understand the difference between progressive and regressive taxes so they can weigh in appropriately when these issues are being considered by local or national lawmakers. **Progressive taxes** place a higher burden on wealthier citizens because the tax rate increases as income increases (e.g. income taxes). **Regressive taxes** are those taxes where the poor pay a higher percentage of their income than do wealthier individuals (e.g., sales tax). Figure 12.2 shows various types of taxes and whether they are considered regressive or progressive. At first glance, it may seem confusing that a sales tax is regressive because it is a set rate for everyone. For example, in a state with a 7% sales tax, all buyers would pay $70 in tax for a new laptop that costs $1,000. However, that $70 impacts a low-income person more than a higher income individual because it represents a higher percentage of a lower income person's overall budget. In other words, a person making $2000 a month will feel that $70 much more than a person making $5,000 a month. The Social Security tax is also regressive because it has a tax ceiling, meaning that individuals are taxed only on the first $110,100 that they make (as of 2012,). Thus, individuals making $1 million a year are taxed only on the first $110,100 of their earnings whereas someone making $50,000 a year is taxed on his or her entire income.

TAXES—WHO CARRIES THE BURDEN?

According to the National Priorities Project, total federal revenues for fiscal year 2012 are projected to be approximately $2.6 trillion. Almost 80% of these revenues are from individual income taxes and the payroll tax that pays for Social Security and Medicare (National Priorities Project, n.d.-a). Since 1960,

Federal income tax	Progressive
State income tax (not all states have one)	Progressive
Sales tax	Regressive
Social Security withholding tax (i.e., the payroll tax)	Regressive
Real estate property tax (local tax)	(Up for debate)
Estate tax	Progressive
Luxury taxes (tax on luxury goods)	Progressive
"Sin" taxes (e.g., tax on cigarettes/alcohol)	Regressive
Corporate income tax	Progressive (except when corporations pay less due to tax loopholes)

Figure 12.2
Types of Taxes.

the burden of taxation has increasingly been shifted from corporations to the individual. Between 1960 and 2010, corporate income taxes went from 23% of total federal revenues to 7% of total federal revenues (National Priorities Project, n.d.-b). There has been some recent media attention focused on large multinational conglomerates like General Electric (GE) that pay little to no taxes despite the fact that the top tax bracket for U.S. corporations is 35%. This is possible due to tax breaks by the government as well as corporations who hire tax attorneys who are very skilled at finding loopholes in the tax system. The practice of the government giving subsidies and tax breaks to corporations has been termed "**corporate welfare**." Many companies like GE avoid paying taxes by moving their business overseas. *ABC News* reported that in 2010, GE earned $14.2 billion in profits, but instead of paying taxes, it received a $3.2 billion tax benefit because the majority of its profits were offshore (Tapper, 2011). Warren Buffett, one of the richest people in the world, famously remarked that his receptionist pays a higher percentage of her income in taxes than he does, which he believes is unfair. Other millionaires agree and have started a new website called Patriotic Millionaires for Fiscal Strength, which urges the president and government leaders to increase taxes for people making over $1 million a year.

Meanwhile, individual income taxes have remained relatively stable over the years. There are many questions that get debated politically related to taxation such as: Who should bear the burden of taxation in American society? How much should they be asked to pay? To what extent should policy makers use the tax system as a way to redistribute wealth and lessen economic inequality? And finally, how should Americans spend their public resources? NASW's (National Association of Social Workers) policy statement on poverty and economic justice indicates the profession's support for "federal tax, budget, and spending mechanisms that help to narrow gaps in the resources available to people" as well as "an adequate safety net for those unable to provide for themselves" (National Association of Social Workers, 2009, p. 261).

Human Rights & Justice

Practice Behavior Example: Engage in practices that advance social and economic justice.

Critical Thinking Question: Who should bear the burden of taxation in the United States in your opinion? How would you change tax policy in the United States if you had the power?

SPENDING

Now that we have covered how money comes into the government, we can focus on the spending side of the equation. Recently, vigorous debate in the nation's capitol has focused on government spending due to heightened concerns over the growing national debt in light of the current economic recession. For fiscal year 2012, spending by the federal government is budgeted at just under $3.7 trillion, which represents almost one-quarter of the total U.S. gross domestic product (GDP) (National Priorities Project, n.d.-c). Many are not aware that there are three pieces of the pie when it comes to spending by the federal government:

- mandatory spending (about two-thirds of the budget);
- discretionary spending (about one-third of the budget);
- interest paid on the national debt (about 5% of the budget).

Mandatory spending in fiscal year 2012 is approximately $2.4 trillion (National Priorities Project, n.d.-c). This is the part of the budget that funds the nation's **entitlement programs** such as programs for older adults (Social Security), health care programs (Medicare and Medicaid), programs that provide income support (Veterans Benefits; Supplemental Nutrition Assistance Program; unemployment compensation; Supplemental Security Income for the aged, blind, and disabled; and student loans) as well as funds for transportation. This part of the budget does not go through the annual appropriation process because these expenditures are mandated by law. **Discretionary spending** in fiscal year 2012 is approximately $1.2 trillion (National Priorities Project, n.d.-c). This is the part of the budget that is negotiated by the president and Congress, who may choose to increase or decrease funding on any of these programs in a given fiscal year. According to data reported by the National Priorities Project, over one-half of discretionary spending has been devoted to national defense in recent years due to U.S. involvement in Iraq and Afghanistan and increased funding for the Department of Homeland Security. Nonsecurity discretionary spending went to the departments of health and human services, education, housing and urban development, justice, and agriculture. Finally, paying **interest on the national debt** (which now totals about $14 trillion) will cost the U.S. government roughly $240 billion in fiscal year 2012 (National Priorities Project, n.d.).

However, when looking at the federal budget as a whole (mandatory and discretionary spending combined), the four biggest budget items are: Social Security (20%), health care (21%), national defense (20%), and safety net programs (14%) (see Figure 12.3). Federal spending on education (including higher education) is very low at approximately 3% (not shown in the graph).

An important theme of this chapter is that social workers need to be engaged with policy makers regarding spending priorities and how Americans spend their state and federal dollars. Figure 12.4 shows a sample op-ed that could be submitted to a newspaper or online news website, making the case of how Americans need to think differently when it comes to the nation's spending priorities.

> Social workers need to be engaged with policy makers regarding spending priorities and how Americans spend their state and federal dollars.

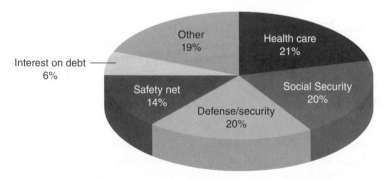

Figure 12.3

FY 2010 Federal Government Spending.

Source: Center on Budget and Policy Priorities. Figures from Office of Management and Budget, 2011. Retrieved from www.cbpp.org/cms/index.cfm?fa=view&id=1258

Think Seniors Are the Victims in the Current Federal Budget Debate? Think Again

One of the hottest political issues in the coming election year will no doubt be how to shore up the Social Security program when the baby boomers start to retire in mass. This is an important issue that must be addressed, but it greatly overshadows a little known fact—that it is children who get the short end of the stick when it comes to federal spending. The bulk of U.S. federal spending goes to defense, Social Security, and Medicare. Children are not a budget priority despite decades of solid research showing the importance of investing in children ages 0–5, which are critical years for brain development.

According to a 2010 report from the Urban Institute and the Brookings Institution, in 2009, less than 10% of federal budget outlays were devoted to children. To put this another way, in 2007, total public spending (federal/state/local) on children was $10,642 per child whereas public spending on older adults was $24,300 per adult. More shockingly perhaps is their finding that children's share of domestic federal spending shrunk by 6 percentage points between 1960 and 2009 whereas spending on the *nonchild* portions of Social security, Medicare, and Medicaid doubled during this time period. Is this the result of societal attitudes that devalue children or the fact that senior citizens are a strong and mobilized voting bloc?

According to professor Lilian Katz, an expert in early childhood education, "Each of us must come to care about everyone else's children. . . . The good life for our own children can be secured only if a good life is also secured for all other people's children." Indeed other Western industrialized countries in Europe and Scandinavia have made this paradigm shift as demonstrated by public policies that invest in children such as family allowances (a monthly stipend given to families regardless of income that helps to cover the cost of raising children), universal health care, government subsidized child care for working parents, and paid family leave, to name a few.

In comparison, U.S. rankings on international comparisons of child poverty, infant mortality, and student performance in math and science are embarrassingly poor. Federal and state governments have often failed the young by allowing millions to forgo health care coverage, ignoring countless children who attend highly segregated, substandard schools, and looking the other way when children are failed by the state child welfare agencies designed to protect them.

A recent story of a 4-year-old child who was killed by her mother, after being abused and severely malnourished, made front page news in the *New York Times*. The mother has been charged with murder, the grandmother with manslaughter. However, because this family was involved with child protection authorities, two city child welfare workers are being prosecuted for criminally negligent homicide.

For decades, child welfare advocates such as the Child Welfare League of America and the Children's Defense Fund have worked tirelessly to galvanize lawmakers to focus more on the welfare of children and the challenges facing child welfare systems that are severely under-resourced. However, there is one concrete step that could set us on the right path in seriously improving the lives of our nation's children. President Obama should convene a White House Conference on Children (WHCC), which would bring together child welfare experts from across the country to review the current state of children in the United States and identify strategies for improvement. **Starting in 1909, this conference was held every 10 years**. **However, the last one was held in 1970**. Positive outcomes of previous conferences include the creation of the Child Welfare League of America; improvements in state regulation of child labor; the creation of the American Pediatric Society; and efforts to end the systematic institutionalization of children.

A White House Conference on Children would help to shine a spotlight on the needs of children. It could also help educate lawmakers on two important programs for children ages 0–5 that are supported by loads of research and offer a lot of bang for the buck: (a) early childhood education programs and (b) home visiting programs, which provide support and parenting education to new parents. Even a divided Oregon state legislature sees the light. This session, they passed a joint memorial (HJM 12) urging the U.S. Congress to convene a WHCC.

Our politicians often talk endlessly about "family values" echoing that "children are our future." In actuality, the United States is a nation that had a Society for the Prevention of Cruelty to Animals before a Society for the Prevention of Cruelty to Children. The United States is one of only two nations in the world that has failed to ratify the U.N. Convention on the Rights of the Child (the other is Somalia). And the United States is a nation that puts children at the bottom of the barrel when it comes to federal spending. A federal bill calling on the president to convene a WHCC failed in the 111th Congress.

Perhaps a new consciousness will emerge in the United States, expressed eloquently by former author and activist Pearl S. Buck: "If our American way of life fails the child, it fails us all." Making sure that our parents and grandparents are taken care of in their golden years is priceless. Making sure that our children get a good start in life—equally priceless.

Figure 12.4

FUNDING FOR FEDERAL PROGRAMS

Most federal programs are either entitlement programs or block grant programs. An **entitlement program** is a program that eligible individuals or beneficiaries have a legal right to receive; in other words, they are "entitled" to receive these benefits if they meet eligibility requirements. However, do not let the terminology confuse you. Many entitlement programs such as Social Security, Medicare, and unemployment insurance are social insurance programs, which means that people have paid into these programs; in other words, people are not getting something for nothing. Social Security and Medicare are perhaps the most well-known entitlement programs because of their popularity and the high cost of these social programs, particularly now that the baby boomers are starting to retire en masse.

Because entitlement programs are under the realm of mandatory spending, they do not go through the annual appropriation process in Congress; so the cost of these programs are more difficult for the government to control. This causes much consternation for political conservatives who complain about the inability of the government to continue to pay for these costly social programs. Some entitlement programs are administered through state governments in a cost-sharing or matching funds framework, such as Medicaid (health care for low-income or disabled people) in which the state may pay 30%–40% of patient care costs whereas the federal government will pick up 60%–70% of the cost. Generally, in entitlement programs, there are some minimum standards imposed on states about services and populations that must be included, but states also have some flexibility to serve additional populations depending on their ability to generate the state financial resources to trigger the federal match.

Block grant programs have been increasingly popular in recent years due to efforts by federal lawmakers to reign in federal spending. Block grant funding is when the federal government gives states a specific lump sum to administer a particular program. Advocates of block grants like that states are given flexibility and decision-making power in designing the program and spending the funds to best suit local needs. Critics argue that block grants devolve responsibility for certain social problems from the federal government to the states, which in some cases are less sensitive to the needs of low-income individuals.

Also, block grants can be used to decrease funding for a specific program. Block grants are finite, so when the need exceeds the amount of the resources in the program either the services end or the implementing partners have to come up with additional resources to serve the clients from some other source, which could be state or local government funds, collecting client fees based on a sliding scale, or public-private partnerships. In fact, one strategy used by fiscal conservatives is to try to turn an entitlement program into a block grant program in order to shrink the size and funding of that program. Perhaps the best example of this occurred in 1996 when the nation's welfare program (Aid to Families With Dependent Children, or AFDC) was replaced with the TANF program. This ended the federal entitlement of public assistance to poor children and families, a practice that had been in place for 60 years in the United States. Figure 12.5 provides an overview of various types of federal funding, which can be a bit confusing.

WHY IS THE U.S. GOVERNMENT IN DEBT?

Many Americans grumble when the federal government is in debt, but when lawmakers begin talking about cutting specific programs, the lawmakers are usually greeted with resistance from their constituents. Before exploring the

Federal funds are distributed to states and communities through a variety of mechanisms. Each is designed to serve a particular purpose, and each comes with its own set of rules and requirements. Understanding the various types of funds is important because the funding mechanism of a particular funding source has an impact on the strategy employed to access funds. Major types of federal funding sources are listed here.

Entitlement programs guarantee that all individuals who meet the eligibility criteria are served. Some federal entitlement funds flow directly to state agencies, which are responsible for operating the particular program or turning the funds over to local agencies to operate the program; in other states, city or county governments run the program. States may also use federal entitlement funds to contract with private nonprofit agencies to perform specific activities that are part of the state plan.

Formula or **block grants** provide states with a fixed allocation of funds to states based on an established formula that may, for example, be linked to a state's poverty rate. On a regular basis, states must submit a general plan describing the broad functions and population to be served by the state program to the federal agency that oversees the program. Like entitlements, block grants flow directly to state agencies that are responsible for operating the particular program, subgranting the funds through a proposal process, or otherwise turning the funds over to local governments or nonprofit agencies. Unlike entitlements, however, formula grants do not guarantee to cover everyone who is eligible.

Discretionary or **project grants** fund a wide range of targeted federal efforts, from preventing juvenile delinquency to improving infant health outcomes. Depending on the program requirements, state and local governments, community-based organizations, or coalitions of community groups and agencies can apply directly to the sponsoring federal agency to gain access to these funds through a competitive bidding process. Application for discretionary grants does not guarantee an award, and the amounts received by grantees are not predetermined by a formula.

Contracts between the state or federal government and other private or public agencies require the provision of specified services and often incorporate specific performance standards that contractors must meet.

Demonstration grants are pilot projects generally involving a small number of sites in an effort to learn about the effectiveness of a new program or approach. An effective demonstration grant program may lead to further funding in the form of discretionary grants. Demonstration grants also are awarded on a competitive basis and can go to state and local governments or to community-based organizations, depending on the program's eligibility requirements.

Direct payments are funds paid by the federal government directly to individual beneficiaries who satisfy federal eligibility requirements. These programs may, however, be administered by an intermediate state agency.

Figure 12.5

Major Types of Federal Funding.

Source: http://www.afterschool.gov/docs/federalFunding.html

rather complicated question of why the United States is in debt, it is important to understand the difference between national debt and deficit. The government runs a **deficit** when its spending exceeds its revenues in a given year. For example, in fiscal year 2011, the federal government ran a $1.1 trillion deficit. A surplus is a year when revenues exceed spending. The last time the federal government had surpluses occurred during the Clinton administration. However, the **national debt** is the total money owed by the government over many years. Thus, when the United States has many years of running deficits, the accumulation becomes its national debt. The U.S. federal government is currently about $15.7 trillion in debt (as of June 2012). To see the current status of the U.S. debt, visit www.usdebtclock.org.

When the U.S. government cannot pay for the programs and services that it needs to provide, it must borrow money. It does this by selling Treasury securities and savings bonds to other federal government agencies, individuals, corporations, state and local governments, associations, public and private organizations, as well as people, businesses, and governments from other countries. These various entities lend money to the U.S. government so that the government can pay its bills, and over time the government must pay the money back with interest. Some Americans would be surprised to learn that a number of foreign countries own a significant amount of U.S. debt, over $5 trillion as of March 2012. According to the Treasury Department, the countries that own the most U.S. debt are China and Japan.

One way that the U.S. Congress has tried to keep the federal government from getting too much in debt is to pass a law enforcing a **debt ceiling**, a cap on the amount of debt the federal government can legally borrow. The debt ceiling is currently set at $14.2 trillion. This has created a standoff between President Obama and Republicans because the Obama administration has requested that the debt ceiling be raised so that the United States can continue to pay its bills. The debt ceiling has been raised many times over the years. Economists argue over whether running deficits is harmful to the U.S. economy, and deficit spending is often recommended during an economic recession to help spur economic activity. Fiscal conservatives argue that it is irresponsible for the government to be in debt in the same way that private individuals should not be in debt. On the other hand, running up high deficits is a strategy often employed by conservatives in order to cut government programs that the country cannot afford (called "starve the beast" strategy) in their efforts to shrink the size of government.

So, the simple answer to the question of why the U.S. government is in debt is that it spends more money than it takes in. President Obama and the U.S. Congress have been grappling over ways to bring the national debt down. Possibilities include raising revenues (taxes), cutting spending, or a combination of the two. Conservatives are urging the president to cut spending and are adamantly opposed to raising taxes on the wealthy. They argue that the rising costs of the Social Security and Medicare programs are unsustainable and that the U.S. government must get government spending under control. Liberals argue that the United States is in this position due to the economic recession caused by the greed of Wall Street as well as heavy deficit spending under President Bush who cut taxes on the wealthy while entering the country into two wars that the United States could not pay for. They further argue that it is unfair to balance the budget on the backs of the poor and the middle class and advocate bringing down the deficit by raising taxes on the wealthy and cutting defense spending by bringing the troops home and ending the wars. This is yet another example of how intertwined politics and economics are in the United States.

Human Rights & Justice

Practice Behavior Example: Advocate for human rights and social and economic justice.

Critical Thinking Question: In the age of the Tea Party and calls for a smaller government, how can social workers convince policy makers to keep their commitment to the social safety net for the nation's most vulnerable citizens?

STATE BUDGETS

Although the focus of this chapter is on understanding the federal budget, there are a few important points to keep in mind when it comes to **state budgets**. In state budgets, there are generally three pots of money: social services, education, and public safety. And one major difference between the federal government and state governments is that states cannot run deficits or accumulate debt—when

Cross roads metaphor showing the raising taxes or cutting spending dilemma faced by U.S. policymakers.

they are out of money, they must cut vital state services. The current economic recession has been devastating for many states for several reasons. First, they rely on funding from the federal government, and when the federal government is struggling financially, this trickles down to state and local government. Additionally, many states rely on state income taxes, sales taxes, and property taxes, and when there are high rates of unemployment and home foreclosures, this results in less revenue for states. Like the federal government, states are also in the position of making tough decisions on whether they need to raise revenues (taxes) or cut services and programs that serve vulnerable populations.

AMERICAN EXCEPTIONALISM OR WELFARE EXCEPTIONALISM?

The term **American exceptionalism** has become part of the American lexicon in recent years as lawmakers and others have sought to make sense of the United States and its place in the world. The term has an interesting history and means different things to different people, although it seems to attempt to define what makes America special or unique compared to other nations. Sociologist Seymour Martin Lipset (1996) wrote that "the nation's ideology can be described in five words: liberty, egalitarianism, individualism, populism, and laissez faire" (p. 19). This term also has religious overtones because according to research, many Americans believe that God has granted America a special role in human history (Tumulty, 2010). Some tend to embrace this terminology whereas others are uncomfortable with the idea that the United States is superior to other nations around the world. The term has become very political and has been used to frame some lawmakers (including President Obama) as anti-American when they fail to embrace this idea.

However, two sociologists used the term **welfare exceptionalism** to describe the reluctance of the United States to become a welfare state similar to other Western industrialized countries in Europe (Amenta & Skocpol, 1989). It is important for the social work profession to explore why the richest country in the world has such high rates of poverty and income inequality. When examining how the United States compares to other nations, the United States

Two sociologists used the term *welfare exceptionalism* to describe the reluctance of the United States to become a welfare state similar to other Western industrialized countries in Europe.

is often compared to other nations in the OECD, or the Organization for Economic and Cooperation and Development. Countries in the OECD are among the most wealthy and developed and are committed to democracy and the market economy. According to the latest data from the OECD (2011a), out of the 34 OECD countries, the United States ranks:

- second in highest household income (after taxes and benefits), after Luxembourg
- fourth highest on level of income inequality
- fourth highest on rate of poverty (17.3% of poor people compared to an OECD average of 11.1%)
- highest of all of the OECD countries in percentage of citizens volunteering time, giving money, and helping strangers
- highest in obesity.

So, the United States ranks extremely high in household income compared to other countries, yet has high levels of poverty and income inequality. What explains this? One explanation is that there is a fairly consistent relationship between tax policy and income inequality. As Figure 12.6 shows, in most cases, countries that have high taxes on individuals and corporations rank low in

OECD Countries with highest tax burden (2009)	Gini Index (lower value means low inequality)		
Denmark	48.1	.25	low
Sweden	46.7	.26	low
Belgium	43.2	.27	low
Italy	**43.4**	**.34**	**high**
France	42.4	.29	low
Finland	42.6	.26	low
Austria	42.7	.26	low
Norway	42.9	.25	low
Hungary	39.9	.27	low
OECD Countries with lowest tax burden (2009)	Gini index (higher value means high inequality)		
Mexico	17.4	.48	high
Chile	18.4	.50	high
Turkey	24.6	.41	high
United States	24.1	.38	high
Korea	25.5	.32	high
Australia	25.9	.34	high

Column 1: From OECD (2011b). *OECD tax revenue statistics.* Tax revenues as percentage of Gross Domestic Product (GDP) (Table A—updated with 2011 publication data), over the period 1975–2009. These ratios are calculated by expressing total tax revenues as a percentage of GDP at market prices. Retrieved from www.oecd.org/ctp/taxdatabase.

Column 2: From OECD (2011a). *Society at a glance 2011—OECD social indicators.* Data on Income Inequality, EQ1.XLS. Retrieved from www.oecd.org/els/social/indicators/SAG.*

Figure 12.6

OECD Countries Comparison: Taxation and Income Inequality.

*OECD (2011), Revenue Statistics 2011, OECD Publishing http://dx.doi.org/10.1787/rev_stats-2011-en-fr

income inequality. For example, Denmark ranks highest in terms of tax revenues generated and also ranks lowest on the Gini index, a measure that is used to assess a nation's level of income inequality. It is fairly striking that the four countries with the lowest taxes (Mexico, Chile, Turkey, and the United States) are the four countries that rank highest on the Gini index (meaning that these are the OECD countries with the highest levels of income inequality). The only outlier is Italy, which has a high tax rate but also has a high level of income inequality.

Another explanation for the high level of income inequality in the United States is that not all Americans enjoy the same level of prosperity when the economy as a whole grows. According to researchers from the Center on Budget and Policy Priorities, in 2007 the share of the nation's income flowing to the top 1% of households was 23.5%, a larger share than at any point since 1928. According to Feller and Stone (2009):

> The uneven distribution of economic gains in recent years continues a longer-term trend that began in the late 1970s. In the three decades following World War II (1946–1976), robust economic gains were shared widely, with the incomes of the bottom 90 percent actually increasing more rapidly in percentage terms, on average, than the incomes of the top 1 percent. But in the three decades since 1976, the incomes of the bottom 90 percent of households have risen only slightly, on average, while the incomes of the top 1 percent have soared.*

When discussions of economic inequality arise, there is often someone who will state that it is impossible for societies to reach full economic equality. While this is true, it is also true that many countries do have some control over the *degree* of inequality they are willing to accept. So a better question to ask would be: How much inequality are Americans prepared to accept as a society? And, why has the United States made different choices than many other industrialized nations when it comes to taxation and wealth distribution? Why is the United States "exceptional" in this regard? Possible explanations that have been posited by scholars include the following:

- the United States is less homogenous than other countries in Europe and Scandinavia (i.e., the United States has higher ethnic and religious diversity);
- the U.S. government is highly decentralized and values states' rights, making it difficult to have strong national strategies and policies;
- well-financed corporate interest groups wield powerful influence to bend economic policies in their favor;
- the worship of materialism and wealth in the United States prevents average Americans from challenging policies favoring the wealthy because they themselves aspire to be wealthy. The financial success of famous Americans like Bill Gates and Oprah Winfrey keep this mythology alive;
- the United States is rooted in the value of rugged individualism;
- trade unions are weak in the United States; and
- it has been observed that the United States is the only industrialized nation that does not have a socialist movement or labor party.

Critical Thinking

Practice Behavior Example: Demonstrate effective oral and written communication in working with individuals, families, groups, organizations, communities, and colleagues.

Critical Thinking Question: How successful has the Occupy Wall Street movement been in raising the nation's consciousness about rising levels of income inequality in the United States? In your view, have the protesters effectively communicated their message to the public?

*Center on Budget and Policy Priorities.

POLICIES THAT PROMOTE POVERTY REDUCTION

One of the values of the social work profession is to promote social and economic justice, yet the profession has been accused of neglecting its commitment to the reduction of poverty on a macro level. However, social workers work with low-income individuals and families every day, and it often seems like a daunting task to help people move out of poverty. This is not an easy problem to solve. The way the U.S. government defines who is living in poverty in the United States is political and is not without controversy. The **poverty threshold or poverty line** was adopted in the 1960s and has not been revised since. The formula was based on the idea that the average family spends about one-third of its income on food, so the cost of the least expensive food plan was figured and that number was multiplied by three. The official poverty line adjusts for various factors such as number of children under 18 and household size, and it is adjusted for inflation based on the consumer price index. According to the U.S. Census Bureau (2011), the poverty line was as follows (income before taxes):

- single person—$11,702
- single parent with one child—$15,504
- single parent with two children—$18,123
- family of two adults with two children—$22,811

The poverty line is an **absolute measure** of poverty, which means that if you are below that line, you are in poverty, but if you are a few dollars above that line, you are not. Some feel that the poverty line underestimates the number of poor people in the United States whereas others feel it is an overestimate. Because of these criticisms, in November 2011, the U.S. government released an "experimental poverty measure" to try to get a more accurate picture of who is poor; however, it will not yet replace the current official measure. The experimental measure will include government benefits that people receive such as food stamps, account for regional differences in cost of living, and will factor in expenses such as healthcare and taxes. According to the U.S. Census Bureau, in 2010, 15.1% of people in the United States were living below the poverty line, which represents 46.2 million people (U.S. Census Bureau, 2010). When describing people who are poor in the United States, generally two groups of people are considered: (a) the working poor and (b) those who are unemployed. Decades of research has consistently found that the following groups are disproportionately represented among the poor: women (called the "**feminization of poverty**"), children, Blacks, and Latinos. One in five children in the United States are poor, and the rate increases for children of color (one in three for Black and Latino children) (National Poverty Center, n.d.).

In order to address poverty, it is important to understand why people are poor and advocate for sound social policies. There are many researchers, advocacy groups, and poverty research centers doing important work in this regard in order to gain more knowledge about this rather complex social problem (see Figure 12.7). The causes of poverty are often multifaceted. Social work professor Mark Rank attempts to explore the causes of poverty in his book titled *One Nation Underprivileged: Why American Poverty Affects Us All* (2004). The premise of his book is that the dominant perspective in the United States has been that of poverty as an individual failing rather than the result of structural

The premise of Rank's book is that the dominant perspective in the United States has been that of poverty as an individual failing rather than the result of structural failings at the economic, political, and societal levels.

Coalition on Human Needs
National Alliance to End Homelessness
National Coalition for the Homeless
The Alliance to End Hunger
National Low Income Housing Coalition
Half in Ten Campaign
The Urban League
National Center for Children in Poverty, Columbia University
National Poverty Center, University of Michigan
Center for Poverty Research, University of Kentucky
Institute for Research on Poverty, University of Wisconsin–Madison
West Coast Poverty Center, University of Washington

Figure 12.7

Poverty: Advocacy Organizations and Research Organizations.

failings at the economic, political, and societal levels. He points to the impact of discrimination, the inability of the labor market to provide enough decent paying jobs, and an American economy that has increasingly produced large numbers of low-paying jobs, part-time jobs, and jobs lacking in benefits. According to Rank, the U.S. has historically focused on *who* loses out at the economic game rather than *why* the game produces losers in the first place. The model that he puts forward is as follows:

- Opportunities and the acquisition of human capital (i.e., education, skills) are strongly influenced by your parents' social class.
- Lack of human capital places individuals in a vulnerable state when detrimental events and crises occur; life crises are experienced more often and with greater intensity.
- Structural forces ensure that there will be losers in the economic game.

Rank also includes data that show that a majority of Americans will experience poverty at some point during their adult years as well as the societal costs to poverty (e.g., higher health care costs, less productive workers, and high rates of criminal activity).

There are three primary strategies that have been used in the United States to address poverty. The **alleviative approach** relies on programs that ease the suffering of the poor but do not ameliorate the causes of poverty (e.g., public assistance). The **preventive approach** attempts to prevent poverty from occurring in the first place and often employs social insurance strategies (e.g., Social Security). The **curative approach** targets the root causes of poverty and involves structural changes in society that would result in very low levels of poverty (e.g., high taxes and redistribution of wealth similar to the system used by many European countries). A number of strategies have been recommended by experts as sound antipoverty strategies:

- The federal earned income tax credit (EITC): This has been touted as one of the best antipoverty tools in existence today. The EITC decreases the tax burden on people making low and moderate incomes; qualified workers receive a tax rebate from the federal government that exceeds the taxes they paid. In 2008, the average EITC was $2,659. For some families, the credit is enough to lift them over the poverty line.

- Asset building strategies such as the use of individual development accounts (IDAs): Low-income people are encouraged to save, and whatever they put in is matched (by an outside funder), helping it to grow more quickly over time; funds can be used to buy a home, start a business, or to finance a college education.
- Micro-finance programs: Banks provide low-interest loans to poor people to help them start a business (see Illustration 12.1).
- Substantial investments in public and higher education.
- Raising the minimum wage or passing living wage ordinances (living wages are higher than minimum wages because they factor in how much money is needed to meet one's basic needs adequately).
- Promoting unionization.
- Cash transfer programs: This is being piloted in New York City and involves providing financial incentives or rewards to low-income people when they engage in certain behaviors (e.g., ensuring their child has good school attendance, receiving preventive medical care, participating in job training or education).

Diversity in Practice

Practice Behavior Example: Recognize the extent to which a culture's structures and values may oppress, marginalize, alienate, create, or enhance privilege and power.

Critical Thinking Question: Of the three approaches to poverty—curative, alleviative, and preventive—which do you think the United States relies on most heavily? Which of the antipoverty strategies discussed at the end of this chapter could be most successful in the United States?

Two U.S. presidents, Franklin Delano Roosevelt and Lyndon B. Johnson (LBJ), chose to prioritize poverty and to address it by passing far-reaching social welfare legislation. LBJ went as far as to declare a war on poverty. But since then, there has been no serious effort to address this social problem systematically as a nation, and this issue is often left off of the political agenda. It is up to social workers and other committed advocates to focus lawmakers' and the greater public's attention onto this problem that most people would rather ignore.

Muhammad Yunus: "Banker to the Poor"

Economics professor Muhammad Yunus established the Grameen Bank in Bangladesh in 1983, because he believed that credit is a fundamental human right and that poor people can be reliable borrowers and successful entrepreneurs. His objective was to help poor people escape from poverty by providing low-interest loans that they could afford and teaching them financial principles needed to successfully run their own small business. He started out focusing on providing loans to women because women were more likely to focus on the needs of their family.

Dr. Yunus started in Bangladesh loaning money to basketweavers in the 1970s, and in 1983 he formed the Grameen Bank (which means Village bank). Today the practice of **micro-lending** or **micro-credit** has spread to the rest of the developing and nondeveloping world. According to the Grameen Bank website, the bank now has over 2,500 branches and serves over 8 million borrowers, collecting an average of 1.5 million in weekly installments. It reports that 97% of the borrowers are women and 97% of the loans are paid back. To learn more, visit www.grameen-info.org/.

Mr. Yunus was awarded the Nobel Peace Prize in 2006.

Illustration 12.1

The following questions will test your knowledge of the content found within this chapter. For additional assessment, including licensing-exam type questions on applying chapter content to practice behaviors, visit **MySearchLab**.

1. Which of the following would be advocated by an individual or organization with a Keynesian economic philosophy?
   a. Low taxes on individuals and corporations
   b. Minimal government regulations for those working in the banking/financial industry
   c. Privatization of the Social Security system
   d. The use of public work projects during an economic recession

2. Regressive taxation places a higher tax burden on:
   a. low income Americans
   b. older Americans
   c. wealthier Americans
   d. corporations

3. A _____ is when the government spends more than it takes in during a given year.
   a. debt
   b. deficit
   c. surplus
   d. debt ceiling

4. Countries that have a high level of income equality tend to have:
   a. low taxes
   b. high taxes
   c. high poverty rates
   d. a philosophy of rugged individualism

5. The Supplemental Nutrition Assistance Program, formerly called the Food Stamp Program, is an example of the _____ approach to poverty.
   a. curative
   b. human capital
   c. alleviative
   d. preventive

6. _____ is the study of the relationship between a nation's political and economic systems.
   a. Corporate welfare
   b. Welfare exceptionalism
   c. Discretionary spending
   d. Political economy

7. In your opinion, which issues deserve more funding than others when thinking about how Americans divide up the funding "pie" in the United States? How should Americans prioritize when it comes to government spending? In other words, how do Americans decide which issues are more important than others? Work with a classmate and come up with a list of the top three issues that the United States should prioritize from a social work perspective.

MYSEARCHLAB CONNECTIONS

Reinforce what you learned in this chapter by studying videos, cases, documents, and more available at **www.MySearchLab.com**.

Watch and Review

Watch these Videos

* Working Poor
* Republicans and Democrats Divide on Tax Cut (2008)
* Raising the Minimum Wage
* The Bailout Hearings

Read and Review

Read these Cases/Documents

Δ Andrew Carnegie, "Wealth," North American Review (1889)

Δ Bob Stinson, Flint Sit-Down Strike (1936)

* Caroline Manning, The Immigrant Woman and Her Job (1930)

* Huey Long, "Share Our Wealth" (1935)

Explore and Assess

Explore these Assets

* Comparing Economic Policy (interactive case study)
* Interactive Case Study: Comparing Social Welfare Systems
* Interactive Case Study: Evaluating Federal Spending and Economic Policy
* Interactive Case Study: Growth of the Budget and Federal Spending, The
* Interactive Case Study: You Are the Mayor and Need to Get a Town Budget Passed

Research these Topics

Understanding "Political Economy"

Understanding State and Federal Budgets—Revenues and Spending

Exploring Income Inequality and Poverty Through a Social Work Policy Lens

Assess Your Knowledge

Go to **MySearchLab** to test your knowledge of key topics in this chapter with topic-specific quizzes. Conclude your assessment by completing the chapter exam.

---

* = CSWE Core Competency Asset   Δ = Case Study

13

A Look to the Future

Competencies in This Chapter (With Practice Behaviors)									
X	Professional Identity		Ethical Practice	X	Critical Thinking		Diversity in Practice		Human Rights & Justice
	Research-Based Practice		Human Behavior	X	Policy Practice		Practice Contexts		Engage, Assess, Intervene, Evaluate

244

First they ignore you. Then they laugh at you.
Then they fight you. Then you win.

—Gandhi

Social workers often feel overwhelmed and disillusioned when thinking about being a change agent in the legislative and/or political arena. It is normal to ask: "Can I really make a difference politically?" Countless books and articles have been written to describe the rise in the number of Americans who feel alienated from the government and the political process. Research from the American National Election Studies shows that the public's trust in government has waned significantly since the 1960s (see Chapter 5 for more on this). Many Americans have come to believe that politicians are corrupt and only cater to powerful, special interests. These feelings are understandable. However, it is crucial to consider the fact that if social workers remove themselves from the political process in anger, frustration, and disgust, it is typically people at the margins who end up suffering the most. Despite the fact that there are some actual and perceived barriers to social workers' political participation on behalf of vulnerable groups, it is imperative that social workers use political advocacy as one of the many tools in their toolkit when seeking change at the macro level.

If social workers remove themselves from the political process in anger, frustration, and disgust, it is typically people at the margins who end up suffering the most.

Social workers have an ethical duty and a moral obligation to share their experiences, expertise, and research with legislators so they have the information they need to make good decisions in the area of social welfare policy. There are many examples throughout history of legislation that made a dramatic difference in people's lives. It is not helpful when the social work profession enters into a false debate over whether the profession should emphasize micro-level social work or macro-level social work. The beauty of social work, and what sets it apart from most other professions, is that it includes both. In the words of social work professor Don Schweitzer of Pacific University Oregon, "There is no such thing as a micro social worker or a macro social worker—you are a social worker!" (Personal communication, n.d.).

In this book, a number of stories were told of advocates and organizations that attempted to get a piece of legislation passed into law. Though each story is unique, a number of important themes emerged. One theme is that most of the change that comes about in the legislative arena is a result of **many committed individuals and groups working together**. Chapter 7 of this book tells the story of how the Paul Wellstone and Pete Domenici Mental Health Parity and Addiction Equality Act of 2008 was passed into law by committed individuals, organizations, and lawmakers who worked together to make it illegal for insurance companies to discriminate against those suffering with mental health disorders. Political and social change requires resources and this includes time, people, and money; thus, the more "people" resources you have at the table, the better. Even though there is some truth to the adage "One person can make a difference," the real story seems to be, "Groups of individuals working together really make the difference." Working for change as part of a group is more fun, and it provides advocates with the support they need when things get tough and they feel disillusioned.

Another theme is that organizations that are able to hire **paid, professional staff with expertise in lobbying and running an effective campaign** will often be more successful. The success of the Death with Dignity campaign in Washington State is a great example of this because advocates were able to raise enough money to hire professionals with expertise in running an effective

Tactics	
☐ Coalition building	☐ Direct lobbying
☐ Earned media	☐ Grassroots lobbying
☐ Paid media	☐ Educational outreach
☐ Visibility	☐ Online advocacy/social media
☐ Political dissent	☐ Paid communication
☐ Providing testimony	☐ Fund-raising activities

media campaign, including television ads. Professional lobbyists and campaign workers have the knowledge and expertise required to mobilize volunteers, build relationships with legislators and other important decision makers, raise money, and develop professional media materials. It is important to know what work can be done by volunteers and where professional people are needed. This is often vital because in many cases, the opposition is better financed.

Yet another lesson that can be learned from the stories in this book concerns the **importance of employing many different tactics in order to win** and the increasing reliance on social media in order to connect with people, educate others, and mobilize them for action. In most of the stories told in this book, a combination of the above tactics were employed in order to achieve a legislative win.

Finally, perhaps the biggest lesson we can learn from most stories involving social and political change is that **those seeking policy change must be persistent and patient** because success does not usually happen overnight. Most stories of social and political change involve a number of ups and downs until a win is achieved. Initially, many social work students operate from the fallacy that micro- and mezzo-level change is easier to achieve than macro-level change. However, after getting some experience at the micro level, new social workers soon discover that helping individuals and families to make changes is equally challenging and that change at this level also can be painstakingly slow. In both cases, it is important to set small achievable markers of success along the way until the big win is achieved.

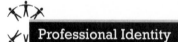

Professional Identity

Practice Behavior Example: Serve as representatives of the profession, its mission, and its core values.

Critical Thinking Question: Do you think that macro-level social work is more challenging and daunting than micro-level social work? Why or why not?

Perhaps social workers will be encouraged by the results of a study published in the journal *Political Psychology* that found positive benefits for those who engage in political activism.

A few of the stories in this book involve advocates who have yet to achieve their "big win" such as the DREAM Act youth activists, the Mad as Hell doctors, and those working to get the United States to ratify the UN Convention on the Rights of the Child. However, they can each point to progress that has been made along the way, such as the number of people who have been educated about the issue, the growth of their organization (e.g., development of a website, growing number of supporters/volunteers), and the skill development of the participating individuals who are part of their movement or cause. In sum, though some legislative change efforts involve sweeping, monumental, or landmark changes, **most change happens incrementally**.

Perhaps social workers will be encouraged by the results of a study published in the journal *Political Psychology* that found positive benefits for those who engage in political activism. Coauthor Tim Kasser explains, "There is something about activism itself that is beneficial for well-being. We found that activists were feeling more autonomy and more personal growth. They also

felt they had better relationships, more purpose in life, and they liked themselves better" (Petre, 2010).

HOT-BUTTON POLITICAL ISSUES ON THE HORIZON OF INTEREST TO SOCIAL WORK

In the coming years, the United States will be confronted with a number of
critical issues that pertain to its many vulnerable populations.

IMMIGRATION

Immigration will continue to be an important issue politically because those
from both sides of the political spectrum agree that the immigration system is
broken and in need of reform. Congress has been split between those who want
to punish and/or deport those who are here with no legal status and those
who advocate a path to citizenship for the roughly 11 million undocumented
immigrants residing in the United States. There are plenty of innocent people
caught in the crosshairs of this debate including those who were brought here
by their parents when they were children (see Chapter 8 on the DREAM Act)
who now want the opportunity to go to college and work in the country that
is their home. Since 2001, the DREAM Act has not been passed by Congress.
Social workers serve immigrants (both documented and undocumented) in
many settings and should be part of the discussion and solution. The National
Association of Social Workers (NASW) has gone on record as supporting the
DREAM Act and has the following policy position:

> NASW supports immigration and refugee policies that uphold and sup-
> port equity and human rights, while protecting national security. The so-
> cial work profession recognizes that the challenge of competing claims is
> formidable; however, immigration policies must promote social justice
> and avoid racism and discrimination or profiling on the basis of race,
> religion, country of origin, gender, or other grounds. NASW has a special
> interest in the impact of refugee and immigration policies on families
> and children and supports policies that encourage family reunification
> and ensure that children do not grow up unduly disadvantaged by the
> immigration status of their parents. (*Social Work Speaks, 2009–2012*)

OLDER ADULTS AND AGING

Many social workers are concerned about whether the United States will be
sufficiently prepared for the graying of America in the coming years as a result
of the millions of baby boomers who will be retiring from the U.S. workforce.
Many questions will need to be addressed by American policy makers such as:
Will the Social Security and Medicare systems continue to be financially sound?
Will the government support and fund home health care programs that will allow older adults to receive care at home when feasible and appropriate instead
of being forced into institutionalized care? How will the country support adults
who are caregivers for their aging relatives? Can Americans have rational conversations about policies focused on end-of-life care without it devolving into

diatribes against "death panels"? NASW's policy position on end-of-life care includes the following statement: "NASW does not take a position concerning the morality of end-of-life decisions, but affirms the right of any individual to direct his or her care wishes at the end of life" (*Social Work Speaks, 2009–2012*).

EQUAL RIGHTS FOR LGBT INDIVIDUALS

Some have characterized rights for LGBT (lesbian, gay, bisexual, and transgender) individuals as the civil rights issue of our time. In the coming years, America will continue to debate equal rights for LGBT individuals in many areas such as marriage, parenting, and workplace discrimination. Violence against LGBT individuals has been a huge concern as the country has witnessed many high-profile cases of students in colleges and public schools who have taken their own life as a result of bullying and intimidation by their classmates. One major step forward was the passage of the Matthew Shepard and James Byrd, Jr. Hate Crimes Prevention Act in 2009 that gives federal officials the power to investigate and prosecute crimes of violence when the victim was chosen because of the actual or perceived gender, sexual orientation, gender identity, or disability.

The Employment Non-Discrimination Act (ENDA), which has yet to pass, would make it illegal to discriminate in the workplace on the basis of sexual orientation and gender identity or expression. The Human Rights Campaign is the premiere advocacy group in the United States for LGBT individuals, but other advocacy groups can be found at the local level in most states. NASWs policy position on lesbian, gay, and bisexual issues is as follows:

> In coalition with other mental health and human services professions, NASW supports antidiscrimination legislation at the national, state, and local levels. NASW opposes laws that allow discrimination against lesbian, gay, and bisexual people, including in immigration, employment, housing, professional credentialing, licensing, public accommodation, child custody, and the right to marry. NASW encourages the adoption of laws that recognize inheritance, insurance, same-sex marriage, child custody, property, and other relationship rights for lesbian, gay, and bisexual people (*Social Work Speaks, 2009–2012*).

RETURNING VETERANS

You may be surprised to learn that the Department of Veterans Affairs (VA) is the largest employer of social workers with master's degrees in the United States. Today, there are over 2 million veterans of the Iraq and Afghanistan wars. Returning veterans face a variety of challenges after returning home, which may include posttraumatic stress disorder (PTSD) and traumatic brain injury, unstable housing and/or homelessness, mental health disorders, physical injury, permanent physical disability, addictions, and a range of difficulties adjusting to civilian life. Social workers who work with veterans are in the position to advocate for them to ensure that veterans and their families have the resources and support that they need when veterans return home. The social work profession must also grapple with issues concerning the morality of war and may engage in conversations about military spending levels in comparison to spending on public welfare and spending for the public good.

POVERTY AND INCOME INEQUALITY

Poverty and income inequality are rarely seriously addressed by U.S. leaders and policy makers at the local and national level. This is despite the fact that according to the U.S. Census Bureau, 46.2 million Americans were living below the poverty threshold in 2010 (one in six), and it was worse for other vulnerable groups. In 2010, 27% of African Americans were poor, 27% of Latinos, 32% of single-mother homes, and 22% of children (DeNavas-Walt, Proctor, & Smith, 2011). This is also despite the fact that income inequality has risen significantly in recent years. According to a report by the Center on Budget and Policy Priorities, the top 1% of households took home 20% of income in 2010 (Shaw & Stone, 2012). Couple this with recent data from the Institute for Policy Study's 17th annual Executive Compensation Survey, which found that, in 2009, CEOs of major U.S. corporations averaged 263 times the average compensation of American workers; in the 1970s, few executives made over 30 times what their workers made (Anderson, Collins, Pizzigati, & Shih, 2010).

There are a number of national organizations that advocate for low-income individuals such as the Coalition on Human Needs, the Half in Ten Campaign, the National Alliance to End Homelessness, the Alliance to End Hunger, the Center for American Progress' Task Force on Poverty, and the National Urban League. There are also poverty research centers located at Columbia University, the University of Kentucky, University of Michigan, University of Washington, and the University of Wisconsin–Madison.

Various strategies to help move people out of poverty that advocates point to include: raising the minimum wage, living wage ordinances, promoting unionization, investing in improving education at all levels (including early childhood education), asset-building strategies such as the use of individual development accounts (IDAs), micro-credit programs to help spur entrepreneurship among the poor, expanding the earned income tax credit and child credit, affordable housing programs, and experimental programs that are showing promise such as the Harlem Children's Zone and the conditional cash transfer program being piloted in New York City, called Opportunity NYC.

THE WELFARE OF CHILDREN

Chapter 9 outlined the many challenges facing children and youth in the United States, including the fact that the U.S. has failed to ratify the UN Convention on the Rights of the Child. However, it is a little known fact that children get the short end of the stick when it comes to federal spending. The bulk of U.S. federal spending goes to defense, Social Security, and Medicare. Children are not a budget priority despite decades of solid research showing the importance of investing in children ages 0–5 because these are critical years for brain development. According to a 2010 report from the Urban Institute and the Brookings Institution, in 2009, less than 10% of federal budget outlays were devoted to children (Rennane, Isaacs, Steuerle, & Ehrle Macomber, 2010). To put this another way, in 2007, total public spending (federal/state/local) on children was $10,642 per child whereas public spending on older adults was $24,300 per adult. More shockingly perhaps is its finding that children's share of domestic federal spending shrunk by 6 percentage points between 1960 and 2009 whereas spending on the *nonchild* portions of Social Security, Medicare, and Medicaid doubled during this time period. It is hard to know whether this is due to societal attitudes that devalue children or the fact that senior citizens are a strong and mobilized voting bloc.

REFORMING GOVERNMENT SO THAT IT OPERATES IN THE INTEREST OF THE PEOPLE

Having people disillusioned, uninformed, and disengaged works well for those in power.

There are a number of organizations that are working to reform the political process in the United States in order to remove corruption and the influence of powerful, special interests, and to help create a system of government that protects the interests of average Americans. Having people disillusioned, uninformed, and disengaged works well for those in power. If the system were more fair and accessible to average Americans, one would likely see more people involved in the affairs of their community and government at all levels, which is a sign of a healthy democracy. These initiatives include:

- abolishing the Electoral College and electing the president by national popular vote (www.nationalpopularvote.com);
- publicly financed campaigns (getting big money out of politics);
- ethics reforms (curtail influence of lobbyists and special interests);
- term limits for those who serve in Congress;
- more political parties to end the dominance of the two-party system in the United States;
- eliminating barriers to voting and registration;
- improving media coverage of politics; and
- strategies to increase levels of civic engagement, particularly for those groups who tend to be less active such as young people and those with lower SES.

GETTING GOVERNMENT TO INVEST IN THE SOCIAL WORK PROFESSION

Most policy change efforts by social workers address a wide variety of social problems that are experienced by the clients they serve. Most of the time, these legislative efforts focus on issues of social and economic justice, and social workers see their role as advocating for children, aging adults, those suffering from mental disorders, and families living below the poverty line, just to provide a few examples. Indeed the bulk of this book is devoted to these issues.

However, there are times when the focus of the change effort is the profession itself, and social workers are in the position of advocating for themselves. Workforce issues, such as recruitment and retention of social workers, are a continuing challenge faced by the social work profession. Other professions have been successful in increasing the status of their profession by unionizing and educating lawmakers about the challenges they face. For example, nurses made great strides in raising awareness about the crisis the profession was facing in terms of having a shortage of nurses in the United States in order to meet the need. Social workers are facing this same type of crisis in the coming years, yet the public is largely unaware. One interesting development is the Congressional Social Work Caucus that was created in the 111th Congress by social workers and congressman, Ed Towns (D-NY). The purpose of the caucus is to

In March 2011, the Congressional Social Work Caucus (CSWC) was launched. The CSWC is made up of members of Congress who either (a) are social workers or (b) support the social work profession. It is chaired by Congressman Ed Towns (D-NY) who is a professional social worker. As of March 2012, there were over 60 members in the Caucus. The purpose of the CSWC is to represent the interests of over 600,000 social workers in the United States and the clients they serve. CSWC does this by expanding congressional internship opportunities for social work students, monitoring legislation designed to assist individuals and families in need, working with the media, bringing together experts on various issues of interest to social work, educating others about the scope of the profession, and convening regular briefings on Capitol Hill. Thus far, the CSWC has held three congressional briefings on: The Social Work Reinvestment Act; Implications of Health Care Reform on the Social Work Profession; and Prevention, Treatment, and Services Research Funding in the National Institute of Mental Health Budget. For more on the CSWC, please visit: http://www.socialworkreinvestment.org/2011/caucus.html

Figure 13.1

The Congressional Social Work Caucus.

educate lawmakers on Capitol Hill about issues of importance to the social work profession (see Figure 13.1).

However, when social workers focus too much on efforts to promote or protect the profession, they can be criticized for serving their own interests at the expense of their clients. Others argue, however, that the social work profession cannot effectively serve its clients if it fails to retain social workers who are overburdened by student loan debt and leave the profession due to low salaries. They point to other professions, such as teaching and nursing, that have done a much better job of advocating for better salaries and working conditions. This has enabled other professions to recruit more attractive candidates to their fields. They are quick to point out that a highly trained and highly qualified workforce is better for service recipients. But this debate raises some important questions. For example, when state and federal resources are scarce, should social workers fight to preserve/enhance funding for social welfare programs, or should they prioritize funding that supports the social work workforce? Or, can they do both?

Professional Identity

Practice Behavior Example: Practice personal reflection and self-correction to assure continual professional development.

Critical Thinking Question: Social workers are great advocates for other people. Why is it difficult and/or important for social workers to advocate for themselves and their profession?

The NASW is the organization most devoted to advocating for social workers in the United States. The **Social Work Reinvestment Act** is a federal piece of legislation that is asking the U.S. Congress to "invest" in social work and to recognize the value of the profession in serving those in society who are most vulnerable. In order to ensure that the social work profession can be effective, social workers need to be compensated fairly, have reasonable caseloads, and work in programs with adequate resources. Important policy issues for social workers include title protection, student loan forgiveness, and funding to support research in their field.

One way for social workers to effect change politically is to get involved with legislative activities in their state NASW chapter. Many NASW chapters have a legislative committee that is charged with getting legislation passed in their state legislature. It is not uncommon for state chapters of NASW to

Pennsylvania (2008): An individual is a social worker if he or she is licensed by the PA Department of State as a licensed social worker or a licensed clinical social worker or if he or she has received a bachelor's, master's, or doctoral degree from an accredited school of social work or social welfare.

Florida (2009): When the Board of Clinical Social Work, Marriage and Family Therapy, and Mental Health Counseling receives a complaint, information, or otherwise has reason to believe that a person has been or is using the title of social worker or holding himself or herself out to the public as a social worker in violation of Section 491.016, F.S., the available information shall be transmitted to the unlicensed activity office for investigation and any authorized, appropriate action in accordance with Section 456.065, F.S.

Oregon (2009): Senate Bill 177 protects the title "social worker" so that employers/individuals cannot use the title unless the person has a degree in social work and is held accountable to professional standards. SB 177 establishes a voluntary registration of bachelor's level social workers (RBSW) and licensure for non-clinical master's level social workers (LMSW) (previously there was only licensing for clinical social workers). In order for someone to use the title "social worker", he or she must be regulated by the state. SB 177 does not prevent someone with a social work degree from referencing his or her academic credentials. SB 177 also mandates a license to practice master's level clinical social work and prevents individuals who have lost their license due to serious misconduct from continuing to practice clinical social work.

Figure 13.2

Examples of Recently Enacted Legislation That Focuses on Title Protection for Social Workers.

propose legislation that offers loan forgiveness to those with a social work degree who agree to work in underserved areas. A number of states have focused on passing legislation that protects the title of "social worker" to help ensure that consumers are being treated by someone who is qualified, has the appropriate degree and training, and must abide by an ethical code. Social workers get miffed when a child protection caseworker is taken to task in the media, and they are referred to as a "social worker," when in reality many caseworkers do not have a degree in social work. Figure 13.2 describes three states that recently passed title protection laws related to the practice of social work.

WHAT ARE THE BIGGEST PROBLEMS FACING THE SOCIAL WORK PROFESSION?

Legislation is always introduced to address a perceived problem(s). In the case of social work, a number of problems facing the social work profession prompted the drafting and introduction of the Social Work Reinvestment Act (SWRA). The heart of the problem centers on the fact that social workers provide an important and necessary role in American society, and although there is a large demand for their services, there are barriers that make social work an impossible career choice for many people. Because of low starting salaries, high levels of student loan debt, and safety concerns, the profession has a difficult time recruiting and retaining talented, highly qualified people.

According to the Bureau of Labor Statistics, employment of social workers is expected to increase by 25% during the 2010–2020 decade, which is faster than average for all occupations. Additionally, employment of child, family, and school social workers is expected to grow by about 20%, mental health and substance abuse social workers by almost 31%, and health care social workers by about 34%. Much of this demand is fueled by the aging baby boom generation.

Despite this demand for social work services, many students do not consider a career in social work due to low starting salaries and fears that they would be unable to pay off their student loans. A report titled "Paying Back, Not Giving Back: Student Debt's Negative Impact on Public Service Career Opportunities (2006)" from the U.S. Public Interest Research Groups (PIRG) confirms these fears. According to this report, 37% of public institution 4-year graduates and 55% of private-college graduates have too much debt to manage as a starting social worker. According to the Project on Student Debt (an initiative of the Institute for College Access and Success), college seniors who graduated in 2008 carried an average of $23,200 in student loan debt, a 24% increase from 2004. Pell Grant recipients, who come from families with lower incomes, are much more likely to borrow, and borrow more.

The Social Work Reinvestment Act (SWRA) is also concerned with workforce improvements such as fair compensation, assuring safety in the workplace, manageable caseloads, and having a more diverse workforce. According to a 2009 study by the NASW Center for Workforce Studies, 6% of social workers make less than $20,000 a year, 18% earn between $20,000 and $39,999 a year, and 34% earn between $40,000 and $59,999 a year (National Association of Social Workers, 2010). The act seeks to ensure that social work research is translated into practice. Research is essential in testing social work interventions to ensure that they are effective in meeting the needs of individuals, families, groups, and communities. According to NASW, the National Institutes of Health (NIH) devotes less than 1% of its research budget to social work research (National Association of Social Workers, 2009).

OVERVIEW OF THE SOCIAL WORK REINVESTMENT ACT

The Social Work Reinvestment Act (SWRA) is named after two pioneers of social justice, Dorothy I. Height and Whitney M. Young Jr. They were both active leaders in the civil rights movement in the United States. This act (H.R. 1106 and S. 584) was introduced in the 112th Congress by U.S. Senator Barbara Mikulski (D-MD) and U.S. Representative Edolphus Towns (D-NY), both of whom are social workers. The language of the bill was crafted by Representative Towns and Senator Mikulski with input from various organizations such as NASW, the National Council of Negro Women, the National Association of Black Social Workers, and the ANSWER Coalition, which is a group of social work organizations focused on social work education, practice, and research (Association of Baccalaureate Social Work Program Directors [BPD], Council on Social Work Education [CSWE], Group for the Advancement of Doctoral Education [GADE], National Association of Deans and Directors of Schools of Social Work [NADD], NASW, and Society for Social Work and Research [SSWR]).

The SWRA urges the federal government to "invest" in the profession of social work and to address the impending shortage of social workers in the coming years.

The SWRA urges the federal government to "invest" in the profession of social work and to address the impending shortage of social workers in the coming years by doing the following:

- establish a social work reinvestment commission to study current trends and needs. This commission will be used to develop strategies and recommendations, which will be presented to Congress and the executive branch.
- provide funds for grants that will focus on workforce improvements, high caseloads, fair market compensation, social work safety, supervision, and working conditions (up to $1 million each).
- provide funds for 25 grants to social workers for postdoctoral research activity to further the knowledge base of effective social work interventions ($5 million total over 4 years). At least 10 of these grants to be awarded to grantees employed by historically Black colleges or minority serving institutions.
- provide funds for 20 grants to institutions of higher learning to support recruitment and education of social work students from high need and high demand areas at the bachelor's, master's, and doctorate levels as well as the development of faculty (up to $100,000 each). At least four grants to be awarded to historically Black colleges or minority serving institutions.
- provide funds for six grants available to not-for-profit or public, community-based programs of excellence to further test and replicate effective social work interventions from the areas of aging, child welfare, military and veteran's issues, mental and behavioral health and disability, criminal justice and correctional systems, health, and issues affecting women and families (up to $500,000 each).
- create a national coordinating center to bring together universities, research entities, and social work practice settings to identify key research areas to be pursued, select research fellows, and organize other efforts.

Policy Practice

Practice Behavior Example: Analyze, formulate, and advocate for policies that advance social well-being.

Critical Thinking Question: Do you think the SWRA should be a policy priority for the social work profession? Or, should issues affecting vulnerable people in the United States be prioritized?

WHAT STRATEGIES HAVE BEEN USED BY THE ANSWER COALITION TO PASS THE SWRA?

NASW has used a multifaceted approach in its attempts to get the SWRA passed into law.

1. **Lobbying legislators:** This has been an important tactic used by advocates of the SWRA. The ANSWER Coalition works with NASW, which has a team of lobbyists that work on this legislative effort. Members of the ANSWER Coalition met with key members of Congress and staff during the 110th and 111th Congress, and letters were sent to each senator and representative urging his or her support of the SWRA. The NASW chapter executive directors are also an integral component of this strategy. In addition, NASW members and other social workers set up lobbying visits in their districts or when they visit Washington, DC.

   All 56 NASW chapters have worked in support of SWRA, contacting and visiting members of Congress. NASW (and members of Congress) sent a letter to President Obama urging him to establish the

Elizabeth Hoffler, MSW, ACSW, Lobbyist for the National Association of Social Workers.

social work reinvestment commission in the Department of Health and Human Services. When Dr. Height was still living, she personally contacted members of Congress and the executive branch in support of the SWRA. Congressman Towns wrote a letter to the secretary of Health and Human Services urging her to establish the social work reinvestment commission. Finally, NASW and CSWE hired outside lobbying firms to promote the profession and social work education in federal legislation.

2. **Grassroots communication and social media:** The ANSWER Coalition has put a lot of effort into educating social workers about SWRA. Part of this education process involves speaking with NASW members, fellow social workers, and allied organizations about the workforce challenges facing the profession and how the legislation will help overcome those challenges. ANSWER Coalition members and NASW staff travel to chapters and other venues to speak about the legislation and hold meetings with external organizations and individuals.

   They have also educated others by launching a website called SocialWorkReinvestment.org (see http://www.socialworkreinvestment .org/), launching social media outlets that highlight the SWRA (http://www.socialworkblog.org/advocacy/category/social-work-reinvestment-act/), and creating numerous grassroots documents to inform social workers and other stakeholders about the SWRA (e.g., a fact sheet, biography sheets on Dr. Height and Whitney Young, action postcards, a petition, and newsletter articles). Much of the grassroots communication involves urging NASW members to contact their senators and representatives. The response rate of action alerts and calls to action has been high, and over 100,000 pieces of grassroots communications (emails, letters, and postcards) have been sent to Congress in support of the legislation. This does not include additional phone calls. Videos in support of the SWRA were also created. To see a video of NASW lobbyist Elizabeth Hoffler explaining the act, go to: http://www.youtube.com/watch?v=xfv_pt-GDiw.

3. **Allied support:** It has been important to have sister social work organizations support the legislation, as well as other external organizations. The following organizations formally support the SWRA
   • Action Network for Social Work Education and Research
   • Association of Baccalaureate Program Directors
   • Association of Oncology Social Work
   • Clinical Social Work Association
   • Council on Social Work Education
   • Group for the Advancement of Doctoral Education in Social Work
   • Institute for the Advancement of Social Work Research
   • Latino Social Workers Organization
   • National Association for the Advancement of Colored People
   • National Council of Negro Women
   • National Urban League
   • National Association of Social Workers
   • National Association of Black Social Workers
   • Social Welfare Action Alliance
   • Society for Social Work and Research
   • Society for Social Work Leadership in Health Care
   • Young Women's Christian Association

4. **Providing testimony, hearings, and briefings on Capitol Hill:** NASW provided testimony on a couple of occasions to the Subcommittee on Labor, Health and Human Services, Education, and Related Agencies in Congress. It also helped to coordinate the first hearing held on the profession of social work in the U.S. Congress, entitled "Caring for the Vulnerable: The State of Social Work in America" (more information, including the webcast, can be found at: http://edlabor.house.gov/hearings/2008/07/).

5. **Attaching the SWRA to other legislation:** Congressman Towns proposed that the social work reinvestment commission be included as an amendment to the Patient Protection and Affordable Care Act. Some components were included in the health care reform bill that was signed by President Obama and passed into law.

WHAT HAVE BEEN THE BIGGEST BARRIERS TO THE PASSAGE OF THE SWRA?

In the 111th Congress, the original strategy was to pass the full legislation as it was originally introduced. The ANSWER Coalition's first goal was to pass the bill in the House of Representatives, followed by the Senate, and ultimately get it signed by the president. This requires a significant number of cosponsors in both chambers, support from the committees of jurisdiction, and widespread grassroots momentum. However, the main objections to the legislation have been due to fiscal constraints within the federal government. As a result, some fiscally conservative members of Congress did not want to spend over $43 million on the demonstration programs included in the bill. Thus, a new strategy was developed.

The ANSWER Coalition came to the conclusion that the most prudent approach would be to work to pass a "commission-only" bill. This means that it would focus predominately on using this legislation to create the social work reinvestment commission, which is budget neutral or requires "such sums as necessary." This newly created commission would later be able to provide information that would be necessary to fund future demonstration programs. The SWRA was introduced in the 110th and 111th Congress, with the ultimate goal of passage into law. The ANSWER Coalition worked closely with Representative Towns and Senator Mikulski to make this a reality. In August 2010, members of Congress wrote a letter to President Obama encouraging him to establish the social work reinvestment commission via executive order.

On November 17, 2010, Congressman Edolphus Towns, the House sponsor of the Dorothy I. Height and Whitney M. Young, Jr. Social Work Reinvestment Act, held a congressional briefing on the legislation to highlight the critical role that social workers play in U.S. society and the necessity of reinvesting in the profession in order to provide the social safety net that has become increasingly important to individuals and communities in the United States. A number of social work academics and leaders spoke at this event. Unfortunately, the SWRA did not pass in the 111th Congress, but it was reintroduced in the 112th Congress on March 15, 2011, which is World Social Work Day. NASW and the ANSWER Coalition will be working hard in the coming years to build the political momentum needed to get this bill through the U.S. Congress, including mobilizing social workers across the nation to get involved by writing, calling, and visiting their members of Congress to tell them personal, compelling stories about the challenges they are facing whether it be low salaries, high levels of student loan debt, high caseloads, or safety concerns (please visit http://www.socialworkreinvestment.org/SWRI/default.html to learn about the current status of the SWRA in the 112th Congress).

Tactics Used to Get the SWRA Passed

☑ Coalition building

☑ Earned media (letters to the editor actions that lead to media coverage)

☐ Paid media (paying for TV/radio ads)

☐ Visibility (rallies, marches)

☐ Political dissent (e.g., civil disobedience, protest)

☑ Providing testimony in a legislative committee hearing

☑ Direct lobbying (in-person lobby visits, sometimes by a professional lobbyist)

☑ Grassroots lobbying (e.g., urging people to call, write, and email legislators)

☐ Educational outreach (town halls, house parties, community forums)

☑ Online advocacy (using social media)

☐ Paid communication (paid staff who call voters, materials mailed out)

☐ Fund-raising activities

ALL SOCIAL WORK IS POLITICAL

Critical Thinking

Practice Behavior Example: Use critical thinking augmented by creativity and curiosity.

Critical Thinking Question: In your opinion, is all social work political?

The first chapter of this book proposed the question, "Is all social work political?" This question is certainly up for debate, but the author of this book would argue in the affirmative. It is almost impossible to identify any realm of social work practice that is not impacted by the legislative process. For example, social workers in most states must abide by laws that require them to be licensed by the state they work in and to get continued training, many work in organizations that receive government funding, and most social workers are impacted by various laws and regulations that affect how they carry out their practice with individuals, families, and communities.

Maryann Mahaffey (1925–2006) is recognized by NASW as a "social work pioneer." She had a distinguished career as a social worker that included working as a social work professor at Wayne State University, publishing a book titled *Practical Politics: Social Work and Political Responsibility*, serving as the first female president of NASW, and serving as a member of the Detroit City Council for 31 years, including 11 years as its president. She was passionate about social workers being involved in the political process, and the following quote (to the right) is from her book that was published in 1981:

A social worker brings to the political process something that's unique, that no one else has. Anyone else can learn how to play games, you know power games. Anybody else can learn to negotiate. Anybody can learn to do the power manipulations. Those are techniques and skills that can be learned fairly easy. What the social worker brings is a value system that, if implemented, along with the skills, makes the difference.

One of the strengths of social work is the broadness of the profession, yet this strength can also be a weakness because it can be quite challenging to unify social workers who work in diverse fields of practice ranging from children and families and mental health to criminal justice and poverty and homelessness. The critical challenge for social workers in the new millennium is to figure out how to come together in order to become a visible and powerful political force in the U.S.

The following questions will test your knowledge of the content found within this chapter. For additional assessment, including licensing-exam type questions on applying chapter content to practice behaviors, visit **MySearchLab**.

1. Which of the following statements from Kasser's study about the benefits of political activism is false?
   a. It leads to better relationships.
   b. People feel more purpose in life.
   c. People like themselves better.
   d. It leads to better health.

2. According to the Census Bureau, in 2009, one in _____ Americans were living below the poverty threshold.
   a. two
   b. three
   c. seven
   d. ten

3. The Employment Non-Discrimination Act (ENDA) would make it illegal to discriminate in the workplace on the basis of
   a. sexual orientation
   b. gender
   c. ethnicity
   d. disability

4. Which of the following statements about efforts to pass the Social Work Reinvestment Act (SWRA) is false?
   a. Political dissent was used as a tactic.
   b. Advocates lobbied members of Congress.
   c. Social media was used as a tactic.
   d. Social workers provided testimony on Capitol Hill.

5. According to the Bureau of Labor Statistics, the employment of social workers is expected to grow by _____% during the 2010–2020 decade.
   a. 12
   b. 16
   c. 20
   d. 25

6. A variety of organizations have voiced their support of the Social Work Reinvestment Act (SWRA). This is an example of which of the following tactics?
   a. Direct lobbying
   b. Paid communication
   c. Visibility
   d. Coalition building

7. This chapter profiled a number of critical policy issues of interest to social workers in the coming years. Which issues are you most passionate about? Is there an issue of interest to you that was not listed in this chapter?

Reinforce what you learned in this chapter by studying videos, cases, documents, and more available at **www.MySearchLab.com**.

Watch and Review

Watch these Videos

* Military Families
* Gay Marriage
* Who Is the Middle Class? (2008)

Read and Review

Read these Cases/Documents

* Human Rights and Justice

Explore and Assess

Explore these Assets

* Career FAQ: Social Work Licensing and Legal Regulations

Research these Topics

Hot-Button Political Issues on the Horizon of Interest to Social Work

What Is the Social Work Reinvestment Act?

Political Strategies and Tactics Used by the Advocates Profiled in This Book

Assess Your Knowledge

Go to **MySearchLab** to test your knowledge of key topics in this chapter with topic-specific quizzes. Conclude your assessment by completing the chapter exam.

---

* = CSWE Core Competency Asset   Δ = Case Study

References

Chapter 1

Abromovitz, M., & Bardill, D. R. (1993). Should all social work students be educated for social change? *Journal of Social Work Education*, 29(1), 6–18.

Andrews, A. B. (1998). An exploratory study of political attitudes and acts among child and family services workers. *Children and Youth Services Review*, 20, 435–461.

Byers, K., & Stone, G. (1999). Roots of activism: A qualitative study of BSW students. *The Journal of Baccalaureate Social Work*, 5(1), 1–14.

Code of Ethics of the National Association of Social Workers. (2008). *Approved by the 1996 NASW Delegate Assembly and revised by the 2008 NASW Delegate Assembly*. Retrieved from http://www.socialworkers.org/pubs/code/code.asp

Council on Social Work Education. (2008). *2008 EPAS handbook*. Retrieved from http://www.cswe.org/File.aspx?id=13780

Dickinson, J. C. (2007). A survey of social policy placements in BSW education. *Journal of Policy Practice*, 6(1), 47–63.

DiNitto, D. M. (2011). *Social welfare: Politics and public policy* (7th ed.). Boston, MA: Pearson.

Epstein, W. M. (1992). Professionalization of social work: The American experience. *The Social Science Journal*, 29(2), 153–166.

Ezell, M. (1993). The political activities of social workers: A post-Reagan update. *Journal of Sociology and Social Welfare*, 20(4), 81–98.

Figueira-McDonough, J. (1993). Policy practice: The neglected side of social work intervention. *Social Work*, 38(2), 179–188.

Hamilton, D., & Fauri, D. (2001). Social workers' political participation: Strengthening the political confidence of social work students. *Journal of Social Work Education*, 37(2), 321–332.

Harding, S. (2004). The sound of silence: Social work, the academy, and Iraq. *Journal of Sociology & Social Welfare*, 31, 179–197.

Haynes, K., & Mickelson, J. (2009). *Affecting change: Social workers in the political arena* (7th ed.). Boston, MA: Pearson.

Meyer, Agnes Elizabeth Earnest. (1980). *Out of These Roots*. North Stratford, NH: Ayer Publishing.

Ortiz, L. P., Wirz, C., Semion, K., & Rodriguez, C. (2004). Legislative casework: Where policy and practice intersect. *Journal of Sociology & Social Welfare*, 31, 49–68.

Parker, M., & Sherraden, M. (1992). Electoral participation of social workers. *New England Journal of Human Services*, 11, 23–28.

Ritter, J. A. (2007). Evaluating the political participation of licensed social workers in the new millennium. *The Policy Practice Journal*, 6(4), 61–78.

Ritter, J. A. (2008). A national study predicting social workers' levels of political participation: The role of resources, psychological engagement, and recruitment networks. *Social Work*, 53(4), 347–357.

Shamai, M., & Boehm, A. (2001). Politically oriented social work intervention. *International Social Work*, 44, 343–360.

Spect, H., & Courtney, M. E. (1994). *Unfaithful angels: How social work has abandoned its mission*. New York: The Free Press.

Thompson, J. J. (1994). Social workers and politics: Beyond the Hatch Act. *Social Work*, 39(4), 457–465.

Wolk, J. (1981). Are social workers politically active? *Social Work*, 26, 283–288.

Chapter 2

Day, P. J. (2008). *New history of social welfare* (6th ed.). Boston, MA: Pearson.

Dorothea L. Dix, & Federal Aid. (1927). *Social Service Review, The University of Chicago Press*, 1(1), 117–137.

Jansson, B. S. (2008). *The reluctant welfare state: Engaging history to advance social welfare practice in contemporary society*. Belmont, CA: Brooks/Cole.

Perkins, F. (October, 1962). *The roots of social security*. Retrieved from http://www.ssa.gov/history/perkins5.html

Roosevelt, F. D. (January 11, 1944). *State of the Union Address to Congress*. Retrieved from http://www.presidency.ucsb.edu/ws/index.php?pid=16518

Specht, H., & Courtney, M. E. (1994). *Unfaithful angels: How social work has abandoned its mission*. New York: The Free Press.

The 25 most powerful women of the past century. (November 18, 2010). *Time Magazine*. Retrieved from http://www.time.com/time/specials/packages/article/0,28804,2029774_2029776,00.html?iid=moreontime

Chapter 3

Clark, E. J. (October 20, 2007). What does unite social workers. *Washington Post*. Retrieved from http://www.washingtonpost.com/wp-dyn/content/article/2007/10/19/AR2007101902281.html

Green Party of the United States. (2000). *The ten key values of the green party*. Retrieved from http://www.gp.org/tenkey.php

Libertarian Party. (n.d.). *The libertarian party on today's issues*. Retrieved from http://www.lp.org/issues

National Association of Social Workers. (2012). *Social work speaks (9th edition). NASW Policy Statements 2012–2014*. Washington, DC: NASW Press.

National Election Studies. (2004). *The ANES guide to public opinion and electoral behavior*. http://www.electionstudies.org/nesguide/toptable/tab3_1.htm

Prigmore, C., & Atherton, C. (1986). *Social welfare policy: Analysis and formulation*. Lexington, MA: D.C. Heath.

Ritter, J. A. (2007). Evaluating the political participation of licensed social workers in the new millennium. *The Policy Practice Journal*, 6(4), 61–78.

Rosenwald, M. (2006). Exploring the political diversity of social workers. *Social Work Research*, 30(2), 121–126.

Thyer, B. (2010). Social justice: A conservative perspective. *Journal of Comparative Social Welfare*, 26(2–3), 261–274.

Chapter 4

DiNitto, D. M. (2011). *Social welfare: Politics and public policy* (7th ed.). Boston, MA: Pearson.

Chapter 5

American National Election Studies. *The ANES guide to public opinion and electoral behavior*. Ann Arbor, MI: University of Michigan, Center for Political Studies [producer and distributor]. Retrieved from www.electionstudies.org

Code of Ethics of the National Association of Social Workers. (2008). *Approved by the 1996 NASW Delegate Assembly and revised by the 2008 NASW Delegate Assembly*. Retrieved from http://www.socialworkers.org/pubs/code/code.asp

DiNitto, D. M. (2011). *Social welfare: Politics and public policy* (7th ed.). Boston, MA: Pearson.

Ezell, M. (1993). The political activities of social workers: A post-Reagan update. *Journal of Sociology and Social Welfare*, 20(4), 81–98.

Lopez, M. H., Levine, P., Both, D., Kiesa, A., Kirby, E., & Marcelo, K. (2006). *The 2006 civic and political health of the nation: A detailed look at how youth participate in politics and communities.* Center for Information and Research on Civic Learning and Engagement. Retrieved from http://www.civicyouth.org/PopUps/2006_CPHS_Report_update.pdf

Milbrath, L. W. (1965). *Political participation: How and why do people get involved in politics?* Chicago, IL: Rand McNally.

Ortiz, L. P., Wirz, C., Semion, K., & Rodriguez, C. (2004). Legislative casework: Where policy and practice intersect. *Journal of Sociology and Social Welfare*, 31(2), 49–68.

Ritter, J. A. (2007). Evaluating the political participation of licensed social workers in the new millennium. *The Policy Practice Journal*, 6(4), 61–78.

Ritter, J. A. (2008). A national study predicting social workers' levels of political participation: The role of resources, psychological engagement, and recruitment networks. *Social Work*, 53(4), 347–357.

Rocha, C., Poe, B., & Thomas, V. (2010). Political activities of social workers: Addressing perceived barriers to political participation. *Social Work*, 55(4), 317–325.

Wolk, J. L., Pray, J. E., Weismiller, T., & Dempsey, D. (1996). Political practica: Educating social work students for policy-making. *Journal of Social Work Education*, 32(1), 91–100.

Chapter 6

DeNavas-Walt, C., Proctor, B. D., & Smith, J. C. (2009). *Income, poverty, and health insurance coverage in the United States: 2008.* U.S. Census Bureau, Current Population Reports, P60–236. Washington, DC: U.S. Government Printing Office. Retrieved from http://www.census.gov/prod/2009pubs/p60-236.pdf

DeNavas-Walt, C., Proctor, B. D., & Smith, J. C. (September, 2011). *Income, poverty, and health insurance coverage in the United States: 2010.* U.S. Census Bureau, Current Population Reports, P60–239. Washington, DC: U.S. Government Printing Office. Retrieved from http://www.census.gov/prod/2011pubs/p60-239.pdf

Kaiser Family Foundation. (June, 2010). *Medicaid and the uninsured. The Medicaid program at a glance.* Retrieved from http://www.kff.org/medicaid/upload/7235-04.pdf

Kaiser Family Foundation. (September, 2010). *Medicare at a glance.* Retrieved from http://www.kff.org/medicare/upload/1066-13.pdf

Kaiser Family Foundation. (May, 2012). *Heath care costs: A primer, Key information on health care costs and their impact.* Retrieved from http://www.kff.org/insurance/upload/7670-03.pdf

Liptak, A., & Landler, M. (2012). Supreme Court Upholds Health Care Law, 5-4, in Victory for Obama. *New York Times.* Retrieved from http://www.nytimes.com/2012/06/29/us/supreme-court-lets-health-law-largely-stand.html?pagewanted=2&_r=2&nl=todaysheadlines&emc=edit_th_20120629

Liptak, A., & Landler, M. (2012). A Vindication, With a Legacy Still Unwritten. *New York Times.* Retrieved from http://www.nytimes.com/2012/06/29/us/health-care-ruling-may-secure-obamas-place-in-history.html?src=un&feedurl=http%3A%2F%2Fjson8.nytimes.com%2Fpages%2Fnational%2Findex.jsonp

National Association of Social Workers. (2009). *Social work speaks (8th edition), NASW policy statements, 2009–2012.* Washington, DC: NASW Press.

Nolte, E., & McKee, C. M. (2008). Measuring the health of nations: Updating an earlier analysis. *Health Affairs*, 27(1), 58–71.

Preston, J., & Cushman, J. H., Jr. (2012). Obama to permit young migrants to remain in U.S. *New York Times*, Retrieved from http://www.nytimes.com/2012/06/16/us/us-to-stop-deporting-some-illegal-immigrants.html?nl=todaysheadlines&emc=edit_th_20120616

Physicians for a National Health Program. (n.d.). *Single-payer FAQ.* Retrieved from http://www.pnhp.org/facts/single-payer-faq#what-is-single-payer

Schoen, C., Doty, M. M., Robertson, R. H., & Collins, S. R. (September 8, 2011). Affordable care act reforms could reduce the number of underinsured U.S. adults by 70 percent. *Health Affairs,* 30(9), 1762–1771. Retrieved from http://www.commonwealthfund.org/Publications/In-the-Literature/2011/Sep/Reduce-Uninsured.aspx

Singh, G. K., & Siahpush, M. (2006). Widening socioeconomic inequalities in U.S. Life expectancy, 1980–2000. *International Journal of Epidemiology*, 35(4), 969–979.

Stolberg, S. G., & Pear, R. (March 23, 2010). Obama signs health care overhaul bill, with a flourish. *New York Times.* Retrieved from http://www.nytimes.com/2010/03/24/health/policy/24health.html

Wilper, A. P., Woolhandler, S., Lasser, K. E., McCormick, D., Bor, D. H., & Himmelstein, D. U. (December, 2009). Health insurance and mortality in U.S. Adults. *American Journal of Public Health*, 99(12). September 17, 2009 (Online).

Chapter 7

Advocates renew push for mental health 'parity' bill. (January 8, 2007). *National Public Radio.* Retrieved from http://www.npr.org/templates/story/story.php?storyId=6740128

After 12 years, Wellstone mental health parity act is law. (October 3, 2008). *Minnesota Public Radio.* Retrieved from http://minnesota.publicradio.org/display/web/2008/10/03/parity_finalpassage/?refid=0

Bailout provides more mental health coverage. (October 5, 2008). *New York Times.* Retrieved from http://www.nytimes.com/2008/10/06/washington/06mental.html?_r=1&pagewanted=all

Fairness for mental health. (March 24, 2007). *New York Times.* Retrieved from http://www.nytimes.com/2007/03/24/opinion/24sat1.html?pagewanted=print

Kessler, R. C., Chiu, W. T., Demler, O., & Walters, E. E. (2005). Prevalence, severity, and comorbidity of twelve-month DSM-IV disorders in the National Comorbidity Survey Replication (NCS-R). *Archives of General Psychiatry*, 62(6), 617–627.

Mental health America hails approval of federal parity legislation. (2008). *Mental Health America.* Retrieved from http://www.nmha.org/index.cfm?objectid=C3162C54-1372-4D20-C8E62AB28BB3FF5B

U.S. Department of Health and Human Services. (1999). *Mental health: A report of the surgeon general—Executive summary.* Rockville, MD: U.S. Department of Health and Human Services, Substance Abuse and Mental Health Services Administration, Center for Mental Health Services, National Institutes of Health, National Institute of Mental Health.

Wang, P. S., Lane, M., Olfson, M., Pincus, H. A., Wells, K. B., & Kessler, R. C. (2005). Twelve month use of mental health services in the United States. *Archives of General Psychiatry*, 62(6), 629–640.

Chapter 8

Arizona goes over the edge. (April 17, 2010). *New York Times.* Retrieved from http://www.nytimes.com/2010/04/18/opinion/18sun3.html

Arizona laws decried. (July, 2010). *NASW News*, 55(7), 1.

Border insecurity. (March 4, 2008). *New York Times*. Retrieved from http://www.nytimes.com/

Coming out illegal. (October 21, 2010). *New York Times Magazine*. Retrieved from http://www.nytimes.com/2010/10/24/magazine/24DreamTeam-t.html?pagewanted=all

Grieco, E. M., & Trevelyan, E. N. (2010). *Place of birth of the foreign-born population: 2009*. American Community Survey Briefs. U.S. Census Bureau. Retrieved from http://www.census.gov/prod/2010pubs/acsbr09-15.pdf

Hoefer, M., Rytina, N., & Baker, B. C. (2010). *Estimates of the unauthorized immigrant population residing in the United States: January 2009. Population estimates*. U.S. Department of Homeland Security, Office of Immigration Statistics. Retrieved from http://www.dhs.gov/xlibrary/assets/statistics/publications/ois_ill_pe_2009.pdf

National Association of Social Workers (n.d.). *Provide legal, earned pathway to citizenship: Co-sponsors needed for DREAM Act. Action Alert*. Retrieved from http://capwiz.com/socialworkers/issues/alert/?alertid=15429636

National Council of La Raza. (2008). *Five facts about undocumented workers in the United States*. Retrieved from http://www.nclr.org/index.php/publications/five_facts_about_undocumented_workers_in_the_united_states

National Park Service, U.S. Department of the Interior. (n.d.). *Jim Crow laws*. Retrieved from http://www.nps.gov/malu/forteachers/jim_crow_laws.htm

Preston, J. (July 31, 2006). Sheriff defies immigrants by billboard and by blog. *New York Times*. Retrieved from http://www.nytimes.com/2006/07/31/us/31sheriff.html

Preston, J., & Cushman, J. H., Jr. (2012). Obama to permit young migrants to remain in U.S. *New York Times*. Retrieved from http://www.nytimes.com/2012/06/16/us/us-to-stop-deporting-some-illegal-immigrants.html?nl=todaysheadlines&emc=edit_th_20120616

Preston, J., & Cushman, J. H. (June 15, 2012). Obama to permit young migrants to remain in U.S. *New York Times*. Retrieved from http://www.nytimes.com/2012/06/16/us/us-to-stop-deporting-some-illegal-immigrants.html?_r=2&nl=todaysheadlines&emc=edit_th_20120616

Chapter 9

Addy, S., & Wight, V. R. (February, 2012). *Basic facts about low-income children, 2010*. National Center for Children in Poverty. Retrieved from http://www.nccp.org/publications/pub_1049.html

Child Welfare League of America. (September, 2002). *Research to Practice Initiative, Child Welfare Workforce, Research Roundup*. Washington, DC: Child Welfare League of America. Retrieved August 20, 2008, from http://www.cwla.org/programs/r2p/rrnews0209.pdf

Dr. Henry Kempe, et al. (July 7, 1962). The battered-child syndrome. *Journal of the American Medical Association*, 181, 105–112.

Home School Legal Defense Association. (2002). *United Nations special session on children set to meet*. Retrieved from http://www.hslda.org/docs/nche/000010/200205060.asp

Mishel, L., Bernstein, J., & Shierholz, H. (2009). *The state of working America 2008/2009*. Economic Policy Institute. Retrieved from http://www.stateofworkingamerica.org/tabfig/2008/08/18.pdf

Senate Resolution 133. *Library of Congress (THOMAS)*. Retrieved from: http://thomas.loc.gov/cgi-bin/query/z?c104:S.RES.133:

United Nations. (2007). *World population prospects: The 2006 revision, pages 103–107*. Retrieved from http://www.un.org/esa/population/publications/wpp2006/WPP2006_highlights_rev.pdf

Unless otherwise noted, the figures in this section are from Children's Bureau. U.S. Department of Health and Human Services, Administration on Children, Youth, and Families. (2010). *Child maltreatment, 2009*. Washington, DC: U.S. Department of Health and Human Services, Administration on Children, Youth, and Families. Retrieved December 1, 2011, from http://www.acf.hhs.gov/programs/cb/pubs/cm09/index.htm

U.S. Department of Health and Human Services, Administration for Children, Youth, and Families, Administration on Children, Youth, and Families, Children's Bureau. (2011). *Child maltreatment 2010*. Retrieved from http://www.acf.hhs.gov/programs/cb/pubs/cm10/cm10.pdf#page=31

Chapter 10

Administration on Aging, U.S. Department of Health and Human Services. (2010). *A profile of older Americans: 2010*. Retrieved December 1, 2011, from http://www.aoa.gov/AoARoot/Aging_Statistics/Profile/index.aspx

Compassion & Choices. (2008). *Washington becomes second state to legalize aid in dying: Campaign has moved patients' rights forward*. Retrieved from http://www.compassionwa.org/docs/press/first_state.pdf

Compassion & Choices. (2009). *First terminally ill Washingtonian uses death with dignity act*. Retrieved from http://www.compassionandchoices.org/documents/WA-Release%201st%20patient%20used%20the%20law.pdf

Congressional Budget Office. (2010). *CBO's 2010 long-term projections for social security: Additional information*. Retrieved December 2, 2011, from http://www.cbo.gov/doc.cfm?index=11943

Death with Dignity Report. (2012). *Characteristics and end-of-life care of 460 DWDA patients who died after ingesting a lethal dose of medication, by year, Oregon, 1998-2009*. Retrieved from http://public.health.oregon.gov/ProviderPartnerResources/EvaluationResearch/DeathwithDignityAct/Documents/year14-tbl-1.pdf

National Center on Elder Abuse. (n.d.). *Types of elder abuse in domestic settings*. Retrieved December 1, 2011, from http://www.ncea.aoa.gov/Main_Site/Library/Statistics_Research/Abuse_Statistics/Statistics_At_Glance.aspx

National Center on Elder Abuse Fact Sheet. (2005). *Elder abuse prevalence and incidence*. Retrieved December 1, 2011, from http://www.ncea.aoa.gov/Main_Site/Library/Statistics_Research/Abuse_Statistics/Statistics_At_Glance.aspx

Quill, T. E., & Battin, M. P. (Eds.). (2004). *Physician assisted dying: The case for palliative care and patient choice*. Baltimore, MD: The Johns Hopkins University Press.

Washington State Medical Association. (2008). *As I-1000 signatures are counted, Washington state Medical Association opposition to physician-assisted suicide reiterated*. Retrieved from http://noassistedsuicide.com/release9.html

Chapter 11

Activists vow to fight on after court puts same-sex marriages on hold. (August 17, 2010). *CNN*. Retrieved from http://www.cnn.com/2010/US/08/17/same.sex.marriage/index.html?hpt=T1

Court strikes down ban on gay marriage in California. (February 7, 2012). *New York Times*. Retrieved from http://www.nytimes.com/2012/02/08/us/marriage-ban-violates-constitution-court-rules.html?_r=1&src=twrhp

For mentally ill, death and misery. (April 28, 2002). *New York Times*. Retrieved from http://www.nytimes.com/2002/04/28/nyregion/for-mentally-ill-death-and-misery.html?pagewanted=1

Malamud, M. (2010). Calif., Fla. Appeals ruling affirm NASW Amicus Briefs: Florida's ban on gay adoption violates the state's guarantee of equal protection of the law. *NASW News*, 55(10).

National Association of Social Workers. (November, 2007). *In the Supreme Court of the United States,* Patrick Kennedy v. State of Louisiana. Retrieved from http://www.deathpenaltyinfo.org/nasw-07-343-11-14-07.pdf

National Association of Social Workers. (2008). *In the Supreme Court of the United States,* Terrance Jamar Graham v. State of Florida *and* Joe Harris Sullivan v. State of Florida. Retrieved from http://www.americanbar.org/content/dam/aba/publishing/preview/publiced_preview_briefs_pdfs_07_08_08_7412_PetitionerAmCu4HealthOrgs.authcheckdam.pdf

Proposition 8 trial pauses, but not for ruling. (August 4, 2010). *New York Times.* Retrieved from http://www.nytimes.com/2010/01/28/us/28prop.html?fta=y

Rhode Island child advocate sues state. (July 19, 2007). *National Public Radio.* Retrieved from http://www.npr.org/templates/story/story.php?storyId=12091975&sc=emaf

Suit says state is segregating the mentally ill. (July 1, 2003). *New York Times.* Retrieved from http://www.nytimes.com/2003/07/01/nyregion/01MENT.html

Chapter 12

Afterschool.gov. (n.d.). *Federal funding basics.* Retrieved from http://www.afterschool.gov/docs/federalFunding.html

Amenta, E., & Skocpol, T. (1989). Taking exception: Explaining the distinctiveness of American public policies during the last century. In F. G. Castles (Ed.), *The comparative history of public policy.* New York: Oxford University Press.

Center on Budget and Policy Priorities. (2011). *Policy basics: Where do our federal tax dollars go?* Figures from Office of Management and Budget, 2011. Retrieved from http://www.cbpp.org/cms/index.cfm?fa=view&id=1258

Feller, A., & Stone, C. (2009). *Top 1 percent of Americans reaped two-thirds of income gains in last economic expansion.* Center on Budget and Policy Priorities. Retrieved from http://www.cbpp.org/files/9-9-09pov.pdf

Lipset, S. M. (1996). *American exceptionalism: A double-edged sword.* New York: W. W. Norton.

National Association of Social Workers. (2009). *Social work speaks, eighth edition. Poverty and economic justice* (p. 261). Washington, DC: NASW Press.

National Priorities Project. (n.d.). *Federal discretionary and mandatory spending.* Based on figures from the Budget of the U.S. Government, FY 2012, Analytical Perspectives. Retrieved from http://nationalpriorities.org/en/resources/federal-budget-101/budget-briefs/federal-discretionary-and-mandatory-spending/

National Priorities Project. (n.d.-a). *Federal revenues.* Based on figures from the Budget of the U.S. Government, FY 2012, Historical Table 2.1. Retrieved from http://nationalpriorities.org/en/resources/federal-budget-101/budget-briefs/federal-revenues/

National Priorities Project. (n.d.-b). *Individual and corporate income taxes 1934-2016.* Based on figures from the Office of Management and Budget, Budget of the U.S. Government, Historical Tables, FY 2012. Retrieved from http://nationalpriorities.org/en/resources/federal-budget-101/budget-briefs/federal-revenues/

National Poverty Center. (n.d.-c). *Poverty in the United States frequently asked questions.* Table, Children Under 18 Living in Poverty, 2008. Data based on report from the U.S. Census Bureau. Retrieved from http://npc.umich.edu/poverty/#5

OECD. (2011a). *Society at a glance 2011—OECD social indicators. Key findings: United States.* Retrieved from http://www.oecd.org/dataoecd/38/53/47573390.pdf

OECD. (2011b). *Tax revenue statistics.* Tax revenues as percentage of GPD, Table A, 1975-2008. Retrieved from http://www.oecd.org/ctp/taxdatabase

Rank, M. (2004). *One nation underprivileged: Why American poverty affects us all.* New York: Oxford University Press.

Tapper, J. (March 25, 2011). *General electric paid no federal taxes in 2010.* Retrieved from http://abcnews.go.com/Politics/general-electric-paid-federal-taxes-2010/story?id=13224558

Tumulty, K. (November 29, 2010). American exceptionalism: An old idea and a new political battle. *Washington Post.* Retrieved from http://www.washingtonpost.com/wp-dyn/content/article/2010/11/28/AR2010112804139.html?id=ST2010112901818

U.S. Census Bureau. (2010). *Income, poverty, and health insurance coverage in the United States, 2009.* Retrieved from http://www.census.gov/newsroom/releases/archives/income_wealth/cb10-144.html

U.S. Census Bureau. (2011). *Poverty thresholds by size of family and number of children, 2011 table.* Retrieved from http://www.census.gov/hhes/www/poverty/data/threshld/

Chapter 13

Anderson, S., Collins, C., Pizzigati, S., & Shih, K. (2010). *Executive excess 2010: CEO pay and the great recession, 17th annual executive compensation survey.* Institute for Policy Studies. Retrieved from http://www.ips-dc.org/reports/executive_excess_2010

Bureau of Labor Statistics, United States Department of Labor (2012). *Occupational outlook handbook, 2012–13 edition: Social Workers.* Retrieved June 13, 2012, from http://www.bls.gov/ooh/community-and-social-service/social-workers.htm

DeNavas-Walt, C., Proctor, B. D., & Smith, J. C. (September, 2011). *Income, poverty, and health insurance coverage in the United States: 2010.* U.S. Census Bureau, Current Population Reports, P60–239. Washington, DC: U.S. Government Printing Office. Retrieved from http://www.census.gov/prod/2011pubs/p60-239.pdf

Mahaffey, M. (1981). *Practical politics: Social work and political responsibility.* Washington, DC: NASW Press.

National Association of Social Workers. (2009). *Social work reinvestment: A national agenda for the profession of social work, transition document to the new administration.* Retrieved from http://www.socialworkers.org/advocacy/resources/TransitionBook.pdf

National Association of Social Workers. (2009). *Social work speaks (8th edition), NASW policy statements, 2009–2012.* Washington, DC: NASW Press.

National Association of Social Workers. (2010). *2009 Compensation & Benefits Study. Summary of key compensation findings.* Retrieved from http://www.socialworkers.org/pressroom/2010/salarystudy2010.pdf

Petre, R. (2010). Smile, you're an activist! *In These Times.* Retrieved from http://www.inthesetimes.com/article/5955/smile_youre_an_activist

Rennane, S., Isaacs, J., Steuerle, C. E., & Ehrle Macomber, J. (2010). *Kids share 2010.* Urban Institute and Brookings. Retrieved from http://www.urban.org/UploadedPDF/412140-kids-share-2010.pdf

Shaw, H., & Stone, C. (2012). *Incomes at the top rebounded in first full year of recovery, new analysis of tax data shows.* Center on Budget and Policy Priorities. Retrieved from http://www.cbpp.org/cms/index.cfm?fa=view&id=3697

The State PIRGs' Higher Education Project. (2006). *Paying back not giving back: Student debts' negative impact on public service career opportunities.* Retrieved from http://www.pirg.org/highered/payingback.pdf

Photo Credits

Chapter 1: p. 1 Jessica Ritter, Ph.D., MSSW; p. 12 © Stephen Coburn/ Shutterstock

Chapter 2: p. 17 Lydon Baines Johnson Library photo by Yoichi Okamoto; p. 22 The Library of Congress Prints and Photographs Division [LC-USZ61-144]

Chapter 3: p. 36 Lindsay Douglas/Shutterstock.com; p. 42 Shutterstock.com

Chapter 4: p. 53 Jessica Ritter, Ph.D., MSSW; p. 58 Official White House Photo by Chuck Kennedy

Chapter 5: p. 77 Courtesy of the Offices of Congresswoman Barbara Lee; p. 95 Courtesy of the Offices of Congresswoman Barbara Mikulski

Chapter 6: p. 98 Jessica Ritter, Ph.D., MSSW; p. 105 Jessica Ritter, Ph.D., MSSW

Chapter 7: p. 119 GWImages/Shutterstock.com; p. 125 abd/Shutterstock.com

Chapter 8: p. 142 Ryan Rodrick Beiler/Shutterstock.com; p. 155 Jessica Ritter, Ph.D., MSSW

Chapter 9: p. 165 Jessica Ritter, Ph.D., MSSW; p. 181 Jessica Ritter, Ph.D., MSSW

Chapter 10: p. 186 The Library of Congress Prints and Photographs Division [LC-USZ62-123278]; p. 195 AP Photo/Richard Sheinwald

Chapter 11: p. 208 George Tames/The New York TImes/Redux Pictures; p. 221 Steve Heap/Shutterstock.com

Chapter 12: p. 225 Sjgh/Shutterstock.com; p. 236 Lightspring/Shutterstock .com

Chapter 13: p. 244 Ryan Rodrick Beiler/Shutterstock.com; p. 255 Jessica Ritter, Ph.D., MSSW

Index

Page numbers followed by "f" indicate figure; and those followed by "t" indicate table.